'Compelling and thought-provoking reading. Sarah Maddison shows that Western systems can never replace the community-driven solutions of Indigenous peoples.'
— Jackie Huggins AM, Co-Chair of the National Congress of Australia's First Peoples

'Timely and important: Aboriginal policy has long suffered from the failed white "we know what's best for you" mentality. Only when those in power and wider society recognise that Aboriginal people are the best placed to solve issues within our own communities will progress be made!'
— Professor John Maynard, University of Newcastle

'Sarah Maddison raises vital questions in relationship to the future we will share. While Indigenous people across Australia strive for, and demand sovereign rights, white Australia needs to come to terms with its own past and its place within and on Indigenous country.'
— Professor Tony Birch, Victoria University

**Other books by Sarah Maddison**

*Beyond White Guilt: The real challenge for black–white relations in Australia*

*Black Politics: Inside the complexity of Aboriginal political culture*

*Silencing Dissent: How the Australian government is controlling public opinion and stifling debate* (with Clive Hamilton)

# THE COLONIAL FANTASY

## WHY WHITE AUSTRALIA CAN'T SOLVE BLACK PROBLEMS

## SARAH MADDISON

ALLEN&UNWIN

SYDNEY • MELBOURNE • AUCKLAND • LONDON

First published in 2019

Allen & Unwin
83 Alexander Street
Crows Nest NSW 2065
Australia
Phone:   (61 2) 8425 0100
Email:   info@allenandunwin.com
Web:     www.allenandunwin.com

A catalogue record for this
book is available from the
National Library of Australia

ISBN 978 1 76029 582 0

Set in 11/15 pt Minion Pro by Midland Typesetters, Australia
Printed and bound in Australia by Pegasus Media & Logistics

10 9

The paper in this book is FSC® certified.
FSC® promotes environmentally responsible,
socially beneficial and economically viable
management of the world's forests.

Aboriginal and Torres Strait Islander people are warned that this book contains the names of deceased persons.

. . . all they seem'd to want was for us to be gone.

Captain James Cook, 30 April 1770

Let us go. Let us go. Give us that space to go, think and develop a way that was there before.

Yingiya Mark Guyula<br/>Yolŋu Nations Assembly<br/>(quoted in Wahlquist 2016a: 1)

# CONTENTS

# CONTENTS

# PREFACE

# WHO IS INDIGENOUS?
# WHO ARE SETTLERS?

Language is important. Both black and white identities in Australia have been constructed through the language of colonialism. Before the British invasion of these territories there were no 'Indigenous' or 'Aboriginal' people. These were generic European terms applied to the over 500 small, autonomous clan groups or nations on this continent and its islands, each with their own language, laws, customs and culture. Indigenous peoples have a unique relationship to the territory and to the nation—not one of 'consent' as might be ascribed to other cultural minorities who have willingly chosen to be a part of the settler society, but as dispossessed First Nations who have never willingly ceded their lands or their autonomy (Short 2008: 19).

Wherever possible in this book, when I am referring to or quoting an Indigenous person I use their preferred nation or clan affiliation. Throughout the book I otherwise use the terms 'Indigenous', 'Aboriginal' and 'Torres Strait Islander' as appropriate, as well as the term First Nations, an identifier that is increasing in usage among Aboriginal and Torres Strait Islander peoples. Internationally, a growing number of Indigenous peoples use the terms 'nation' and 'nationhood' to refer to themselves, accompanying the politics of resurgence discussed throughout the book (Cornell 2015: 2). Each of these forms of Indigenous identity is constructed and lived in the highly politicised context of contemporary settler colonialism. Gamilaroi journalist and founder of IndigenousX, Luke Pearson (2017e), explains the choices he has made in how he identifies:

> I am Aboriginal, but not an aboriginal or Aborigine. I am Indigenous, but not indigenous. I am First Nations, but not a First Australian (if anything, Indigenous people are the last Australians, as we were the last to be granted citizenship rights). I am Gamilaroi. That's just me though, every other Indigenous person has their own views and preferences for terminology that they use.

Note that Pearson points out that the terms 'Indigenous' and 'Aboriginal' are capitalised because they are used as proper nouns to signify the political sovereignty of these groups.

The sovereignty of Aboriginal and Torres Strait Islander peoples over these territories, and the identities that arise from connection to land and territory, persist despite the fact that hybridity is now a central component of contemporary Indigenous identity. Bundjalung poet and teacher Evelyn Araluen (2018: 13), born and raised on Dharug country, understood from childhood that being Aboriginal 'meant we were here before the tall ships came. Bits of us. But bits of us came on those tall ships too.' Yet this recognition of different 'bits' of identity does not displace the claim to a full Indigenous identity (rather than the racialised fractions of settler-imposed and highly offensive identity categories such as half-caste, quarter-caste or octoroon), which remains a powerful statement against colonial assimilation. Being Indigenous *and* whatever other ethnicity might come with a person's family history recognises Indigeneity as something to 'cherish and encourage' rather than stamp out (Goninan 2018: 95). Kamilaroi and Dunghutti woman Marlee Silva (2018: 216) recalls her father making this point by pouring milk into cups of black coffee, telling her, 'It doesn't matter how much milk you add: they'll never not be coffee.'

I use the terms 'settler' and 'non-Indigenous' in relation to any individual or group of people who came to Australia at any time after the first invasion in 1788. The term 'settler' is intended to be discomforting, deliberately underscoring the nature of non-Indigenous people's relation to this territory and its peoples as a further impetus towards decolonial transformation

(Snelgrove et al 2014: 2). Settler Canadian authors Emma Battell Lowman and Adam Barker (2015: 1) suggest that non-Indigenous people

> need a term that can help us see ourselves for who we are, not just who we claim to be. For that we need a term that shifts our frame of reference away from our nation, our claimed territory, and onto our relationship with systems of power, land, and the people on whose territory our country exists.

Settlerness is often bound up with whiteness, and settler privilege and white privilege tend to be deeply connected.[1] The relationship between Indigenous and non-Indigenous people in Australia is often described as a relationship between black and white constituencies. But it is also important to note that the extent to which settlers benefit from colonisation is modified to varying degrees by their skin colour and cultural background (not all settlers are white or Anglo), and by class, gender, sexuality and physical ability. Settlers are a diverse and multi-ethnic group, whose identities have been shaped by settler colonialism in a range of ways, but who in different ways are all complicit in sustaining colonial relationships (Battell Lowman and Barker 2015: 69).

Beyond their use as descriptors, however, the terms 'Indigenous' and 'settler' also convey the reality of the power relations that produce, and are reproduced in, settler colonial societies. As with any implied binary, there are problems with this pairing—as noted, many Indigenous people share settler heritage and in both groupings an individual's identity is complex and layered. But as political signifiers these terms reject any idea of neutrality in the relationship. We are none of us outside or above these relationships. Migrants are still settlers, white progressives are still settlers, and as Corey Snelgrove (in Snelgrove et al 2014: 5–6) has argued—'There are no good settlers; there are no good colonisers.' Settlers are complicit in the ongoing dispossession of Indigenous peoples. Potawatomi environmental justice advocate and philosopher Kyle Powys Whyte (2018) argues that settler privilege means that some combination of our economic security, citizenship, relationship to land and place, mental and physical health, cultural integrity and spiritual life, family values and career aspirations are *literally not possible* were it not for the dispossession of Indigenous peoples. The challenge for settlers who are cognisant of this privilege—potential allies to Indigenous struggles—is to find ways to become more than 'sympathetic beneficiaries of colonialism' and embrace legitimately decolonising approaches. While settlers can—and do—evade thinking about the violent circumstances that cause us to be here, thinking more consciously of ourselves as settlers may give us pause to consider how it is that we can feel at home on the homelands of others.

I am a white, settler writer, and it is this perspective I inevitably bring to my work. Self-identifying as a settler still carries the risk of what non-Indigenous political scholar Alissa Macoun (2016) describes as 'colonising white innocence', becoming little more than a performance of political consciousness used to exonerate oneself from responsibility in the relationship with Indigenous peoples. But there is possibility in the term too; thinking through what it means to be a settler involves engaging with the recognition that 'living on another Indigenous nation's territory also carries an obligation to support those defending their homelands' (Corntassel in Snelgrove et al 2014: 25). It mandates political action. In this sense, an identity as 'settler' cannot be decontextualised, and must not displace Indigenous peoples' own articulations of Indigenous–settler relations. This book seeks to foreground precisely these articulations.

The research that has informed this book represents a deep dive into a wide range of media from the past eight years, including both mainstream and Indigenous media sources, in search of voices and perspectives that are not always heard or amplified. Media might seem a strange location to look for diverse voices, but the wealth of new online media sources, including Indigenous-led platforms like IndigenousX, means that Aboriginal and Torres Strait Islander peoples of all ages, from all over the continent, are contributing to reporting and public debate like never before. Mindful of the concern that settler colonial theory has a tendency to overshadow Indigenous voices, it has been the explicit intention in this book to foreground these voices and perspectives as they examine the core issues that continue to structure Indigenous–settler relations.

The first four chapters of the book examine the central claims Aboriginal and Torres Strait Islander peoples have made upon the settler state—for recognition, self-determination, representation and land. The last four consider some of the policy regimes deployed by the settler state to maintain the

colonial fantasy—intervention, incarceration, closing the gap and reconciliation. In each chapter, diverse First Nations voices and perspectives are
brought to the fore in the hope that readers will understand that what may
appear to them a radical position is in fact widespread, coherent and practical and should be taken seriously as a genuine alternative to the constantly
failing status quos upon which the state and mainstream population rely.

# INTRODUCTION

## AUSTRALIA'S SETTLER PROBLEM

26 January 2018. Soaring temperatures do not deter tens of thousands of people, Indigenous and non-Indigenous, from turning out at the Invasion Day march and rally in the centre of Melbourne. Invasion Day. Not Australia Day. Because for Aboriginal and Torres Strait Islander people there is little reason to rejoice when modern-day Australia continues to celebrate the day the British first invaded this continent.

The speeches are fiery, and none more so than the words from the MC, young Yigar Gunditjmara and Bindal woman Tarneen Onus-Williams. From the steps of Victoria's Parliament House, Onus-Williams invoked an anger felt by many Indigenous people in Australia when she declared:

> We have organised this rally to abolish the day. Again, we have not organ-
> ised this for change the date. We have organised this to abolish Australia
> Day because fuck Australia. Fuck Australia, I hope it fucking burns to
> the ground.

The backlash was predictable. Former Victorian premier Jeff Kennett insisted that Onus-Williams should be removed from her position on the Koorie Youth Council—the representative body for Aboriginal and Torres Strait Islander young people in Victoria. Conservative Bundjalung commentator, Warren Mundine, told the media he thought that governments should stop funding groups like the Koorie Youth Council when they appointed 'haters' who had 'no scruples about taking taxpayers' money and then spitting in their faces.' Other conservatives wailed on social media about people who 'hate Australia', disparaging Onus-Williams in ways that frankly do not need to be repeated. Yet the conservative backlash garnered its own backlash from Aboriginal and Torres Strait Islander peoples and their allies, and within days the hashtag #IStandWithTarneen was trending on Twitter.

Given the opportunity to clarify her views, Onus-Williams refused to apologise for her statement, instead insisting her words needed to be understood in context:

> It was a metaphor, not actually a statement to be taken literally. I just want everything, all the governments to fall apart, because our people are dying and nobody cares and the whole system needs to change. The leaders of this country continue to ignore and oppress us. I am sick of our people getting locked up and dying in custody, of our young people suiciding.
>
> I don't have all the answers of what is going to liberate us. I just know the current system isn't working. Since colonisation nothing has worked for blackfellas on this land (quoted in Cunningham and Carey 2018).

And here, precisely, is the point—both the point of this book and the point of a resurgent Aboriginal and Torres Strait Islander movement in Australia. The current system—the settler colonial system—is not working. It has never worked for Aboriginal and Torres Strait Islander peoples. Yet despite incontrovertible evidence of this failure, the nation persists in governing the lives of Aboriginal and Torres Strait Islander peoples in ways that are damaging and harmful, firm in its belief that with the right policy approach, the right funding arrangements, the right set of sanctions and incentives, Indigenous lives will somehow improve. This is the colonial fantasy.

At the heart of the colonial fantasy lies the belief that colonialism is already over. Those of us educated in the Australian school system were taught that Australia began as a penal colony, with the territories acquired by the British subsequently revealed and mapped by explorers, populated by squatters, and made rich off the sheep's back and in the heady days of the gold rush. Aboriginal and Torres Strait Islander people barely featured in this narrative, and when they did it was as a curious footnote to the story of the birth of a 'new' nation. The territories invaded by the British were treated as though they were *terra nullius*—land belonging to no one—with the violence that was done to First Nations peoples recounted as an unfortunate but inevitable chapter situated in a long-ago history. In this story, the idea of Australia as a colony ended at Federation, when the six self-governing British colonies (Queensland, New South Wales, Victoria, Tasmania, South Australia and Western Australia) united as the Commonwealth of Australia, with the terms of their new federal relationship outlined in the Australian Constitution.

Much of this story is, however, a lie. The arrival of the British was more than the benign settlement of empty land, but instead introduced a particular type of colonialism to these shores—penal colonies yes, but also something more. The land that the British invaded clearly belonged to the people living here, as many early accounts of the colonies attest, but this did not deter the new arrivals. The early invaders came with the specific intent of taking the land in order to *settle* it. In other words, they came to stay. As with settler colonial societies elsewhere in the world, the British colonisers (and their generations of descendants), would eventually relinquish their identification with the empire that dispatched them, in favour of an identification with their new homeland and the society they would construct here (Battell Lowman and Barker 2015: 27).

The frustration for the new arrivals is that they have never been able to truly naturalise this new identity or their presence on this territory. What reveals the lie in the classroom story of Australian settlement is the survival and resistance of Aboriginal and Torres Strait Islander peoples. The presence of Aboriginal and Torres Strait Islander peoples is a constant reminder that settler society has been imposed on Indigenous lives and territories. This fact frustrates the completion of the colonial project. Non-Indigenous Australian historian Patrick Wolfe's seminal formulation of settler colonialism rests on the central insight that settler colonies were and are premised on the *elimination* of Indigenous societies (Wolfe 1999: 2), whether by their physical obliteration or by absorbing them into the wider population.[2] This is the part of the story not told in our schools. Unlike other forms of colonialism where the intent was to extract the resources of a territory (often using Indigenous peoples as enslaved or exploited labour), a settler colony like Australia seeks to acquire land and in doing so to *replace* the Indigenous population with the peoples, institutions and structures of the new nation.

As with other settler colonial societies, Australia too sought first to destroy and later to assimilate Aboriginal and Torres Strait Islander peoples in order to eliminate the Indigenous presence and its constant reminder of colonial illegitimacy on newly acquired territory.

Federation did not end this story. Federation was not the end of colonialism. While the British colonies ended at Federation, colonialism has continued in a relationship that many Aboriginal and Torres Strait Islander peoples still experience as an occupying power living on their lands. Indigenous people see the anxiety this causes for non-Indigenous people, as Waanyi and Juru medical anthropologist Gregory Phillips (2018: 103) points out:

> White Australia's biggest fear and justification for denying Aboriginal prior ownership and brilliance is not only because they are jealous of it, and cannot comprehend it, but because they fear this land won't ever be their true spiritual home—that we might tell them to go back to Europe.

Progressive Australians—those who seek to reform and improve society rather than protecting the status quo—desperately want their position as an occupying power to be resolved. One way to achieve this would be to have Aboriginal and Torres Strait Islander people enjoy the status and quality of life enjoyed by most Australians. Like many others I have spent years believing that with the right attitudes and policies Indigenous people might one day accept us as colleagues, allies, friends and family, with a legitimate place on these territories. Like many others I have sheltered this belief with a faith that Australian democracy was fundamentally benign and benevolent, and that the problem lay with ideological approaches and policy settings that could be contested and corrected as part of the normal business of electoral politics. I bolstered this belief with the view that once the policy settings were right, Aboriginal and Torres Strait Islander peoples would be able to thrive as equal citizens with other Australians. This set of beliefs is common among progressive Australians and it blinds us to the obvious lack of evidence for this position. Or more accurately, perhaps, what blinds us is that part of the colonial fantasy that believes colonialism is almost complete, that the coloniser will (one day soon!) cease to be an invading force and that all peoples living on these stolen territories will share in the nation's riches and rewards. This is what non-Indigenous political theorists Elizabeth Strakosch and Alissa Macoun (2012) describe as the 'vanishing endpoint' of settler colonialism—a desired moment of completion that is forever pushed further into the future.

This dream of colonial completion sits uneasily between the drive for the *elimination of* Indigenous peoples and the contradictory but persistent faith that the right policy settings will resolve the difficult *relationship with* Aboriginal and Torres Strait Islander peoples. In practice this contradiction means that seemingly progressive policies, which produce moments of apparent hope—the 1967 referendum, the bridge walks in 2000, the 2008 apology to the Stolen Generations—in fact do little to change the relationship or transform Indigenous lives. The 1967 referendum did not transform the place of Aboriginal and Torres Strait Islander peoples in Australian society, nor did a decade of reconciliation, and nor did an apology for past wrongs. Although each of these initiatives was a genuine expression of the hope felt by progressive Australians that the relationship between Aboriginal and Torres Strait Islander peoples and others in Australia might be improved, this hope is always trounced by the underlying desire for colonialism itself to be completed. This book explains why such moments can never complete the Australian colonial project, and why something far more radical is required.

THINGS ARE GETTING WORSE, NOT BETTER
As I began to write this book in 2017, Australia marked a number of significant anniversaries: the tenth anniversary of the Northern Territory Intervention, the twentieth anniversary of the tabling of the *Bringing Them Home* report in federal parliament, the twenty-fifth anniversary of the *Mabo* High Court decision and the fiftieth anniversary of the 1967 referendum. Each of these events were imagined, at the time, as a turning point in the relationship between Aboriginal and Torres Strait Islander peoples and the Australian settler state. Several of them—the 1967 referendum and the *Mabo* decision in particular—are still considered high-water marks in the relationship, while others—most notably the Northern Territory Intervention—are considered low points. As Gamilaroi man and founder of IndigenousX Luke Pearson (2017f) observes, each anniversary passed

during 2017 provided an opportunity for the nation to reflect and to ask 'how far have we come in 50 years? In 25, 20 or 10 years?' Pearson suggests that the 'age-old Western belief in the inexhaustible march towards progress' would lead many to assume that the issues marked by these milestones—Indigenous poverty and disadvantage, child removal, dispossession, recognition—had all been addressed or at least improved in the intervening decades.

And yet, as 2017 passed without a promised referendum on the recognition of Aboriginal and Torres Strait Islander peoples in the Australian Constitution—indeed, as the federal government rejected the proposals from the Indigenous-led Referendum Council on exactly this question—Pearson observed that 'the relationship between government and Indigenous groups feels like it may have reached a new low.' 2017 was, in fact, a year that the Australian Director of Human Rights Watch, Elaine Pearson, described as 'particularly dismal' for Indigenous peoples' rights (Hocking 2018).

That there is deep pain and much suffering in many Indigenous communities in Australia goes almost without saying. The successes of a burgeoning Indigenous middle class do not obscure the fact that for the majority of Aboriginal and Torres Strait Islander people, government policies and programs have made little positive difference to their quality of life. Over many decades, Australian government policies in the Indigenous affairs domain have been marked by two things: constant churn and reinvention; and constant resistance to the one thing that Aboriginal and Torres Strait Islander people want, indeed the one thing that has made a difference elsewhere—the ability to control and manage their own lives. On this second point, Bunuba woman and Aboriginal and Torres Strait Islander Social Justice Commissioner, June Oscar (2017b) is clear:

> Since the arrival of the British on our shores in 1788, Aboriginal and Torres Strait Islander peoples have consistently called for greater control over our destinies, for the ability to live freely and equally, and for greater recognition of our rights as the First Peoples of this land. This has remained an unresolved source of pain for our people . . . Today, nearly 230 years later, too many of our peoples are still not able to feel at home in the place we call our own. The political systems and institutions of this country remain inadequate at providing us with a voice in the matters that affect our lives.

> Our people seek an answer to our powerlessness, not extra rights. We seek a resolution that is not confined by the parameters of government, but is driven by the will of our people. This is self-determination.
>
> So long as we fail to address this question as a nation, so long as we suppress the desires of Aboriginal and Torres Strait Islander people for a greater say—the policies, the programs directed at us will flounder.

Oscar's claims are far more than mere speculation. International evidence confirms that Indigenous communities begin their revival at the point where they acquire the sort of territorial autonomy that enables them to control their own affairs in areas such as health, education and economic development (Fournier 2005: vii). Indeed, Stephen Cornell (2004: 2) argues that in the United States, self-determination has been the only overarching policy that has shown 'sustained evidence of actually improving the condition of Native[3] peoples', precisely because self-determination has put 'substantive decision-making power in Aboriginal hands.' Drawing on decades of research on the resurgence and success of Native Nations, Cornell (2004: 12) argues that three important things happen when Indigenous peoples gain power over their own affairs:

> First, bureaucratic priorities are replaced by Indigenous priorities, thereby gaining Indigenous support for initiatives and programs. Second, decisions begin to reflect local knowledge and concerns. One of the great fantasies of colonialism, still alive in the Indigenous affairs bureaucracies of the world, is the idea that 'we know what's best for you.' But we don't . . . And the third thing that happens is that decisions get linked to consequences . . . when Indigenous peoples themselves are in charge, they pay the price for bad decisions and reap the rewards of good ones . . . Jurisdiction, in other words, creates accountability.

In Australia, however, Indigenous affairs policy has gone in exactly the opposite direction, continuing to exert ever more heavy-handed controls over Aboriginal and Torres Strait Islander people and communities despite all evidence that this approach is failing miserably.

The endless renovation and relentless paternalism of Australian Indigenous policy has always been justified as a response to the so-called 'Aboriginal problem', which—it was assumed—could only be solved by the exercise of settler colonial authority. In a lecture in 2000, Yawuru man, and now federal senator, Patrick Dodson argued that for all governments, at all stages in Australia's post-invasion history, policy has been about 'their solutions to us as the problem':

> The problem of our being here.
> The problem of our disposal!
> The problem of our assimilation!
> And the problem of having us appreciative of all that governments have done 'for our own good' (Dodson 2000: 13).

There can be little doubt that Australia does indeed have a problem with Aboriginal and Torres Strait Islander people. Judging by the heat and volume of public debate, the endless moral panic, and the constant readjustment to policy settings, it is a very big problem indeed. The concern of this book, however, is to point out that the problem Australia thinks it has is not the real problem at all.

## AN ABORIGINAL PROBLEM OR A SETTLER PROBLEM?

In 2014, Arrernte Elder Rosalie Kunoth-Monks appeared on the ABC television program Q&A. In response to a question about whether documentaries such as John Pilger's Utopia encouraged or deterred activism on Indigenous 'problems', Kunoth-Monks issued a powerful reply:

> I am an Arrernte, Alyawarre First Nations person, a sovereign person from this country . . . Don't try and suppress me and don't call me a problem. I am not the problem. I have never left my country nor have I ceded any part of it. Nobody has entered into a treaty or talked to me about who I am. I am Arrernte, Alyawarra female elder from this country. Please remember that. I am not the problem (quoted in Bond 2016).

Like many other First Nations people before her, Kunoth-Monks was rejecting the framing of the 'Aboriginal problem' in Indigenous–settler relations. Since at least the 1800s, colonial and then Australian governments have used the language of the 'Aboriginal problem' as shorthand for recognising that the continuing existence of Indigenous peoples constitutes some kind of 'ongoing political difficulty' that the state needs to 'do something about' (Strakosch and Macoun 2012: 44). Suggestions that contemporary problems of so-called 'community dysfunction' are really the result of pre-colonial cultural norms, exacerbated by the damage caused by alcohol and violence (Sutton 2009), have been championed by conservative commentators including those associated with organisations such as the Institute of Public Affairs and the Bennelong Society (see for example Brunton 1993; Johns 2001). Palawa sociologist Maggie Walter (2018: 259) suggests that Aboriginal and Torres Strait Islander people are missing from the portrait of Australia created by Indigenous data, 'except as a problem.' As Patrick Dodson (2018: 65) has argued, however, 'No fair-minded Australian could think we want to be in this sad state by our own desire.'

Nevertheless, as Luke Pearson argues (2016a), it serves the interests of governments to perpetuate the view that the 'problem' is in fact Indigenous people themselves, who are cast as 'too backwards, too primitive, too greedy, too drunk, too everything bad to make use of the government's good will.' Keeping the focus on Indigenous people absolves the settler state of responsibility, casting government actions as benevolent and charitable rather than harmful. As Pearson argues:

> So long as we are seen as the problem, there is literally nothing that the government cannot justify, there is no level of incompetence or racism from the government that cannot be justified, and there is no amount of arguing from anyone else that will be seen as anything other than 'reverse racism', wanting 'free handouts' and refusing to accept responsibility.

Munanjahli and South Sea Islander academic Chelsea Bond (2018) describes this dynamic as providing 'the very foundation' of the relationship between Aboriginal and Torres Strait Islander people and the state; a relationship that is 'serving the interests of the colony financially and politically.' If Indigenous peoples and cultures are to blame for their own suffering, the settler state can avoid addressing the structural roots of these problems and deny the fact that structural change is needed if the situation is ever to change. The evident fact that Indigenous peoples do not thrive in situations of ongoing colonialism makes a lie of both the banality of colonialism and the benevolence of settlers themselves.

Framing 'the problem' as having its locus in Aboriginal and Torres Strait Islander society and culture rather than in settler structures, also allows settlers to ignore the fact that the same patterns of struggle and disadvantage are evident in *all* settler colonial societies, and in widely diverse Indigenous cultures. Mohawk scholar Taiaiake Alfred (2017b: 2) makes this observation of the Canadian settler colony, arguing that while many people have devoted considerable energy and vast amounts of money 'trying to fix the problems' faced by First Nations there, Canada, like Australia, has seen things 'getting worse, not better.' Alfred contends that the reason for such persistent failure is that even progressive activists or allegedly more progressive governments are 'working on the wrong problem, one that has been defined in a way that prevents its solution.' Alfred makes this point about Canada, but I have substituted Australia in the quote below to make the parallel completely evident:

> It may be difficult for non-Indigenous people to accept that [Australia] exists as a result of the illegal dispossession of Indigenous people. [Australians'] prosperity is derived from the fraudulent taking of Indigenous nations' lands and the marginalization of Indigenous peoples in their own homelands. The mentalities and self-images of [Australians] support these hard truths: the forced acculturation and imposed redefinition of Indigenous people away from their true selves to serve the needs of the mainstream society; the economic exploitation of their lands; the denial of First Nations' inherent right to govern themselves; the creation of dependency that has generated psychological and social problems arising from alienation or active oppression. This is [Australia].
>
> [Australia] is the problem. There is no [Indigenous] problem. [Indigenous people] are not the problem . . . If we want to solve the so-called [Indigenous] Problem, what we need to do is fix [Australia], and the relationship it has to its Original People and the land.

What Alfred (2017a), describes as the 'Coloniser Problem', has proven toxic to Aboriginal and Torres Strait Islander people. Wiradjuri journalist Stan Grant (2016a: 1) suggests that for Indigenous people in Australia, the harms done to Aboriginal and Torres Strait Islander peoples are 'the images that give shape to Australia.' For Grant, these images include seeing the physical scars of my loved ones: bodies marked by knife wounds, broken bones, missing fingers, and dark ink tattoos. These tell stories of lives at the coalface of bigotry and poverty. It is hearing stories of people arrested and chained like dogs to trees left to burn in the blazing summer sun. It is stumbling on a book as a child and seeing Aboriginal people chained and bound to each other, staring blankly at a world that could not see them as anything but a problem to be solved or a people to be extinguished.

If the problem is understood as a coloniser or settler problem rather than an Indigenous problem, then the possible solutions to the problem look radically different to the solutions Australia has been pursuing to date. The settler problem cannot be addressed through assimilation, welfare quarantining or efforts to 'close the gap', and nor will it be resolved through apparently more progressive approaches of reconciliation or constitutional recognition. None of these strategies attend radically enough to the foundations of the relationship between Indigenous peoples and settler colonial states. Yellowknives Dene scholar Glen Coulthard has argued that even though contemporary colonial states no longer reinforce their power over Indigenous people through policies 'explicitly oriented around the genocidal exclusion/assimilation double' they continue to reproduce these same power relations 'through a seemingly more conciliatory set of discourses and institutional practices that emphasize [Indigenous] *recognition* and *accommodation*.' Regardless of this change of emphasis, however, Coulthard argues that 'the relationship between Indigenous peoples and the state has remained *colonial* to its foundation' (2014: 6). As Tanganekald, Meintangk and Bunganditj scholar Irene Watson (2007a: 29) has suggested, we 'need to move beyond the conversation of the Aboriginal problem to a discourse on the problem of colonialism.'

What makes the ongoing project of settler colonialism visible to settlers is Indigenous resistance. At every stage of the colonial project, Aboriginal and Torres Strait Islander people have resisted and—more frustratingly for the colonial endeavour—they have survived. The sustained denial of either colonial oppression or Indigenous sovereignty does not make either disappear (Simpson 2014; Veracini 2015). The persistence of Indigenous peoples, despite everything the settler has thrown at them, continues to frustrate the desire for colonial completion. Consistent, powerful assertions of Indigenous identity and sovereignty continue to challenge the legitimacy and confidence of settler identity and institutions. This has been the case since the moment of invasion. From the outset, as non-Indigenous anthropologist Deborah Bird Rose (1991: 46) has pointed out, Indigenous people 'got in the way' of the coloniser 'just by staying at home.' Aboriginal and Torres Strait Islander peoples are still at home in this continent, despite all the settlers' efforts to dispossess and displace them. The fantasy of colonial completion remains just that, and fuels an endless cycle of contestation between coloniser and colonised. For Aboriginal and Torres Strait Islander peoples, this contestation is increasingly framed around a refusal of settler norms and practices, and a resurgence of Indigenous culture and self-determination.

## RESISTANCE, REFUSAL, RESURGENCE

Despite the colonisers' myth of their peaceful settlement of the continent, Aboriginal and Torres Strait Islander peoples have forcefully resisted the colonial presence since the moment of invasion. As non-Indigenous historian Henry Reynolds (2013: 111) has argued:

> The evidence is bountiful and it is clear. Aboriginal resistance to the intrusion of settlers into their country was widespread and persistent. It was common to almost every part of Australia and continued for well over a century. It was one of the most enduring features of the nation's history.

For over 230 years, Aboriginal and Torres Strait Islander peoples have continued to contest settler control over their lives. As Patrick Dodson (2000: 14–15) has argued, Aboriginal and Torres Strait Islander peoples have been, and continue to be

> an affront to the foundational thinking and perception that underpins the British mould of Australian institutional principles of society. The confidence of the nation to celebrate with some pride its achievements is always tempered with the concern that the issues of unfinished business between us would surface and detract from the moment.

As colonisation unfolded across the continent that would become known as 'Australia', colonisers hoped that Aboriginal and Torres Strait

Islander people would become a mere footnote to a triumphalist history. Aboriginal and Torres Strait Islander peoples would not let this be so. Throughout the twentieth century and into the twenty-first, Indigenous peoples have resisted and contested colonial domination. I have written elsewhere (Maddison 2009) of the healthy diversity of views among Indigenous leaders and activists on a range of political issues. Nevertheless, across the decades and around the continent it is also possible to observe an overarching consistency in Indigenous views of colonialism. Achieving independence from settler authority and control has been a 'defining characteristic' of the Indigenous rights movement in Australia (Burgmann 2003: 60). In New South Wales in the 1920s, the Australian Aboriginal Progressive Association formed under the leadership of Wonnarua and Worimi man Fred Maynard, demanding land for every Aboriginal family in the state and pioneering the call for Aboriginal control of Aboriginal affairs (Maynard 1997). In Victoria in the 1930s Yorta Yorta leader William Cooper and the Australian Aborigines League rejected settler control of Indigenous lives, and made the demand that Indigenous peoples should govern themselves central to their campaigning (Attwood and Markus 2004: 15). When the Australian Black Power movement emerged in the late 1960s it embraced Cooper's emphasis on the need for 'thinking black' and explicitly rejected settler control and assimilation. From the late 1970s onwards, right across the Australian continent, Aboriginal and Torres Strait Islander groups and organisations demanded the recognition of rights that stemmed from their prior occupation of the territories colonised by the British.

Wirdi woman from Wangan and Jagalingou country, Murrawah Johnson, suggests that what it means to be Black Australia today has been shaped by these 230 years of resistance, by 'brave decisions to not comply with the invading colonial-settler forces.' Johnson (2017: 5) situates her own struggles in this history, arguing that:

> Every win our freedom fighters made became the statements of defence of country, or markers of advancement back to our freedom, to reclaiming our people and families, cultures and stories, places and land. The strikes, the walk-offs, and the resistance to the destruction of our ways of life and our very survival have guided us . . . We record these moments as 'our' Black History. This is an account of the resistance to colonial powers.

Recent years have seen a shift in emphasis in Aboriginal and Torres Strait Islander resistance. While for much of the period from the 1960s to the turn of the twenty-first century, effort and energy has been directed at national politics, and particularly towards changing the policies of the federal government, more recently there has been a profound shift in emphasis. In response to the seeming imperviousness of settler structures and institutions, there has been a growing call for Indigenous people to turn away from these hostile political environments in favour of decolonising programs focused on local, place-based politics and cultural rejuvenation (Elliott 2016: 413). This turn, also evident in other settler colonial societies, is significant for its renewed emphasis on Indigenous autonomy and nationhood, and the foregrounding of surviving Indigenous languages, cultural practices, geographies and modes of political organising. This trend is neither complete or exclusive, but it is seeing 'growing numbers of Indigenous nations pursuing their own political goals and engaging in innovative political action and institution building' (Cornell 2015: 6).

Colonisation is not the only story to be told of Indigenous lives, and there is a danger in suggesting that it is. It is one thing to understand the power of colonialism and the importance of Indigenous resistance to that power. Such an understanding, however, limits an understanding of the freedom of those who have been colonised, framing all Indigenous actions as a response to, or as an outcome of, settler power (Alfred 2013b). In fact, as Geonpul scholar Aileen Moreton-Robinson (2003: 128) argues, in their engagement with white settler culture, Indigenous people

> have learnt to create meaning, knowledges and living traditions under conditions not of our own choosing as strategies for our survival. Our cultural forms take account of the ambiguous existence that is the inevitable result of this engagement . . . there is no single, monolithic form of Indigenous resistance, rather than simply being a matter of overtly defiant behaviour, resistance is re-presented as multi-faceted, visible and invisible, conscious and unconscious, explicit and covert, intentional and unintentional.

Understanding Indigenous resistance in terms of refusal and resurgence suggests the vitality and independence of these practices.

By refusing to 'consent to the apparatuses of the state', Indigenous peoples are able to articulate political projects that draw from pre-colonial political traditions and thereby resist settler domination (Simpson 2016: 328). Audra Simpson (2016: 327–8) points to the practices of refusal she has observed in her own Kahnawà:ke Mohawk polities, describing 'the very deliberate, wilful, intentional actions that people were making in the face of the expectation that they consent to their own elimination as a people.' Simpson describes 'refusal', as

> a political and ethnic stance that stands in stark contrast to the desire to have one's distinctiveness as a culture, as a people, recognised. Refusal comes with the requirement of having one's *political* sovereignty acknowledged and upheld, and raises the question of legitimacy for those who are usually in the position of recognizing: What is their authority to do so? Where does it come from? Who are they to do so? (Simpson 2014: 11).

In practising refusal, Indigenous people turn away from the settler state and its offer of 'recognition' that does little to disrupt the structural arrangements of settler colonialism. Where participation in settler politics and institutions remains necessary—and at times even beneficial—a politics of refusal encourages an ongoing, watchful, and critical mode of conduct (Elliott 2016: 415). Chelsea Bond (2016: 4) suggests that the settler state fails to see Indigenous acts of refusal for what they are, choosing instead to label Indigenous people as 'divisive or aggressive' or as 'playing the victim.' What these labels ignore, Bond maintains, is that whenever Indigenous people 'refuse to accept the "gifts" of the state . . . refuse to comply, perform or play on their terms' it is because they recognise that

> there is something deeply wrong with the systems and structures that seek to demean and diminish us as Indigenous peoples. In denouncing these we are asserting both who we are as Indigenous people, but also rejecting the authority of these [settler] systems and structures.

Like refusal, resurgence also resists a politics of recognition that seeks to 'pacify and co-opt Indigenous leadership' (Alfred 2013a). Indigenous resurgence means actively restoring and regenerating Indigenous nationhood, focusing on transformative alternatives to settler colonial dispossession

(Corntassel 2012; Snelgrove et al 2014: 2). Like refusal, resurgence signals a turn *away* from settler institutions, values and ethics and a turn *towards* Indigenous institutions, values and ethics, 'reframing the conversation around decolonization in order to re-center and reinvigorate Indigenous nationhood' (Snelgrove et al 2014: 18). Taiaiake Alfred and Cherokee scholar Jeff Corntassel (2005: 612) argue that resurgence—'Indigenous pathways of authentic action and freedom struggle'—begins with 'people transcending colonialism on an individual basis', with ripple effects 'from the self to family, clan, community and into all of the broader relationships that form an Indigenous existence':

> As Indigenous peoples, the way to recovering freedom and power and happiness is clear: it is time for each one of us to make the commitment to transcend colonialism as *people*, and for us to work together as *peoples* to become forces of Indigenous truth against the lie of colonialism. We do not need to wait for the colonizer to provide us with money or to validate our vision of a free future; we only need to start to use our Indigenous languages to frame our thoughts, the ethical framework of our philosophies to make decisions and to use our laws and institutions to govern ourselves (Alfred and Corntassel 2005: 614).

Resurgence should not be understood only as practices of cultural revival, although such practices are certainly important. What Michi Saagiig Nishnaabeg scholar Leanne Betasamosake Simpson (2017: 48–9) has described as 'radical resurgence' is predicated on 'an extensive, rigorous, and profound reorganisation of things.' Simpson contends that 'cultural resurgence' can be dangerously compatible with settler colonialism because it does not contend with dispossession. While Simpson also acknowledges that, in Indigenous thought, culture and politics are inseparable, and that community-based language revival projects (as an example) are 'inherently political and cultural', she also observes that adding the modifier of 'cultural' depoliticises resurgence in ways that enable it to be co-opted by the modes of recognition offered by the settler state (Simpson 2017: 50). 'Political resurgence', by contrast, 'is seen as a direct threat to settler sovereignty.'

Radical resurgence also has specific political goals concerned with the decolonisation of political relationships between Indigenous peoples and settler states through the revival of Indigenous self-government. Indigenous peoples the world over seek recognition as distinct political entities with control over their lands, governance of their internal affairs, and the ability to define and pursue their own interests, even as Indigenous nations continue to exist within encompassing settler states. Resurgent self-government means Indigenous nations are increasingly turning away from a focus on changing settler government policy and towards Indigenous agendas and action, 'giving political force to Indigenous nationhood' through the intentional processes of 'identifying as a nation, organising as a nation, and acting as a nation' (Cornell 2015: 3–6).

How a more radical, structural transformation of the relationship between Aboriginal and Torres Strait Islander peoples and the Australian settler state might occur is uncertain, and yet in some important ways this work is already underway. Renowned writer of Aboriginal, West Indian and Irish descent Tony Birch (2018) has argued that settler colonial societies are 'incapable of countenancing either the relinquishment of power, or the contemplation of genuine remorse.' Like most dominant political systems, settler colonialism remains pervasive, naturalised and invisible to those who enjoy its benefits (Snelgrove et al 2014: 9). But there is a risk that highlighting the structural nature of settler colonialism will cast it as unchangeable (Strakosch and Macoun 2017: 36). This is far from the case. As the non-Indigenous theorist of settler colonialism Lorenzo Veracini (2015: 102) has argued, 'structures can be torn down; hegemonies can be superseded.'

At the nub of a politics of resurgence is the argument behind the subtitle of this book: white Australia can't solve black problems. White Australia can't solve black problems because white Australia *is* the problem. Many scholars, activists and analysts—Indigenous and settler alike—maintain a degree of faith in the liberal settler order, or at least a belief that working with the liberal settler order is the only viable political option. This is a view to which I subscribed for many years, but which I can no longer hold. As Yawuru man Michael 'Mick' Dodson (2007: 5) has argued, there is little evidence that the settler state has the capacity to support Indigenous aspirations 'let alone recognise and respect our sovereign status.' This book explains why.

WHITE COMPLICITY AND THE COLONIAL FANTASY

The majority of Australians resist the idea that their country is a contemporary coloniser, despite the evident fact that there has been no structural decolonisation and little restitution of the majority of stolen land (Strakosch and Macoun 2017: 35). There is a deep reluctance to let go of the historical narratives that legitimate the settler presence on the continent, and which downplay the resulting harms done to Aboriginal and Torres Strait Islander peoples. In what Euahleyai and Kamilaroi legal scholar Larissa Behrendt (2003: 20) has described as 'the pervasiveness of Australia's psychological *terra nullius*', settler Australia remains attached to the 'deeply ingrained conviction' that, really, we 'couldn't have been all that bad' (Read 2010: 293). As Stan Grant (2016b: 2) observes, *terra nullius* still 'holds us in its grip. Australia clings to the idea of settlement while Indigenous people know the reality of invasion.'

Enough has been written elsewhere, including by me, on what it might take to change the hearts and minds of settler Australians such that they might more willingly embrace moves for Indigenous justice. For many years this has seemed an important task in a context where the political endgame was 'better' Indigenous policy, produced more consultatively but nonetheless within the settler structure. As non-Indigenous social movement scholar Verity Burgmann (2003: 49) has suggested, the 'Aboriginal movement' has been 'the most beleaguered' of any of the social movements she has researched, both because of its 'extremely limited' support base, and because decades of government policy have contributed to the fragmentation of Indigenous communities, which has, in turn, 'rendered political mobilisation difficult.' As a tiny percentage of the overall population, Burgmann (2003: 50) considers the movement 'powerless within the parliamentary political system.'

In the context of Indigenous resurgence, however, a different analysis is possible. The 'fragmentation' of Indigenous communities may be reimagined as the resurgence of Indigenous clan and nationhood. The parliamentary political system becomes less relevant when Indigenous peoples are turning away from that system and towards their own institutions, values and ethics. A decolonising approach to Indigenous politics, and specifically to the relationship between Aboriginal and Torres Strait Islander peoples and the Australian settler state, requires an unsettling of both the institutional structures of settler domination and of the assumptions and certainties that underpin settler political analyses (Elliott 2016: 423). None of this relies on the changed hearts and minds of non-Indigenous Australians. For First Nations, these changes are already happening. Non-Indigenous Australians need to get out of the way.

As the Unangax critical race scholar Eve Tuck and non-Indigenous cultural theorist Wayne Yang (2012: 10) argue in their precisely titled essay 'Decolonisation is not a metaphor', what they describe as 'settler moves to innocence' involve strategies that seek to relieve settlers of 'feelings of guilt or responsibility' without requiring them to give up land or power or privilege; 'without having to change much at all.' Decolonising will require change, and it will require of settlers that we give up power and privilege. Being an ally means more than just befriending Indigenous people. It means developing relations of accountability, and it means respecting Indigenous laws and jurisdiction. It means not just advocating for the return of 'remote' land, land that is 'over there', but thinking about what it means to live and work on Indigenous territories wherever we are on the continent, and what we may have to give up for this ongoing occupation. This requires considerable 'unlearning' on the part of all settlers, that can only happen through action, specifically through activism with and in support of Indigenous peoples. The process of 'unsettling the settler within' cannot be seen as an end in itself, but only as an opening for further action that benefits Indigenous peoples (Davis et al 2017: 394). As Clare Land (2015) has argued so compellingly, even solidarity must be decolonised.

In Australia, progressive non-Indigenous perspectives have not tended to be decolonial. Campaigns focused on achieving reconciliation, apology, recognition and even treaty, are often based on a desired imagined future in which there is a unified political community. Progressive policy has been limited to forms of redress intended to complete the colonial project and allow both Indigenous and non-Indigenous peoples to 'move forward as an inclusive Australian nation' (Strakosch 2016: 29). Despite good intentions, this approach merely perpetuates the colonial fantasy. Decolonisation, as Tuck and Yang (2012: 36) argue, requires 'a different perspective to human and civil rights based approaches to justice', an approach that necessitates 'relinquishing settler futurity, abandoning the hope that settlers may one day be commensurable to Native peoples.'

In pursuing this approach, I am mindful that I cannot afford to adopt for myself a version of Macoun's (2016) 'colonising white innocence.' Like other white progressives I am, as Fiona Probyn (2004: par 17) has argued, very much a part of the problem that I am trying to articulate. Aileen Moreton-Robinson (2000) has long made the point that it is not only conservatives and nationalists who seek to preserve white virtue. Moreton-Robinson (2000: 186) has written of the complicity of white feminists in the oppression of Indigenous women, challenging white feminists to 'theorise the relinquishment of power' so that 'feminist practice can contribute to changing the racial order.' So too, progressives of other kinds need to recognise their investment in a longed-for colonial redemption through apparently benevolent settler acts of apology and reconciliation (Strakosch and Macoun 2012). Macoun (2016: 86) argues that for critical scholars such as me, 'Assuming one's criticality can be a way of not admitting one's complicity.' Her analysis is incisive:

> Some white progressives interested in justice for Indigenous peoples tend to see our great political challenge to be mobilising the goodwill of other non-Indigenous people; sharing what we know and believe in order to turn those that are uneducated or unwilling or inactive into allies willing to add the strength of their numbers to Indigenous struggles.

This story that progressives tell ourselves is 'powerful and appealing', a story we 'can cling tightly to' even as we see its limits. And its limits are evident. As Macoun goes on to point out:

> Every person in Australia is always-already engaged with and in race-based colonial systems of rule and what many of us consider to be problematic political relationships; some of us have more opportunities to ignore or evade this reality than others. No politically pure or righteous way of being, acting or thinking as a white person or non-Indigenous person can exempt us from our political context, even though it is a context we collectively create, recreate, and may hope to change.

The move to colonising white innocence occurs when educated white progressives (like me) assume that we are somehow 'fundamentally different from other non-Indigenous people' and that we are somehow the solution to a problem that 'lies in the hearts and minds of others, rather than in our own institutions, knowledges, and practices.' We cannot, Macoun insists, 'see ourselves as agents of progressive futurity and not also of colonial institutions and racial power.' We cannot 'make ourselves the subjects and heroes of our own stories' (Macoun 2016: 95).

I do think progressive settlers, including settler scholars, have a role. I agree with Macoun (2016: 98–9) that settler scholars should not assume that Indigenous peoples will automatically experience our interventions as benevolent. However, for many years I have also taken very seriously another message I have heard from innumerable Aboriginal people; that is, that they are tired of being asked to educate white people. As Bidjara/Pitjara and Biri/Birri Gubba Juru historian and activist Jackie Huggins (1998: x) has argued specifically about Indigenous women, it is 'too much' to expect Aboriginal women 'to be continually explaining their oppression.' This is not to suggest that settler scholars should ever presume to displace the voices of Indigenous scholars. But it is to say that settler scholars have a responsibility to use their racial and institutional privilege to share the burden of educating non-Indigenous populations, while also holding and creating space for Indigenous critical engagement with their work. Many progressive or concerned settler Australians feel confused, hopeless and unable to identify a position that will support Indigenous peoples or bring change. It is my hope that this book will help facilitate a reorientation in non-Indigenous concern, away from ideas about improving Indigenous policy or services, and towards a recognition of the resurgence that is already underway in Aboriginal and Torres Strait Islander nations around the continent. Figuring out how we can get out of the way of Indigenous aspirations, and what we must give up to do so, is an urgent political task.

## ANGER, RESISTANCE, PERSEVERANCE

Listening to Indigenous voices from across the country it quickly becomes evident that Aboriginal and Torres Strait Islander people are calling for radical change in their relationship with the Australian settler state. While in mainstream circles at least, the call for decolonisation is usually regarded as a fringe position, in Indigenous circles it is far from marginal. From their

lived experiences Aboriginal and Torres Strait Islander people describe the
paternalism, the ongoing inequity, the harms, and the endless frustrations
caused by the colonising relationships they endure. Is it any surprise that
Aboriginal and Torres Strait Islander people are demanding structural
change? In the context of ongoing settler colonial injustice, Coulthard
(2014: 22) suggests that Indigenous peoples' anger can be seen as 'a sign
of moral protest and political outrage' that should be embraced as a sign of
critical consciousness.

Stan Grant (quoted in Mitchell 2016: 2) understands the righteousness of
this anger. In the wake of the Don Dale Youth Detention Centre revelations
(discussed in Chapter Six), he describes himself as struggling 'to contain a
pulsating rage':

> I have moved from boiling anger to simmering resentment but the feeling
> has not passed nor do I wish it to. Even as I write, my words are powered by
> a coursing fury. My hands hover above the keyboard in a clenched fist.
>
> This is an anger that comes from the certainty of being. This is an anger
> that speaks to my soul. This anger I know to be just.

Gunai/Kurnai, Gunditjmara, Wiradjuri and Yorta Yorta writer and
activist Nayuka Gorrie (2016:4) articulates some of the reasons for this
anger:

> Black rage is justified. Everyday we walk around on stolen land—it might be
> our own, or we might have been dispossessed so cows, coal mines and white
> people could exist on it or for our 'protection'. We go to schools where the
> most we can hope for is at least one other black person in our cohort; that no
> one will catch us lip-synching the anthem; that we do reasonably okay in an
> education system that was first used as a tool for assimilation.
>
> We might then go on to jobs where we are the only black people and feel
> utterly isolated. We will sit through this nation celebrating colonialism every
> year on January 26. We will experience racial profiling by every system we
> come into contact with. We go to more funerals than we can remember and
> are constantly mourning someone.

As with Tarneen Onus-Williams, sometimes Indigenous anger finds
public expression in resistance to the compulsory celebration of Australian
nationalism. Former rugby league player turned boxer, Wiradjuri man Joe

Williams, made headlines in 2016 calling for Indigenous sports stars not to stand during the national anthem. Williams argued that his stance was 'for our future':

> I believe that national anthem does not represent our people. That every time we see the flag raised, it shows the Union Jack. And to us that represents bloodshed and torture and rape of mass people, by the thousands. How disrespectful do you think it is to our people that have to stand through that? (quoted in Murphy-Oates 2016: 2).

Musician Dan Sultan, who is of Arrernte, Gurindji and Irish descent also weighed into the ongoing national debate about Australia Day, arguing:

> It is what it is, whether people want to believe it or not. It's completely beside the point. It's the fucking history of this country. It's not our opinion, it's fucking what happened, and *is* happening . . . If there's anyone out there whose connection to this place is so fucking fragile and flimsy that someone giving them a history lesson about the place that they apparently love so much is threatening, then they can go fuck themselves. They're not patriots, they're nationalists and they're racists (quoted in Cunningham 2017: 1).

Alongside anger there is frustration, because Aboriginal and Torres Strait Islander people have been making the same claims, articulating the same problems, over many generations. As Arrernte man William Tilmouth argues, settler colonialism is present in all current approaches to Indigenous policy, where he detects 'a little heartbeat of assimilation in opposition to everything we try or aspire to achieve.' For Tilmouth, it is evident that 'more of the same will only lead to the same results, of more failure.' A commitment to change must mean 'governments stepping back, relinquishing agency and decision-making back to the community in order for them to have the chance to decide what they want to do with their lives, and what is best for them' (quoted in Children's Ground 2017). June Oscar (2017) suggests that too many Aboriginal and Torres Strait Islander people

> . . . feel at unease at the ever increasing role of governments and other agents in our lives. Daily experiences of racism and disadvantage are the norm and eat away at our health and wellbeing. It is sad that we live in a world so

desensitised to our trauma that 10 year olds committing suicide are met with expectation and not surprise.

This is an indictment on our country. This is the story of Australia. Brick by brick, structures have been built on our ancestral homes, leaving little room for our cultural way of life.

At times, these experiences of living as an Indigenous person in the Australian settler state are overwhelming. Gamilaraay writer Natalie Cromb (2017c: 1) describes herself as 'drowning':

I am drowning under the weight, the exhaustingly heavy weight of the constant and brutal hits that keep coming. I find myself both breathing deeply in anger and suffocating all at once. The feeling is difficult to enunciate, because it's all internalised as I continue to rise each morning and smile at my daughter, and maintain the façade that the world is good so I can shelter her as long as possible and give her the childhood she deserves, while inside I am crying . . . I feel rage so powerful and overwhelming I feel like I am burning up.

Bunurong writer Bruce Pascoe (2017: 3) feels the exhaustion of decades of struggle:

Every day I wake up to dawn on the river and I strap myself up for the battle. Most Aboriginal people do. The war is still in progress, every day we have to bolster the defence of the past and protect the future of our children and grandchildren.

There is little trust in government, and many questions to be asked. Gregory Phillips (2018: 99) describes the relationship between Aboriginal and Torres Strait Islander people and the Australian settler state as one akin to a violent domestic relationship in which 'white Australia abuses Aboriginal people and blames us for not accepting their benevolence and favour.' As Stan Grant (2016c: 2) points out, Aboriginal and Torres Strait Islander people 'fear the state' and 'have every reason to. The state was designed to scare us.' Reading transcripts from the 2015 Joint Select Committee on Constitutional Recognition of Aboriginal and Torres Strait Islander Peoples, Cobble Cobble woman and lead advocate for the

Referendum Council, Megan Davis (2016a) found herself frequently brought to tears. The testimony of witnesses, their feelings of 'hopelessness, abandonment, and despair' that spoke of 'the unfreedom that defines their existence', led Davis to conclude that 'for Indigenous Australians the system is broken.' She asks in response to this brokenness, 'How can this be of no concern to anyone in positions of power? What kind of system blithely ignores these perceptions?' Darumbal and South Sea Islander journalist Amy McQuire (2017a: 3) points to government dishonesty as a contributing factor, asking:

> In all the decisions made by government affecting us, how often have they lied? How often have they dispossessed us, how often have they reneged on already one-sided agreements? How often have they used the very race powers in the constitution to deny our own rights, and why would government ever seek to amend this so it doesn't happen again?

Luke Pearson (2016b: 3) asks of the settler state, 'Do you really think that we are upset over what happened "200 years ago", or what started 200 years ago?':

> You cannot 'get over' a colonial past that is still being implemented today. You cannot come to terms with a national history that the nation refuses to acknowledge ever happened. We cannot 'reconcile' what happened yesterday when we are too busy bracing ourselves for what will inevitably come tomorrow.

As Irene Watson (2009: 46) points out, the Australian settler state is yet to answer the most significant question of all: 'by what lawful process do you come to occupy our lands?' Watson (2018) points to the flawed and racist assumptions at the heart of the colonial project:

> The assumption that the coloniser could subjugate us to their way of being, to dismantle our relationships to our laws and our lands, is a denial of our ways of existence. The assumption that the coloniser could deny our existence, our ways of being and our relational legal systems is an act of racism.

These assumptions remain structured into the relationship between Aboriginal and Torres Strait Islander peoples and the Australian settler state.

Mick Dodson (2007: 5) has expressed the view that Indigenous peoples in Australia are 'getting slaughtered by the colonial imperative to steal our land, to strip our culture, and to demoralise us as peoples and nations.' Yet as Dodson also points out, Indigenous people 'have always resisted' and will continue to resist 'as nations, forever connected to the land and fortified by our law and culture, to make decisions for ourselves in determining our future.'

Aboriginal and Torres Strait Islander people know that they are not the problem. Aboriginal and Torres Strait Islander peoples have clear ideas of what is needed. Chief executive of the National Aboriginal Community Controlled Health Organisation (NACCHO), Arrernte woman Pat Turner, makes a call for resurgence, contending that

> what our people and our communities have to do is just take total control of their own affairs. Don't wait for government, don't wait for them to provide the solutions. Work it out ourselves and just move on (quoted in Pearson 2017f).

While acknowledging that there will always be dissent among Aboriginal and Torres Strait Islander peoples (as there is in any polity), it is also fair to say that many Indigenous people today express their primary political aspiration as being for 'decolonisation'. The many voices you will encounter in this book may not be the ones preferred by the mainstream media, many of whom express far less challenging views, but these voices are today much, much more widespread than is generally acknowledged.

In the present political moment, the idea of decolonising Australia may seem pure fantasy. Replacing colonial authority with revitalised, self-governing relationships seems an aspiration beyond reach. How could such a radical restructuring take place? How could it be possible for Indigenous nations to reconstitute and govern themselves? Would the settler state simply abandon Indigenous nations to their own fates?

There are no easy answers to any of these questions, and what answers there may be must be determined community by community, clan by clan, nation by nation, by First Nations themselves. But there are answers to be found. As Veracini (2015: 106) has argued, 'Contrary to what the settler common sense may assert, settler colonial ways of belonging are not inevitable or natural; they are merely one possibility among many.' Between assimilation and secession there are an infinite number of possible configurations to the relationships between Aboriginal and Torres Strait Islander peoples and the settler state (Bradfield 2006: 81). Any new political arrangements need not, indeed cannot, originate from the settler state but may instead exist alongside it (Strakosch 2015: 186).

White Australia cannot solve black problems because white Australia *is* the problem. As Waanyi writer Alexis Wright has argued, 'Too many non-Indigenous people have tried to save us and have failed' (2006: 107). By now this fact is patently, irrefutably established. Aboriginal and Torres Strait Islander peoples are the only possible authors of their future. For First Nations peoples to recover from the multiple harms of settler colonialism *they* must change the terms of the relationship and take control of the structures, systems and services that they need, free from the control and interference of the settler state. Progressive settler Australians must learn to get out of the way, to be allies and accomplices without speaking for or over Aboriginal and Torres Strait Islander peoples. Structural change is needed, and this can only happen when settlers let go of the fantasy of colonial completion.

Let me explain why.

# CHAPTER 1

## RECOGNITION

As Senator Patrick Dodson took up the role of co-chairing a new Joint Select Committee on Constitutional Recognition in 2018, the fifth government-sponsored process since 2011 to consider the issue of Aboriginal and Torres Strait Islander recognition in the Australian Constitution, he found himself again questioning what it is about this issue that has proven so difficult for successive governments to resolve. For Dodson (2018: 60), the issues are clear:

> First Nations are simply asking parliament for recognition of who we are. We are seeking recognition of our sovereign status. We are seeking acknowledgment of our joint histories and the appalling injustices that we have suffered. We are sovereign peoples. We are the First Peoples of this country.

For others, however, the issues seem far more difficult, which at least partly explains why they have been on the political agenda for so long. Recognition of the Indigenous peoples of the continent in the nation's founding document is considered by many to be part of Australia's 'unfinished business' of reconciliation. Without treaties or other forms of agreement, the lack of constitutional recognition of Indigenous Australians is seen to perpetuate settler injustices. As legal scholar George Williams (2013: 14) has suggested, there is a popular view that it 'does not speak well of our nation' that Australia has thus far failed to recognise Aboriginal and Torres Strait Islander peoples in the Constitution. The colonial fantasy is writ large in such arguments, which rest on the idea that Indigenous recognition would 'complete' the nation, and that the failure to do so would be 'catastrophic for the national psyche' (Parker 2016: 101).

Exactly what form that recognition should supposedly take has never been resolved. Until 2017, a government-funded campaign organisation—'Recognise'—attempted to galvanise national enthusiasm for Indigenous constitutional recognition even though no clear model or question had been agreed. Over time, however, it became apparent that many Aboriginal and Torres Strait Islander people did not in fact support the idea. The desire for recognition within a constitution that many First Nations see as an illegitimate document was not as widely shared among Indigenous people as the settler state had presumed. Former chief executive officer of the National Centre of Indigenous Excellence, Yuwallarai woman Kirstie Parker (2016: 101) pointed out that many Indigenous critics who 'live catastrophe every day' were not persuaded that non-recognition would in fact be the psychic catastrophe that was suggested.

Such criticism created doubt about the entire recognition proposal. As Amy McQuire (2015a: 4) asked, if the campaign for recognition did not have overwhelming support from Aboriginal and Torres Strait Islander people 'what point is there to it at all?' Instead, in place of a demand for constitutional recognition came renewed calls for a treaty or treaties between Aboriginal and Torres Strait Islander nations and the Australian state that could create a new framework for Indigenous–settler relationships.

Australia is not alone in these struggles over recognition, which have become central to the global Indigenous rights movement over the last three decades. Recognition-based approaches to Indigenous–state relations have emerged in Asia, northern Europe, across the Americas, and throughout the South Pacific, including in Australia and Aoteaora New Zealand. Diverse in scope and scale, these new regimes claim to recognise forms of political autonomy, land rights and the cultural distinctiveness of Indigenous peoples and nations 'within the settler states that now encase them' (Coulthard 2014: 2). As Audra Simpson (2014: 23) has suggested, recognition is 'to be seen by another as one wants to be seen', not only as an individual but as part of a group that is formally and officially seen in politics. In the Australian context Patrick Dodson (2000: 13) argues that it has 'always been' the hope of Aboriginal and Torres Strait Islander peoples that governments would see them 'as the first Australians, with our Indigenous rights, obligations, and responsibilities respected and recognised.'

Yet, this apparently benign notion is profoundly challenging to the colonial fantasy. For the settler state to recognise Indigenous peoples *as they want to be seen* would require recognition of the fact that colonisation involved the forcible acquisition of First Nations territories without consent. For the settler state to recognise Indigenous peoples *as they want to be seen* would require recognition of First Nations sovereignty, enabled through territorial self-government—the central defining claim of the global Indigenous rights movement—in ways that would threaten the stability of the colonial fantasy (Jung 2011: 241; Watson 2007a: 20). In its pursuit of colonial completion the settler state wants only to draw Indigenous peoples *into* the colonial order in order to eliminate that political challenge. Indigenous demands for recognition of sovereignty thus become cloaked by what Henry Reynolds (2013: 236) describes as settlers' 'muffled demands for assimilation'.

But if someone has stolen your car would it really be enough for them to say 'I recognise that you were the original owner of the car' but still refuse to give it back? As Irene Watson (2007b: 28) argues:

> We have in Australia two ways, two different frameworks; one that refuses to recognise the existence of the other, stating that to 'give recognition' would be to fracture the state's very foundation. But how does a thief recognise the victim of the theft, if not to give back what they have stolen and to no longer hold claim over the object of the theft?

For the Australian settler state, like other settler colonial orders, such questions are a conundrum, as the colonial fantasy affords only a very limited view of what recognition might entail.

The counter to the settlers' limited view of recognition is a decolonising view that places far greater demands on the settler order. A decolonising view does not assume the legitimacy of settler state sovereignty over Indigenous peoples, and instead requires a genuine redistribution of both resources and political power, such that Indigenous peoples are able to terminate both their dependant relationship on the state and the colonial relationship itself (Short 2005: 275). As Djiniyini Gondarra of the Yolŋu Nations Assembly asserts, for Yolŋu peoples recognition means, 'All of Arnhem Land, we still maintain our law, maintain our language and have our land . . . We have not been conquered. We need our society recognised' (quoted in Fischer 2014a: 6).

## RECOGNITION STRUGGLES: CITIZENS TO SOVEREIGNS

Like the struggles of Indigenous peoples elsewhere in the world, Aboriginal and Torres Strait Islander struggles for recognition have taken many forms. Indigenous peoples have been both forcibly *included* in the settler state (and therefore have struggled for autonomy and self-government) and been damagingly *excluded* from the state (and therefore have struggled for the full rights of citizenship). As Elizabeth Strakosch (2015: 27) points out, although both settler and Indigenous energy is directed towards the debate about which form of recognition is more just, this contest leaves settler political structures fundamentally intact. For Aboriginal and Torres Strait Islander peoples, these two forms of recognition—either as sovereigns or as citizens—often require quite divided loyalties, which will occasionally come into conflict with each other (Chesterman 2005: 31). Yet, as I have discussed elsewhere (Maddison 2009), these demands for both sovereignty and citizenship have long been accommodated within Aboriginal and Torres Strait Islander political culture, although not without tension.

Aboriginal and Torres Strait Islander people first began demanding recognition as citizens in the 1920s, motivated by the experiences of poor treatment meted out to Indigenous ex-servicemen returning from World War I. Activists such as Fred Maynard, who established the Australian Aboriginal Progressive Association at the end of 1923, were dismayed to find that upon their return from active service they were denied full citizenship. These issues prompted the first wave of citizenship struggles, which continued during the inter-war period with the 1938 Aboriginal Day of Mourning conference. The development of Aboriginal citizenship, wrested from governments over decades of activism that has often been rendered invisible in history, was the result of civil rights activism that broke new ground in Australian politics. By 1948 the *Nationality and Citizenship Act* had created the category of Australian citizen, which included Aboriginal people by virtue of the fact that they had been born in Australia. In reality, however, Aboriginal and Torres Strait Islander peoples were recognised as citizens 'in name only' (Chesterman 2005: ix), and remained excluded from many rights and entitlements through a 'mosaic of discriminatory laws and administrative practices' (Cunneen 2005: 48). More substantive changes to the citizenship status of Aboriginal people did not emerge until the 1960s after the restrictions that had been enshrined in various 'protection'[4] acts began to be wound back (Peterson and Sanders 1998: 14).

While the 1960s were the culmination of the 30-year struggle for Indigenous citizenship recognition, it was also the period during which a different recognition struggle came to the fore. Even as citizenship became more inclusive, many Aboriginal and Torres Strait Islander people came to see it as an 'ambiguous achievement' reliant on forfeiting the possibility of sovereign recognition (MacDonald and Muldoon 2006: 210). The high point of Indigenous citizenship struggles was the 1967 referendum, which saw the Australian Constitution amended to permit the Commonwealth government to make laws for Aboriginal people and to allow Aboriginal people to be counted in the census. Despite much myth-making about the significance of the 1967 referendum, it is not the case that these changes to the Constitution conferred any new rights or afforded Aboriginal and Torres Strait Islander peoples any new legal or political status. Rather, the significance of this vote was in the 'symbolic affirmation of Aboriginal people's acceptance into the national community' (McGregor 2011: 141).

The granting of full citizenship to Aboriginal people came during a period in which assimilation remained official government policy, and so for many Indigenous activists there was a deep suspicion that civil rights were granted as part of this assimilationist program. As Trawlwoolway and Pinterrairer man and long-time sovereignty activist Michael Mansell notes, 'There is indeed a fine line between gaining equality through citizenship, and succumbing to assimilation forces' (2003: 9). Mer scholar Kerry Arabena also suggests that citizenship still implies a process of redefining Aboriginality so that Indigenous people may be better integrated into the 'colonial, corporate, globalised culture' of modern Australia (2005: 50). However, non-Indigenous law and politics scholar John Chesterman (2005: 21–2) makes two important distinctions between civil rights and assimilation. The first is philosophical, as the acquisition of civil rights in a settler society does not *necessitate* the sacrificing of cultural identity. Indeed, it is evident that Aboriginal and Torres Strait Islander peoples around Australia have maintained cultural autonomy in concert with the exercise of civil rights—evident in the kinds of refusal discussed in the introduction to this book. The second distinction that Chesterman outlines notes that Indigenous activists campaigning for civil rights were explicit in retaining this distinction themselves, separating their campaigns for equal rights from assimilatory policies and the desire to remove cultural distinctiveness. Campaigns for civil rights were undertaken during a period when white racial ideas and attitudes dominated the political climate. During a period in history that Wiradjuri woman and now federal MP Linda Burney recalls as Australia's equivalent to South African apartheid, the 1967 referendum was 'a high watermark for the relationship between Aboriginal and non-Aboriginal people' (Burney quoted in Thorpe 2017e: 2). For many Aboriginal and Torres Strait Islander people, campaigning for civil rights was a tactical consideration that sat alongside their abiding view of themselves as sovereign and distinct peoples (Attwood 2003: 78).

Nevertheless, for many Indigenous people, like Mick Dodson (1997: 57), although the 1967 referendum 'provided a ticket of entry into the political system', this was only a 'concession ticket' with entry to 'the back stalls at some of the shows.' As Michael Mansell (2003: 8) argues, citizenship

> is not offered without strings attached—it comes at a heavy price. The price to be paid . . . is the abandonment of indigenous sovereignty, and with it the loss of self-determination. Any rights would be limited to those granted by the parliaments or recognised by white law.

The challenging reality for those who had campaigned for citizenship recognition, was that including Indigenous people *within* the settler order only entrenched settler authority (Strakosch 2015: 22). Recognition as citizens could not be the goal for those who questioned the legitimacy of such authority. Indeed, granting citizenship recognition to Indigenous peoples can be seen as an act of absorption within, and redemption for, the settler colonial state (Short 2008: 20–21). Sovereignty campaigners pointed out these shortcomings in citizenship recognition, and by the time of the 1967 referendum, the frontline of struggles for Indigenous recognition had moved on to embrace claims for self-determination and the recognition of sovereignty. Many Aboriginal and Torres Strait Islander people were deeply disillusioned following the referendum, having hoped, as the late Wiradjuri poet and author Kevin Gilbert (2002 [1973]: 101) explained, that 'at last a new deal for black people was imminent.' In the years that followed 1967, struggles for recognition began to focus more explicitly on Indigenous claims as 'a colonised people demanding liberation' rather than as an excluded minority seeking civil inclusion (McGregor 2011: 164). The tension between inclusion and non-inclusion became explicit, as claims for *equality within* the Australian state were increasingly rejected in favour of claims for recognition as a *separate entity* that called into question the legality of Australian institutions to rule over Indigenous lives (Behrendt 2003: 14).

In the post-1967 period, Indigenous struggles increasingly focused on calls for recognition of an abiding sovereignty over unceded First Nations territories. Larissa Behrendt argues that 'just because non-Aboriginal Australia refuses to recognise our sovereignty does not mean that it does not exist' (1995: 99). Behrendt articulates the aspirations of many when she writes:

> In the heart of many Aboriginal people is the belief that we are a sovereign people. We believe that we never surrendered to the British. We never signed a treaty giving up our sovereignty or giving up our land . . . It always was Aboriginal land. It will always be Aboriginal land (1995: 97–98).

As a concept within the lexicon of First Nations struggles for recognition, 'sovereignty' has been attached to various visions of Indigenous autonomy and self-determination (Behrendt 2003: 96). In its most important sense, Indigenous sovereignty does not *require* recognition. For many Aboriginal and Torres Strait Islander peoples, sovereignty 'is not reliant on either European law or occasional state paternalism' . . . it is 'actual', 'spiritual', 'psychological' and 'legal'; it is 'enacted in the daily struggles of Indigenous people striving to retain autonomous lifestyles' (Birch 2007: 107). Indigenous sovereignty is 'carried by the body' (Moreton-Robinson 2007b: 2); it 'simply exists' despite the settler view that Aboriginal laws are 'no longer relevant' (Watson 2007b: 24). This means that, for many Aboriginal and Torres Strait

Islander people, life is lived on 'two levels', one within a nation that regards itself as the sovereign authority over Indigenous lives, and the other 'as a *functioning* sovereign Indigenous being' (Brady 2007: 140). Indigenous sovereignty in this sense defies any possibility of colonial completion. Aboriginal and Torres Strait Islander people do not need to engage in political struggle in order to refuse the settler logic of elimination. They just need to *be*.

But as well as being a lived experience, sovereignty *is* a political claim upon the settler state. It is a rejection of settler authority over Indigenous lives and lands, and it is a demand for land and autonomy. Sovereignty struggles have animated landmark moments in Indigenous refusal and resistance. In 1972 the establishment of the Tent Embassy in Canberra was started with a single sign saying 'Sovereignty', and in 2006, Tent Embassy activists declared 26 January (officially Australia Day, but long known as Invasion Day or Survival Day to Aboriginal people) 'Sovereignty Day', issuing a call for 'Aboriginal Sovereign nations to stand up against the illegal occupation of our country.' Indigenous claimants have tested the legality of British assertions of sovereignty in court, notably in *Coe vs Commonwealth* (1979). These tests have, unsurprisingly, failed in the settler institutions in which they were heard,[5] and in 1983 a Senate Standing Committee also found that 'sovereignty does not now inhere in the Aboriginal people' and recommended constitutional change that would permit the negotiation of a new relationship between Indigenous peoples and the settler state (Senate Standing Committee on Constitutional and Legal Affairs 1983). Indigenous people then had to wait until the 1992 *Mabo* judgment to have some degree of legal recognition for the fact that they had never relinquished their land nor ceded their sovereignty. However, the *Mabo* decision also found that the acquisition of Australia had been an Act of State that rendered future claims to Indigenous sovereignty 'non-justiciable'—an issue unable to be heard in any court. Gumbainggir activist and historian Gary Foley further argues that the legislative response to the *Mabo* decision—the 1993 *Native Title Act*—amounted to 'an absolute denial of Aboriginal sovereignty' (2007: 118).

The question of what recognition of Indigenous sovereignty might mean in practice in Australia remains unanswered. In international law, sovereignty is understood as pertaining to the possession of absolute authority with complete jurisdiction over internal and external populations within territorial boundaries. First Nations sovereignty claims may be more nuanced and complex than this, deriving from the fact that sovereignty is still exercised in many Indigenous communities where Indigenous modes of governance continue despite the imposition of settler law (Cunneen 2005: 54). Behrendt (2003: 97–8) suggests that calls for a separate Indigenous state are 'not in the sense of a separate country' but rather a claim to jurisdiction at a community level and a vision of national political recognition that would enable negotiations between Indigenous nations and other governments. Irene Watson (2007a: 20) argues that Indigenous sovereignty is 'different' from state sovereignty because 'there is not just one sovereign state body but hundreds of different sovereign Aboriginal peoples', underscoring the ways in which Indigenous sovereignty 'embraces diversity, and focuses on inclusivity rather than exclusivity.'

This is not as unimaginable as many might think. Despite a constant emphasis on national unity and singularity, the unified Australian settler state is in fact a relatively recent construct. In 1901 the coming together of the Australian Federation saw sovereignty divided between federal and state governments in the rule book known as the Australian Constitution. At least one way through the political impasse created by the colonial fantasy is to think creatively about how sovereignty could be divided again in order that Aboriginal and Torres Strait Islander peoples might run their own affairs (Reynolds 1998: 213). As Michael Mansell (2016c: 268) has argued, even the creation of an Aboriginal State would not signal the breakup of Australia. Mansell contends that Australian federalism is designed to accommodate such division, and that a 'distinct people will want to remain part of something that treats them well.' The idea that sovereignty might be shared is not threatening to many Aboriginal and Torres Strait Islander people. For example, senior Gumatj ceremony man, Djunga Djunga Yunupingu (quoted in Davidson 2018a) has described sovereignty as 'a gift for the Australian people.' At the ceremonial welcome to the 2018 Garma Festival at Gulkula in north-east Arnhem Land Yunupingu explained to the visitors, 'Our ancient sovereignty is here . . . It is here and it is for all Yolngu people to appreciate but we want all people to walk with us. Two laws, two people, one country.'

Anaywan man and contemporary sovereignty activist Callum Clayton-Dixon (2015) has set out what he sees as the 'core principles and elements' expressed by Aboriginal people articulating the meaning of sovereignty:

Sovereignty is the foundation of all Aboriginal rights, and responsibilities;

It's the inherent right we have to determine the future of our lands and lives;

Aboriginal sovereignty finds its roots in our connection to kin and country, the ancient reciprocal relationship we have with our lands;

It manifests in our song, dance and story, our language, ceremony and customary law;

Aboriginal sovereignty is shared by the individual, the family, the clan, the tribe, and the nation;

Our sovereignty has endured since the first sunrise; and

It's the vision for Aboriginal people to take our place among the nations and peoples of the world, not beneath them.

Aboriginal sovereignty is not an abstract, absurd concept based in conspiracy theory and legal mumbo jumbo. And it shouldn't be dismissed as such.

Settler colonial logic has, to date, dictated that debate about Indigenous sovereignty is pushed to the political margins. Aileen Moreton-Robinson (2007a: 101, 102) suggests that the continuing refusal of First Nations sovereignty shapes an Australian politics that is driven by 'white anxiety of dispossession' and 'white colonial paranoia'; simplistic responses to political complexity. The call to recognise Indigenous sovereignty 'interrupts the colonial process' (Watson 2007b: 40). Moreton-Robinson (2007b: 3) asks, 'if Indigenous sovereignty does not exist, why does it constantly need to be refused?' She answers with the argument that: 'The possessive logic of patriarchal white sovereignty is compelled to deny and refuse what it cannot own—the sovereignty of the Indigenous other' (Moreton-Robinson 2015: 179).

Callum Clayton-Dixon (2015) suggests that Indigenous sovereignty tells Aboriginal and Torres Strait Islander peoples to ask two questions. The first is, 'what must we do ourselves?' and his answers concern the kinds of practices of resurgence outlined in the Introduction to this book: going back to country, reviving language, and not being reliant on government or corporate funding. For Clayton-Dixon, sovereignty is about 'rekindling that which made our families, our clans, our tribes, our nation strong and proud' as a means of '(re)creating a viable alternative to assimilation.'

But Clayton-Dixon's second question for Aboriginal and Torres Strait Islander peoples is 'what do we want from the coloniser?' He argues that Indigenous people

> must be specific in our demands, going beyond the slogans 'land rights' and 'treaty now'. We know we want the return of land and political empowerment. But what land do we want returned, and what rights do we want over that land? How are we to exercise political power and decision making about our future as a people? What model will deliver the most land and the most power in the most secure way possible? Is it a treaty? Dedicated Aboriginal seats in the parliament? National uniform land rights legislation?

Clayton-Dixon maintains that the recognition of Indigenous sovereignty is 'what stands in the way of assimilation' as the abiding opposition to the logic of elimination. In pursuing its desire for colonial completion, however, the Australian settler state has instead pursued a very limited notion of Indigenous recognition.

## CONSTITUTIONAL RECOGNITION
The proposed 'recognition' of Aboriginal and Torres Strait Islander peoples in the Australian Constitution was seen by many as an effort to address an historical oversight. There is no record of Aboriginal and Torres Strait Islander people playing any role in the drafting of the Constitution, nor was their consent sought regarding the creation of a new nation on Indigenous ancestral lands (Davis and Williams 2015: 24). In fact, the only references to Aboriginal people were in Section 51 (xxvi), which empowered the federal parliament to make laws with respect to the 'people of any race, other than the aboriginal race,' and Section 127, which excluded Aboriginal people from being counted in the national census. And while neither section actually excluded Aboriginal and Torres Strait Islander people from Australian citizenship, they both suggested that Indigenous peoples were not really a part of the Australian nation (McGregor 2011: xvii–xx).

The modest reforms in the 1967 referendum were an attempt to address this exclusion, but there was a widespread view that more needed to be done. As Tanya Hosch (2013: 27), a Torres Strait Islander woman and former co-director of the Recognise campaign, argued in 2013:

> . . . by remaining silent about the Indigenous history of this land, our Constitution is saying one of two things. Either that this chapter didn't happen. Or that it is unimportant. We know both to be patently untrue. Australia's history did not begin in 1901. Nor in 1788. It spans tens of thousands of years and more than 1500 generations. And it encompasses the oldest living cultures in human history.

For other Indigenous people, the possibility of constitutional recognition was born from a desire to grasp certainty in the ever-changing legal world of the settler state. As Warlpiri man Jacob Jungarrayi Spencer argues:

> Our laws have always been there, that's never changed, but Kartiya (European) law, every few years it changes when the government changes . . . we Yapa people want to see what's right for us in that Constitution, and we want our voice to be put in place and be heard (quoted in Fitzpatrick 2017a).

Suggestions that the Australian Constitution be amended in order to better recognise Indigenous peoples are not new. The third part of the Keating government's response to the 1992 *Mabo* High Court decision, and the subsequent *Native Title Act 1993* was a promised social justice package outlined in the Aboriginal and Torres Strait Islander Commission (ATSIC) report, *Recognition, Rights and Reform*. This report noted 'overwhelming support' for constitutional reform and recommended that government fund a process to canvass the opinion of Indigenous communities and facilitate local conventions and negotiations at which Aboriginal and Torres Strait Islander people were adequately represented. This proposal (along with the rest of the social justice package) was never implemented. New calls for constitutional change came in 2000 as part of the Council for Aboriginal Reconciliation's 'roadmap to reconciliation', which recommended that parliament prepare legislation for a referendum to recognise Aboriginal and Torres Strait Islander peoples as the First Peoples of Australia (Appleby and Brennan 2017: 5–6).

It was still some years before the contemporary conversation about constitutional recognition was initiated and it was not until 2010 that the then
prime minister, Julia Gillard, commissioned an 'Expert Panel' of Indigenous
and non-Indigenous experts to undertake nation-wide consultation on
the issue. The Panel released its report in January 2012, recommending the
repeal of two provisions in the Constitution that allow racial discrimination
(Section 25 and Section 51 [xxvi], the so-called 'race power'), and the creation
of a new section recognising that 'the continent and its islands now known
as Australia were first occupied by Aboriginal and Torres Strait Islander
peoples'; acknowledging their continuing cultures, languages, heritage,
and relationship to their traditional lands and waters; and proposing that
the federal parliament have powers to make laws for the 'advancement' of
Aboriginal and Torres Strait Islander peoples. The Panel further proposed
two additional sections prohibiting racial discrimination and providing for
the recognition of Indigenous languages. Significantly, however, the Panel
rejected the call from many Aboriginal and Torres Strait Islander people that
a referendum should consider the 'constitutional recognition of the sovereign status of Aboriginal and Torres Strait Islander peoples' on the grounds
that such a proposal 'would be highly contested by many Australians, and
likely to jeopardise broad public support' for the reforms (Expert Panel on
Constitutional Recognition of Indigenous Australians 2012: xvi, xviii).

After the release of the Panel's report, the organisation YouMeUnity, which
had been the public face of the Expert Panel, was rebranded 'Recognise',
and given the task of leading the campaign for a successful referendum.
Between 2012 and 2017 (when it was quietly folded back into Reconciliation
Australia) Recognise was funded by government to campaign in support of
recognition despite the fact that there was no agreed proposal or referendum
question. Recognise also promoted the contested view that constitutional
recognition had widespread Indigenous support (see Maddison 2017 for
discussion).

In the background to the Recognise campaign and the attention it
garnered from the mainstream media, there was a steadily rising volume
of Indigenous dissent about the desirability of some ill-defined form of
recognition. Without a definitive model, a simplistic idea of recognition was 'shopped around for public consumption as a no-brainer and

uncontroversial', a strategy that 'inadvertently raised the ire of a battle-weary [Indigenous] polity' (Davis 2015b: 2). Suspicion and cynicism grew, and Indigenous critics named the logic of elimination they saw at the heart of the Recognise campaign. Megan Davis (2016a: 4) noted that mainstream media coverage was ignoring 'the growing resistance to being "recognised" by the settler state' such that 'the subjects of recognition are all but erased from the process.' Michael Mansell (2016b: 47) described constitutional recognition as 'anti-sovereignty' because it endorses the status of Aboriginal and Torres Strait Islander peoples as 'mere citizens instead of as a distinct sovereign people', an approach he describes as 'intellectually shallow and politically short-sighted.' Similarly, Euahlayi activist Ghillar Michael Anderson (2014a: 25) argued that:

> The real hidden agenda of the proposed referendum is to coerce Aboriginal Nations and Peoples to become part of the Australian Constitution and, by doing so, consent to be governed. The Commonwealth Government can then claim that Aboriginal nations and peoples have acquiesced . . . [and] everything Aboriginal people have fought for until this day will be given up.

For Mansell, any question put to a referendum will still be 'implicitly endorsing the right of white people to decide our fate', while he noted that Aboriginal and Torres Strait Islander people have 'had 220 odd years to rethink that strategy' (quoted in McQuire 2015b).

Davis suggests that backlash against the Recognise campaign effectively 'galvanised a resistance movement' (2016a: 5). In July 2015, following a meeting of 40 Aboriginal and Torres Strait Islander representatives at Kirribilli House in Sydney, attended by both the then Prime Minister Tony Abbott and the Leader of the Opposition Bill Shorten, four key attendees—Davis, Patrick Dodson, Noel Pearson and Kirstie Parker—wrote a letter to the prime minister requesting 'a proper Indigenous process' that would determine 'where Indigenous people stand' on the question of constitutional recognition. This proposal, for a so-called 'black process' was initially rejected by government, however in December 2015 (after a change of prime minister) it was announced that a Referendum Council would be established to conduct a series of regional Indigenous-only meetings, culminating in a national Aboriginal and Torres Strait Islander Convention, eventually held at Uluru in May 2017.

Central to tensions between supporters and critics of the Recognise campaign was an understanding that passing any referendum in Australia is enormously difficult. Since Federation, only eight of 44 referendums have succeeded, and in each successful case the proposed change had bipartisan support. This fact was certainly 'intimidating' according to Davis (2016a: 8), but the challenge of persuading conservatives to vote in support of Indigenous recognition risked a situation in which 'huge pressure will be placed on the mob to accept something they don't want, for fear of disappointing the settlers.' Aboriginal and Torres Strait Islander peoples experienced pressure to accept that

> something is better than nothing; symbolism is better than nothing; go for something now and get what you want in 20 years; go for minimalism and bargain for more off the euphoria of a win; if you walk away you risk race relations; if it fails it risks race relations; symbolism will close the gap; symbolism will improve health and wellbeing; recognition will complete the Constitution; recognition will create a unified and reconciled nation (Davis 2016a: 8).

In contrast, the type of recognition likely to receive Indigenous support was generally described as 'meaningful', with high-profile leaders advocating for both symbolic and substantive measures of recognition (Davis and Williams 2015: 136). As Megan Davis and Marcia Langton (2016: 5) contend, the plea from Aboriginal and Torres Strait Islander people over the years has been

> to adjust Australia's constitutional arrangements so that our people can take better control of our lives and own the responsibility for our children's futures. The kind of recognition first peoples seek is one of empowerment and making space for the first peoples to play an active role in the nation.

Davis suggests that the type of recognition on offer could range from weak (a few words of recognition of a fact, preoccupation, dispossession and survival) to strong (treaties, constitutional recognition of treaty rights or Aboriginal rights or Indigenous parliaments). Weak forms of recognition, for Davis, have 'never been a significant part of Aboriginal advocacy' (Davis 2016a: 9). It was with these sentiments in mind that the Referendum Council began its work.

## THE REFERENDUM COUNCIL AND THE STATEMENT FROM THE HEART

As the official 'black process', the work of the Referendum Council provided the first opportunity for Indigenous people in Australia to deliberate together and provide advice on what kind of recognition would be meaningful to them. The process was carefully designed and managed through a series of twelve dialogues held in regional centres around the country. Each dialogue involved no more than 100 invited participants, 60 per cent of whom came from traditional-owner groups; 20 per cent from community organisations; with the remaining 20 per cent of places reserved for key individuals. In each location, the Council worked with a local host organisation to ensure proper local representation, with balance sought between gender and across age groups and representation for the Stolen Generations prioritised. The meetings themselves took place over three days and were conducted as facilitated deliberative dialogues in which delegates were supported to understand the history of Australian constitutional reform and assess different options in terms of what they would mean for their communities. At the conclusion of the dialogues delegates were asked to confirm a statement of their discussion and to select ten representatives for the final convention to be held at Uluru (Hobbs 2017a: 1).

Four key proposals that were broadly common to both the Expert Panel's recommendations and the work of the 2015 Joint Select Committee were taken to the regional dialogues. These proposals included a statement acknowledging Aboriginal and Torres Strait Islander peoples as the First Australians (which could be placed in the Constitution or outside it); amending the existing 'race power' (Section 51(xxvi) of the Constitution), or deleting it and inserting a new power for the Commonwealth to make laws for Aboriginal and Torres Strait Islander peoples; inserting a guarantee against racial discrimination, Section 116A, into the Constitution; and deleting Section 25, which contemplates the possibility of a state government excluding some Australians from voting on the basis of their race. The Council also included a fifth option, which had emerged after the Expert Panel's work had concluded: providing for a First Peoples' Voice to Parliament, and the right to be consulted on legislation and policies that relate to Aboriginal and Torres Strait Islander peoples (Referendum Council 2017b: 6). During the dialogues, the Referendum Council adopted the same four principles that had been used to guide the Expert Panel's assessment of proposals for constitutional reform, meaning that each proposal must:

- contribute to a more unified and reconciled nation;
- be of benefit to and accord with the wishes of Aboriginal and Torres Strait Islander peoples;
- be capable of being supported by an overwhelming majority of Australians from across the political and social spectrums; and
- be technically and legally sound (Referendum Council 2017b: 5).

At the Uluru Convention, however, proposals were assessed according to a set of guiding principles that had been distilled from the regional dialogues, and which were supported by international standards pertaining to Indigenous peoples' rights and international human rights law. Whereas the Expert Panel principles had emphasised national unity and reconciliation, the Uluru Convention principles emphasised sovereignty and Indigenous rights. The Convention principles proposed that an option should only proceed if it:

- does not diminish Aboriginal sovereignty and Torres Strait Islander sovereignty.
- involves substantive, structural reform.
- advances self-determination and the standards established under the *United Nations Declaration on the Rights of Indigenous Peoples.*
- recognises the status and rights of First Nations.
- tells the truth of history.
- does not foreclose on future advancement.
- does not waste the opportunity of reform.

- provides a mechanism for First Nations agreement-making.
- has the support of First Nations.
- does not interfere with positive legal arrangements (Referendum Council 2017b: 22).

The dialogues attempted to negotiate a path through two positions on sovereignty: the first, that the Australian polity would not be willing to surrender parliamentary sovereignty; and the second, that Aboriginal and Torres Strait Islander peoples are not willing to cede their own sovereignties. During the dialogues, participants attempted to 'reclaim the debate' about Indigenous recognition in the Australian Constitution, speaking against any form of minimalist or weak recognition and expressing the desire to 'get out from under the European terms of the Australian Constitution' (Murphy et al 2017). The dialogues also embraced the idea of an Indigenous 'voice to parliament' through which Indigenous people would be able to provide direct input to legislative and policy decisions that would impact upon the lives of their communities (Davis 2017a: 3).

On 26 May 2017, the fiftieth anniversary of the 1967 referendum, the delegates at the Uluru Convention concluded three days of deliberations and released the Uluru Statement from the Heart:[6]

## ULURU STATEMENT FROM THE HEART

We, gathered at the 2017 National Constitutional Convention, coming from all points of the southern sky, make this statement from the heart:

Our Aboriginal and Torres Strait Islander tribes were the first sovereign Nations of the Australian continent and its adjacent islands, and possessed it under our own laws and customs. This our ancestors did, according to the reckoning of our culture, from the Creation, according to the common law from 'time immemorial', and according to science more than 60,000 years ago.

This sovereignty is *a spiritual notion: the ancestral tie between the land, or 'mother nature', and the Aboriginal and Torres Strait Islander peoples who were born therefrom, remain attached thereto, and must one day return thither to be united with our ancestors. This link is the basis of the ownership of the soil, or better, of sovereignty.* It has never been ceded or extinguished, and co-exists with the sovereignty of the Crown.

How could it be otherwise? That peoples possessed a land for sixty millennia and this sacred link disappears from world history in merely the last two hundred years?

With substantive constitutional change and structural reform, we believe this ancient sovereignty can shine through as a fuller expression of Australia's nationhood.

Proportionally, we are the most incarcerated people on the planet. We are not an innately criminal people. Our children are aliened from their families at unprecedented rates. This cannot be because we have no love for them. And our youth languish in detention in obscene numbers. They should be our hope for the future.

These dimensions of our crisis tell plainly the structural nature of our problem. This is *the torment of our powerlessness.*

We seek constitutional reforms to empower our people and take *a rightful place* in our own country. When we have power over our destiny our children will flourish. They will walk in two worlds and their culture will be a gift to their country.

We call for the establishment of a First Nations Voice enshrined in the Constitution.

Makarrata is the culmination of our agenda: *the coming together after a struggle.* It captures our aspirations for a fair and truthful relationship with the people of Australia and a better future for our children based on justice and self-determination.

We seek a Makarrata Commission to supervise a process of agreement-making between governments and First Nations and truth-telling about our history.

In 1967 we were counted, in 2017 we seek to be heard. We leave base camp and start our trek across this vast country. We invite you to walk with us in a movement of the Australian people for a better future.

Convention delegate, Arrernte woman Rachel Perkins (2017: 3), described the Statement as an 'historic consensus' that 'unifies the aspirations
and dreams of our mobs from all corners of the country' and provided a
new starting point for 'pragmatic and principled change for the benefit of
all Australians.' With its emphasis on structural reform, others were quick
to recognise that the proposed reforms were intended to 'restore collective political power and control to Aboriginal and Torres Strait Islander
peoples themselves' (Lino 2017: 2). Yet despite the intent at the heart
of the Statement, Referendum Council co-chair, Pat Anderson, suggests that
the proposals were actually 'very modest', noting that

> for Australia, it seems like we're doing something extraordinary, and we're
> not. [...] It might seem we're asking for too much, but in fact, what we might
> ask for and what is happening is just the same for other Indigenous peoples
> in the world. 'Hear us, we're here. We have things to tell you. We have to be
> part of the policy-making and the legislation that affect us' (quoted in *NITV
> News* 2017b: 3).

For Megan Davis (2017a: 2), Uluru 'disrupted the recognition project'
and 'brought clarity and coherence' to a debate that had 'rambled on for
ten years.' And rather than being new or unexpected, Davis saw the reform
proposals as sitting 'in a continuum of Aboriginal advocacy for structural
reform' from the 1963 Yirrkala Bark Petitions, to the Barunga Statement of
1988, the Eva Valley Statement of 1993, the Kalkaringi Statement of 1998,
the report on the Social Justice Package by ATSIC in 1995 and the Kirribilli
Statement of 2015.[7]

At the end of June 2017, the Referendum Council released its final report,
which made two recommendations. The first recommendation was for a
referendum to be held that would embed the 'Voice to Parliament' in the
Australian Constitution. The 'Voice' was envisaged as a representative body
that would recognise the status of Aboriginal and Torres Strait Islander
peoples as the First Peoples of Australia and provide the ability to monitor
the use of the heads of power in Section 51 (xxvi) and Section 122. The
Council report was emphatic that the Voice to Parliament was 'the only
option for a referendum proposal that accords with the wishes of Aboriginal
and Torres Strait Islander peoples.' The role of the proposed Voice to

Parliament will be discussed further in Chapter Three. The second recommendation from the Referendum Council was that all Australian parliaments pass an extra-constitutional 'Declaration of Recognition' using 'inspiring and unifying words' to bring together the three parts of our Australian story: our ancient First Peoples' heritage and culture, our British institutions, and our multicultural unity.' The Council further noted that the Statement from the Heart had called for the establishment of a Makarrata Commission with the function of supervising agreement-making and facilitating a process of truth-telling, confirming that the negotiation of treaties was overwhelmingly supported by delegates at all regional dialogues. However, the report also acknowledged that it lay outside the Council's terms of reference to recommend the creation of such a commission, which could instead be pursued by Aboriginal and Torres Strait Islander peoples as legislative initiatives outside of the Constitution (Referendum Council 2017b: 2).

In the weeks following the release of the Statement from the Heart and the subsequent report from the Referendum Council there was hope that this process had finally shifted the debate on constitutional reform from weaker forms of recognition to the more meaningful, substantive reforms that Aboriginal and Torres Strait Islander people desired (Hobbs 2017a: 3). Les Malezer, Australian delegate to the United Nations Permanent Forum on Indigenous Issues and a Butchulla and Gubbi Gubbi man, suggested it would be 'shallow and hypocritical' for the federal government to fund the work of the Referendum Council only to ignore its recommendations. Michael Mansell agreed, claiming that although government might be reluctant to allocate more resources to follow through on the work of the Council there would be an obligation to fund further efforts anyway (both cited in Wahlquist 2017b: 5). A meeting of some of Australia's most senior Indigenous leaders, called by Aboriginal and Torres Strait Islander Social Justice Commissioner June Oscar and Reconciliation Australia co-chair Tom Calma, also called on the federal government to 'actively back' the proposal for an Indigenous Voice to Parliament (quoted in Fitzpatrick 2017c).

Yet despite this pressure, Aboriginal and Torres Strait Islander people found themselves again disappointed. In October 2017, some five months after the release of the Referendum Council report, the prime minister rejected its proposals. Prime Minister Malcolm Turnbull determined that the Voice to Parliament 'would inevitably become seen as a third chamber of Parliament' and that this was 'inconsistent' with principles of political equality. Turnbull declared the proposal was neither 'desirable or capable of winning acceptance' from the Australian people (Turnbull 2017). For many Aboriginal and Torres Strait Islander people the rejection was devastating. After months of work, and the achievement of a fragile consensus at Uluru, the project of Indigenous constitutional recognition seemed to have ended. Noel Pearson accused the government of being 'egregiously dishonest' and dog-whistling in their argument against the Voice to Parliament, while Megan Davis accused them of 'deliberate mischief intended to mislead the Australian population' (quoted in Hunter 2017). The fact that the decision was first leaked to the media then announced in a media statement rather than being communicated directly to the members of the Referendum Council only poured salt into the wounds of dismissal and disrespect.[8]

Davis (2016a: 13) had earlier made clear that many Indigenous leaders would rather leave the project of constitutional reform to another generation than compromise on the kind of recognition that was meaningful to them. She pointed out that Aboriginal and Torres Strait Islander peoples comprise a 'politically astute polity fluent in the betrayals of political leaders.' For the settler state, however, such betrayals are part of the normal business of politics, where meaningful recognition is considered a risk to the unity of the Australian body politic (Lino 2017: 4).

Perhaps tellingly, the government rejection of the Statement from the Heart engaged only with the proposal for a Voice to Parliament. The proposal for a Makarrata Commission to oversee processes of agreement-making and truth-telling was ignored altogether. The question remains as to whether makarrata—a treaty or set of treaties—might enable the recognition of Indigenous sovereignty alongside the sovereignty of the settler state.

TREATY TIME?
The stalking horse to the Recognise campaign was always the question of treaty. Soon after the contemporary conversation about Indigenous constitutional recognition was initiated, talk of negotiating a treaty or treaties instead of seeking inclusion in the settler constitution began to emerge.

By the time the Referendum Council began its work, treaty was the dominant topic of concern—a position borne out in each of the regional dialogues.

Australia stands alone among other British settler colonial states for its lack of treaty relationships with Indigenous peoples. Internationally, treaties have long been used as a means of reaching a settlement between Indigenous peoples and colonisers. They are formal, negotiated agreements, that acknowledge Indigenous peoples as the original owners and occupiers of the land (Hobbs 2016: 1). The content of treaties varies considerably from historical treaties to some of the modern-day treaties still being negotiated in parts of Canada, but in general terms they tend to focus on land, resources, reparations and the recognition of Indigenous self-determination, representation and decision-making. Treaty-making has not necessarily resulted in material benefit for Indigenous peoples, and indeed treaties were often tools that legalised Indigenous dispossession. Yet despite significant shortcomings in the negotiation, content and subsequent honouring of treaties, the fact remains that in many cases it is the existence of treaties rather than the making of subsequent law and policy that continue to define the nature of the relationship between Indigenous peoples and the settler states that occupy their territories. In the United States, for example, it has been the *fact* of treaty-making that 'confirmed a nation-to-nation relationship between the negotiating tribal and non-tribal parties' (Wilkins 2002: 42), and which has allowed Native Nations to exercise increasing autonomy from the state in the present day. In Australia, however, not only were no treaties ever negotiated with the several hundred Aboriginal and Torres Strait Islander nations on the continent at the time of the British arrival, but the question of negotiating a contemporary treaty or treaties has been highly contentious and divisive.

Discussion of treaties in Australia has a long history. Gunditjmara playwrite and musician Richard Frankland (2017) points to the existence of Indigenous treaties 'long before the white man came to our lands' and suggests what treaties between Indigenous people and the settler state might offer the contemporary relationship:

> This story begins thousands of generations ago. There were treaties here then, between us, our mob, nation to nation agreements, tribe to tribe agreements,

clan to clan agreements—treaties. Treaties on boundaries, treaties on food, partners, ceremony, ritual, hunting grounds, engineering, farming, trade . . . the list goes on. A treaty was an agreement then and now it is the same . . . For me, a treaty is ultimately about hope. A treaty is a light that shines in the distance, and that light that may help us as a nation to acknowledge the atrocities of the past, and plant seeds here in the present for future generations to grow trees, a forest, perhaps even change the cultural tapestry of our nation.

The desire for a treaty or treaties between Aboriginal and Torres Strait Islander peoples and the settler state has been a longstanding aspect of political debate. In 1979, the National Aboriginal Conference (NAC), a national representative body created by the federal government to provide a forum for the expression of Indigenous views, recommended that a Treaty of Commitment be entered into between the Australian government and Aboriginal nations. This proposal recommended that a word from an Indigenous language should be used to describe this process, and chose the word 'makarrata', discussed further below. The NAC proposal included the need to address issues of prior ownership, compensation, the return of lands, reserved Indigenous seats in parliament, and the return of artefacts and human remains from museums (Luke Pearson 2017c: 2). A few years later, the Treaty '88 campaign disrupted the national story of peaceful settlement being celebrated during Australia's bicentennial by bringing about 50,000 Aboriginal people together (nearly a fifth of the total national population at that time) to converge on the 26 January settler celebrations (Burgmann 2003: 66). Kevin Gilbert, in consultation with the Sovereign Aboriginal Coalition, developed a draft treaty that called for the creation of a sovereign and autonomous Aboriginal State, which comprised a land base of 'not less than forty percent of the land mass of each "Australian State"' (Gilbert 1987: 111). Also in 1988, the then prime minister, Bob Hawke, was presented with the Barunga Statement, which called on parliament 'to negotiate with us a Treaty recognising our prior ownership, continued occupation and sovereignty and affirming our human rights and freedom.' Hawke acquiesced to this demand and signed a statement in which he undertook to negotiate a treaty with Indigenous people—a promise on which he would later renege.

The question of a treaty was again revived in 2000 when the Council for Aboriginal Reconciliation's final Document Towards Reconciliation recommended that a treaty be negotiated. As will be discussed further in Chapter Eight there was widespread scepticism among Aboriginal and Torres Strait Islander people about the merits of the reconciliation process. Nevertheless, by the end of the Council for Aboriginal Reconciliation's life the majority of Indigenous political leaders were calling for a treaty or treaties to be negotiated as a part of, what they described as, the 'unfinished business' of reconciliation (Short 2008: 152). Yet again, however, the settler response was to foreclose the discussion. In the official Commonwealth Response to the Council for Aboriginal Reconciliation Final Report (2002: 23), the government rejected a treaty on the grounds that '. . . such a legally enforceable instrument, as between sovereign states, would be divisive, would undermine the concept of a single Australian nation . . .' For many Aboriginal and Torres Strait Islander people, the settlers' refusal to negotiate a treaty expressed their reluctance to acknowledge that there has been a war that still needs concluding (Burgmann 2003: 66). Here again is the colonial fantasy at play; the settler cannot negotiate over something they do not acknowledge.

The desire for treaty negotiations was taken up at state level in Victoria in 2016[9] and was briefly advanced in South Australia before a change of government put an end to the process there. In New South Wales the Labor Opposition suggested they would advance a treaty should they win office in 2019 and in mid-2018 the Northern Territory also committed to advancing a treaty in that jurisdiction. The success or failure of these processes remains to be seen, and for many Indigenous people evaluation will rest on the capacity of state and territory governments to genuinely recognise Indigenous self-determination. As Harry Hobbs argues, 'Simply calling an agreement a "treaty" will not make it so' (2016: 2). What is hoped is that a treaty that will deliver land, resources and genuine self-determination will be 'far more beneficial than any constitutional recognition could possibly be' (Mansell 2016a: 2).

The proposal that emerged from the Uluru Convention was for a Makarrata Commission, to oversee a process of agreement-making, rather than a treaty. These words are not completely synonymous. Makarrata is a Yolŋu word that refers to a process of conflict resolution and peacemaking following a dispute (Luke Pearson 2017c: 1). Yolŋu leader Galarrwuy Yunupingu (2017) has written eloquently of the ways in which the principles of makarrata have guided Yolŋu people in the resolution of disputes for centuries:

First, the disputing parties must be brought together. Then, each party, led by their elders, must speak carefully and calmly about the dispute. They must put the facts on the table and air their grievances. If a person speaks wildly, or out of turn, he or she is sent away and shall not be included any further in the process. Those who come for vengeance, or for other purposes, will also be sent away, for they can only disrupt the process.

The leaders must always seek a full understanding of the dispute: what lies behind it; who is responsible; what each party wants, and all things that are normal to peacemaking efforts. When that understanding is arrived at, then a settlement can be agreed upon. This settlement is also a symbolic reckoning—an action that says to the world that from now on and forever the dispute is settled; that the dispute no longer exists, it is finished.

For many Aboriginal and Torres Strait Islander people, including long-time sovereignty activists, the proposals in the Statement from the Heart were a welcome step. Michael Mansell (2017a: 2) suggests that from the 'ashes of the burnt referendum' on constitutional recognition there was a new opportunity: 'for Aboriginal people to more seriously negotiate for parliamentary support for a treaty and a truth telling review.' Galarrwuy Yunupingu (2017) also recognises the opportunities of the post-Uluru moment, suggesting that this is a moment for the Australian settler state to deal with its relationship with Aboriginal and Torres Strait Islander peoples or to 'turn its back on these issues, leaving these challenges for the next generation' Murrawarri man Fred Hooper, a Dubbo delegate to the Uluru Convention, agrees, noting that a treaty negotiation process is the only way to deal with the nation's 'unfinished business', including an acknowledgement that 'this land wasn't peacefully settled' (quoted in Lawford 2017a). Recognition is central to these claims, but not in a way that implies inclusion in the settler state.

For Aboriginal and Torres Strait Islander peoples, the negotiation of treaties remains important as a means of resisting the incorporation inherent to settler colonialism, and for acknowledging the reality of their political experience. Indigenous people seek treaties to provide some measure of historical justice in recognition of the claim that the settler unjustly appropriated their land. Long-term Gunai and Mara activist Robbie Thorpe argues that there has 'been a war trying to exterminate our people' since Indigenous territories were invaded, and that 'the reason to have a treaty is to end that war' (Thorpe quoted in Donnelly 2016). Stan Grant (2016b: 2) makes a similar point, suggesting that a treaty 'is about finally and truly expunging the stain of *terra nullius* – the belief that this was an empty land free for the taking.' As Liya-dhälinymirr Djambarrpuyŋu man Yingiya Mark Guyula argues, a treaty is needed to 'recognise our power, recognise who we are, recognise that we were here before any law that came and ruled all over us' (quoted in Wahlquist 2016a: 1).

Despite the relentless pressures of settler colonialism, Aboriginal and Torres Strait Islander peoples remain committed to pursuing their political autonomy. Kombumerri scholar Mary Graham describes the negotiation of treaties as a 'maturing process' for the states that do it. Graham suggests that there could be 'hundreds of treaties on the ground, perhaps on a national level there could be a charter of treaties, with a treaty commission that could oversee the legalities.' Importantly, Graham stresses, the content of each of these treaties 'would have to be in the hands of local people' (quoted in *Koori Mail* 2013c: 18). In practical terms, negotiating treaties would also enable land settlements, power sharing, and genuine forms of self-determination and Indigenous decision-making. For Matthew Dhulumburrk Gaykamaŋu of the Yolŋu Nations Assembly, Indigenous people need a treaty in order to stop the kind of 'one-sided talk' that government currently uses to direct policy that 'never ends in things that work' (quoted in Fischer 2014a: 6). This, for Gary Murray from the Victorian Traditional Owner Land Justice Group, might be the thing that 'strengthens' Indigenous people, 'picks them up out of the gutter and makes it work better' (quoted in Wahlquist 2016b: 2).

Certainly a treaty would not solve all the ills of settler colonialism. It would not eradicate racism, heal intergenerational trauma, or deal with systemic problems in education, media representation or the criminal justice system. But a treaty framework might, as Luke Pearson (2016a) suggests, help to create opportunities 'for true social, cultural and economic developments that are not reliant on being given permission, on having to argue for basic human rights, or on new names for old approaches with every change in government.' Or as Richard Frankland (2017) argues, while treaties would 'not be the ultimate answer to all the ills we face as a people', they could 'change the cultural tapestry of this nation' and provide a foundation for building 'culturally safe social orders, structures and events that take into account our cultural shape, ways and needs.'

Despite settler resistance to the negotiation of treaties, however, it is not necessarily the case that treaties with Indigenous peoples would fracture Australian national unity—that unity is already fractured through our federalist structure. The Australian Constitution already acknowledges 'multiple political communities'; the sovereignty of the nation is complemented, not undermined, by the sovereignty of the states. In this sense, advancing the calls for a Makarrata Commission as outlined in the Uluru Statement, as a form of federalism, 'keeps faith' with Australia's constitutional tradition (Lino 2017: 2). There is a significant risk that the colonial fantasy would come into play in ways that would undermine the potential power of treaty, that the makarrata idea of 'coming together after a struggle' would be interpreted as another opportunity to draw Aboriginal and Torres Strait Islander people into the settler state and complete the colonial project. As non-Indigenous legal scholars Harry Hobbs and George Williams (2018: 14) argue, a treaty is 'a marriage not a divorce.' Like any marriage, a treaty or treaties between Aboriginal and Torres Strait Islander peoples and the Australian state could enable more or less independence and autonomy for the partners.

The rejection of the Uluru Statement means that much political energy will be expended just to get government to the negotiating table. Referendum Council advocate and Torres Strait Islander Thomas Mayor (2018) calls on all Australians to join with First Nations to 'knock on the constitutional door with raucous passion'. Yet even if these efforts prove successful, it is likely that the settler state would diminish the transformative capacity of any treaty negotiations, undercutting their decolonising potential. As Strakosch (2015: 70–1) has pointed out, despite some benefits, the experience in other settler colonial states shows 'how effectively colonisation can proceed *through* treaties and recognition', precisely because the settler desire will always be 'aimed at colonial completion and the "solving" of the "Aboriginal problem". As a result, there is a significant risk that huge amounts of time, energy and goodwill will be directed towards the negotiation of a treaty or treaties, but that Aboriginal and Torres Strait Islander peoples and the Australian settler state will be negotiating towards quite different ends. While the settler state will see a successful treaty as a (re)assertion of their legitimate authority over Indigenous lives, and therefore as a possible moment of colonial completion, Aboriginal and Torres Strait Islander peoples will seek agreements that recognise their sovereignty and continue to call the legitimacy of the entire colonial project into question.

What is clear, however, is that regardless of the attitude of the settler state, Aboriginal and Torres Strait Islander peoples will continue to contest state legitimacy and resist state efforts directed at colonial completion. As Gary Foley has argued, the failure to resolve the question of settler legitimacy will 'ensure that the contest over sovereignty will continue for many generations to come' (2007: 139). Indigenous resurgence shows a different path ahead. As Irene Watson (2002), suggests:

> We must reclaim our being as independent nations, in control of our territories where we live under our laws of respect for all things with our relationship to the natural world. If we were to have all of that returned to us what would be left to agree to? Peaceful coexistence perhaps.

Perhaps resurgence lies with the kind of agreement recently signed between sixteen Indigenous nations from across the Murray–Darling Basin. The treaty, known as the Union of Sovereign First Nations of the Northern Murray–Darling Basin, unifies the groups in the hope of creating more bargaining power and economic opportunities. For signatory Fred Hooper (quoted in Wainwright 2017), chairman of the Northern Basin Aboriginal Nations (NBAN), the treaty meant that 'for the first time in this country we are not standing alone':

> We have a whole heap of nations who are standing up and saying we have never ceded our sovereignty, we've never acquiesced our colonial title to the Crown of England . . . We're hoping that it can show the rest of Aboriginal Australia that we can do things between ourselves . . . We have a wealth of knowledge that we have to take advantage of and promote and I think this is the start of something like that.

# CHAPTER 2

# SELF-DETERMINATION

As sovereign peoples who have never ceded their territories, Aboriginal and Torres Strait Islander peoples have continued to demand their right to govern themselves. Throughout the twentieth century, Indigenous political struggles against dispossession and settler domination were increasingly articulated as a right to self-determination, which is defined in Article 1 of the United Nations Covenant on Civil and Political Rights as the right of all people to 'freely determine their political status and freely pursue their economic, social and cultural development.' Regardless of the judgments of settler institutions, Aboriginal and Torres Strait Islander people still determine themselves to be sovereign peoples, and have struggled to sustain and develop their own jurisdiction. By the 1960s, settler intellectuals such as C.D. Rowley and H.C. Coombs were also arguing that the continuing vitality of Indigenous cultural life should be recognised and encouraged, and that settler legal and administrative structures could and should accommodate Indigenous social and political life (Kowal 2015: 5). By the 1970s, Aboriginal and Torres Strait Islander voices could no longer be ignored, and the election of the Whitlam Labor government in 1972 saw the formal introduction of a policy of Aboriginal 'self-determination', which was to remain the dominant political framing of the settler policy regime for the next 30 years.

Yet despite the rhetoric, the Australian settler state did not in fact allow a formal policy of self-determination to displace its colonial ambitions. The Australian version of self-determination, which remained official government policy until 2005, was always more rhetorical than real, characterised by weak and compromised philosophical underpinnings that meant Indigenous aspirations for autonomy were buried in practices that remained fundamentally assimilationist (Maddison 2009). Self-determination policies under Whitlam were seen as an attempt to 'level the playing field'. As Stan Grant (2016c: 51) notes, however, these policies in fact sought to 'create pathways for Aboriginal families to merge more successfully with . . . "mainstream Australia."' Despite an emphasis on Indigenous participation in decision-making, Australian self-determination policy did not break with the 'proselytising intent of the modernising project' of settler colonialism, nor did it disrupt the power relationships that underpinned the colonial project (Brigg and Murphy 2011: 22). By the time the Howard government unleashed a radical change of policy direction in Indigenous affairs in 2007, the concept of self-determination had become a political and ideological football. As Megan Davis argued in 2012, the language of self-determination was 'eviscerated from the lexicon of Australian politicians, policy makers and political commentators, inelegantly dismissed as a "failed experiment" and antithetical to Aboriginal economic development.'

Such statements again reveal the colonial fantasy. While written off as an 'experiment' in settler politics, for Aboriginal and Torres Strait Islander peoples, self-determination remains the only acceptable framework for negotiating Indigenous governance. The right to self-determination is the right to make the decisions that affect all other freedoms and rights of Indigenous peoples. It 'remains fundamental to the aspirations of Aboriginal communities' (Davis 2012: 24) because, as Luke Pearson (2017a) insists, 'nothing less than Aboriginal control of Aboriginal affairs will do.' This is a view that has been sustained over decades, with Kevin Gilbert (2002 [1973]: 160) arguing back in the 1970s that 'the only thing years of white administration have proved to us is that it doesn't work, it can't work.' As Gumbayyngirr man and former Australian senator Aden Ridgeway (2000: 188) has noted, Australian governments have had 'report after report' that consistently advocate the same principle, that is, that 'Indigenous disadvantage can only be improved when Indigenous people are given greater control over the decisions that impact on their daily lives.' In 2017 the Statement from the Heart maintained that Aboriginal and Torres Strait Islander peoples sought a 'better future' through 'self-determination', but as far back as 1991 the report of the Royal Commission into Aboriginal Deaths in Custody (RCIADIC), included nineteen recommendations related specifically to self-determination, maintaining that the control of Indigenous lives must be returned to Indigenous hands.

Australia is out of step with other countries, including other settler colonial states, in its attitude to self-determination policy. As Davis (2012: 24) argues:

> The right to self-determination is taken seriously in most states of the world that have indigenous communities because self-determination in its true form is intended to enhance democracy and enhance political participation and therefore improve health and well-being.

The domestic policies of several countries around the world include concrete measures intended to advance the right to self-determination as established in the United Nations Declaration on the Rights of Indigenous Peoples,[10] but despite eventually signing the Declaration in 2008, Australia is not one of them. Instead, Australia has effectively rejected self-determination, with the term itself now 'pilloried' as a 'wishy-washy, pie-in-the-sky, lefty concept' (Davis 2016a: 2–3). Australia has promoted an 'impoverished', 'one-dimensional' and 'state-centric' form of self-determination that has proven 'unable to facilitate freedom or choice for many Aboriginal people' (Davis 2012: 24).

In a context of Indigenous resurgence, however, the actions and policies of the state in this regard become less and less significant. In Australia, New Zealand, Canada and the United States, Indigenous peoples are working to reclaim *self-government* as an Indigenous right and practice. Stephen Cornell describes this as the latest phase in the self-determination movement, as Indigenous nations have shifted their focus from a demand for Indigenous recognition and rights from the settler state and towards the actual exercise of those rights, whether recognised or not. The movement for self-government is 'less likely to be national than local: It is about distinct groups, communities, tribes or nations engaging the practical tasks of governing. It pays less attention to overall patterns of Indigenous rights than to localized assertions of Indigenous decision-making power.' Still, despite this localism, there is a common theme:

> The assertion of genuine decision-making authority over lands and other natural resources held to be an Indigenous patrimony, over the internal affairs of Indigenous communities, over the nature and processes of economic development on their lands, over cultural properties and the management of cultural heritage, over the organization of self-government, and over other matters that directly affect Indigenous welfare (Cornell 2015: 1–2).

Where self-determination is an aspiration, Cornell contends, self-government is 'doing it.'

## AUSTRALIAN SELF-DETERMINATION

Worimi historian John Maynard points out that Aboriginal people were calling for self-determination as early as the 1920s (Maddison 2009: 32). However, these demands did not receive widespread political attention until several decades later, when they were re-articulated under the banner of the Australian 'Black Power' movement, which rejected any form of white paternalism and called for Aboriginal control and autonomy (Attwood 2003: 322–4). Gary Foley reminds us that Black Power was 'always about self-determination . . . about Aboriginal people assuming responsibility and control of their own affairs' with the express desire being to 'put the resources into the hands of the communities themselves, cut out the middle man and . . . let the communities make their own mistakes' (Foley quoted in ABC 2003).

The eventual introduction of a formal policy of self-determination was seen by both settlers and many Indigenous leaders as a progressive step in reforming the settler colonial relationship. Self-determination was thought to have 'vindicated' the belief in a continuing Indigenous social solidarity that had survived the regimes of protection and assimilation that sought to devalue and eliminate Indigenous political difference. The new policy framework would instead invite Aboriginal and Torres Strait Islander people to 'make choices' about 'the terms and the pace of their adaptation to the settler-colonial society that encapsulated them' (Rowse 2002: 230). At the time, this new approach seemed almost revolutionary. In hindsight, however, such a constrained approach to self-determination was never likely to be transformative.

Over time, the Australian version of self-determination came to mean different things in practice. In some parts of Australia it meant the decline and eventual withdrawal of missions, in other places it meant the emergence of Aboriginal-controlled organisations. Some Aboriginal and Torres Strait Islander people gained limited rights or ownerships of their lands. The assumption from the outset was that the new policies would allow Indigenous people to make decisions about their own priorities and lifestyles. What quickly became evident, however, was that Australian governments did not intend to deal with Aboriginal people on a nation-to-nation or government-to-government basis, but would instead insist on maintaining a 'top-down approach' to self-determination (Brennan et al 2005: 32); clearly a contradiction in terms. Aileen Moreton-Robinson (2005: 63) suggests that government policies of self-determination were more concerned with organisational and community management than with placing meaningful political and economic power in Aboriginal hands. This approach meant that aspirations for self-determination in practice were in fact 'buried' in assimilatory practices that remained driven by the logic of elimination (Young 2005: 120). This profound *lack* of self-determination at the heart of policies ostensibly espousing self-determination continued to frustrate Indigenous desires and aspirations to exercise their sovereignty as First Nations through genuine control over their governance arrangements and the delivery of services to their communities (Maddison 2009).

The drive for self-determination is not just about a desire for political autonomy. Both Indigenous and non-Indigenous advocates believe that by putting control of Indigenous affairs in Indigenous hands, self-determination will enable Aboriginal and Torres Strait Islander people to more effectively address the social challenges that many communities were experiencing. Writing in the early 1970s, the late Wiradjuri poet Kevin Gilbert observed that 'Aboriginal life is an ocean of suffering, maladjustment, ill-health, dreadful conditions, stunted wasted lives, dying babies and frustration' (Gilbert 2002 [1973]: 141). Gilbert claimed that, 'dependence on "handouts" had sapped the initiative and the substance of blacks' and advocated for a radical political autonomy, arguing that 'what blacks really want' is a combination of 'land, compensation, discreet non-dictatorial help and *to be left alone* by white Australia', insisting, 'You'll never heal a wound if you keep picking at it' (2002 [1973]: 175, emphasis in the original). More recently, Yolŋu leader Gularrwuy Yunupingu has made similar claims, arguing that, 'Governments must stop babysitting us because we are not children. But if treated like children, people will behave like children. It is time for us to be given responsibility in the right way' (2007).

These arguments are well-established. In the 2006 *Aboriginal and Torres Strait Islander Social Justice Report*, the then Social Justice Commissioner, Kungarakan man Tom Calma, pointed out that the irony of failing to treat Aboriginal people as 'partners and equal participants in creating a positive life vision' is that this approach 'fosters a passive system of policy development and service delivery while at the same time criticising Indigenous peoples for being passive recipients of government services' (ATSISJC 2007b: 18). Waanyi author Alexis Wright (2006: 107) has also observed that Aboriginal and Torres Strait Islander people have been left with the 'chaos' caused by two centuries of non-Indigenous 'solutions' and wonders why non-Indigenous Australia cannot just embrace 'the Indigenous vision' of political autonomy and community repair. As Mick Dodson has argued, 'You can't fix community problems, they belong to communities. Communities have got to fix them. What you can do is help them. Give them the power and the resources to do what needs to be done' (quoted in Maddison 2009: 31). Yuin man Gerry Moore, CEO of the Secretariat of National Aboriginal and Islander Child Care (SNAICC) argues that while government can 'chuck as much money at problems as they like' outcomes for Aboriginal and Torres Strait Islander people will only improve

> when our communities are leading discussions; when our knowledge, expertise and understanding is being utilised. It should always be about community-led decision-making and community control . . . Ensuring that Aboriginal and Torres Strait Islander people and organisations have control over decisions that affect their children is vital in supporting, healing and strengthening our families (Moore 2016: np).

Yorta Yorta man Paul Briggs has made a similar point, suggesting that without genuine self-determination, Indigenous people become 'consumed' by a dependency on government, draining them of their capacity to develop their own solutions to social problems (quoted in Maddison 2009: 32).

A central plank of Australian self-determination policy was the creation of the Aboriginal and Torres Strait Islander Commission (ATSIC) in 1989. With both an elected arm and a bureaucratic arm, ATSIC was intended to provide both representation and service delivery to Aboriginal and Torres Strait Islander people around the continent. In mainstream political circles and in the media, ATSIC was generally spoken about as though it really was a model that advanced Aboriginal and Torres Strait Islander self-determination. There was a widely held perception that ATSIC had responsibility for most issues affecting Aboriginal and Torres Strait Islander people, despite the reality that the organisation in fact had only limited control over important policy areas or over government funds directed to Aboriginal and Torres Strait Islander issues (Patterson 2017: 14). Indeed, despite a deep appreciation of many of the things that ATSIC offered, most especially an elected representative interface with the federal government, most Indigenous people did not consider ATSIC to be an autonomous or Indigenous organisation. Rather it was understood as a 'creation of non-Aboriginal Australia' (O'Shane 1998: 6) that hovered in 'uncertain space' between a dominant state and the possibility of genuine self-determination (Bradfield 2006: 88). As Irene Watson (2007a: 24) has argued:

> Aboriginal people were given an under-resourced white model to perform the impossible task of caring for Aboriginal Australia. From the beginning the ATSIC project was doomed to fail and, when it did, white racism laid the blame in black hands.

There was considerable anger when ATSIC was abolished in 2005, leaving Aboriginal and Torres Strait Islander people without a representative voice (something I will explore further in the next chapter).

Other problems also undermined the Australian approach to self-determination. The new policy regime led to complicated interactions between Indigenous nations, groups and communities that were both different from one another to begin with, and had subsequently endured diverse and varying impacts of colonisation over time. For some Indigenous nations, the Australian model of self-determination was marked by a clash between traditional structures of community governance and control, and newly imposed settler structures such as elected community councils. Non-Indigenous community educator Richard Trudgen (2000: 55) observes that there was an assumption that, as the missions withdrew from communities in north-east Arnhem Land, the Elders would take control of the new community councils. In most cases, however, this did not happen because the new 'Balanda [white] processes' were only understood by some of the younger, Western-educated Yolŋu. As a result, traditional models of social organisation were undermined at a time when stability was desperately needed. In other parts of the country, the preceding protectionist regimes, such as missions, had not only done irrevocable damage to traditional governance norms and practices, but their withdrawal also meant that their imposed governance arrangements were revoked, in some cases leaving a significant social void (Sutton 2001: 128). Although many communities clearly prized the restoration of their autonomy above all else, in Noel Pearson's view, many communities 'threw the baby out with the bathwater' by destroying the 'moral and cultural order that the churches had given to communities' (2007: 28). At the same time, however, the new policy regime saw an influx of non-Indigenous bureaucrats and managers to Indigenous lives and communities, which further undermined Indigenous leadership and governance practices (Trudgen 2000: 56).

The weak form of self-determination adopted in Australia did little to foster Indigenous autonomy and break the habit of dependency on government that bedevilled some communities. In Australia, self-determination was 'entirely recoded' as an issue of 'policy self-management rather than political autonomy' (Strakosch 2015: 70). As a result of these inherent weaknesses, the Australian version of self-determination eventually came under fire from all sides, including critique from prominent Indigenous leaders and commentators, and from all political directions. Some pointed to the policy's 'carefully circumscribed remedialism', while others pointed to the apparently 'corrosive welfare economies' that self-determination has fostered (Strakosch 2015: 2). This latter critique, led by Noel Pearson, linked the introduction of self-determination with what Pearson described as 'institutionalised dependency', which he argued had been created by a regime of 'passive welfare' (2007: 17). Pearson claimed that the collapse of social norms and the rise of ills such as violence, suicide, alcoholism and child abuse in some Indigenous communities are recent rather than historical phenomena, dated to the rise of 'victim politics' in which the 'increased recognition of black rights' was accompanied by 'a calamitous erosion of black responsibility' (2007: 26). Interestingly, Pearson's proposed solution to these ills was a new form of Indigenous-led paternalism—a proposal not necessarily at odds with arguments for returning the control of Indigenous affairs to Indigenous hands. Certainly, that was the way that Pearson understood his proposals, evident in the title of his self-published report *Our right to take responsibility* (2000).

For the opportunistic, conservative Howard government, however, Pearson's proposals provided ammunition for their more widespread reforms in Indigenous affairs, including the abolition of ATSIC and later the Northern Territory Intervention. In 2005 when ATSIC was abolished, self-determination was proclaimed a failure by the Howard government, to be replaced by 'neo-colonial rule from Canberra' leading to a new policy regime with 'frightening similarities' to the 'highly destructive' assimilation regime of an earlier time (Altman 2017a: 5). For many Aboriginal and Torres Strait Islander people, the abolition of ATSIC was 'the stuff of nightmares' as the stripping of representative and legislative rights and powers demonstrated yet again 'just how Indigenous people are at the mercy of the government' (Cromb 2017a: 1).

Former Aboriginal and Torres Strait Islander Social Justice Commissioner, Mick Gooda has pleaded with government to let Aboriginal and Torres Strait Islander people 'take control of their affairs' in ways that are 'culturally relevant and meaningful' to them. Gooda argues that, 'For Indigenous governance to be effective it is not enough to import foreign governance structures into communities and expect that those communities will be able to function effectively within those structures' and contends that the correct role for government is to support Aboriginal and Torres Strait Islander communities to govern themselves (quoted in *Koori Mail* 2012c: 27). Such an approach has thus far proven irreconcilable with the desire for colonial completion, which continues to deny Indigenous peoples the capacity to pursue self-determination through their own national sovereignties and associated governance.

## INDIGENOUS NATIONHOOD AND GOVERNANCE

Indigenous calls for self-determination originate in Aboriginal and Torres Strait Islander peoples' ongoing sovereignty and their existence as self-governing political entities or 'nations' that have survived colonisation. The colonial gaze has generally overlooked the diverse, complex and sophisticated forms of Indigenous governance that have been maintained in various parts of the continent, which have appeared 'invisible, unknowable, and underdeveloped' to settler eyes. This apparent unknowability—erroneously interpreted as a governance *tabula rasa*—has been used by the settler state as justification for inscribing liberal norms and institutions of statecraft onto Indigenous polities, in ways that have been disempowering and deeply problematic (Smith 2008: 78).

Since the advent of formal self-determination policy in Australia in the 1970s, governments have grasped for 'cultural models' of Indigenous political organising, without which they had 'no intellectual basis' for understanding or recognising the political and cultural differences that they ostensibly respected (Rowse 2001: 104). A fundamental problem with the Australian settler state's approach to Indigenous self-determination was the desire to constitute the scale of the Indigenous group or nation in ways that did not disrupt the structures and rhythms of the bureaucratic apparatus of the state. This is, of course, entirely contrary to the principles of self-determination and self-government, which dictate that Indigenous peoples must identify for themselves what constitutes their operative political communities. Determining their political communities—operationalising jurisdiction over their Indigenous nations—is a crucial and practical matter of political reform (Russell 2005: 136–7). In the context of Indigenous nationhood on the Australian continent, self-determination can only be understood in localised and highly context-specific ways (Davis 2012: 24).

This is not to suggest that Indigenous nationhood has remained fixed over time, preserved as some kind of 'cultural museum'. Rather, there is a long history on this continent of 'highly sophisticated innovations' in Indigenous governing institutions (Smith 2008: 107), which have continued to adapt to the pressures and demands of settler colonialism. Over generations, First Nations have experimented with various means of determining regions, from the geographic to the social and political, recognising the ways in which both contemporary political and economic ties as well as historical foundations form the 'cultural geography' underpinning their collective alliances (Smith 2007: 28–30). This has certainly been the case for the Yolŋu clans of north-east Arnhem Land, the Pitjantjatjara people from the Western Desert and the Tiwi of Bathurst and Melville islands, among others who have managed to organise politically above the level of the local community. Nations such as the Ngarrindjeri or Gunditjmara have survived as organised groups that can still draw on pre-colonial conceptions of the collective self and can build to some degree on older structures of decision-making (Cornell 2015: 8). What is distinctive about groups such as these is that, as a result of the ways in which colonisation rolled across Indigenous territories, they have maintained some integrity in their kin, language and spiritual associations (Bern and Dodds 2002: 175).

Indigenous nations in other parts of the country have had to focus on reconstituting their interests in the wake of colonial destruction. Careful work has been needed to determine who rightly belongs in a regional alliance, who should be included and who should be excluded, and it is these decisions that ought to determine the physical boundary of a region rather than the other way around (Smith 2007: 41). A political community or nation has to be realised in the minds of its members, with enough significance to 'sustain allegiance and shape action' (Cornell 2015: 6). It is difficult work to (re)determine the boundaries of such an entity in a settler colonial context that intentionally disrupted Indigenous governance arrangements, taking land, relocating and containing populations, overriding social and political organising, and prohibiting languages and cultural practices. As Cornell (2015: 6) argues, 'Claiming or revitalizing an Indigenous nationhood has to confront the embedded legacies of these processes.' To do so means determining the appropriate basis for collective political action and self-government, whether that be by kinship, language, geography, shared history or some other criteria. Cornell suggests that groups engaged in this work of political reconstitution should consider what they need to achieve beyond identifying as a nation. His research (2015: 12) suggests that the key processes involve 'organising as a nation' (How will they make the decisions they view as theirs to make? How will they enact the political community they claim? How will they govern?) and 'acting as a nation' (developing policy and strategy, and delivering the outcomes: law, justice, economy, resource stewardship, cultural revitalisation, productive intergovernmental relationships, the intergenerational transmission of knowledge, and so on). It is in acting as a nation that Indigenous peoples are most likely to come into conflict with settler governments as they test the jurisdictional limits of the settler order (Cornell 2015: 17).

One example that is often cited is the Murdi Paaki Regional Assembly in western New South Wales, a 'regional, representative, community-controlled organisation that gives voice and decision-making authority to a range of Aboriginal communities across a vast and diverse area' (Jeffries et al 2011: 118). The Assembly developed out of an earlier regional council, and it is still hoped that it may one day transition to a regional authority model, much like the one in the Torres Strait. Through efforts like these, Indigenous nations are being re-imagined and transformed, and Indigenous people are reasserting the legitimacy and cultural basis of these institutions and their decision-making authority (Smith 2008: 76). As Diane Smith (2007: 45) has pointed out, there is a 'two-way trajectory' in Indigenous govern-ance arrangements that balances 'residential decentralisation and local autonomy' with 'political centralisation and regional alliances.' Smith and Hunt (2008: 11) see Indigenous governance as an important site for 'the unfinished business of post-colonial struggle' in which the 'balance of power and relationships between Indigenous Australians and the Australian state' are constantly contested and renegotiated (2008: 13).

Reconstituting Indigenous nationhood in these ways provides a basis for Aboriginal and Torres Strait Islander nations to exercise self-determining *governance* over the territories in which they have *jurisdiction*. Meaningful governance is impossible without the recognition of Indigenous jurisdic-tion. Morgan Brigg and Lyndon Murphy (2011: 28) suggest that jurisdiction is not the same thing as sovereignty, as it need not refer to absolute control over a particular territory. Instead, jurisdiction refers to 'matters of authority, power, and control' that translate to 'the legitimacy to act authoritatively and confidently in relation to a given geographical space or set of processes and practices.' Jurisdiction in this sense necessitates the asking of ques-tions that should inform any negotiation about governance arrangements:

'Who has jurisdiction for this program or for this site? Whose ideas and values are at play in the management of this site? Whose knowledge arbitrates decisions within this program?' Brigg and Murphy (2011: 28–9) suggest that asking these questions helps to distinguish issues of Indigenous 'participation' within settler jurisdictions from genuine forms of 'control and empowerment.' Participation, they point out, is 'far from control', but the settler order tends to frame problems only in liberal terms and then seek Indigenous participation in subsequent programs, thereby subsuming Indigenous values and ideas as the logic of elimination drives the progressive assimilation of difference.

In Australia, however, self-determination was advanced through the regional structure of ATSIC (discussed further in the next chapter), and through the supposed empowerment of Indigenous organisations intended to function as organs of self-determination. Settler colonial logics saw the fragmentation of the Indigenous 'sector' from a period of vocal, pan-Indigenous national unity in the 1970s, into a multitude of local service delivery organisations. While in some ways this represented the instantiation of Indigenous nationhood, in effect this saw the dilution of challenges to settler colonial domination. This uniquely Australian mode of 'corporate self-determination' proved problematic in multiple ways, not least because it tended to reduce 'good governance' to successful compliance with corporate regulation and an audit culture (Davis 2012: 24). As Patrick Sullivan (2011: 55) points out, self-determination was 'least challenging for settler interests' when it was understood primarily as local self-governance. Indigenous jurisdiction was obscured in another moment of fantasised colonial completion.

The establishment of Indigenous organisations provided an avenue for asserting Aboriginal and Torres Strait Islander rights to self-determination, and a vehicle for the development and delivery of culturally appropriate services. Early organisations, such as the Aboriginal legal and medical services, were intended to be as much about autonomy and self-determination as they were about service provision (Briskman 2003: 31–3). The settler colonial logic of elimination derailed these aspirations, and through the incorporation of Aboriginal organisations, many previously autonomous leaders and activists found themselves 'integrated into the very structure of oppression that they are trying to combat' (Jones and Hill-Burnett 1982: 224). Indigenous governance organisations found themselves 'between a rock and a hard place', with increasingly divergent goals and aspirations between Indigenous communities and the settler state (Hunt 2008: 27).

Over the decades since the introduction of a formal policy of self-determination, and in the years since that policy was abandoned, Indigenous organisations have struggled to exercise jurisdiction in their communities and provide culturally appropriate services to Aboriginal and Torres Strait Islander people. As Alexis Wright points out, however, (and writing specifically about organisations in the Northern Territory), these organisations 'keep doing this better than anyone else' despite the gross power imbalances of the settler colonial regime, which remains 'the crippling factor, and it keeps pulling us down' (Wright 2016: 2). David Ross, Director of Aboriginal Peak Organisations Northern Territory (APO NT), argues that, 'Many Aboriginal organisations are strong, operating well and need little assistance' (quoted in *Koori Mail* 2014d: 34). Operating effectively is not enough to stop these organisations falling victim to the policy churn that is endemic to Indigenous affairs. As yet another example, many Aboriginal community organisations were threatened by the 2014 introduction of the Abbott government's Indigenous Advancement Strategy (IAS), which pooled Indigenous funding, took a 'razor' to Aboriginal community organisations and programs, and put out to tender much of the $4.8 billion these organisations relied on, effectively gutting Indigenous communities of control over their services (Davis 2017b: 2). The IAS has been criticised at all levels, for lacking coherent policy logic, poor communication and chaotic implementation. A 2017 review by the Australian National Audit Office found that the program's planning, design and implementation had been rushed through the Department of the Prime Minister and Cabinet's grants administration processes, and

> fell short of the standard required to effectively manage a billion dollars of Commonwealth resources. The basis by which projects were recommended to the Minister was not clear and, as a result, limited assurance is available that the projects funded support the department's desired outcomes (ANAO 2017: 8).

Indeed, the IAS came under specific criticism from UN Special Rapporteur Victoria Tauli-Corpuz who described it as bureaucratic, rigid and as wasting considerable resources on administration (quoted in *NITV News* 2017a).

Integrating economic activity with Aboriginal and Torres Strait Islander peoples' cultural priorities and effective governance systems has been recognised as one of the greatest challenges that Indigenous people face (Dodson and Smith 2003: 6). Wiradjuri man Geoff Scott, formerly the CEO of both the New South Wales Aboriginal Land Council and the National Congress of Australia's First Peoples, argues that, 'It's no secret strong and effective governance brings with it sustainable economic, social and cultural outcomes', but contends that for these outcomes to be achieved the focus needs to shift 'back to developing credible and legitimate governance structures . . . accepting responsibility as the First Peoples of this country and demonstrating that fact' (quoted in *Koori Mail* 2012c: 27). This type of economic self-determination is evident in initiatives such as the Torres Strait Economic Development Summit. Seisia man Joseph Elu, chairman of the Torres Strait Regional Authority (TSRA), explained that the objective of the Summit was 'to provide our region's community leaders with the opportunity to consider key principles that will contribute to local growth, jobs and long-term prosperity' and provide 'a unique opportunity to discuss key principles for a strategic approach to economic and industry development in the Torres Strait' (quoted in *Koori Mail* 2014e: 26). But these opportunities for advancing economic development through self-determination are increasingly rare. As South Sea and Torres Strait Island man Wally Tallis (2017), general manager of Indigenous Business Australia, argues:

> The current government's engagement with Aboriginal and Torres Strait Islander peoples around things like policy and delivery for programs like Closing the Gap do not satisfactorily incorporate our voices and beliefs. These are generally the first things forfeited in the government's blinkered pursuit of a single policy approach. Proper engagement with defined or select groups of Aboriginal and Torres Strait Islander people is all too rare, which hinders what many of our mobs have been calling for for some time: stop the paternal control and work with us.

There is no guarantee that a shift in jurisdiction will result in sustainable economic development, but self-government is the only condition in which such development is possible. Returning accountability for decision-making to Indigenous nations is key to this. As Stephen Cornell (2006: 16–17) has argued:

> the divorce between those with the authority to make decisions and those bearing the consequences of those decisions has resulted in an extraordinary and continuing record of central government policy failure.

Despite radical changes in policy, government rhetoric still seems to support Indigenous aspirations for self-determination. In the 2017 *Closing the Gap* report (DPMC 2017b: 10), government described the *Empowered Communities* policy framework that aims to 'empower Indigenous people to build positive futures for themselves and their families and build trust between communities and governments'. The approach claims to 'put Indigenous culture and participation front and centre in the decisions of government', moving from 'an application driven, transactional approach to one of partnership, transparency and shared accountability'. The report maintains that government is 'shifting to a new way of engaging' and 'using different approaches in different regions across the country'.

And yet, on the ground, this is far from the reality. Non-Indigenous development studies scholar Mark Moran (2018) observes that the introduction of Empowered Communities produced a 'Swiss cheese jurisdiction' that was far less effective than the Indigenous leaders of the initiative had hoped for. Moran believes there is an important role for government in helping to resolve 'durable territorial jurisdictions' that will enable a more hands-off approach based on intergovernmental funding transfers (from federal government to Indigenous jurisdiction) instead of program and organisational funding. Moran suggests that this kind of model would both increase local autonomy and provide 'non-judgmental inclusivity' for those people living within jurisdictional boundaries.

Such reforms are both delicate and urgent. Writing of the communities of Papunya and Maningrida, the non-Indigenous anthropologist Jon Altman (2017a: 5) notes that the shift to self-determination in 1972 came off the back of 'overwhelming political acceptance that the colonial development

project at these iconic government settlements had failed.' Over a decade
after self-determination was abandoned, to be replaced by the neoliberal
paternalism of the Intervention (to be discussed further in Chapter Five),
Altman (2017a: 9) reports that in many remote communities, poverty is
worsening and social conditions are in further decline. After the 'flattening'
of Indigenous governance arrangements that had been 'slowly and collabo-
ratively built over decades', Altman asks:

> Where to now? How can the emerging governance for destructive depend-
> ence be radically shifted so that communities regain control and govern for
> forms of development that accord with local aspirations in all their diversity?
> How can the Australian state ever be trusted to deal with its remote-living
> Indigenous citizens with appropriate poverty alleviating duty of care?

He wonders what will happen when the dominance of the current policy
regime is reversed:

> Will flattened people and institutions magically bounce back as if nothing
> has happened? Will the community organisations that delivered positive
> outcomes, demeaned as worthless by the Australian state and its compliant
> supporters, somehow automatically reconstitute?

Altman is pessimistic about the future, suggesting 'it could take a long
time for diminished local organisational capacity to be repaired.' While
this is doubtless true, it is also the only place to start. Research from the
Indigenous Community Governance Project a decade ago indicated that
getting Aboriginal and Torres Strait Islander people 'back in the driver's seat
in making decisions about their governance' was the 'only effective path' to
breaking the cycle of Indigenous poverty and marginalisation (Hunt and
Smith 2007: 2). Self-determination remains at the heart of Aboriginal
and Torres Strait Islander ambition, and while Australia has been drastically
out of step in this regard to date, there are still strengths to build upon and
successes to replicate.

## SELF-DETERMINATION AS RESURGENCE
Over a decade ago, Hunt and Smith (2007: 27) questioned whether conditions existed in Australia that would enable Indigenous leadership and

decision-making to be adequately exercised. Since then, the settler state has only ramped up its intrusion into Indigenous lives, and further undermined Indigenous autonomy. The argument of this book, however, is that the settler state will *always* act in this way, either overtly as in the present or, more covertly, through the relentless assimilatory undercurrents of policy regimes like the Australian version of self-determination.

The alternative path to self-determination is Indigenous resurgence. Taiaiake Alfred and Jeff Corntassel (2005: 611–12) argue that:

> Current approaches to confronting the problem of contemporary colonialism ... are, in a basic way, building not on a spiritual and cultural foundation provided to us as the heritage of our nations, but on the weakened and severely damaged cultural and spiritual and social results of colonialism. Purported decolonization and watered-down cultural restoration processes that accept the premises and realities of our colonized existences as their starting point are inherently flawed and doomed to fail.

While Alfred and Corntassel (2005: 611–12) suggest that there is no 'neat model' of resurgence, they do point to 'directions of movement, patterns of thought and action that reflect a shift to an Indigenous reality from the colonized places we inhabit today in our minds and in our souls.' Central to these transformative practices is a regeneration of place and nation-based Indigenous identities that are expressed and governed through culturally appropriate political formations (Battell Lowman and Barker 2015: 112). These practices do not rely on the settler state for validation or the provision of funding, but instead are evident in efforts towards the recuperation of Indigenous languages, philosophy and laws to shape practices of jurisdiction and governance (Alfred and Corntassel 2005: 614). In terms of self-determination and governance, Indigenous resurgence involves Aboriginal and Torres Strait Islander people developing governance arrangements that 'embody their own values, norms, and views about how authority and leadership should be exercised' (Hunt and Smith 2007: 24).

As Alexis Wright has suggested, settler governance is 'the wrong system of governance for people who have been working to their own governing system for thousands of years' (Wright 2016: 1). Kevin Gilbert pointed out over three decades ago that 'the toughest thing that blacks are going to have to come to grips with' is the 'psychological damage done to individuals and communities' as a result of post-colonial dependency. Gilbert argued that even though 'the white man put you there, psychologically' even if he wanted to 'he can't get you out' (Gilbert 2002 [1973]: 200).

Around the continent, Aboriginal and Torres Strait Islander people are using various tools to advance Indigenous resurgence, working both with and against settler institutions. In 2016, Yingiya Mark Guyula was elected to the Northern Territory seat of Nhulunbuy as an independent candidate. Guyula actively campaigned on a platform of Indigenous sovereignty intended to empower Indigenous communities of Arnhem Land with 'law-making jurisdiction over its land and seas', 'policing and judicial powers within its boundaries', 'control of resources from regions land and seas', 'taking control of tax regimes', and 'being a "nation within a nation", in line with the US ethos for Native American nations.' In what had been a very safe Labor seat, with a margin of 13.7 per cent, Guyula won the vote in every single Yolŋu community and ultimately won the seat by a small margin, a victory seen by some commentators as an 'explicit rebuke of the ongoing project of colonisation' and 'a significant moment in the long history of Indigenous campaigns for political, economic and cultural independence' (McLoughlin 2016a: 2, 5).

In other parts of the continent, Aboriginal and Torres Strait Islander peoples have come together to articulate their commitment to self-determination through resurgence. For example, Ghillar Michael Anderson (Convenor of the Sovereign Union of First Nations and Peoples in Australia) wrote of the 2014 Freedom Summit:

> It is clear that the uniform position of the great majority at the Freedom Summit, held in Alice Springs last month, was their determined resolve to confirm that no Aboriginal/Original Nation or People in this country has voluntarily ceded its sovereignty to the invader British/Australian society, nor has been conquered in any declared war . . . The most significant point that came from the Freedom Summit was that we will determine the pathways to self-determination; we will establish and direct policy for our people, and in doing so all delegates agreed that we must go home to our respective Nation's communities and convene meetings to seek guidance on their views of what types of independence and policy direction we

take . . . The Sovereign Union itself is made up of member states which are asserting independence and are working to be self-determining, through their own governance structure, in accordance with their ancient law and culture (Anderson 2014b: 24).

Anderson observed three groups of people at the Freedom Summit, each engaged in resurgence from a different starting place, dependent on their own experiences of colonisation. Firstly, he quoted the words of a young Gamilaroi delegate to the Summit, Paul Spearim, who had argued that many Indigenous people had been

dispersed and displaced by the tyranny and genocidal objectives of previous government policies, which sees fragmentation in our communities particularly in the east and south, where white people have impacted most to date, with our culture and languages torn from us.

This group was engaged in resurgence through 'striving to locate that which was lost. Whilst we live in cities and regional areas we do want our culture and language back.' Secondly, Ghillar observed those who spoke of being descendants of the Stolen Generations and the pain that they showed when speaking of being 'disconnected to their country.' Ghillar reported that one delegate in that group described their Indigeneity as being like 'a leaf on a dying tree' that 'fears the sudden wind of change' that might result in them being 'lost forever.' Finally, Ghillar noted the delegates who were

firmly grounded in their law and culture . . . secure in their identity, with a true sense of who they are and where they belong with language, law and culture intact. These people are connected to country through their law. They have greater opportunity to assert sovereignty over their own territories, waters and natural resources.

Across these differences, Ghillar expressed the hope from the Summit that groups would be able to support one another to pursue sovereignty and self-government with proprietary interests in land and the struggle to secure adequate resources to provide 'health, housing, economic development and future political pathways' in ways that Indigenous peoples themselves determine (Anderson 2014b: 24).

Megan Davis (2012: 24) argues that the right to self-determination 'as configured in international law, translated by the state and adopted by Indigenous communities' has had particular impacts on women and girls. The state-centric version of self-determination adopted in Australia saw Indigenous governance remain 'overly reliant on the state and state legislative acts and institutions and consequently calibrated according to the male experience'. Davis says:

> Less attention was paid to how the right should be managed internally within groups themselves, especially in regard to Aboriginal women's status. We know this because for over three decades, Aboriginal organisations, corporations and councils—the groups that make up the collective 'self'—have to a large extent ignored the marginalisation and violence experienced by Aboriginal women.

This analysis suggests that there will also be gender-specific dimensions to practices of Indigenous resurgence, and indeed these are evident. Fiona Hamilton (2017a) a Tasmanian Aboriginal woman of the Trawlwoolway nation, now working as a community family violence educator in the Northern Territory's Barkly region, draws parallels between the violence of settler colonialism and other forms of violence against women. Hamilton suggests that 'for a good many Aboriginal and Torres Strait Islander women, there is little difference between being caught in a violent relationship and the relationship we must have with structures and systems, and their agents, to save our own lives and the lives of our children'. She argues that:

> The consequences of colonisation and all that it has brought to Aboriginal and Torres Strait Islander peoples cannot be ameliorated by reducing the status and agency of our peoples. It's that simple. Structures and systems that do this are further damaging us, even when they are pre-supposed or designed to empower us. [. . .] What is important to us as First Nations peoples is continuance. This is the conditions of systems and structures being set right to enable us to continue culturally, spiritually, socially and economically. This is equity for us. Aboriginal women and children cannot secure 'continuance' under the current conditions, and this situation plays out across the country. We cannot free ourselves from family violence whilst we are co-opted into systems and structures that model it, sustain it and in many cases drive it.

Resurgence may be linked to cultural practices that are deeply traditional, such as in the program at Ali Curung, north of Alice Springs where Graham Beasley takes young people out onto country to teach them traditional survival techniques. Beasley links this explicitly to self-determination, saying, 'For years and years we lived off the land ourselves' and encourages young people to pursue their own autonomy, telling them that if they know their country, 'You can't go hungry. You can't get lost' (quoted in *Koori Mail* 2016b: 21). Resurgence may also be associated with practices that are not so explicitly connected to traditional Indigenous culture. For example, the Wiradjuri DJ, music curator and writer Hannah Donnelly describes the curation of the Sovereign Trax playlist on the digital music platform SoundCloud as a contribution towards 'decolonising the conversation of how we consume music in this country and how we support and listen to our First Nations artists.' Donnelly argues that Aboriginal and Torres Strait Islander people

> can actively participate in decolonisation through music by playing, selecting and listening to First Nations artists . . . This shifts how Indigenous people are represented by national narratives, to become accountable to Indigenous sovereignty, rather than being positioned as a minority in settler colonial structures . . . It is for our own mob to listen to our own music and support each other, but it's definitely aimed at other people . . . it's a way of sharing stories (quoted in Reich 2017).

In the Atherton Tablelands in Queensland, the Yidinji, Narjon and Mbarbarum nations have advanced a community power project that is allowing Indigenous communities to take their power back 'both literally and figuratively' through renewable energy that is owned, managed and controlled by communities. Representing these nations, Mbarbarum man Eddie Turpin (2017) has linked this initiative with practices of resurgence, arguing that 'Setting up a community energy project allows us to live back on country. We can raise our children on their land and give them a cultural upbringing that allows them to understand who they are and where they come from.' For these nations, renewable energy is just a first step:

> Building renewable energy projects, which are owned and managed by our community, mean that in the long term we can start to build other projects

that will increase our capacity and employment in the region. We've been working on Ranger programs, food production and other farming opportunities . . . Self-determination for our Mob is a critical factor in all of this. All we want is to be able to run our own affairs, look after our kids, care for country and create sustainable futures for our communities.

These are just a handful of examples of the ways in which Indigenous resurgence might be practised by different Indigenous nations around the continent. While settler colonial ideas and values have come to dominate the governance landscape, these remain fundamentally incompatible with Indigenous ideas and values, creating the 'antagonistic intimacy' of Indigenous–settler relations (Brigg and Murphy 2011: 25). Indigenous lives have been ceaselessly impacted upon by the successive governments of the settler order, and Aboriginal and Torres Strait Islander people have articulated a range of political demands in their struggles against these impacts. One constant has been Indigenous calls for self-determination (Luke Pearson 2017a: 6). Practices of political and cultural resurgence suggest some of the ways in which self-determination will be practised with or without engagement from the settler state.

In the long term, however, the ability to live genuinely self-determining lives will depend on a careful disentangling of Indigenous and settler modes of governance, and extensive work to reconstitute Indigenous jurisdiction in places where colonialism has damaged systems of authority and decision-making in communities. This work is not unthinkable or undoable, but it will need resourcing and support. As Plangermairreenner man Jim Pura-lia Meenamatla Everett has argued (quoted in McConchie 2003: 60), Aboriginal and Torres Strait Islander people need 'to be given back the resources to live a cultural life in a modern world without being told by government how to do it.'

# CHAPTER 3

# REPRESENTATION

Aboriginal and Torres Strait Islander peoples need to be able to speak to the settler state. Regardless of any future political autonomy that may be achieved by Indigenous peoples as self-determining nations and communities, the settler state will remain an encompassing political reality. The fact of this relationship means there will always be a need for a political interface between Indigenous peoples and the state. Indigenous nations will always need to represent themselves to and within the settler order. Exactly how that representation should best take place, however, has been hotly contested over many decades.

The small size of many Indigenous clans and nations makes effective political representation difficult, sometimes creating tension between Aboriginal and Torres Strait Islander peoples about what form of representation might best capture their diverse institutions and values (Bern and Dodds 2002: 164). These dynamics have frequently been exploited by the settler state, which finds it easier to contain and suppress a divided and voiceless Indigenous population. As Wolfe (2016: 32) has argued, settler democracy will always be an oxymoron for Indigenous peoples, as it is this same democracy that has pursued their elimination. The question as to whether and how the distinct lack of Aboriginal and Torres Strait Islander voices in settler political institutions should be formally addressed remains unresolved, meaning that any position taken by the settler state 'cannot be neutral or apolitical' (Patterson 2017: 7).

One thing that has been important to Indigenous peoples seeking to engage with government has been the right to choose their own represent- atives. Aboriginal and Torres Strait Islander peoples have had some form of elected national representation almost continuously since the 1970s, first with the National Aboriginal Consultative Committee (NACC), 1973–77, then its replacement, the National Aboriginal Conference (NAC), 1977–85. Two years after the NAC was wound up the Hawke Labor government announced their intention to develop another representative body, which eventually began operation as the Aboriginal and Torres Strait Islander Commission (ATSIC) in 1990. ATSIC survived until its abolition by the Howard government in 2005. In the wake of ATSIC there was another dif- ficult period in which no elected representative body existed, replaced by Howard with a handpicked advisory council. In 2010 the Rudd government created the National Congress of Australia's First Peoples (Congress), after a process of extensive consultation with Aboriginal and Torres Strait Islander peoples around the continent. In 2013, Prime Minister Tony Abbott created a separate, hand-picked Indigenous Advisory Council, which continued to operate in parallel to Congress under Prime Minister Malcolm Turnbull, but had no representational basis.

It is clear that these organisations and mechanisms have not always— or even often—been perceived as adequate by Aboriginal and Torres Strait Islander people. There have been many calls to improve the representational interface between Indigenous peoples and the settler state. As Noongar, Wangai and Yamatji man and federal MP Ken Wyatt has argued, 'You have to involve Aboriginal people in the process of decisions that impact on them' (quoted in Gredley 2017). Co-chair of National Congress, Amangu and Wajuk man Rod Little, has argued that Indigenous people 'need a new rela- tionship that respects and harnesses our expertise, and guarantees us a seat at the table as equal partners when governments are making decisions about our lives' (quoted in *Koori Mail* 2017: 5). Little's co-chair, Jackie Huggins, agrees, arguing that Aboriginal and Torres Strait Islander people are 'tired of being marginalised, tired of being ignored', and that they deserve 'much, much better' (quoted in Maxwell 2016b: 5).

Exactly what 'much better' representation would look like remains contested. As Morgan Brigg and Lyndon Murphy (2003: 30–1) suggest, there is always a risk for Aboriginal and Torres Strait Islander people that their participation in the administrative arrangements of the settler state will see them 'trading in "whitegoods"', legitimating 'institutional and internal assimilationist policies and practices' at the expense of 'Aboriginal history and experience with white institutions.' Nevertheless, in 2017 the Statement from the Heart called for a constitutionally entrenched 'Voice to Parliament' that would represent, and provide advice on, Indigenous interests. As discussed in Chapter One, this proposition was swiftly rejected by the Turnbull government, with claims that such a body would effectively create a third chamber of parliament and undermine parliamentary sovereignty (Turnbull 2017). The perceived threat to parliamentary sovereignty clearly derives from the settler logic of elimination, which understands the recognition of continuing and distinct Indigenous political interests as a challenge to the fantasy of colonial completion. Indeed, an examination of previous representative structures for Aboriginal and Torres Strait Islander peoples shows that each has fallen prey to the same logic.

## REPRESENTATION IN PARLIAMENT

Unlike Australia's closest settler colonial relative, New Zealand—which has seven reserved Māori seats—no Australian parliament has in place any special measures to secure the election of Aboriginal and Torres Strait Islander peoples. In the absence of such measures, Aboriginal and Torres Strait Islander peoples have, until very recently, been largely absent from these institutions. Since Federation, Aboriginal and Torres Strait Islander people have been poorly represented—or not represented at all—in the nation's state, territory and Commonwealth legislatures. It is possible that this absence reflects a poor fit between Indigenous culture/s and democratic political representation (see Rowse 2001), however, from at least the 1930s Aboriginal and Torres Strait Islander people have expressed a desire for greater involvement in government and representation in parliament (see Attwood and Markus 1999, 2004). Indeed, William Cooper gathered (on foot!) 2000 signatures for his petition to the King calling for Aboriginal representation in parliament—a labour frustrated by the then federal government, which declined to forward the petition to the King given that, in their view, appointing an Aboriginal representative to parliament was 'a constitutional impossibility' (Atkinson 2008: 307).

At the time of writing, there is the highest number of Indigenous parliamentarians in the federal parliament than at any time since Federation. Nevertheless, Australia's parliaments have remained fundamentally white institutions. Until relatively recently, there had only ever been two Indigenous people in Australia's federal parliament: Jagera man Neville Bonner was a senator from 1971 to 1983, and Gumbaynggirr man Aden Ridgeway from 1998 to 2005. This was despite the fact that, since the mid-1970s, Indigenous candidates had been contesting parliamentary elections in increasing numbers. The relatively small number of Indigenous Australians compared with the wider population (around 3 per cent) suggests that even on a proportional basis Indigenous people would not be present in our parliaments in large numbers. Nevertheless, if federal parliamentary representation were to more closely reflect the Indigenous population we could expect to see three Indigenous members in the House of Representatives and one senator (Lloyd 2009: 1). In fact, the Australian federal parliament has come close to these numbers. In 2010, Ken Wyatt became the first Indigenous person in Australia to be elected to the House of Representatives, joined there in 2016 by Wiradjuri woman Linda Burney. The Senate has seen Gidja, Iwaidja and Yawuru woman Nova Peris take and leave her seat (2013–16), along with Jagera and Mununjahli woman Joanna Lindgren (2015–16). At the time of writing senators include Yawuru man Patrick Dodson (filling a casual vacancy in 2016) and Yanyuwa woman Malardirri McCarthy, who was elected in the 2016 general election.[11]

Although this number of Indigenous parliamentarians is a relatively recent achievement in the federal parliament, it remains questionable whether representation within settler institutions can ever have meaningful impact on the standing of Indigenous people. On the one hand, as Anne Phillips has argued, without the direct involvement of parliamentary representatives who share a history of 'subordination, exclusion or denial' it is likely that 'the policy process will be inherently paternalistic and the policy outcomes almost certainly skewed' (Phillips 2001: 26). This is certainly the view of many Aboriginal and Torres Strait Islander people, such as Michael Mansell, who argues that because the mainstream media is 'committed to the parliamentary process' they cannot 'ignore black parliamentarians just because they're black' (quoted in *National Indigenous Times* 2008: 18). This view is echoed by Ken Wyatt (also the Minister for Indigenous Health and Aged Care under Turnbull—the most senior position ever held by an Indigenous parliamentarian), who suggests that Aboriginal and Torres Strait Islander people gain respect and influence when they are 'elected equal to any other peer . . . by virtue of the fact that we've been able to tell people that we're worthy of their support.' For Wyatt personally, this has been 'a very powerful journey' through which he has been able to say, 'I have a voice, I have ideas and I have plans for the future' (quoted in Thorpe 2017d). In her maiden speech in the Western Australian parliament, Gidja woman Jarlbinymiya Josie Farrer (who broke new ground by speaking in her own language[12] to thank the people of the Kimberley for electing her) under-scored the importance of Indigenous representation in settler parliaments by arguing that 'the Parliament belongs to everybody, it's not just a place to make laws' (quoted in Maxwell 2013a: 17). Farrer had argued during the campaign—the first in which both the Liberal and Labor parties had fielded Indigenous candidates in the same seat—that 'Indigenous peoples are learning and understanding that this is the best way to fight' (quoted in Bamford 2017).

Yet this is certainly not the view of all Aboriginal and Torres Strait Islander people, and many remain highly critical about the potential impact of parliamentary representation. One long-time Indigenous activist, for example, has suggested that the pressures on Indigenous parliamentarians mean that they are forced to 'cooperate in their own oppression', while another suggests that the 'quality people' in the Northern Territory parliament are often 'hamstrung' by party control (Crawshaw and Cubillo quoted in Maddison 2009: 234). Others question whether parliamentary representation can ever adequately reflect 'the differences in the makeup and the cultural fabric of Aboriginal people right across the country' (Barbara Shaw quoted in Guivarra 2017).

For Indigenous parliamentarians themselves, the experience of seeking representation in settler political institutions can be deeply conflictual. Political institutions, such as parliaments, tend to perpetuate the dominant culture through the maintenance of norms and practices that are seen as universal, thereby erasing their cultural underpinnings (Reilly 2001: 78). More targeted approaches to Indigenous inclusion in mainstream politics, including systems of designated seats for Indigenous peoples, such as in New Zealand, and separate Indigenous parliaments, such as those adopted by Finland, Norway and Sweden for Sami peoples, do not necessarily prove more effective, as their reliance on the existence and mobilisation of political elites is challenging in situations like Australia, where the historical exclusion of Indigenous peoples from national politics would likely make implementation slow and difficult (Iorns Magallanes 2005: 107).

Mainstream political parties also have a problematic relationship with Indigenous representation and representatives. The majority of Indigenous federal parliamentarians have been elected as members of either the Labor or Liberal parties, with Aden Ridgeway the notable exception with his election as a member of the now defunct Australian Democrats. Around Australia, there has never been a coordinated effort by Aboriginal groups, communities or organisations to stand independent candidates in federal or state parliaments (Reilly 2001: 85) and nor has a significant Indigenous political party ever emerged (Bennett 1989: 121).[13] Despite this, proposals to ensure the preselection of greater numbers of Indigenous candidates to winnable seats have been slow to emerge. As the number of parliamentarians has grown, however, there have been efforts at the internal reform of the parties. Labor parliamentarians Patrick Dodson and Linda Burney were instrumental in establishing a national caucus aimed at increasing representation, voter enrolment and party representation among Aboriginal and Torres Strait Islander people (Chan 2017). Dodson sees this initiative as an indication that there is a new 'openness' about issues of concern to Aboriginal and Torres Strait Islander people that makes parliamentary politics more attractive, while Burney contends that 'creating a permanent forum within the party for Aboriginal people and Aboriginal issues . . . is making a difference and having Aboriginal voices at the table will attract Aboriginal people to the party' (both quoted in Thorpe 2017a).

This optimism about the capacity for party reform is not necessarily widely held, with other Indigenous politicians articulating political aspirations rooted in Indigenous culture rather than party loyalty. In the 2016

Northern Territory election, Yolŋu man Yingiya Mark Guyula (2016) stood as an independent candidate endorsed by the Yolŋu Nations Assembly, arguing:

> Since the first NT legislative council in 1947, we Yolŋu have been voting for ALP and CLP politicians to speak on our behalf, but their policy is governed according to the Monarch of the Commonwealth of England, created by a King 800 years ago, or more. That's why our voices through politicians, (both Yolŋu and Balanda[14]) have never been listened to, because that law is not ours. It operates according to the (foreign) Westminster system of law. Sadly, some Indigenous candidates will stand for ALP and CLP parties this year, but they will be controlled by a foreign sovereignty . . . I will represent my people according to the Yolŋuw madayin system of governance created by a mimay (unseen creator), created ever since time began, and handed through Djaŋ'kawu and Barama/Lany'tjun. I am proud to be a Yolŋu leader/ elder. I have knowledge systems passed on to me by fathers. I will represent my people with the Djirrikay (proclamation) according to the Yolŋu Ŋärra (parliament) of this land . . . the voices of my people, of Arnhem Land and Australia wide, our voices have never really got through to the parliament house in the way it was meant to be. Our voices and our cause have been misinterpreted and twisted around and the politicians we have voted in before have always thought of how Yolŋu people should live. It's always been said 'I think this is what is good for you', rather, I want to go in there and say 'this is what we know we need for our children, this is what we know we need for our community'.

The experiences of the first Indigenous parliamentarian in Australia's national parliament, Neville Bonner, were instructive in this regard. Bonner attempted to balance his representation of Indigenous people and issues with his support for the conservative ideology of his party and ended up pleasing nobody. At first he displeased other Aboriginal people by support- ing conservative state and federal Indigenous affairs policies, and in the end confounded and alienated his conservative Queensland Liberal Party col- leagues by becoming more vocal about Indigenous rights (Reilly 2001: 85). Initially convinced that the needs and interests of Aboriginal people would be best served by working within the institutions of white society, Bonner appeared 'obliged to defend, against a sceptical Indigenous constituency, the dignity and efficacy of parliament' (Rowse 1997: 97). He rejected claims that he was an 'Uncle Tom' or what he termed a 'tame cat liberal', stressing that he had exercised his 'right of conscience' to vote against his party on 23 occasions (quoted in Rowse 1997: 98). In a tribute to mark the twenty-second anniversary of Bonner's inaugural speech to parliament, Aden Ridgeway argued that Bonner's time as a senator 'highlighted the unique difficulties facing Indigenous people when they need to choose between their political parties and the priorities of their people' (Ridgeway 2003). Ridgeway went on to quote Bonner in a 1995 interview, a dozen years after he had left the parliament, as saying:

> I would not recommend with a clear conscience that Indigenous people join any one of the major political parties, because political parties in this country want bottle-drawn seats, hands in the air at the right time. You have no freedom to express yourself against the party (Bonner quoted in Ridgeway 2003).

It is concerns such as these that have led to calls for reform of the Australian parliamentary system to include reserved seats for Indigenous representatives as per the system in Aotearoa New Zealand. One of the clear advantages that a system of reserved seats might offer is a greater level of clarity about the status of parliamentarians elected to such seats as unambiguously representing Indigenous people rather than party or wider electorate issues. The creation of dedicated seats is seen as doing more than increasing the number of Indigenous representatives in a parliament. It is also an irrefutable expression of the formal political relationship between Indigenous peoples and the settler state (Lloyd 2009: 1). Wiradjuri academic Jessa Rogers (2017) is 'perplexed' that there has yet to be a serious discussion about creating dedicated seats for Aboriginal and Torres Strait Islander parliamentarians when she observes that Indigenous peoples in other parts of the world have 'gained a voice in their national political institutions' through such systems. Rogers argues that the Statement from the Heart makes clear that 'Aboriginal and Torres Strait Islander voices need to be heard' not through 'mere symbolic recognition' but through 'meaningful change that will allow us, and our children, a true voice in our own country.' For Rogers, reserved seats remain an option that the nation 'should carefully consider.'

Certainly some parliamentarians are bringing the language of resurgence and decolonisation into settler parliaments. In her 2017 maiden speech, the first Indigenous woman elected to the Victorian parliament, Gunai and Gunditjmara woman Lidia Thorpe (2017), argued that:

> Our First People must be at the centre of decision-making processes. We need a clan-based treaty to ensure self-determination is at the heart of our future. We are not a problem to be fixed. We are the custodians of this land and the oldest living culture in the world. We must be heard. For those who feel they are not being counted, for those who have lost the will to fight and for those who are no longer with us, I will be that voice. I will fight for you. You have my word, and I will never sell you out.

Time will tell whether these decolonial aspirations are able to survive—and possibly create change—in a colonial institution.

## REPRESENTATION OUTSIDE THE PARLIAMENT

In their efforts to create effective political relationships with the settler state, Aboriginal and Torres Strait Islander peoples have commonly worked through extra-parliamentary representative bodies. As noted above, Aboriginal and Torres Strait Islander peoples had some form of elected national representation from the mid-1970s to 2005, and then again since 2010. At least in theory. The reality is that these organisations have all seen their representative legitimacy 'undermined from the outset', both because they were creations of the settler state, and because they each struggled to adequately represent the diversity of Indigenous cultures, communities and nations across the continent. Representative bodies from the 1970s, such as the NACC and its successor the NAC, came to be seen as 'impotent' organisations that had been designed to contain Indigenous challenges to settler legitimacy (Bradfield 2006: 84). The NAC and the NACC were not sufficiently connected to, or representative of, Aboriginal communities and organisations. Settler logics were also at play, with government expecting both the NACC and the NAC to be advisory bodies only, while Aboriginal and Torres Strait Islander peoples continued to struggle for self-determination through these models of representation—efforts that were 'destined to disappoint' (Beresford 2006: 122). Attempting to organise political representation through national bodies has risked obscuring Indigenous cultural diversity and leaving many clans, nations and communities feeling invisible or unrepresented.

ATSIC was created in 1989 to recognise the unique place of Indigenous peoples in Australian history and contemporary society and to address both historical disadvantage and ongoing discrimination (Jonas and Dick 2004: 8). Among other things, the design of ATSIC was intended to manage the tension between the localism of Indigenous politics and the perceived need for national representation and a national voice. The ATSIC model managed these complexities by creating a system of regional representation (originally spread over 60 regions but reduced to 35 following a 1993 review), with nearly 800 positions for elected representatives, in an attempt to connect local governance to national representation through the intermediate level of regionalism (Sanders 2004: 56–7). The reality, however, was that this structure did not come nearly close enough to accommodating or representing the cultural diversity of Aboriginal and Torres Strait Islander peoples at the local or community levels. ATSIC regional councils were created by the settler state as merely the 'institutional face of diversity' (Smith 1996: 30) rather than as bodies that could genuinely represent Indigenous nationhood.

ATSIC certainly had its critics among Aboriginal and Torres Strait Islander people. Gary Foley (2007: 130) has argued that the announcement of the creation of ATSIC was aimed at 'placating' the Indigenous activists planning to demonstrate at the settlers' bicentennial celebrations. Beyond concerns with such political machinations lay a deeper critique of the lack of cultural fit between ATSIC and the Aboriginal and Torres Strait Islander communities it would attempt to represent. As Charles Perkins (1992: 228) articulated at the time, ATSIC was 'a creation of white politicians and bureaucrats . . . not an initiative of the Aboriginal people.' It was 'a colonialist model that served to entrench white values and ways of being' (Watson 2007a: 24). As Patrick Dodson has argued, political institutions like ATSIC, created by the settler state, 'lacked the integrity of the Aboriginal cultural position and the authority and leadership of traditional leaders to make decisions in relation to their own people on the ground' (quoted in KALACC 2006: 20). Jim Pura-Lia Meenamatla Everett (quoted in McConchie 2003: 62) expressed concern that organisations like ATSIC were

> moulded into the administration of government to implement the govern-
> ment's policies down into the Aboriginal communities. They do not come
> and sit with the elders and find out what we want and hear our voice . . .
> If we think we need white man's money to develop our culture into our
> communities, then we ought to throw our culture away, because we've lost
> if we think we need money to keep culture alive!

Nor did the ATSIC structure deal effectively with the representation, needs or status of Aboriginal women (see ATSIC 1995; Davis 2008).

Despite these criticisms, however, the creation of ATSIC was also seen—at least at first—as 'the great hope for Indigenous participation in the legislative and policy process', valued for—among other things—being 'the first national representative body that gave Indigenous people both advisory and decision-making capacity' (Cromb 2017a: 2). As Natalie Cromb (2017a: 2) has argued, this 'very real power' was an effort to level the playing field in Indigenous affairs, and was 'a far cry from the power-less positions experienced in negotiations by Indigenous representative bodies up until that time.' Nevertheless, in 2004 the Howard government announced that they would abolish ATSIC, disregarding the findings of a review they had themselves commissioned, which had unambiguously supported continuing and strengthening ATSIC's mandate and functions (Jonas and Dick 2004: 7). Howard claimed that Aboriginal and Torres Strait Islander people supported the decision to abolish ATSIC because they 'felt an absolute disconnect' with the organisation, arguing that 'ATSIC was not serving them well' (Howard and Vanstone 2004).

It was certainly the case that not all Aboriginal and Torres Strait Islander people were fans of ATSIC, but this assessment only tells a part of the story. There was much in the structure and functioning of ATSIC that was always supported by Indigenous people, and while allegations of fraud and other criminal charges levelled at some of the organisation's senior leader-ship were debilitating and damaging to the organisation's reputation, the point has frequently been made that it was inappropriate to do away with a whole level of governance due to the alleged corruption of a small number of representatives. As Irene Watson (2007a: 23) points out, Aboriginal and Torres Strait Islander people were blamed for all of ATSIC's perceived failings, while the critical gaze 'was not once turned upon the state—the state which, in any event, held power to determine a different course for ATSIC, in terms of it being a failure or a success.' ATSIC was blamed for lack of progress in areas where it had never had any program responsibility and this supposed failure was in turn used to explain the poor living conditions and short life expectancies of many Indigenous people. This political sleight of hand caused outrage among Aboriginal people. As Bill Jonas and Darren Dick argued:

> It is one thing to suggest that ATSIC could perform its obligations to Indigenous peoples better; it is another thing entirely to suggest that there should not be a national representative body through which Indigenous people can participate in government decision making about their lives (Jonas and Dick 2004: 14).

And while Howard was correct in saying that many Indigenous people were unhappy with aspects of ATSIC's functioning, after its abolition Indigenous peoples faced an uncertain future without any form of national representation. There was a perception that ATSIC was abolished after a 'witch hunt', which led to calls for future bodies to be enshrined in treaties or through constitutional reform to ensure that they 'could not be so easily put to the axe as ATSIC was' (Cromb 2017a: 3).

Howard caused great offence by determining that Aboriginal people should no longer be represented through separate institutions. At the media conference announcing ATSIC's abolition he claimed that

> the experiment in separate representation, elected representation, for indigenous people, has been a failure. We will not replace ATSIC with an alternative body (Howard and Vanstone 2004).

In response, Larissa Behrendt (2004: 3 *inter alia*) reiterated the need for a proper political interface between Indigenous peoples and the settler state:

> ATSIC was not just an experiment in public administration. It was an attempt to provide a representative voice to Indigenous people in the

development of policy and program delivery. One of its real strengths was that it provided a voice—an independent voice—at the national level ... In areas such as native title, Australia's obligations under international human rights conventions and the protection of rights within the Australian legal system, Indigenous people had a view that conflicted with the federal government's. That view was often voiced by ATSIC.

The end of ATSIC also saw an 'exodus' of Indigenous people from the public service, reversing the trend of previous years, which 'created a knowledge-and-skills deficit and crippled the quality of advice to government.' This void, according to Megan Davis (2016a: 2), has been largely filled by 'faceless, unnamed drivers of my people's destiny' who 'shrewdly resist' an alternative policy approach that prioritises Aboriginal and Torres Strait Islander autonomy and self-determination. As Davis suggests, the attitude seems to be 'How dare Aboriginal people conceive of solutions to their own problems?'

In the post-ATSIC era, successive governments have departed from 'structural solutions' to the need for national Indigenous representation, re-centralising decision-making and relying on government-appointed bodies for advice: the National Indigenous Council during the Howard years, and the Prime Minister's Indigenous Advisory Council during the Abbott/Turnbull years (Patterson 2017: 12). Natalie Cromb (2017a: 2), who describes the abolition of ATSIC as 'the stuff of nightmares', considers these handpicked bodies to be a 'failed notion.' Cromb argues that without the legitimacy that comes from elected representation, government-appointed bodies can only provide advice without 'any real leverage or negotiating power' over decision-making. As activist and pastor Geoffrey Stokes (2005: 24), former convenor of the Coalition of Goldfields Aboriginal People commented, without a body like ATSIC in place it quickly became 'impossible to get first-hand advice to the Federal Government on our needs and aspirations.'

In the years following the abolition of ATSIC, Aboriginal and Torres Strait Islander people attempted to regroup and plan their own replacement national representative body. After extensive consultations with Aboriginal and Torres Strait Islander people around the continent, a new model was launched in 2010—the National Congress of Australia's First

Peoples. The design of the new body eschewed ATSIC's regional model by instead basing representation in three chambers to which members were elected based on three separate criteria. Chamber 1 was made up of representatives from national Aboriginal and Torres Strait Islander organisations and peak bodies; Chamber 2: All other Aboriginal and Torres Strait Islander organisations; and Chamber 3: Individual Aboriginal and Torres Strait Islander people, eighteen years and older, with assured gender equity in each chamber. Key architects of the model, the then Aboriginal and Torres Strait Islander Social Justice Commissioner, Tom Calma, and his non-Indigenous colleague Darren Dick (2011: 175) described the role of the new body as being to 'represent a national perspective on Aboriginal and Torres Strait Islander issues' rather than to 'represent Aboriginal and Torres Strait Islander peoples across the nation.' They saw this distinction as critical, with fundamental implications for how the organisation was designed. Representing *a national perspective* on Aboriginal and Torres Strait Islander issues requires 'engagement practices that can draw from the wealth of knowledge across Aboriginal and Torres Strait Islander communities, industry and organisations', whereas national representation itself would require 'a more traditional constituency-based approach with representatives selected on the basis of geographical, cultural or political factors.'

The design of the new Congress also sought more independence from government, with the specific ambition that it might thus avoid the fate of ATSIC, which was abolished at the stroke of a pen. Rather than a future as a government-funded non-government organisation, the architects of the new model imagined a future in which the new organisation would be fully self-funded. Unfortunately, this ambition proved impossible to realise after the then Minister for Indigenous Affairs, Jenny Macklin, rejected the proposal to create an Investment Future Fund that would fast track financial independence. At the time Macklin (2009a) stated that Congress would be funded in the same way as 'other national peak bodies' as long as the organisation could 'demonstrate that they are representative and that funding is used responsibly.' This decision undermined the new organisation's independence from the outset, leaving it beholden to government for financial support (Appleby and Brennan 2017: 6). Indeed, after just three years, the new Congress found itself under threat from the newly elected Abbott government, which had re-formed the federal government's Indigenous Advisory Council (IAC).The then co-chair, Kirstie Parker, maintained that the government would be foolish not to listen to the views of the (at that stage) 6500 Aboriginal and Torres Strait Islander people and their families, and the 172 peak, state, regional and local organisations that had signed up to be members of Congress. These members, Parker suggested, had 'an expectation' that 'their views and perspectives will be taken into consideration by the new Government', and urged that the relationship between government, Congress, the IAC and other Indigenous community organisations be 'a respectful and genuine one' (quoted in Maxwell 2013d: 9). Parker's co-chair, Butchulla and Gubbi Gubbi human rights advocate Les Malezer set the challenges faced by Congress in a wider context of political turmoil regarding Indigenous representation following the election of the Abbott Coalition government in 2013, arguing that:

If we interpret their actions, it's quite clear it is to take the legs out of Aboriginal leadership, to shut down the voice and decision making of Aboriginal and Torres Strait Islander peoples, and take it off the political agenda (quoted in Graham 2014: 7–8).

These concerns were prescient. Funding to Congress was slashed by the Abbott government in 2014, in a move that observers believe showed 'how little respect' government had for Indigenous aspirations for a national representative voice (Cromb 2017a: 2). Having already been without operational funding since 2013, further cuts meant Congress had to radically scale back its structure and functions, which were reduced to four meetings of the national board per year. The low esteem in which Congress was held by government was made further evident in Prime Minister Turnbull's *Closing the Gap* report in 2017, in which he thanked the National Congress of Australia's First Peoples 'for their leadership in bringing together the Redfern Statement alliance' but maintained that they would 'work with a diversity of representatives to ensure a broad range of views are heard on key issue such as health, justice, education and employment' (DPMC 2017b: 10).

The Redfern Statement to which the *Closing the Gap* report referred was an important statement from Congress and other organisations during the 2016 federal election campaign. The Statement called on government to develop a relationship with Aboriginal and Torres Strait Islander people 'based on meaningful respect and to start developing policy with us, rather than doing things to us' (Rod Little quoted in Maxwell 2016b: 5). The co-chairs of Congress both placed an emphasis on the need for a 'new relationship' with government. Jackie Huggins emphasised the need for a genuine partnership and a commitment to ongoing structured engagement', while her co-chair Rod Little argued that:

> After 25 years, eight Federal election cycles, seven Prime Ministers, eight Ministers for Indigenous Affairs, 400 recommendations, and countless policies, policy changes, reports, funding promises and funding cuts it's time to draw a line in the sand. [. . .] We need a new relationship that respects and harnesses our expertise, and guarantees us a seat at the table as equal partners when governments are making decisions about our lives (both quoted in Briscoe 2017).

The Redfern Statement also made specific demands in relation to the need for ongoing national representation for Aboriginal and Torres Strait Islander peoples, arguing:

> It is critical that Australia's First Peoples are properly represented at the national level to ensure meaningful engagement with Government, industry and the non-government sectors to advance the priorities of our people.
>
> Since 2010, the National Congress of Australia's First Peoples (Congress) has gone some way to fill the gap in national representation since the demise of the Aboriginal and Torres Strait Islander Commission in 2005.
>
> However, there remain too many gaps in adequate national level representation for Aboriginal and Torres Strait Islander people—particularly for employment and education. Without Congress or equivalent national bodies where Aboriginal and Torres Strait Islander leaders are supported to engage with Government it will be difficult for the next Federal Parliament to meet the multi-partisan priority and commitment to work 'with' Aboriginal and Torres Strait Islander people (Aboriginal and Torres Strait Islander Peak Organisations 2016: 7).

The statement called on the government to restore full funding to the National Congress of Australia's First Peoples, arguing that it was a 'mistake' to defund the organisation 'just as it is beginning to emerge':

Without support, Congress' ability to do its job of representing Aboriginal and Torres Strait Islander interests is severely compromised. Congress must be supported to provide a mechanism to engage with our people, develop policy, and advocate to Government. Congress should be supported to reach sustainability and independence as soon as possible (Aboriginal and Torres Strait Islander Peak Organisations 2016: 7).

Government attitudes towards Congress would not seem to suggest that such funding will be forthcoming. Allowing Congress to wither away sits well with the settler logic of elimination. In the face of this uncertainty the Uluru Statement called for an entirely new mode of Indigenous representation and interface with the settler state.

## A VOICE TO PARLIAMENT?

The political uncertainty that has bedevilled Aboriginal and Torres Strait Islander representative bodies since the 1970s, leaving them dependent on the goodwill of the settler state and the government of the day, lends weight to the proposal in the Statement from the Heart for a 'voice' to parliament to be entrenched in the Australian Constitution. Arrernte woman and Uluru Convention delegate Rachel Perkins (daughter of the late activist and ATSIC commissioner Charlie Perkins) (2017: 2), argued that Aboriginal and Torres Strait Islander people want 'a voice that cannot be struck down at government whim. A voice that is embedded in the Constitution.' Perkins asks, 'What could be more meaningful recognition than the opportunity to be heard and have a say on laws and policies made about us?'

The report of the Referendum Council (2017b: 14) describes the proposed Voice to Parliament as a model for 'the enhanced participation of Aboriginal and Torres Strait Islander peoples in the democratic life of the Australian state, especially the federal Parliament.' And while the report concedes that such a proposal is 'not a new one' it maintains that:

The Voice was the most endorsed singular option for constitutional alteration. A constitutionally entrenched Voice appealed to Aboriginal and Torres Strait Islander communities because of the history of poor or non-existent consultation with communities by the Commonwealth. Consultation is either very superficial or it is more meaningful, but then wholly ignored. For Dialogue participants, the logic of a constitutionally enshrined Voice—rather than a legislative body alone—is that it provides reassurance and recognition that this new norm of participation and consultation would be different to the practices of the past.

The proposals for the Voice to Parliament emerged because, as Davis (2016a: 3) observed of the hearings of the 2015 Joint Select Committee on Constitutional Recognition of Aboriginal and Torres Strait Islander Peoples, the Indigenous polity was 'telling the democratic representatives that they have no voice', which meant they 'feel like they have no control over their lives'. Responding to this gulf in legitimate representation, the proposal for a constitutionally enshrined voice was ultimately intended to 'bring leadership authority, decision-making and consultation back to the polities who constitute Aboriginal and Torres Strait Islander communities nationally'. The Voice should be exactly that: a loudspeaker with which to communicate the decisions made by and about the multiple and varied Indigenous communities around the continent, through 'the decision-making structures that they trust or desire' (Davis 2016a: 10).

The Referendum Council reported that participants in the dialogues saw a constitutionally entrenched Voice to Parliament as 'a way by which the right to self-determination could be achieved' (2017b: 29). Noel Pearson (2017: 3) advocated strongly for the Voice to Parliament proposal, arguing that the proposal 'gained consistent support' at all the regional dialogues because:

> Blackfellas want to be empowered in their affairs. They want to influence political decision-making about their rights and the future of their people. They want grassroots local voices to be heard. And they don't want any such representative institution abolished at government whim.

Pearson maintained that the Voice would be like 'the Tent Embassy in stone', allowing the Indigenous voice to 'get out from under the fringes, out of the fringes and the shadows, and be put in the centre of action, the democratic action in this country (Pearson quoted in Australian Broadcasting Corporation 2017c). Patrick Dodson (2018: 64) has made a similar point, arguing that, 'Without an institution of our making, First Nations people are subjected to a public-sector dependency syndrome, governed by distant and detached bureaucrats.'

This concern about the decisions made by government drove the second motivation behind the proposed Voice. Participants in the Referendum Council dialogues sought a means of preventing further discrimination against Aboriginal and Torres Strait Islander people through government policy. There is considerable history of the Australian parliament passing discriminatory laws that have affected the lives of Aboriginal and Torres Strait Islander people—most recently the 2007 Intervention legislation (discussed further in Chapter Five), which required the suspension of the federal *Racial Discrimination Act 1975*. Both the Expert Panel and the Joint Select Committee that had examined constitutional recognition had suggested that future discrimination could be prevented by entrenching a constitutional protection against racial discrimination, a proposal that alarmed constitutional conservatives who saw it as a 'one clause bill of rights.' Through the Referendum Council dialogues, Aboriginal and Torres Strait Islander people proposed an alternative, namely to have this history of discrimination 'dealt with by their own political empowerment' (Appleby 2017: 2). The Referendum Council report noted that the Voice would not be a 'foolproof' way of preventing any future parliament from passing laws that would discriminate against Aboriginal and Torres Strait Islander peoples. However, the report also noted that the 'potential' for the Voice to have 'additional functions' that would in turn provide Aboriginal and Torres Strait Islander people with an 'active and participatory role in the democratic life of the state' was viewed as 'more empowering than a non-discrimination clause (Section 116A) or a qualified head of power' in the Constitution (Referendum Council 2017b: 14).

Not everyone was convinced by the proposed Voice. Aboriginal politics scholar Lyndon Murphy, writing with Kombumerri scholar Mary Graham and non-Indigenous scholar Morgan Brigg (Murphy et al 2017), suggest that the proposal would be merely a 're-enactment' of previous advisory structures including the NACC, NAC, ATSIC and the IAC and, like the others, 'might provide advice to the parliament, but would play second fiddle to parliamentary sovereignty.' Michael Mansell (2017a: 2) argues that the Voice to Parliament proposal 'was never going to have legs' and 'always lacked merit' because it 'subordinates' Aboriginal and Torres Strait Islander people, reducing them to 'advisers instead of decision makers.'

Mansell (2017b: 1) did not buy the argument that 'constitutionalising the body elevates its standing and guarantees its potency', contending that it would always be only 'an *advisory* body, no matter how it is set up', and maintaining that while advocates for the proposal believe that 'getting the right words in the constitution' would force governments to listen to the new body, 'precedent says otherwise' (Mansell 2017b: 2). Mansell instead advocated for a decision-making body that could 'feasibly take charge of Aboriginal affairs' such that government could eventually 'be eased out of policy and funding decisions' while lobbying for a treaty and for designated Indigenous seats in parliament. This need not be an either/or decision. The Voice to Parliament could have a role to play even in a context of resurgent Indigenous nationhood and self-government. Aboriginal and Torres Strait Islander governments would still need to speak to the settler state.

Indeed, the Referendum Council (2017b: 29–30) report itself noted a range of possible concerns with the proposed model, along with caveats on what would be required for the Voice to have legitimacy:

> There was a concern that the proposed body would have insufficient power
> if its constitutional function was 'advisory' only, and there was support
> in many Dialogues for it to be given stronger powers so that it could be
> a mechanism for providing 'free, prior and informed consent'. Any Voice
> to Parliament should be designed so that it could support and promote a
> treaty-making process. Any body must have authority from, be repre-
> sentative of, and have legitimacy in Aboriginal and Torres Strait Islander
> communities across Australia. It must represent communities in remote,
> rural and urban areas, and not be comprised of handpicked leaders. The
> body must be structured in a way that respects culture. Any body must also
> be supported by a sufficient and guaranteed budget, with access to its own
> independent secretariat, experts and lawyers.

Noel Pearson has not shied away from the fact that his proposals for an Indigenous voice to parliament emerged in discussions with constitutional conservatives. He makes clear that he found agreement with conservatives on the proposition that 'if the High Court should not decide what is in the interests of indigenous people in contentious political and policy matters, then surely indigenous people themselves should be guaranteed a fair say. The Constitution might be amended simply to guarantee the indigenous voice in indigenous affairs' (Pearson 2016). Yet, as has now become apparent, even a more conservative proposal—at least in constitutional terms—ultimately failed to find support within the current settler colonial order.

In his statement rejecting the Statement from the Heart, Prime Minister Malcolm Turnbull argued that:

> The Government does not believe such an addition to our national representative institutions is either desirable or capable of winning acceptance in a referendum.
>
> Our democracy is built on the foundation of all Australian citizens having equal civic rights—all being able to vote for, stand for and serve in either of the two chambers of our national Parliament—the House of Representatives and the Senate.
>
> A constitutionally enshrined additional representative assembly for which only Indigenous Australians could vote for or serve in is inconsistent with this fundamental principle. It would inevitably become seen as a third chamber of Parliament (Turnbull 2017).

The decision outraged those who had been involved in the Referendum Council process, including Megan Davis. Davis (2017b: 2) pointed to the context in which the Referendum Council's work had taken place, highlighting the previous lack of consultation with Aboriginal and Torres Strait Islander people during the work of the Expert Panel, and the impact of the Coalition government's Indigenous Advancement Strategy, which had stripped Aboriginal and Torres Strait Islander communities of funding and control (discussed in Chapter Two). Davis argued that the regional dialogues made it apparent that pursuing 'recognition' amid 'the chaotic and destructive paternalism of Commonwealth public policy' meant that 'the experience of voicelessness and powerlessness became inextricably linked to the solutions designed by the dialogues.' Davis asks, 'Surely it comes as no surprise that compelling the government to listen to communities and give them a voice in decisions about their lives was the highest and singular priority?'

The settler state needs a political interface with Aboriginal and Torres Strait Islander peoples, but its own logics see it unable to allow that interface to develop on Indigenous terms or in ways that reflect Indigenous culture and cultural diversity. After the deep disappointment following Turnbull's rejection of the Statement from the Heart, his successor, Scott Morrison, added insult to injury by appointing former prime minister Tony Abbott a 'special envoy' in Indigenous affairs. This move, described by Luke Pearson (2018a) as 'patronising and bewildering', was widely condemned by First Nations leaders on the grounds that Abbott had done considerable damage to Indigenous policy during his own brief term as prime minister (see Koslowski 2018). Indeed, an appointment such as this is a very long way from the structures of governance and representation devised by Aboriginal and Torres Strait Islander peoples to reflect and represent their own values, in keeping with their own cultural and political institutions, which have commonly been disavowed by the settler state. Government ministers have, for example, 'lashed out' at clan-based councils in remote communities, labelling them 'communist collectives' and 'gatekeepers' that perpetuate 'cultural museums' (Smith 2007: 35–6).

The rejection of the Statement from the Heart and the proposed Voice to Parliament, combined with Abbott's 'special envoy' appointment, carries on this practice of settler disavowal. The logic of elimination cannot tolerate the persistence of political difference, whiteness cannot recognise Indigenous values and modes of governance as its equal. The colonial fantasy imagines Aboriginal and Torres Strait Islander peoples as just another cultural minority. As Lyndon Murphy and colleagues (2017) point out, 'the institutions of the state reflect the ideals, interests, preferences, habits and cultural biases of those who brought this system to these shores. If Indigenous people are seeking to assert their voice, it should be a voice that is authored by themselves rather than prompted by colonisers.' Again, the way forward seems to lie in Indigenous refusal and resurgence rather than further effort to invent a mode of political engagement that requires the stamp of settler approval.

# CHAPTER 4

---

# LAND

In 2017 the Anangu people made the decision to permanently close Uluru to tourists wishing to climb the rock. In explaining this decision, Pitjantjatjara and Yankunytjatjara man Sammy Wilson (2017) from the Uluru–Kata Tjuta National Park board and the Central Land Council articulated the differences in Indigenous and settler relationships to land:

> Whitefellas see the land in economic terms where Anangu see it as Tjukurpa [sacred laws]. If the Tjukurpa is gone so is everything. We want to hold on to our culture. If we don't it could disappear completely in another 50 or 100 years. We have to be strong to avoid this. The government needs to respect what we are saying about our culture in the same way it expects us to abide by its laws. It doesn't work with money. Money is transient, it comes and goes like the wind. In Anangu culture Tjukurpa is ever lasting.

Wilson argued that the decision by Anangu to close the rock to climbing, after years of feeling too intimidated to do so, is a decision 'for both Anangu and non-Anangu together to feel proud about.' Wilson proposed that, 'Closing the climb is not something to feel upset about but a cause for celebration.'

Land is at the centre of the troubled relationship between Aboriginal and Torres Strait Islander peoples and the Australian settler state. The need for new territory in order to create an economic base for the settler society is the primary motive behind the logic of elimination. The taking of Indigenous lands underpins the destructive, immoral exchanges that are intrinsic to settler colonial societies, and which have wrought incredible damage to Indigenous peoples and communities (Lyons et al 2017: 8). The threat posed by the continuing existence of Indigenous polities within newly claimed territorial boundaries makes the intensity of the settler drive for land inherently genocidal. As Wolfe (2006: 387) argues, if land is life, or at least necessary for life, then contests over land become contests for life.

In settler colonial societies, Indigenous and settler identities coalesce around crucial differences in their relationship to land. In settler society and politics, land is both an economic resource and demarks the boundaries of sovereign authority over a particular territory. Colonialism seeks to turn land into a commodity providing power and profit to the colonisers, creating a home and economic stability for settlers. Indigenous conceptions of land tend to be starkly different. For Indigenous people, land is what sustains communities and identity, and forms the basis of social life (Battell Lowman and Barker 2015: 48). The collective Indigenous 'self' derives its identity from a particular place or territory (Russell 2005: 155). As Larissa Behrendt (1995: 15) explains, 'Aboriginal people believe the land gives life. The attachment of Aboriginal people to their land and the importance of land in Aboriginal life cannot be overemphasised.'

Custodianship of land is a foundational element of Aboriginal and Torres Strait Islander cosmology and cultural practice. It is the 'central organising principle of society' (Goodall 1996: 18), and relationships to land are understood as relations of care and responsibility rather than ownership and exploitation. Settlers have commonly misunderstood these relations, either romanticising them as some sort of universal, anti-capitalistic spirituality or deriding their significance as primitive, anti-development ignorance (Maddison 2009: 74). Yet it is precisely this deep connection to land that is most threatening to the colonial fantasy, challenging both the settler's access to land as an economic resource and—more significantly—the settler's dream of complete sovereign authority over the territory.

Continued settler control over Indigenous-owned land remains the constant provocation at the heart of settler colonial relationships (Tully 2000: 39–40). Political struggles to regain rights and authority over land have been at the centre of Aboriginal and Torres Strait Islander politics, stemming both from the cultural significance of land and the pressing need to secure a resource-base for economic development. While there have been some significant reforms, ostensibly designed to return land to the control of Aboriginal and Torres Strait Islander peoples, the logics of settler colonialism that underpin reforms in land rights and native title have at every stage undercut their capacity to restore Indigenous self-government.

SETTLER REFORM AND CONTEMPORARY DISPOSSESSION

Henry Reynolds describes colonisation in Australia as 'one of the greatest appropriations of land in world history' (Reynolds 2013: 248). Despite orders that the establishment of penal colonies take place with the consent of the Indigenous inhabitants, early British arrivals took the attitude that the continent of Australia was *terra nullius*.[15] This set the stage for more than two centuries of land struggles, including the long frontier wars that Reynolds claims were inevitable in the face of the colonisers' 'legal fantasies' about the vacant status of the territory (Reynolds 2013: 163–4); wars that dispossessed Aboriginal and Torres Strait Islander peoples of their land, brought disease and alcohol, and saw Indigenous people incarcerated in order to access land for farming.

Aboriginal and Torres Strait Islander people mounted a sustained resistance against the dispossession of their land. The settler state's response to this resistance, however, was not to concede Indigenous rights to land, but instead to turn contested areas into reserves where Indigenous people could be kept separate from white society, occasioning further forced and violent removals (Burgmann 2003: 70). It was not until the 1960s that struggles for the recognition of the prior and distinct nature of Indigenous landholding at last gained political traction. In 1963 the Yolŋu sent bark petitions to Canberra in protest over the mining of their land on the Gove Peninsula, and in 1966 the Gurindji staged a walk-off from the Wave Hill station and demanded the return of their land—both events that garnered national political attention. Further south, these landmark protests sparked the first pan-Indigenous movement. Demands for land rights found expression at the Tent Embassy in Canberra, established on the lawns of (now old) Parliament House in 1972, and in the courts. The landmark judgment in *Milirrpum vs Nabalco Pty Ltd and the Commonwealth* (1971), flowing from the Yolŋu protest at Yirrkala, accepted that Indigenous peoples did indeed have a system of land ownership, but determined that the communal nature of that ownership, which bore little resemblance to Western property law, meant it could not be recognised. Nevertheless, relentless pressure from Indigenous activists and their allies eventually produced a long overdue settler response, notably through the *Aboriginal Land Rights Act (Northern Territory) 1976*. The recognition of land rights changed the lives of many Indigenous people who were able to take renewed control over their lives and communities, returning to live on and care for country from which they had previously been removed (Central Land Council 1994: vii).

Yet while these new legal regimes were of vital importance, they remained limited in their scope. It was generally assumed that land restoration would lead to economic development for Indigenous peoples, despite the fact that returned land was generally remote, arid and of low commercial value (Altman et al 2005: 3). Where there is value in land, Indigenous access to it remains limited. For example, the terms of land ownership under the Northern Territory *Land Rights Act* specify that the federal government retains ownership of subsurface minerals in Aboriginal land, meaning that First Nations have, for the most part, not shared in the vast profits that have been extracted from their lands. Land rights regimes also tend to neglect Indigenous water rights, with perpetual water rights awarded to farmers and irrigators. The icing on the cake was the politically hostile environment in which land rights were legislated, which saw relentless opposition to land claims. In the Northern Territory, the Country Liberal Party (CLP) government (in power from 1974 to 2001) opposed every single land claim made by Aboriginal groups, engaging in litigation estimated to have cost over $10 million. The Northern Territory government's attitude turned something that was intended to be beneficial for Indigenous economic development into a 'legalistic battlefield' (Central and Northern Land Councils 1991: 4).

In the 1992 *Mabo* case (*Mabo and others vs Qld [No. 2]*) the High Court of Australia determined that the communal ownership of land by Aboriginal people in fact constituted a unique form of title that had existed prior to colonisation. But while *Mabo* provided a belated acknowledgement of wrongful dispossession, the settler response was ambivalent at best. The 1992–93 cabinet papers reveal government concern in the wake of the *Mabo* decision focused primarily on how they might avoid the 'uncertainty' that could be created by Aboriginal and Torres Strait Islander peoples seeking to establish title to land. Corporate interests were also unsympathetic, with industry actively lobbying to block any strong form of native title recognition by transforming their own commercial concerns into an alleged national crisis (Short 2008: 45). The mining industry in particular was vocal in its opposition to the *Native Title Act* during its 1993 negotiations, first seeking to prevent the introduction of the legislation, and later lobbying government for amendments on the grounds that the proposed act was 'unworkable and an impediment to development' (Howlett 2006: 13). Indeed, the then Minister for Aboriginal Affairs, Robert Tickner, has suggested that there is little appreciation of the 'vitriol, intolerance and scaremongering that went on in the debate on Mabo', particularly after the 'spoilers and wreckers' in the pastoral and mining industries had sought to influence the political response (quoted in Damien Murphy 2017b: 2).

In 1996 the High Court ruled in the *Wik* decision (*Wik peoples vs Qld*), which held that the granting of statutory interests did not necessarily result in the extinguishment of native title and that pastoral leases did not necessarily confer a right of exclusive possession. The Howard government was quick to respond, developing a highly controversial '10-Point Plan' to provide 'certainty' to pastoralists that eventually became enshrined in the *Native Title Amendment Act 1998*. The amendments further restricted the scope of native title claims and promoted the co-existence of native title with other uses, including through the establishment of Indigenous Land Use Agreements (ILUAs)[16] (Lyons et al 2017: 19). Many Aboriginal people saw the 10-Point Plan as an attack on hard-won native title rights and a 'sell-out of their interests' (Sanders 2005: 153). According to Patrick Dodson, while native title holders are 'the living testimony of their prior occupation of their lands and waters' that decries the notion of *terra nullius*, the 'sinister' application of extinguishment written into native title legislation, which 'requires the consent of the very people that hold the native title', is 'neither honourable, nor generous' but rather a form of 'treachery' that 'brings shame to the Mabo name' (P. Dodson quoted in Caccetta 2017a).

Mick Dodson (2004: 123–26) believes that the consequences of Howard's
response to *Wik* have been far-reaching. He suggests that where the government could have used the *Wik* decision to 'draw Australia together . . .
educating the nation in a calm and factual way' they instead behaved 'in the
style of a colonial power' and 'repudiated any responsibility for land justice'
in this country.

The native title system has had very mixed results for Aboriginal and
Torres Strait Islander peoples around the country, many of whom remain
highly critical of it. Gary Foley (2007: 119) observes that many Indigenous
activists still regard the legislation as a 'sell-out' and 'an absolute denial of
Aboriginal sovereignty.' Patrick Dodson (quoted in KALACC 2006: 41)
contends that the *Native Title Act* is 'a westernised way of corralling and
limiting Aboriginal people's rightful demand for justice and rightful demand
for their lands.' Mick Dodson (2007: 13) describes it as a 'compromised
and complicated' piece of legislation that was 'based on racial discrimination' from the outset. Aileen Moreton-Robinson (2015: xi) describes
native title as advancing the underlying principle of settler colonialism, and
as continuing a process of perpetual dispossession that, at best, results in
'overregulated piecemeal concessions.' At its core, native title continues to
be recognised 'on the terms of the settler state', meaning that it 'does not
substantially disrupt settler interests or sovereignty' (Lyons et al 2017: 13).

This is most evident in the requirement that native title claimants prove
their continuous association with the land over which they are claiming title.
This means that for those First Nations dispossessed of their lands early and
most completely—notably groups in the south-east of the continent—native
title may be placed cruelly out of reach. The burden of proof rests solely
with the Indigenous claimants, whose fate is decided by settler institutions
(Short 2008: 63). Māori justice Joe Williams has argued that this 'surviving
title approach'

> requires the Indigenous community to prove in a court or tribunal that
> colonisation caused them no material injury. This is necessary because the
> greater the injury, the smaller the surviving bundle of rights. Communities
> who were forced off their land lose it. Those whose traditions and lan-
> guages were beaten out of them at state-sponsored mission schools lose

all of the resources owned within the matrix of that language and those traditions. This is a perverse result. In reality, of course, colonisation was the greatest calamity in the history of these people on this land. Surviving title asks Aboriginal people to pretend that it was not (quoted in Cornell 2015: 15).

Native title claims are expensive, taking many years of work with anthropologists and archaeologists, and the outcomes remain very variable. For the groups that succeed, however, the recognition of native title holds considerable meaning and promise. Graham Atkinson, chair of the Dja Dja Wurrung Clans Aboriginal Corporation, who in 2013 were finally recognised as the traditional owners of just over 2665 square kilometres of lands in central Victoria, sees that native title will give his people

> certainty and the opportunity to determine our own sustainable future . . .
> Dja Dja Wurrung's connection to this area for thousands of years is finally
> being acknowledged in the formal recognition that we are the traditional
> owners of this area . . . We will now be able to fulfil our cultural and spiritual
> obligation to look after this country and preserve our culture, not only for
> the future generations of Dja Dja Wurrung people, but for all Victorians
> (quoted in *Koori Mail* 2013a: 28).

Nyikina Mangala traditional owner, Anthony Watson, whose people were recognised as the traditional owners of 26,000 square kilometres of land in the central Kimberley region after an eighteen-year battle, is also optimistic. The claim recognised 40 per cent of the claim area as exclusive possession (the highest form of native title) of the Nyikina Mangala people. Watson hopes that this will give his people

> the respect and recognition of being landowners with rights and interests . . .
> We are not spectators; we are real players and want to be at the forefront
> of any decisions made about what happens on our country . . . We want
> to ensure that native title benefits our people, our country and our culture
> (quoted in *Koori Mail* 2014b: 14).

Many groups recognise a successful native title claim as a beginning rather than an ending. Kerry Blackman, a representative of the Port Curtis

Coral Coast native title groups who were successful in their claim over 4000 square kilometres of land and waters around Gladstone and Bundaberg (thought to be the first successful claim involving multiple language groups), believes that the successful claim is

> just one chapter closing and another one has to open up on our native title sea country rights . . . As we regain some of our land and we work on regaining our languages, it's all about your identity and a sense of belonging—which is powerful. A lot of our first nations people don't have that (quoted in Stunzner and Hendry 2017).

For others, a successful native title claim brings a sense of peace. After eventual success in the Western Bundjalung claim in 2017 (after six years), claimant Dave Walker suggested he would celebrate the victory in the simplest of ways, saying:

> I might just sleep . . . sleep on my land down here tonight on the side of the river. I've got no blanket or anything but I'll just go down and make a fire and just sit up and enjoy it, I think. Because it's our land (quoted in ABC 2017b).

Others, however, see native title as perpetuating settler injustice. BJ Cruse, a Yuin descendent from Eden on the south-east New South Wales coast, objects to the Yuin Nation's native title claim, arguing that native title is 'the most offensive, destructive, immoral legislation that Aboriginal people have ever been confronted with' because it suggests that Indigenous people are actually agreeing 'that all land that has been taken by the Crown up to 1994 is all extinguished—you have no right to it anymore.' Cruse instead advocates for a 'sovereignty treaty that focussed on bringing about peace and allows for greater Aboriginal contribution to the wealth and prosperity for the community in general' (quoted in Brown 2016). Mer and Erub man Charles Passi, son of the only surviving plaintiff in the *Mabo* case, has also contemplated whether legislating for native title in the wake of the High Court decision was an error. At the time, he recalls, the lawyers on the case suggested that the decision had 'unlocked the door' but that it remained for them to 'push the door wide open.' According to Passi, the lawyers suggested it was time to negotiate a treaty, and he now wonders whether, if that advice had been followed, his people would now be 'on a different platform.' Instead, Passi views native title as 'something that birds and animals have with parks and wildlife . . . It's the same thing—it's an area set aside for the use of the natives for that area.' Indigenous people now 'need to draw a line in the sand. We need to be the people that put an end to how our children soak up the poison of the past' (quoted in Archibald-Binge 2017).

The *Native Title Act* did give settlers the certainty they craved, ensuring a stable environment for the management of pastoral land and resource extraction that was important to business, albeit at the cost of Aboriginal and Torres Strait Islander peoples' capacity to negotiate. Although agreement-making processes are available under the native title regime, there are significant barriers to the kind of positive outcomes that claimants hope for. Entrenched disadvantage on the part of many native title claimant groups, combined with procedural limitations in negotiating processes, limit the bargaining power of native title groups (Prout Quicke et al 2017: 2–3). And while First Nations still seek recognition of their rights to govern and steward their land in wholly self-determined ways, the reality is that the granting of native title in fact positions traditional owners as 'bound beneficiaries of the exploited resources on their land' (Prout Quicke et al 2017: 3–4).

The limitations in the *Native Title Act* constrain the ability for First Nations to transform their moral interests in land into legally enforceable rights. Native title agreements do not recognise the right to self-government and the prescribed bodies corporate that act as trustees to manage native title also work to ensure certainty for governments and other parties with interests in land and waters (Hobbs and Williams 2018: 27). Native title remains a weak form of title that can only be claimed in areas where other forms of legal title do not exist, and does not apply where (ongoing) colonisation has disrupted the practice of Indigenous custom. Native title can also be extinguished, and because native title rights tend not to be exclusive, traditional owners have 'little opportunity to control access to land or its use' (Lyons et al 2017: 14). As Irene Watson (2002: 34) has argued, Aboriginal and Torres Strait Islander people may enter the native title process and become a consenting party to the genocide, where one is stamped native or extinguished, but whatever the stamp, once in the process you are open to a determination of extinguishment at a time determined by the state.

As a result, agreements are increasingly being made outside of—or only interacting with—the native title process. A prime example is the South West Native Title Settlement, which Hobbs and Williams (2018) have described as 'Australia's First Treaty'. Due to both its content and the kinds of recognition it provides, it is the largest native title settlement in Australian history. The settlement, made up of six individual ILUAs, encompasses approximately 200,000 square kilometres of land in the south-west of Western Australia and will affect an estimated 30,000 Noongar people. Elsewhere, in Victoria the *Traditional Owner Settlement Act 2010* enables out-of-court settlements for traditional owner groups who agree to withdraw any native title claim and not make any future native title claims.

Outside of the relatively meagre protections that native title offers, Aboriginal and Torres Strait Islander people continue to resist the ongoing dispossession of their lands in various parts of the continent. In 2015, for example, the Western Australian government threatened to close up to 150 of the state's 274 remote communities, after a loss of federal funding. The threatened closures followed the traumatic forced closure and bulldozing of the Oombulgurri settlement in the East Kimberley in 2011, after the community was described by the Western Australian government as 'unviable.' Oombulgurri was part of the Balanggarra native title claim, which was successfully determined in 2013 following a twenty-year fight. That determination could not, however, include the Oombulgurri settlement because the settlement was owned by the state government's Aboriginal lands trust, which effectively extinguished native title over that part of the claim. This 'loophole' in the native title laws allowed the government to forcibly evict Balanggarra traditional owners from their homelands at Oombulgurri, causing ongoing trauma to the displaced community members, many of whom are today homeless and living rough in bigger towns in the regions like Wyndham and Kununurra (Solonec 2014).

For the Aboriginal people potentially affected by new plans for closures the debate was distressing. In a far cry from the optimism he expressed at the Nyikina Mangala native title determination (discussed above), Kimberley Land Council chair, Anthony Watson, argued that closing communities would 'cost Aboriginal people in terms of identity, relationship to country, health, and wellbeing' with these costs being passed on to 'the already under-resourced larger towns, service providers, local governments, housing, health, costing the state for generations to come' (quoted in *Koori Mail* 2015a: 5). The Kimberley Aboriginal Law and Culture Centre (KALACC), which represents traditional owners from the 30 language groups across the Kimberley, argued that the threatened community closures were a 'deep-rooted threat to our fundamental spiritual connection to land . . . that makes us Aboriginal people.' The organisation drew direct connections between the contemporary exercise of colonial power and the horrors of the past, arguing:

> Forced relocations of our people are assimilationist echoes of the colonial past and have no place in the modern world . . . People were forced off their lands in the late 1960s and they all remember the experience. Hundreds of people lived literally in shacks and shanty towns. How can a repeat of that even be contemplated? . . . If people are forced off their land and away from their communities they will lose their identity . . . Culture and land are not liabilities. They are the single biggest asset and strength that we, as Aboriginal people, have (quoted in *Koori Mail* 2015c: 19).

Another mode of contemporary dispossession had earlier emerged in the Howard government's *Aboriginal Land Rights (Northern Territory) Amendment Act 2006*, which introduced the possibility of 99-year leases over communally held Aboriginal land in the Northern Territory. Despite being of great concern to Aboriginal and Torres Strait Islander people around the continent, these reforms were passed after a Senate Committee hearing of only one day—a process that has been condemned as wholly inadequate given the significance of the provisions in the bill. The then Aboriginal and Torres Strait Islander Social Justice Commissioner, Tom Calma, pointed to the international evidence that individualising Indigenous land tenure leads to significant losses of land (ATSISJC 2006a). Calma also expressed the view that leases of 99-years, essentially four generations, with the possibility of back-to-back leases, would have the 'practical effect' of alienating Indigenous communal land (Calma 2007: 4). Alyawarre Elder Rosalie Kunoth-Monks describes the program as 'insidious', effectively reinforcing the settler colonial order through 'land being leased to the landlord rather than a landlord leasing to a business partner' (quoted in Maxwell and Coyne 2013: 9).

Early leases were controversial. In May 2007, the traditional owners of the Tiwi Islands signed over the town of Nguiu in return for $5 million and 25 new houses, allegedly dividing the community amid threats and intimidation (ABC 2007a). The lease deal was strongly criticised by Calma (2007), who claimed that the deal made Nguiu 'open for business to anyone who wants to set up shop.' In his view, the communal rights of landholders had been undermined and the Tiwi people would have 'limited say in what can occur on their land.' Also in 2007, the high-profile Yolŋu leader, Galarrwuy Yunupingu agreed to sign a 99-year lease over the township of Ski Beach on the Gove Peninsula.[17] The resulting memorandum of understanding offered far better terms than the Tiwi lease and enabled Yunupingu's Gumatj clan to retain considerable control over their land. Yunupingu stated that the deal would 'empower traditional owners to control the development of towns and living areas, and to participate fully in all aspects of economic development on their land' (Yunupingu 2007). Other Yolŋu traditional owners were unhappy, however, claiming that it was unacceptable for the government to deal with individuals.

A decade on, however, and it seems that, in some cases, First Nations may have successfully utilised the leasing provisions in the amended *Land Rights Act* to gain greater control over their land. In 2017, in stark contrast to the type of lease proposed by the federal government a decade earlier, members of the Gumatj clan in the community of Gunyangara in north-east Arnhem Land signed a 99-year lease that will give them control over development on their own land. While talks about the leasing arrangement had begun in 2007, the negotiation took over ten years to conclude. Under the original proposal from the Commonwealth, the head lease would have been held by a Commonwealth officer. The Northern Land Council opposed that approach on the grounds that it would strip control from traditional owners. Under the lease that was eventually signed, the head lease will be held by a community entity with the power to make decisions about sub-leases intended to facilitate economic development. In endorsing the new lease, Northern Land Council chair, Samuel Bush-Blanasi contended that 'Aboriginal people themselves will be in control of their own destiny' (quoted in Everingham 2017).

The puzzle in a case such as the Gunyangara lease, however, lies in the pernicious effects of the colonial logics at work. The Gumatj clan have now signed a lease with government for land that always was and always will be their land. If the Gunyangara lease arrangement proves able to support Gumatj self-determination, it may prove to be a genuinely decolonising step. The challenge will be for Gumatj people to protect this new independence from the constant threats and encroachments of the settler regime.

Alexis Wright (2016: 3) has argued that the only thing she has seen work well for Aboriginal people in the Northern Territory is the *Aboriginal Land Rights (Northern Territory) Act 1976*, and this has only been possible because of

> the consistent, focussed and extremely hard work and vigilance by Aboriginal people from the communities, and their land councils to make land rights work. It was never easy. There were always challenges. Always battles. Always threats.

Former CEO of the Northern Land Council, Joe Morrison, notes that he spent most of his two-and-a-half years in the role trying to protect the *Land Rights Act*, rather than focusing on advancing the self-determination of Indigenous people (quoted in Davidson 2016a: 2). These challenges are nowhere more obvious than at the intersection of Indigenous rights and corporate profit in the resources industry.

THE RESOURCE EXTRACTION CONUNDRUM
Aboriginal and Torres Strait Islander people are impoverished *because* of colonisation, *because* of dispossession, *because* of the loss of an economic base in land. Neither land rights or native title have provided an adequate legal framework through which a majority of Aboriginal and Torres Strait Islander people might, if they choose, generate wealth from resource

extraction, agriculture or other economic development on their lands. Much of the wealth generated on lands to which Indigenous people have traditional rights and attachments (in reality the entirety of the continent) continues to flow to government and the private sector (Dodson and Smith 2003: 10). While some Indigenous corporations and native title groups have leveraged agreement-making to considerable financial benefit, far more have been afflicted by the so-called 'resource curse', meaning that their tenure over land containing substantial natural resource wealth has not translated into beneficial outcomes for Indigenous communities (Langton and Mazel 2008). In fact, the potential for wealth from mineral extraction in particular has often led to conflict within and between groups, accompanied by a loss of capacity and skill to engage in traditional economic activities including land and sea management, hunting, harvesting and cultivation (Prout Quicke et al 2017: 13). For many Aboriginal and Torres Strait Islander people, the demand for economic development sits uncomfortably alongside the acts of 'protecting, recovering, gathering together, keeping, revitalising, teaching and adapting' the practices that were nearly destroyed by colonisation (Tully 2000: 59).

At the same time, however, settler colonial developmentalism in Australia has driven relentless expansion of industry, and particularly the resource extraction industry. Developmentalism originated in the doctrine of *terra nullius* and the idea that European invaders had an obligation to develop the allegedly empty land and make use of its natural resources. The priority given to agricultural development over other land uses was a feature of Australian developmentalism, and large landholdings were acquired by wealthy pastoralists across the continent. Mining, however, was undertaken primarily by individual prospectors. As a result, and unlike most other common law jurisdictions, mineral rights came to be held by the state rather than landowners, with the state retaining the power to determine who could mine the land. This has produced a tradition of preferential treatment for miners that continues to this day, despite the fact that most contemporary resource extraction is now undertaken by large multinational corporations (Lyons et al 2017: 11).

Making decisions about mining and other potentially destructive industrial practices is an unenviable task for First Nations concerned about both economic and cultural survival. Decision-makers constantly risk being charged with 'saving the village by destroying it' (Havemann 2000: 25). Within any Indigenous community there may be diverse interests in land, from those whose primary responsibility is to care for and protect it, to those who would prefer to use the land to achieve greater economic independence.

For some Aboriginal and Torres Strait Islander people, resource extraction is seen as an existential threat to their spiritual connections and responsibilities to land. For example, Nawurupu Wunungmurra, a senior Yirritja man from north-east Arnhem Land, expresses concern about the impact of mining, particularly fracking, on the spiritual cycle of Yolŋu through the land's water sources, telling a journalist:

> It's some sort of a hole they've got to dig in and get the oil and the gas, you know—but there's spirits of Yolŋu people in the ground . . . Yolŋu and Balanda are working together now, but there's somebody coming in behind, looking around for oil and gas in north-east Arnhem land. We don't want to be dug out, because we come from the ground and we go back, like the water. We don't want it . . . We're worried, and sad about it (quoted in Davidson 2017a: 1–2).

Another case that has caused controversy is the proposed expansion of the McArthur River zinc mine near Borroloola in the Northern Territory, which has been in the news for over a decade. In 2007 the Northern Land Council and a group of traditional owners from the McArthur River area initiated court proceedings to stop the Territory government-approved expansion of the mine, which would necessitate a 5.5-kilometre diversion of the river itself. The ensuing victory in the Northern Territory Supreme Court was subsequently 'sidestepped' by the Northern Territory government, which intervened with new legislation to provide the mining corporation with 'certainty' (ABC 2007a). As a result, according to Gudanji traditional owner Josephine Davey Green, one of the area's most important sacred sites, the Rainbow Serpent Dreaming, was destroyed, and Davey Green believes that the proposed expansion would damage another sacred site, the Barramundi Dreaming (Bardon 2017a).

The operators of the mine, Glencore Xstrata, are seeking to raise the height of its waste-rock dump from 80 metres to 140 metres, which would make it higher than the Barramundi Dreaming, situated on a rocky ridge behind the mine. For three years prior to the request, parts of the waste-rock dump had been spontaneously combusting, and the mine had also contaminated cattle that wandered onto the site, and fish in McArthur River tributaries, with lead and copper. In 2014, Borroloola Elders from the four clan groups with responsibility for the McArthur River led a protest march to a meeting at which an independent monitor's report detailing contamination in water and fish as a result of the mine was presented. The Elders called for production at the mine to stop until the water contamination and waste-rock fire problems had been resolved. They presented a copy of a community letter and management plan, signed by more than 100 Elders and traditional owners, to Northern Territory government representatives, calling on the government and regulatory agencies to act to protect the community. Senior Garawa man, Jack Green, argued that the damage caused by the mine was far-reaching:

> That river is part of old rainbow snake, and they dug up half his tail and backbone. From that time on, a lot of old people passed away who had been arguing against the mine. We don't have any native title over the mine area, the only protection we have is our sacred site, and that's about it, because they don't care about Aboriginal country. We are all frightened by what has happened to the river and worried about it. Our children used to play and swim in the river but not now. The lead has been leaking out of the mine, and affecting our land and water. Our songline lies along that river. They need to pay us compensation or pack up and get out of our land or both. Our country is beautiful country. We want to keep it that way and the mining company doesn't care (quoted in Maxwell 2014: 19).

In other cases, division among Indigenous communities is exacerbated by pressure to agree to resource extraction, such as in the dispute over a proposed gas hub to be built at James Price Point near Broome. Protest against the proposed development eventually saw the proposal abandoned. In 2017, however, one of the groups opposing the gas hub was found not to be traditional owners of the area. Federal Court Justice Anthony North found that the Goolarabooloo people's connection to the area did not go back far enough and only began with the arrival of their ancestors in the area in the 1930s. Justice North determined that the traditional owners were in fact the Jabirr Jabirr people, who had supported the gas hub development, which included an Aboriginal benefits package worth more than $1.5 billion. Frank Parriman, one of the Jabirr Jabirr people who had negotiated the deal, expressed the view that abandoning the gas hub development had left a generation of Aboriginal people in the area without an economic base. Now, he said, Jabirr Jabirr would 'just like to move on and look after our country' (quoted in Caccetta 2017b).

Such cases are not restricted to mining in remote areas of the Northern Territory or Western Australia. The approval of a mine in north-west Tasmania caused significant division among the Aboriginal people of that state. Circular Head Aboriginal Corporation chair Graeme Heald argued that the mine is 'vital to the growth of Circular Head' and contends that, 'There's got to be a balance, between employment and protection.' In response, Aboriginal Land Council of Tasmania chair, Clyde Mansell, argued that while his organisation is 'not against progress', they were worried that 'the assessments in relation to Aboriginal heritage don't take into account what Aboriginal heritage really means':

> You can look at sticks and stones, pick up an artefact and move it, but that doesn't take into account what heritage really means . . . heritage is also about the right of connection and celebration of our community of that landscape . . . That whole landscape has a long association with traditional people, the spirit of the place, the land ecology, and none of that is being considered at the moment (quoted in Maxwell 2013b: 14).

Concerns such as these are, however, not the only view. In her 2012 Boyer Lectures, Marcia Langton (2013) argued that participation in the Australian resource industry boom was essential for Indigenous livelihoods into the future. She suggests that three important issues have governed the journey that has taken Aboriginal and Torres Strait Islander people out of the extreme poverty and marginalisation that characterised the twentieth century. The first is that Aboriginal and Torres Strait Islander people have many more rights, including native title rights, than they did 50 years ago. These rights have provided a 'seat at the table' to negotiate with the mining industry, which in turn has provided jobs and cultural heritage protections. Second, Langton argues, the mining industry itself has changed its *modus operandi* and now involves Indigenous people through employment and other business opportunities. Third, Aboriginal and Torres Strait Islander people have used their native title rights to 'ensure the sustainability of their ancient ways of life and values' by returning enormous tracts of land to conservation and biodiversity protection.

Langton's arguments have been contested by some Indigenous activists. Former co-chairs of the Australian Nuclear Free Alliance (an organisation that brings together Aboriginal people and civil society groups concerned about the impact of the nuclear industry on Aboriginal lands and communities), Arabana man Peter Watts, Aranda and Luritja woman Mitch (no surname) and Wongutha man Kado Muir (2013) 'take issue' with Langton's suggestion that 'embracing mining is a positive option for Aboriginal people if they are to engage with the modern economy.' They argue:

> Mining generally is an extractive industry, that by its very nature destroys land, often at the expense of spiritual and cultural connections of Aboriginal people. Income generated from mining comes at a cost and often ignores the possibility of creating alternative sustainable economic opportunities that need not rely on extraction as its primary economic base . . . It is important that Aboriginal people have the opportunity to participate in economic development on their country, but this must never be at the expense of custodial responsibilities or community wishes. Mining is inherently short term, but the problems it brings to country last well beyond the life of any mine.

Langton (2013: 2) has criticised what she sees as a widespread depiction of Indigenous people as 'the hapless victims of a voracious and brutal mining industry' while herself suggesting that Indigenous people are hapless victims of what she considers to be manipulation by environmental campaigners who relegate Aboriginal and Torres Strait Islander people to the status of the 'new noble savage.' This has certainly been her criticism of Indigenous activists campaigning against the proposed $22 billion Carmichael mine to be built in the Galilee Basin, west of Rockhampton in Queensland by the multinational corporation, Adani. The Adani mine has encountered years of opposition from a range of stakeholders, including the majority of the

Wangan and Jagalingou traditional owners of the area. The Wangan and Jagalingou Traditional Owners Family Council (W&J) are native title applicants over a large area of Central Western Queensland, including the land that Adani needs to build crucial infrastructure for its mine. W&J contend that if this mine proceeds it will destroy their ancestral homelands, thereby irreversibly devastating culture, customs and heritage, and will also lead to environmental destruction and significant carbon emissions.

Adani has already been granted three mining leases that have been authorised by the National Native Title Tribunal, but the third of these—pertaining to a 27.5 square kilometre area over which native title rights must be surrendered in order to build critical infrastructure for mine operations—was disputed by W&J. Adani sought to negotiate an Indigenous Land Use Agreement that would give them control of the land unencumbered by native title rights. Finalising the ILUA was also critical to Adani gaining finance as many major banks will not finance resource projects without traditional owner consent (Robertson 2017a). The proposed ILUA was voted down by the native title claimant group in 2012 and again in 2014. In the event an ILUA is not achieved, the Queensland government can undertake compulsory acquisition to secure this land for Adani's project (Lyons et al 2017: 16).

The complexity of the Wangan and Jagalingou campaign against the Adani mine is emblematic of the challenges and limitations inherent to the native title regime. Some members of the native title claimant group support a deal with Adani. An April 2016 meeting organised and paid for by Adani and facilitated by Queensland South Native Title Services, recorded a vote of 294 in support of the deal with Adani, and one against. The W&J faction opposed to the deal claim that they stayed away from the meeting to avoid legitimising the process, and have subsequently contested the result (which was the subject of court proceedings in March 2018). Dissenters questioned the legitimacy of those given voting rights at the contested meeting, alleging that many who attended and voted had not previously participated in W&J native title matters (Lyons et al 2017: 16–17). Critics also claimed that Adani had courted a 'block of seven' traditional owners who had been paid inducements to support the deal, and were subsequently used in Adani public relations material (Lyons 2017). In mid-2017, one of this 'block of seven' split from the group supporting the mine, citing concerns about 'the destruction the project will wreak upon the traditional culture and lands of our people' (Craig Dallen quoted in Robertson 2017a: 1). This left the W&J representative group deadlocked with six in favour and six against (Robertson 2017a: 1). At a December 2017 meeting of the W&J, the 120 attendees again voted against the ILUA, and the group immediately filed an injunction against both Adani and the Queensland government to prevent the native title tribunal signing off on the ILUA before the outcome of the court challenge was known. W&J spokesperson Adrian Burragubba maintained that Adani 'want the Queensland government to extinguish our native title while pretending to have our consent. There will be no surrender of our traditional lands and waters' (quoted in Wahlquist 2017f).

The Adani case was further complicated by the February 2017 Federal Court decision in *McGlade vs Native Title Registrar & Ors (McGlade)*, in which several Western Australian ILUAs were challenged by Noongar applicants who argued that the deals should not stand because they did not have the requisite signatures to the agreement. The case arose after several of the Noongar claimants had refused to put their names to the $1.3 billion Western Australian land use agreement that had been negotiated by the South West Aboriginal Land and Sea Council. One of the claimants in the case, Mervyn Eades, argued against the standing of the agreement, suggesting that:

> Our sovereignty cannot be bought for no amount of money . . . They were destined to extinguish our native title rights and all rights to country . . . We will discuss on other terms now and we will be part of the negotiations and not have a deal dictated to us by the state (quoted in Trigger and Hamlyn 2017).

The court agreed that, to have standing, an ILUA required the signature of *all* native title claimants, rather than just some of them, overruling the 2010 *QGC vs Bygrave* case, which had ruled that it is not necessary for all applicants constituting the registered native title claimant to sign an ILUA. While the *McGlade* ruling was only expected to apply to a small number of cases, it clearly had the potential to empower all native title applicants who felt they had been disenfranchised through poor process and unequal negotiating positions.

In the wake of the *McGlade* decision, the W&J immediately sought a court order to strike out what they saw as the illegitimate land use agreement with Adani. In an effort to protect the Adani deal, however, less than two weeks after the *McGlade* decision the federal government introduced the Native Title Amendment (Indigenous Land Use Agreements) Bill 2017 (Lyons et al 2017: 19–20). The Noongar people, who are the subject of the *McGlade* decision, say the government's bill to overturn the ruling denied their native title rights. Mervyn Eades said:

> Native title is being butchered, slaughtered, watered down to the maximum to protect the interests of mining companies and the states and the government not for the rights of our people. They're taking that away from us so they may as well take native title and put it in their pocket and keep it (quoted in Thorpe 2017b).

For the W&J, the Native Title Amendment Bill, and particularly the speed at which it was introduced was 'abhorrent.' Adrian Burragubba argued that 'the Federal Government moved to amend the *Native Title Act* as if there was a state of emergency, but without any evidence of a real problem or justification for the rush.' Burragubba was concerned that the bill seemed to be 'rammed through to the calls of the mining lobby, and in particular Adani and its resource council backers' (quoted in Thorpe 2017b). Wangan and Jagalingou Council spokesperson Murrawah Johnson suggested that the amendments underscored the weakness of the native title regime, arguing that governments 'say that Native Title is the way you can claim that continued connection to your country' but then 'every time there's a win for Aboriginal people the Federal Government go and undermine that through the parliamentary process' (quoted in Hocking 2017a).

The campaign against Adani has been seen as exposing the shortcomings of the native title system by revealing the ways in which the interests of the settler state can converge with mining interests (Lyons et al 2017: 24). Adrian Burragubba has argued that the campaign against Adani is 'a matter of justice' because, 'Every Aboriginal group has a right to stand up and say what mining companies are doing to their sacred land' (quoted in

*Koori Mail* 2015d: 14). But the costs of standing up are considerable. As Lyons et al (2017: 22) note:

> Wangan and Jagalingou people carry the costs of these community conflicts and divisions (as do other Aboriginal people caught up in similar conflicts) in deeply personal ways, including in the form of stress, fatigue and a range of health problems. These impacts double down on people already living with the legacies of violent settler-colonialism.

For Marcia Langton, however, the fight over the Adani mine and opposition to the Native Title Amendment Bill were the result of 'cashed-up green groups' working to

> deliberately thwart the aspirations and native title achievements of the majority of Indigenous people by deception, by persuading the media and the public that a small handful of Indigenous campaigners who oppose the legitimate interests of the majority of their own people, are the truth-tellers and heroes (quoted in Katharine Murphy 2017a: 2).

This, Langton argued, was merely the 'environmental industry' trying to 'hijack' Indigenous concerns in an effort to 'return us to the pre-1992 era of *terra nullius*' (Langton quoted in Murphy 2017a: 2)

Langton's claims are strongly contested by other Aboriginal and Torres Strait Islander people. Tony McAvoy, a leading native title lawyer, Australia's first Indigenous silk, and himself a Wangan and Jagalingou traditional owner involved in the campaign to stop the Adani mine, contends that the campaign is being driven by 'proud and independent people' who he considers among the best-informed Indigenous litigants in the country. McAvoy suggests that Langton's claims that W&J are 'somehow puppets' of environmentalists is disrespectful and offensive, and argues that in fact they are 'very, very aware that our interests of preserving our country are not entirely aligned with the green interests' (quoted in Robertson 2017b).

Langton's contentions also fail to address concerns raised by Indigenous environmental activists who draw concerns with Indigenous sovereignty together with concerns about the environment and climate. Amelia Telford, an Aboriginal and South Sea Islander woman from Bundjalung country who is the National Co-Director of the Indigenous Youth Climate

Network, Seed, which joined forces with environmental groups to campaign against the Adani mine, argued that the proposed mine both 'threatens the rights, the ancestral lands, waters and our climate for local Aboriginal people' and also contributes to the impacts of climate change being experienced by the world's 'most vulnerable communities' (quoted in Thorpe 2017c). Knowledge about the climate and the environment is embedded in Indigenous oral traditions, where songs and paintings contain references to ecological management, including fire-stick farming and the regulation of hunting, fishing and harvesting. In this sense, campaigning to protect the environment may be seen as one aspect of Indigenous resurgence.

LAND EQUALS LIFE
Land is central to Indigenous resurgence. Wendy Brady (2007: 151) understands that Indigenous people 'cannot relinquish our sovereign rights to our lands' because this would mean 'denying our connection to each other and to the land that is the constitution of our identity.' Ngarigu woman and academic Jakelin Troy (2016) argues that the land 'owns' Indigenous people, and suggests that as long as Indigenous people keep their songlines[18] open they will 'never be truly colonised.' Troy contends that songlines 'tell political stories and keep us connected in our struggles for recognition and sovereignty.' As Murrawah Johnson (2017: 6) argues:

The invading colonial project began with a land struggle. As Aboriginal peoples resisted on frontier battle lines all over so-called Australia, these struggles of our old people have become the legacies that have defined generations of our people. While First Nations peoples remain, and until there is restitution and land justice, the land struggle is not over.

For the majority of Aboriginal people, the protection of culture is crucial and will often take precedence over economic development. While he was Aboriginal and Torres Strait Islander Social Justice Commissioner, Tom Calma conducted a survey of traditional owners regarding their attitudes to land and development, which confirmed that while economic development was considered important, the majority of respondents ranked 'custodial responsibilities' as the most important use for their land (ATSISJC 2007b: 1). As the Central and Northern Land Councils (1994: 8) have argued, 'Our land is our life . . . . it also provides our identity and it must be looked after, both physically and spiritually. If we abuse our land, or allow someone else to abuse it, we too suffer.'

The different values accorded to land in Indigenous and settler world-views can place them starkly at odds. As Lyons et al (2017: 10) suggest, it may be impossible 'to draw equivalences between introduced and Indigenous values', with Indigenous worldviews, ethics and political commitments delegitimised by the settler.

The deep clash of values between Indigenous peoples and the settler order over land can be at once deeply damaging to Aboriginal and Torres Strait Islander peoples and the source of much of the drive to refuse settler dominance. For example, traditional owners from Fitzroy Crossing in the Kimberley are working together to protect the Fitzroy River from increasing development pressure. For Walmajarri traditional owner Anthony McLarty, the Fitzroy River 'is one living system. The river gives life and has a right to life, and we are determined to protect it for current and future generations' (quoted in *National Indigenous Times* 2016a). Across the country, Barkandji man William 'Badger' Bates (2017) makes a strikingly similar point. Writing of the Barka (the Darling River), which has been severely damaged by irrigation, Bates links the decline in the health of the river to everything from suicide, increasing crime and diminishing work opportunities. He suggests that:

> When they take the water from a Barkandji person, they take our blood. They're killing us . . . How can I teach culture when they're taking our beloved Barka away? There's nothing to teach if there's no river. The river is everything. It's my life, my culture. You take the water away from us; we've got nothing.

Many Aboriginal and Torres Strait Islander people also link the protection of their lands to future capacities for self-determination. Nari Nari man and chairman of the Murray Lower Darling Rivers Indigenous Nations, Rene Woods, maintains that the Murrumbidgee River is his people's 'life-blood . . . just like our veins', saying that:

> When there's water, there's a whole lot of community spirit lifted, just seeing the country come back and seeing it as good as it can be . . . So we can go and

continue our cultural practices around those water ways, which is crucial to us moving forward and strengthening our connection with country (quoted in Timms and Vidot 2017).

Amy McQuire and Lizzie O'Shea contend, the 'most insidious part of the colonial project' was the attempt to destroy Indigenous knowledge systems based in land:

Aboriginal people had formed a symbiotic relationship with land, sea and sky over tens of thousands of years, and had developed complicated systems of land management and agriculture, interwoven with spirituality. Their children were later told that their people were simply 'hunters and gatherers' and their traditional knowledge, sacred sites and languages were devalued and destroyed (McQuire and O'Shea 2017: 2).

Revitalising these knowledge systems is a central aspect of Indigenous resurgence. Birri Gubba and Kungalu woman, Teila Watson (2017), links the re-centring of Indigenous knowledges with the looming climate crisis. Watson argues that Australia is 'so entrenched in the blood of colonialism that it has been unable to even consider listening to what First Nations people have been saying about care for country.' Watson sees the description of Aboriginal and Torres Strait Islander peoples as 'the oldest continuing culture on earth' being romanticised by settler society in a way that 'embraces cultural practice but can distance us from any possible engagement with our knowledge systems.' The problem, as Watson sees it, is that:

White Australia is often moving towards the future while facing backwards, with a closed mind to anything beyond the limits of the colonial logic. It's this logic that has allowed us to get so far into the destruction of our planet. Surely we cannot believe that this logic will save our future? The only possible, sustainable and empowering future we could have would be one where the sovereignty of our people, our knowledges and of our lands and laws are respected, valued, heard and implemented throughout modern Australian life . . . At the end of the day, if 'Australia' wants to survive and combat global warming, First Nations sovereignty and governance is the best chance it has.

In many cases, efforts to recuperate Indigenous knowledge and share it with future generations are valued more highly than financial compensation. Nywaigi traditional owner and the chair of the Indigenous Reef Advisory Committee to the Great Barrier Reef Marine Park Authority, Phil Rist, points out that the reef is 'such a significant space for all saltwater mob along the east coast.' Despite an assessment that the reef is worth $56 billion as a natural asset, Rist maintains that 'if that comes at the cost of the Traditional Owners' values then it's a net loss.' He argues that

> some of the activities that we've been doing for thousands of years are now gone because of tourism or fishing or some of the other industry that impact on our values. If we can't teach our younger men about hunting turtles and dugongs because they are gone, what's the value in that? (quoted in Copp 2017).

Anangu woman Ruby James, one of the first female Indigenous rangers from Kaltukatjara (Docker River) in the Northern Territory, also links the protection of country to the education of future generations. James hopes that the new Katiti Petermann Indigenous Protected Area at Tjitjingati, a 5 million-hectare site between Uluru and the Western Australian border, will mean they can extend the ranger program and take young people on more trips on country:

> By taking them out on country they see and learn about places. It will allow them to protect their country themselves in time. This is their schooling. This is the education we need our children to have and this is the way we do it (quoted in *Koori Mail* 2015f: 6).

Responsibility to future generations weighs heavily on traditional owners concerned about development on their country. Yawuru man Micklo Corpus camped at Yulleroo, 70 kilometres east of Broome in the Kimberley, for eighteen months while trying to stop coal seam gas mining on his country. Corpus objects to negotiations about fracking on this land, saying:

> It's the white man's way and I understand that, but I don't agree with it . . . I am a traditional owner. This is my country. I have the right and responsibility under traditional law to look after my country . . . The Government

gave approval to [mining company] Buru, saying that there would be little impact on our country. But tampering with our water should be zero tolerance. It's not our place as cultural people to pass on dirty water to our children. We were given clean water and we need to pass that on (quoted in Maxwell 2015b).

Creating employment opportunities on country for future generations is also a priority. Adnyamathanha woman and Nantawarrina ranger Sophia Wilton suggests that 'many young ones are moving to the city and feeling disconnected like I did so we need to make sure when they return home, they have jobs where they can connect with land and culture ready for them' (quoted in Morelli 2017).

Olkola traditional owner and chairman of the Olkola Aboriginal Corporation in Cape York, Mike Ross (quoted in Norman 2018), outlines a vision for his people's land that doesn't involve mining:

Mining doesn't fit in our 10-year plan. We have been doing ecotourism here, we have a carbon trading program, and we have a golden-shouldered parrot committee, and we have Indigenous park rangers. So we've got all these programs happening on our country and we worry what sort of impact mining will have on that. I mean, if you organise a tour, they don't want to see country being mined.

In a landmark case in the National Native Title Tribunal in March 2018, the Olkola Aboriginal Corporation successfully objected to mining exploration permits being issued under 'expedited procedure' in Queensland. This is a bittersweet victory for the Olkola; as Ross points out, his people should have the right to say no to mining on their country without fighting legal battles that are a drain on resources they could be using elsewhere. And while Ross acknowledges that traditional owners 'may want mining', a choice he says is 'up to them', he also says that he has yet to see

any rich Indigenous people from working with mining companies, or traditional owners getting rich from royalties from their country. I see that Indigenous people in Weipa here in the Cape are among the poorest communities in Australia, and they are working with one of the richest bauxite mining companies in the world. So what's going wrong?

Aboriginal and Torres Strait Islander people living in urban centres face particular challenges in terms of their relations to land. The dramatic changes in land tenure that have been won over the past twenty years have had little impact on urban Indigenous lives, despite the fact that Aboriginal and Torres Strait Islander people living in urban areas generally maintain their links with the land or nation of their family (Behrendt 1995: 24). Public debate occurs, as non-Indigenous geographer Libby Porter (2016: 1) has argued, 'as if Indigenous people were not present, and as if cities were not built on Aboriginal land.' Settler property regimes carve up the landscape with titles and fences and planning zones that are all 'imposed on Indigenous lands' and that 'exclude the people from whom the land was stolen.' Unlike Canada and New Zealand, Indigenous people in Australian cities find it 'exceptionally difficult' to gain access to land, with few opportunities for land grants, and limited chance of success in native title claims (Porter 2016: 2). Porter (2016: 4) asks how urban Australia might be different if space were made for Indigenous knowledge, law and cultural perspectives to inform decision-making in urban spaces:

> Imagine if caring for country principles were at the heart of the urban development system. Imagine if the planning and design of public space recognised these are some of the only places that Aboriginal people can access a land base in the city. Imagine if we used density and zoning tools to provide reparation for land theft and to redistribute wealth. Imagine if mainstream urban planning processes recognised continuing co-existing Indigenous methods of land governance. Imagine if we did urban development in a way that honours Indigenous histories, knowledge and relationships with those places.

In urban contexts, the occasional handback of land takes on particular significance. The return of Me-Mel (Goat Island in Sydney Harbour) to Eora people in 2016 was profoundly important. Metropolitan Local Aboriginal Land Council CEO, Nathan Moran, reflects on the 'multiple benefits' to Aboriginal people that came with the handback, pointing out that the Land Council had

> long advocated for a central and visible site for Aboriginal people to show our culture, resilience and innovation, to increase our health and wellbeing through acceptance and acknowledgement as original peoples of Australia,

to celebrate our survival and to end centuries of dislocation from Sydney Harbour.

For Moran, Aboriginal ownership and control of their lands is 'a true model of self-determination' (quoted in Guivarra 2016).

The possibilities inherent in such moments have sometimes been over-shadowed by battles over Indigenous urban spaces. The planned Pemulwuy Project redevelopment of The Block in Sydney's Redfern is a case in point. Chief executive of the Aboriginal Housing Corporation, Michael Mundine, found himself at odds with other Indigenous people who established a Tent Embassy in protest on the proposed development site. For Mundine, the Pemulwuy Project was an opportunity to generate wealth while providing some affordable housing within a mixed retail and commercial develop-ment. He described as 'very sad' the fact that objections to the project meant they were 'fighting black on black' because Aboriginal people 'need to get away from that welfare mentality; we need to empower ourselves' (quoted in Mundy 2014c: 5). For Wiradjuri Elder and Tent Embassy activist Jenny Munro, however, opposition to the development was 'about Aboriginal people's sovereignty. Our law, our land. This is black land' (quoted in Mundy 2014c: 5). Munro contended that the Pemulwuy Project was fundamentally assimilationist and argued that:

> The basic element that assimilationists don't really grasp is that to assimilate into another culture is to commit your own cultural genocide—to turn your back on thousands, if not millions of years of history and heritage. I'm too black to acknowledge that sort of rubbish. Our people have a right to be Aboriginal (quoted in *Koori Mail* 2014c: pp 6–7).

Such conflicts are of course commonplace to settler business and politics, yet they take on a different character when they erupt between Indigenous people. Underlying a politics of decolonisation, Indigenous resurgence and genuine self-determination is a recognition that these disputes are the business of the disputing Indigenous parties to resolve. As we will see in later chapters, settler Australia is endlessly drawn to intervene in black problems in an effort to solve them. History has shown that these efforts do little to benefit Aboriginal and Torres Strait Islander people, and more often than not in fact make the situation far, far worse.

# CHAPTER 5

# INTERVENTION

Settlers have seemed compelled to intervene in the lives of Aboriginal and Torres Strait Islander peoples since the moment of invasion. Early interventions were physically violent, as settlers sought to destroy peoples and cultures they were unable to comprehend. Over time, interventions became less physically violent as settlers developed other modes of eliminating Indigenous peoples—through, for example, surveillance, assimilation and aggressive policing. Settler interventions continue to be multiple, varied and protracted, with the effect—intended or otherwise—of dismantling existing social support systems and 'compounding the agony' of Aboriginal and Torres Strait Islander peoples already traumatised by colonial impacts (Atkinson 2002: 68). Representing these interventions as responses to alleged crises and emergencies within Aboriginal and Torres Strait Islander communities has had the effect of rendering invisible the settler–colonial violence that is inherent to the regulation of Indigenous peoples (Howard-Wagner 2012: 222).

Far from acts of benevolence, however, it is evident that there are settler logics at work in interventionist policies and practices—both logics of elimination and logics of racial superiority. The settler state demonstrates its continuing colonial authority through the process of *acting upon* Indigenous people as subjects of domestic policy (Strakosch 2015). Policies such as the Northern Territory Intervention, which forms the basis of the discussion in this chapter, are 'explicit demonstrations' of colonial authority, used most powerfully in contexts where the state has been unsuccessful in its efforts to erase Indigenous difference, thereby exposing the settler colonial project as incomplete (Macoun and Strakosch 2013: 432). The settler state seeks to reframe the lack of colonial completion as merely a matter of time. Indigenous peoples are cast as 'not quite ready' to enter into sovereign exchange with the settler, meaning that the unequal relationships that characterise colonialism are required to exist 'for a while longer.' This in turn justifies 'intensive work' on Indigenous lives in order to prepare them for the dissolution of colonialism that is forever just around the corner (Strakosch and Macoun 2012: 61).

Central to the desire for colonial completion is the drive to erase Indigenous difference—the more that Aboriginal and Torres Strait Islander people live like settlers, the closer it seems the moment of colonial completion must be. Indigenous peoples and communities—most especially remote communities—are depicted by politicians and mainstream media as places of violence and suffering, thereby legitimising settler claims that the 'good life' is better lived elsewhere and in ways that resemble the settler mainstream (Hinkson 2017a: 3). Settler interventions entail a set of assumptions about what is needed to live a 'good life', including education, employment, housing and freedom from illness and addiction (Kowal 2015: 35). While many Indigenous people may agree with these priorities, they are likely to also prioritise the provision of services through institutions that are culturally appropriate and independent of government. Instead, Indigenous people are racialised as deficient in capacity to manage their own lives. These justifications, based on a belief in settlers' 'good intentions', mask the ways in which the settler colonial state sustains itself through interventions that focus on Indigenous inclusion in programs of governmental 'care' that are only possible through the exercise of settler sovereign authority over Indigenous lives (Strakosch 2015: 27).

The effects on Aboriginal and Torres Strait Islander people have been devastating. As Alexis Wright argues:

> The use of colonial laws and the policies associated with those laws has been, and still is, an abusive weapon, which is rendering more and more Indigenous people powerless, apathetic and tragic (2006: 106).

Aboriginal and Torres Strait Islander people themselves have long acknowledged that the impacts of colonialism have caused damage to their relationships with one another. Intergenerational and multi-layered trauma of the kind created by colonisation is known to produce dysfunctional and sometimes violent behaviour within families and whole communities (Atkinson 2002: 24). This is evident among dominated Indigenous peoples all over the world (Trudgen 2000: 173). Irene Watson (2007a: 30) describes these kinds of violence, through which she sees colonised peoples 'devour' each other, as 'the worst aspect of colonialism.' It is not surprising, Watson argues, that Indigenous peoples in these circumstances should call for protection, and, she believes, the call should be answered.

The question remains, however, exactly how Indigenous people should be protected, and by whom. When the settler state assumes it is their responsibility to protect Indigenous people, Indigenous calls for protection are appropriated in order to disguise the ongoing colonialism manifest in settler responses. Instead these responses are reframed as 'humanitarian intervention' (Watson 2007a: 30–1), and allowed to continue virtually unchecked. What interventionist approaches miss is that Aboriginal and Torres Strait Islander people are proud, not ashamed, of the fact that their cultural values and lifestyles are different to those of mainstream settler society (Altman 2017a: 2–3). This is central to Indigenous refusal and resurgence—Indigenous peoples fight to preserve their distinctiveness even as the settler order persists in its efforts to eliminate the difference it finds intolerable.

Settler culture is still used as a benchmark against which Indigenous peoples and cultures are evaluated and found wanting. The assumed superiority of white settler culture justifies the colonialism that is integral to policies such as the Intervention, and obscures the structural violence inherent in the regulation and control of Indigenous lives and communities (Howard-Wagner, 2012: 222). Indigenous peoples in Australia have found this more explicit expression of settler domination increasingly difficult to contest. Advancing projects of refusal and resurgence has become all the more challenging in the wake of the most recent decade of intensive, destructive, colonial intervention in Aboriginal and Torres Strait Islander lives.

INTERVENTION REDUX

In June 2007, the then prime minister, John Howard, announced an 'emergency intervention' into Aboriginal communities in the Northern Territory in response to the *Ampe Akelyernemane Meke Mekarle 'Little Children are Sacred'* report from the Northern Territory Board of Inquiry into the Protection of Aboriginal Children from Sexual Abuse. This report had been commissioned by the Northern Territory government, in part as a response to allegations of rampant abuse made by the Alice Springs Crown Prosecutor, Nanette Rogers, on ABC Television in 2006 (ABC 2006)[19] and joined a growing list of reports highlighting the same problem in other parts of Australia (see NSW Aboriginal Child Sexual Assault Taskforce 2006; Gordon et al 2002). The *Little Children are Sacred* report confirmed what many Aboriginal people had been saying for years: that many of their communities had broken down to the point that damaging and dangerous behaviour including violence, suicide, alcohol and other substance abuse, and the abuse of children had become endemic. Until this report, however, pleas for help had fallen on deaf ears. As Larissa Behrendt has suggested, this was 'the national emergency that was sitting neglected for over thirty years' (Behrendt 2007: 15). Justifying the Intervention as an 'emergency response' was, in part, possible because of the growing scepticism about self-determination (discussed in Chapter Two), which had been advanced by the Howard government, and given legitimacy by Indigenous voices such as Noel Pearson and Marcia Langton (Kowal 2015: 161). Indeed, Noel Pearson was the only Indigenous person consulted by the Howard government before the announcement of the hastily conceived Intervention.

From the outset, however, the Northern Territory Emergency Response (NTER), known colloquially as the Intervention, was deeply problematic. The *Little Children are Sacred* report, used to justify the Intervention policies, had made an urgent plea for 'radical change' in the way government and other services consult, engage with and support Indigenous people (Nicholson et al 2009: 21). The report's authors argued that previous approaches had left Aboriginal people in the Northern Territory 'disempowered, confused, overwhelmed, and disillusioned', and specifically linked the contemporary challenges in Indigenous communities to a 'combination of the historical and ongoing impact of colonisation and the failure of governments to actively involve Aboriginal people, especially Elders and those with traditional authority, in decision making' (Wild and Anderson 2007: 50). To combat these experiences of disempowerment and exclusion, the report's first and most important recommendation was to address the 'urgent' issue of child sexual abuse through 'a collaborative partnership' and 'genuine consultation with Aboriginal people in designing initiatives for Aboriginal communities' (Wild and Anderson 2007: 7).

What unfolded could not have been further from the recommended approach. The 'emergency response' contained extraordinary provisions including (among other measures) widespread alcohol restrictions on Northern Territory Aboriginal land; paternalistic welfare reforms that would 'quarantine' social security income for approved purchases; measures to enforce school attendance by linking income support and family assistance payments to school attendance; a ban on the possession of X-rated pornography and audits of all publicly funded computers to identify illegal material; and the appointment of 'government business managers' in each of the 73 'prescribed communities' that fell under the Intervention powers. Passing the legislation to introduce the Intervention policies required the suspension of the *Racial Discrimination Act 1975* by prescribing the Intervention as falling under the 'special measures' provision of the Act. The Intervention was to commence immediately, drawing on police and army personnel and a volunteer workforce of doctors and other professionals. A further change, which predated the Intervention but became part of the emergency response, was the abolition of the Community Development Employment Projects (CDEP) program, set to be phased out by 30 June 2008 with CDEP jobs replaced with 'real jobs' or participants moved onto mainstream Work for the Dole arrangements. The abolition of CDEP (discussed further below) was alleged to be necessary in order to create a single welfare system to streamline the quarantining of welfare payments (Hinkson 2007: 1–5).

The distress caused by the announcement of the Intervention was palpable. Warlpiri Elder Harry Nelson, a traditional owner from Yuendumu who had been part of a delegation of Aboriginal leaders who went to Canberra to try and stop the passage of the legislation, was distressed at its passing, saying:

Our dream has been shattered. This is coming from my heart. We can't go home from Canberra and hold our heads up. I've got no answer for my people because the minister wouldn't even meet with us. I feel sad and no good. I fought for my land and they can take away all the houses but they can't take my land. After all these years of fighting for our land and our freedom, this is where we end up (quoted in *National Indigenous Times* 2007: 16).

Rex Wild and Pat Anderson, the authors of *Little Children are Sacred*, were devastated that their report had been used to justify the Intervention, despite their careful recommendations. They told the audience at the 2007 Garma Festival at Gulkula in north-east Arnhem Land that the government response had left them feeling 'betrayed and disappointed, hurt and angry and pretty pissed off.' Anderson noted that, despite government claims the Intervention was a response to their report, there was 'not a single action that . . . corresponds with a single recommendation' (quoted in Ravens 2007: 3). Muriel Bamblett emphasised the dispossession at the heart of the policy, arguing that the legislation

takes control away from Indigenous communities. It allows government bureaucrats to force themselves into our boardrooms . . . It places bureau-crats in charge of our lives . . . This legislation is an attack on our people (quoted in *National Indigenous Times* 2007: 16).

Mick Dodson described the policy as 'heavy handed, ill thought out, paternalistic and draconian', and asked, 'Why do you keep doing this? What's the problem with you people that you always feel you have to come in and fix things rather than support us to fix the things?' (quoted in Maddison 2009: 15). Joe Morrison recalls thinking that the announce-ment of the Intervention heralded 'the beginning of a new relationship with Australia', but not a positive one. For Morrison, the Intervention meant that Aboriginal and Torres Strait Islander peoples' struggle for their 'rightful place in the nation's future had been set back decades' (Morrison 2017: 18).

The new policy regime and its muscular exercise of authority over Aboriginal and Torres Strait Islander lives was certainly the most overt expression of the settler logic of elimination that had been seen in Australia for some decades (Macoun and Strakosch 2013: 431–2). Yolŋu leader Djiniyini Gondarra, who had been an outspoken critic of the Intervention since its inception, compared the implementation of the policy to the invasion of 1788, arguing that the settler state was 'using military law . . . to take away civil and political rights, as well as rights to be self-determining on our own lands' (quoted in *Koori Mail* 2012a: 17). The considerable investment of resources into the Interventions' policies ought to have been welcomed, but in a context where the underlying policy settings were completely at odds with Indigenous aspirations, even these additional resources had to be contested. As Pat Anderson has argued:

> It is not the fact of the intervention, but the kind of intervention that is contentious. No intervention will work if it is an attempt to 'turn the clock back', to go back to a past when the non-Aboriginal state was a presence in every Aboriginal person's daily life (Anderson 2007).

For many of the Aboriginal people subject to the Intervention measures, the immediate impacts of the policy were terrifying. Anangu woman and Mutitjulu resident Dorothea Randall recalls it as 'an experience of invasion', with some members of her community feeling 'so nervous and scared' that they 'ran up to the sand dunes to hide their kids' in fear that they would be taken away as so many had in the past (quoted in Lawford 2017b: 1). Another Mutitjulu resident, Anangu man Gary Cole, highlights the kind of stigmatisation that many Aboriginal men experienced, saying that, 'On that day, every man got accused of being a paedophile . . . So we felt no good, and we still feel no good today that we got accused of something we never ever done. And we'll never ever do' (quoted in Lawford 2017b: 2). Large numbers of Aboriginal people found themselves effectively displaced by the Intervention, choosing to relocate to urban centres rather than living subject to neo-paternalistic controls (Skelton 2008).

The measures in the Intervention, and most particularly the quarantining of welfare payments, were described as 'a return to the ration days' (Billings 2010: 180). Indeed, there was an obvious continuity between earlier policy eras in which the 'captured' Indigenous population was subjected to paternalistic institutions of 'care' designed to 'civilise, modernise and assimilate' that were justified as necessary forms of 'practical care in exceptional circumstances' (Lattas and Morris 2010: 62). Thus, the Intervention could be seen as a different articulation of what remains constant in Australian Indigenous policy: the presumed authority of the settler state to define and act upon Indigenous people. This is not a natural, benign authority but one that is continuous with and remains invested in the original project of settlement: to replace Indigenous people on their land and to naturalise their replacement (Strakosch and Macoun 2017: 35).

Irene Watson (2009: 55) understands the Intervention approach as a 'continuing play for legitimacy' by the settler state, dressed up as a kind of rescue mission for Indigenous women and children, with the effect of making them 'subjects in the tactics of their disempowerment.' For Watson, the Intervention further entrenched the colonial project 'by reviving protectionist policies, this time under the rubric of human rights.'

Not all Indigenous people were critical of the Intervention approach. In the days immediately following the announcement Noel Pearson defended the policy, arguing that the negative reaction was 'a kind of madness', and that he was 'just amazed that anybody would put the protection of children secondary to anything else' (ABC 2007b). Marcia Langton championed the Intervention as 'the greatest opportunity we have had to overcome the systemic levels of disadvantage among Aboriginal Australians' (Langton 2008: 147) and argued that 'those opposed to the intervention are morally and politically wrong' (Langton 2008: 152). Nevertheless, the Intervention approach continued to come in for sustained criticism, including through international scrutiny. The then United Nations Special Rapporteur on the rights of Indigenous peoples, James Anaya (2010), acknowledged that the Intervention policies represented 'a substantial commitment of human and financial resources' but described the 'overtly interventionist architecture' as working to 'undermine indigenous self-determination, limit control over property, inhibit cultural integrity and restrict individual autonomy.' Irene Khan, the Secretary General of Amnesty International, found the fact that Indigenous people in Australia were experiencing human rights violations 'on a continent of such privilege' to be 'not merely disheartening, it is morally outrageous' (AAP 2009).

Many Aboriginal and Torres Strait Islander people had hoped that the end of the Howard government in 2007, and the election of the Rudd government, would herald the end of the Intervention approach. Disappointingly, this was not the case at all. While in Opposition, Labor had supported the passage of the Intervention legislation and upon their election made it clear that they would continue, and expand, aspects of the policy. The new Indigenous Affairs Minister, Jenny Macklin, ordered a review of the Intervention, which found that the policy had 'diminished its own effectiveness through its failure to engage constructively with the Aboriginal people it was intended to help' (Yu et al 2008). But the new government ignored these findings and pressed ahead. Macklin did undertake to rein-state the *Racial Discrimination Act* by the end of 2009, but ultimately was unable to meet her own deadline, instead announcing that the government would 'strengthen the Northern Territory Emergency Response (NTER) to provide the foundations for real and lasting change in Indigenous commu-nities' (Macklin 2009b). In this instance, 'strengthening' meant widening the application of income quarantining measures beyond the prescribed communities to include all areas of the Northern Territory as a 'first step in a national roll out of income management in disadvantaged regions.' For some analysts, the expansion of the welfare quarantining measure amounted to little more than a cynical attempt to 'normalise' the policy by potentially applying it to disadvantaged sections of the non-Indigenous community (Lattas and Morris 2010: 84). Other Intervention measures that continued in the prescribed communities alone included restrictions on alcohol and pornography, the retention of government business manage-ment powers, and the five-year leases over townships as a 'special measure' under the *RDA*.

Before introducing the legislation that would restore the *RDA* (while simultaneously continuing many of the Intervention measures as so-called 'special measures' under the Act) the Rudd government undertook a series of 'redesign consultations' with affected Indigenous people. Problematically, however, it was evident the government was attempting to obtain consent to measures that were in fact already in force, and about which there had been no prior consultation (Partridge et al 2012: 31). The consultation process revealed the extent to which relationships between government and Indigenous communities in the Northern Territory had broken down. One participant, from the community of Ampilatwatja, suggested that the consultation process had come much too late, arguing that

nobody has taken time off from this crazy cash cow, which is the intervention, to come and listen to us. Listen to old women like me and listen to these
wise men. You look at them like they're rubbish. They're not rubbish . . . They
are not rubbish! But that is what the intervention is imparting to us (quoted
in Nicholson et al 2009: 31).

Another participant, from the Bagot community in Darwin, made it clear
that the community saw the continuity between the Intervention policy and
earlier policy regimes:

Because it is wrong in what they are doing because . . . I mean this goes back
to . . . back in the time when you had Native Affairs where the government
was overruling people and then you've got it, it is now 40 years down the
track now, 50 years down the track. I was there in Native Affair times and
if anybody remembers Native Affairs time, and this is exactly what they are
doing to us now (quoted in Nicholson et al 2009: 25).

Despite the deepening resentment towards government that resulted
from the Intervention approach, in 2011 the federal government, then
under the leadership of Prime Minister Julia Gillard, proposed to entrench
the Intervention for a further decade in a suite of bills known as the
'Stronger Futures' legislation. The Stronger Futures laws, described by some
as 'oppressive and racist' (Altman 2017a: 8), came into effect in 2012 despite
the complete lack of evidence for the claim that expanded welfare quarantining, punitive school attendance measures, and penalties for alcohol and
pornography were in any way effective (Perche 2017: 3).

TEN YEARS ON
More than ten years after the introduction of the Intervention its impacts
are still being felt and the effects on those subjected to the policies have been
profound. One delegate at the 2017 Stand Up convention, which brought
together people affected by the Intervention to consider the way forward,
says simply that the stigmatising effects of the policy 'broke' Aboriginal
people (Matthew Ryan quoted in Hocking 2017c). One of the authors of
the *Little Children are Sacred* report, Pat Anderson, argues that ten years
on the Intervention is 'decimating' Indigenous communities, 'killing' them
through 'another form of abuse' (quoted in Fitzpatrick 2017b).

Joe Morrison believes that the 'stain' of the Intervention approach still 'smears the nation', leaving Aboriginal and Torres Strait Islander people 'disengaged from participating in its future, both practically and symbolically.' Morrison sees the situation of Aboriginal people in the Northern Territory as being 'many times worse than it was before the Intervention' (Morrison 2017: 18). Anthropologists Melinda Hinkson and Jon Altman, both long-term critics of the Intervention, document its failings. Hinkson (2017b: 2) is damning, describing the policy as

> a messy conjunction of vigorously pursued ideological campaign, profligate waste of very substantial sums of public money, mismanagement of programs, and, for Aboriginal people, cycles of hope, disappointment, resistance, and despair.

Altman (2017a: 8) considers the Intervention approach to be 'fast entrenching a disaster' through 'a sunken investment of billions in an institutional architecture that is impoverishing and causing harm.' Chief executive officer of the National Aboriginal Community Controlled Health Organisation (NACCHO), Pat Turner, agrees, arguing that the Intervention is 'the worst set of public policy' she has seen in her 40 years in the public sector, insisting that it 'must never ever be repeated' (quoted in Luke Pearson 2017b: 4).

By any measure, the Intervention must be considered a policy failure. A 2015 evaluation undertaken by Stephen Gray from Monash University assessed the Intervention policy against a range of measures, including Closing the Gap targets and broader human rights standards. Noting the problems with evaluating such a complex program, without an established evaluation strategy, and in a context where impartial data was hard to find, Gray and his colleagues assessed the Intervention across measures including employment and economic participation; education; health and life expectancy; safer communities; lowered incarceration rates; general compliance with human rights; racial discrimination; the right to self-determination, the right to be consulted; and the rights of children. They found that the Intervention fell short across every measure they considered: only education scored five out of a possible ten, with the remaining scores ranging between four (for health and life expectancy, general compliance with human rights) down to zero (for lowered incarceration rates). This manifest failure has come at great expense and has produced 'unprecedented levels of surveillance' over the lives of remote-dwelling Aboriginal people as settler logics have become more deeply entrenched. As Melinda Hinkson (2017b: 2) argues:

> Where life in the bush once allowed Aboriginal people some degree of relative autonomy, and indeed the possibility of establishing places and activities beyond the reach of government, today such spaces of hope are difficult to find. The comprehensive intent of the new surveillance landscape is marked by the building of new police complexes, Centrelink offices and residential compounds in larger communities to house the ever-growing volume of work generated for their expanding and extensive bureaucratic machinery.

Other such negative consequences have been extensively catalogued. Non-Indigenous Aboriginal rights campaigner and researcher Paddy Gibson (2017: 2–12) has detailed ten impacts over the ten years of the program:

1. More Aboriginal children are being forcibly removed from their family and culture, as increases in funding are 'focused on surveillance and removal of Aboriginal children, rather than support for struggling families.' The impact of child removals will be discussed further in chapters Seven and Eight.
2. Punitive measures have not increased school attendance. The School Enrolment and Attendance Measure makes welfare payments conditional on school attendance, and the Northern Territory government has run a parallel system of fining parents of truants. Despite these measures, however, the rates of school attendance of Aboriginal children under the Intervention have gone backwards, declining from 62.3 per cent just before the Intervention to 57.5 per cent in 2011.
3. There has been an increase in youth suicide and a huge spike in self-harm.
4. The Intervention housing program has had a minimal impact on overcrowding, although more than 1000 new houses have

now been built in Northern Territory communities since the start of the Intervention. Productivity Commission figures show that the proportion of Indigenous people living in overcrowded housing has decreased from 59 per cent in 2008 to 53 per cent in 2014. Under the Intervention, funding for new housing and for housing maintenance has been contingent on Aboriginal communities signing over township lands, to the Commonwealth, under long-term leases of between 40–99 years.

5. Income management has made life harder for many and remains racially discriminatory. Despite the enormous expense involved in administering welfare quarantining policies, the government-commissioned review of income management in the Northern Territory in 2014 could not find substantive evidence of beneficial change in either individual behaviour or community wellbeing. The evaluation also found that, rather than building capacity and independence, in fact the program has increased dependency on welfare.

6. The abolition of the Community Development Employment Projects (CDEP) has created mass unemployment and exploitation. CDEP was replaced by the Community Development Program (CDP—discussed further below) in 2015. The new program is widely considered more punitive and exploitative than CDEP.

7. Restrictions on courts considering Aboriginal culture, custom and law in bail and sentencing decisions continue. The Intervention 2007 prohibited courts in the Northern Territory from considering Aboriginal culture, custom and law when making bail and sentencing decisions in the Northern Territory. All other groups in Australia have a right for all of their circumstances to be considered when courts are making bail and sentencing decisions—including their culture and customary obligations.

8. The number of Indigenous people in prison has exploded. According to figures from the Australian Bureau of Statistics, the number of Indigenous men in prison in the Northern

Territory has doubled over the past ten years, from 668 in March 2007 to 1327 in March 2017. The number of Indigenous women in prison has increased more than threefold from 30 in March 2007 to 106 in March 2017. The Don Dale Royal Commission investigating abuse of children in youth detention (discussed further in Chapter Six) reports that between 2006 and 2016 the number of children and young people entering detention more than doubled, from 120 to 254. Indigenous adults make up 84 per cent of the Northern Territory prison population and Indigenous children and young people make up 94 per cent of the Northern Territory youth prison population.

9. Discriminatory alcohol bans remain in force and there is no evidence they have reduced harmful drinking. Prior to the Northern Territory Intervention, many remote communities had taken the initiative to have dry areas established or to establish their own alcohol management plans, all of which were overridden by the blanket ban put in place by the Intervention.

10. High rates of family violence have not decreased despite this being one of the central justifications for the Intervention. This problem has not improved under the Intervention and there is evidence to suggest it has become worse. Aboriginal community controlled organisations and many other Aboriginal community leaders have insisted throughout the Intervention that seriously addressing these problems requires respect for self-determination, and the urgent allocation of resources for community-led development.

For older Aboriginal people in particular, the Intervention caused 'deep hurt and distress', reviving traumatic and bitter memories of earlier settler policy regimes. Assimilation policy had treated Aboriginal and Torres Strait Islander people as legal minors, robbing them of hope and leaving them disempowered and angry. The Intervention policies reinforced feelings of vulnerability and a lack of control in the face of state power and structural racism (Altman 2017a: 2-3). Director of the Central Land Council, David Ross, argues that the Intervention is 'an invasion of people's rights and privacy' in what was a drastic backwards step 'for people who had barely 20 or 30 years earlier won back their land under the Land Rights Act' (quoted in Fitzpatrick 2017b).

Equally problematic is the fact that, despite the distress caused by the Intervention, the policies have not achieved their intended outcomes. Luke Pearson (2016a) argues that the 'racist and punitive' policies, based on 'demonisation, racism [and] land grabs' could possibly have been vindicated if 'they had achieved their intended outcomes of keeping women and children and communities safe, getting kids to school and adults to work.' This, however, has not been the case. Despite the focus on child abuse as the original rationale for the Intervention, not one prosecution has resulted from the new policy framework. There is also growing evidence that remote-living Indigenous people in the Northern Territory have become more rather than less impoverished since the policy was introduced in 2007 (Altman 2017a: 3).

In the community of Mutitjulu—the community effectively scapegoated at the start of the Intervention as a means of justifying the 'emergency response'—the anger and cynicism is apparent. Dorothea Randall insists the Intervention has, 'Done nothing, just damage. Ten years and just a big wider gap.' Sammy Wilson questions the motivation of the policy, maintaining that the government 'wanted to close this place down . . . they want to clear this and put an Uluru sunrise place here because there is good sunrises here we are living on. It was about money' (both quoted in Lawford 2017b: 6). The first Indigenous woman in the Australian parliament, former senator Nova Peris, agrees, arguing that the Intervention was 'partly about a land grab under the guise of other things that demonised us all as a race of First Nations people' and that for many Aboriginal people the policy was experienced as 'an act of war declared by the Australian government on Aboriginal people' (quoted in AAP 2017b: 1–2). Chairman of the Mutitjulu Community Aboriginal Corporation, Anangu man Craig Woods, argues that the Intervention 'achieved nothing' and that 'people's wellbeing really hasn't changed' (quoted in Jones 2017).

Many First Nations people also reported feeling stigmatised by the Intervention policies—Aboriginal men in particular felt demonised as alleged paedophiles, while those on the BasicsCard found it humiliating to have to present it while shopping. Warlmanpa and Warumungu woman Kylie Sambo asks, 'Do you know how that feels? That feels very hurtful and very disrespectful to us—because you're here in our country. We're sharing this country with you, and yet you're still treating us like this' (quoted in Luke Pearson 2017b: 2). Yingiya Mark Guyula (2016) lists the Intervention policies as central to his reasons for standing as an independent in the seat of Nhulunbuy. He argues that beyond the policies and programs themselves, the Intervention has subjected Aboriginal people to a range of flow-on effects including constant police intimidation with lower resourcing of legal aid, the threat of 99-year leases or compulsory land acquisition, the 'slander' of Yolŋu culture, and being 'daily subject to permission by mainstream culture for outsiders to assume superiority.' According to Guyula, these effects also coincided with new actions instigated by the Northern Territory government, including the loss of assets from community-controlled Indigenous organisations to create new regional councils, the destruction of bilingual or 'two-way' education policies to be replaced with 'English Only policies' and Direct Instruction teaching methods, and the 'Growth Towns' policy, which diverted government funding away from homelands towards regional centres. Aside from needing what he calls 'real infrastructure' in communities, Guyula maintains that what Yolŋu (and other Indigenous people need) is to 'exit this "mainstream" we're currently in. Our community leaders and our old people need to have that power back to think and make decisions for the community.'

It is evident, however, that despite such critical assessments, and in the face of renewed calls for greater Indigenous independence from the settler state, the Intervention approach is only being intensified. Two areas of policy make this abundantly clear.

First, there is the expansion of welfare quarantining and income management through the re-named BasicsCard, now known as the Cashless Debit Card. As with the earlier iteration of the card, a portion of the welfare recipient's payment is quarantined onto a government-managed EFTPOS card with the intention of preventing people from using their welfare payments to gamble or to buy alcohol or other drugs. In the first iteration of this system, quarantined income was limited to 50 per cent of the recipient's welfare payment. Under the current regime, however, cash withdrawals are limited to 20 per cent, with the remaining 80 per cent quarantined onto the card. This is an administratively burdensome and expensive program, which was allocated $410.5 million over six years in the 2010–11 budget (Buckmaster et al 2012). Despite the cost, however, evidence concerning the efficacy of compulsory income management as a tool for improving Indigenous lives ranges from ambiguous to damning (see Bray 2016 for an overview). A report undertaken by the Australian Parliamentary Library (Buckmaster and Ey 2012: 24) concluded that there is little in the way of 'unambiguous evidence for or against the effectiveness of income management.' This study notes that there is no clear evidence that income management is responsible for a worsening of the situation in areas in which it operates, but also points out that any positive changes have been 'uneven and fragile.' Patrick Dodson acknowledges that he too has heard 'mixed messages' about the effectiveness of income management, leaving him 'not convinced that it's the solution to anything', describing the cashless debit card as 'a public whip to make people comply' (quoted in Wahlquist 2017e: 2). In the face of this ambiguity, there remains clear and publicly expressed opposition to the card, evident at public meetings and through strikes and petitions, which has been 'dismissed and ignored' by government as they continue to expand forms of income management around the country (Klein 2017).

A second area in which it is apparent that Intervention policies are intensifying is in the Community Development Program (CDP). CDP replaced the Community Development Employment Projects (CDEP) program, which was originally a response to community fears that 'passive welfare' in the form of social security payments would create 'harmful personal and social consequences' (ATSISJC 2007b: 39). By 2004 there were over 35,000 Indigenous people participating in CDEP with 70 per cent living in remote Australia and 265 community-based Indigenous organisations administering the scheme and running municipal and other community services (Altman and Klein 2017). The CDEP emphasis on community development attempted to reconcile Indigenous communality with the settler demand for individualised employment. The program was an innovative bridge between the liberal individualism of settler society, underpinned by the individual right to unemployment payments in situations where there were no jobs, and the group right of Indigenous peoples for self-management, supported by part-time employment (Sanders 2006: 47). While critics such as Marcia Langton maintained that CDEP was the 'principal poverty trap for Aboriginal individuals, families and communities' (2002: 10), for many communities, CDEP money underpinned important activities such as ranger programs and cultural tourism.

The abolition of CDEP in 2007 meant that Aboriginal people had to comply with mainstream 'work for the dole' requirements or risk losing their benefits. More than 29,000 Indigenous people are now subject to the new CDP scheme, and 84 per cent of CDP participants are Indigenous. Nevertheless, the activity tests that are required of these participants are neither 'regionally or culturally appropriate' (Klein 2016). Under CDP, welfare recipients (who receive payments well below award wages) are required to work for 25 hours per week to receive their entitlements. This may include municipal work or unpaid work for private companies, without protections under industrial law. When combined with the income management measures described above, CDP workers may receive as little as five dollars cash per hour for their work—well under any award rate—and have no access to superannuation. People subject to the CDP regime can be cut off welfare payments for up to eight weeks if they fail to attend work. Between the program's July 2015 commencement and March 2017 over 200,000 breach notices were issued (Gibson 2017: 7). In 2015 and 2016 financial penalties were applied to 34,000 CDP participants, compared to 104,000 penalties applied to 750,000 job-active participants in non-remote Australia. Drawing on research by Lisa Fowkes and Jon Altman, non-Indigenous development scholar Elise Klein (2016) observes that this is a 33:1 comparative rate, meaning that 'poor Indigenous Australians are penalised for non-participation in a program they are resisting for being unsuitable for their circumstances and inferior to what operated before.' Altman (2017b: 14) considers the imposition of CDP a form of modern-day slavery that fits the International Labour Organization (ILO) definition of forced labour because participants are penalised if they try to exercise their right to withdraw their labour and not turn up to 'work.'

A 2016 report from Jobs Australia, the national peak body for non-profit organisations that assist unemployed people, found that CDP is causing 'severe hardship' in many Aboriginal and Torres Strait Islander communities, due to the high rate of financial penalties; the poor connection with communities, which has led to a lack of community buy-in; and the program's overly complex administrative arrangements, which make compliance even more difficult. Jobs Australia also contended that the scheme failed to adequately understand the realities of the labour market for Indigenous people in remote communities, such that it is 'causing more harm than good' (Jobs Australia 2016: 5). Australian Council of Trade Unions Secretary Sally McManus described CDP as 'a stark reminder that racism still endures' in contemporary settler Australia (quoted in Thorpe 2017g: 1). ACTU National Campaign Coordinator, Kara Keys, a Yiman and Gangulu descendant, did not mince words in her assessment of the program:

> The CDP is causing people to go hungry, costs more than any comparable program and does not achieve its stated goals. The creation and pigheaded defence of this disastrous policy by the Turnbull Government has done lasting damage to countless remote communities who have been robbed of their autonomy. This program needs to be scrapped, and replaced with a model which puts economic autonomy in the hands of Indigenous people. The CDP's paternalistic approach has clearly failed and is causing serious harm (quoted in Hayman-Reber 2018).

The settler order seems immune to such criticism. Despite the evident flaws in the Intervention approach, and the continuing damage to the relationship between Indigenous peoples and the settler state that the policy is causing, the Intervention continues. In these circumstances, Aboriginal and Torres Strait Islander people are left with little alternative than to find other ways of surviving such an oppressive regime.

OUT FROM UNDER

A decade after the Intervention began, it is evident that the policies have done more harm than good. The forceful, coercive, assimilatory and far-reaching effects of the Intervention have been assessed as 'culturally genocidal' (Short 2010: 59). Some of this damage is beyond repair. A founding member of the Intervention Rollback Action Group, Marlene Hodder, maintains that the Intervention has done 'untold damage' to the lives of Indigenous people, by demonising them, creating a lack of respect and increasing racism (quoted in Fischer 2014c: 11). As Melinda Hinkson (2017b: 3) has argued, if the Intervention was 'a dramatic moment of flux and chaos between shifting policy paradigms' what has been displaced in its aftermath 'is any vision of Aboriginal communities as places that sustain distinctive, valued ways of life and where futures might be optimistically imagined and creatively pursued.' The loss experienced in this violent paradigm shift has been all the harder to bear as it has coincided with the deaths of many of the last generation of Indigenous people who remembered a 'radically different way of life' before earlier regimes of settler intervention through government settlements and missions. These losses are of profound significance in the context of Indigenous resurgence, in which the knowledge of distinctive ways of living and relating, both to people and place, is intrinsic to the capacity to (re)imagine Indigenous independence.

From its inception, Indigenous peoples have resisted the Intervention through both legal and political means, and in everyday practices of resistance, non-cooperation and refusal (Howard-Wagner 2012: 237–9). The ongoing lack of Indigenous knowledge and input into the design of policies such as the Intervention have contributed to the renewed calls for 'meaningful change' in the relationship between Aboriginal and Torres Strait Islander peoples and the settler state (Perche 2017: 3). It is clear, however, that such change means very different things for Indigenous peoples and settler institutions. Aboriginal and Torres Strait Islander people are seeking greater independence from the state, and struggling to free themselves from settler interventions and paternalistic controls. Rosalie Kunoth-Monks considers it a battle to protect Aboriginal and Torres Strait Islander cultural difference and political sovereignty:

> We are not about to let our culture die. We have survived this long against brutal and psychological assaults like the NT intervention and we are up and running and we are going to fight . . . It is not colour that counts, it is the policies of this Government that are repressive and the fact they feel they are in control of a section of humanity in this land . . . This land belongs to us, we more than share it . . . It's no good mincing words, the truth is that through propaganda our people have been made to look sub-human, when the most noble people who show absolute control over themselves are First Nations people (quoted in Maxwell 2015a: 3).

Many Aboriginal and Torres Strait Islander leaders and Elders have gone beyond the limits of their tolerance with the current regime. As a group of Northern Territory Elders and community representatives (Gondarra et al 2011) proclaimed in a statement opposing the Intervention:

> We have had enough! We need our independence to live our lives and plan our futures without the constant oppression and threats which have become central to the relationship between Government and Aboriginal communities in the Northern Territory.

What this independence might look like in reality is challenging for settler conceptions of what constitutes a 'good life'—or indeed, a good death. Following the 2017 death of world-renowned Yolŋu musician Gurrumul Yunupingu, Bunurong author Bruce Pascoe used a widely-shared Facebook post to outline his views of Indigenous resurgence and autonomy, even at the end of life. Yunupingu had died at a hospital in Darwin, where he had been taken after being found in poor health on a local beach. He had apparently made the decision to stop participating in renal dialysis, following years of ill health, and according to Pascoe was choosing to die on his own terms:

> Did my brother Yunupingu of the sweet voice want one more round of renal dialysis? No, he wanted to be on the beach with his family. He knew he'd never sing again. He wanted the beach until that too was stolen from him. Lyn [Pascoe's wife] cried when I showed her the [news] report; she cried for the deep insult to a great Australian and his family, for the way white men decided to sully his last day.
>
> If a doctor tells me one more Boag's [beer] will be the death of me, pass it to me brother, pass it to me sister, watch me down it in delicious drafts, pass me another one and take the lid off it slowly so I can see the gas escape from the neck like smoke off a sunset beach fire, laugh and joke . . . But never let middle class Christian sanctimony spoil my last beer or the last skein of smoke from the twilight fire.
>
> Leave me on the beach, that would be grace.

Amidst all the distress caused by the Intervention, high levels of Indigenous disadvantage persist. Where Marcia Langton (2008: 147) had championed the policy as 'the greatest opportunity we have had to overcome the systemic levels of disadvantage among Aboriginal Australians', on the ground in many remote communities very little has changed. The fact of this persistent disadvantage is, however, still used to justify interventionist approaches and to deny Indigenous peoples greater autonomy and independence (Klein 2016: 2). As Yingiya Mark Guyula (2010) has argued, the Intervention process

> has been a huge waste of money that has left our people scared. In fact, the intervention has led to the further destruction of our culture, ceremony and a loss of discipline among our people. The white authorities don't know what is best for us. They only think they do.

# CHAPTER 6

---

# INCARCERATION

The statistics on the over-representation of Aboriginal and Torres Strait Islander peoples in the criminal justice system in Australia are damning. During a 2017 episode of the ABC television program *Q&A*, Noel Pearson described Indigenous Australians as 'the most incarcerated people on the planet Earth', a statement subsequently confirmed in a fact check by legal scholar Thalia Anthony (2017). At the time of the Royal Commission into Aboriginal Deaths in Custody, which reported in 1991, Indigenous people constituted 14 per cent of the prison population, while today they make up 27 per cent. The rate at which Indigenous people are imprisoned has more than doubled over the past 25 years—something that federal senator and former Deaths in Custody commissioner, Patrick Dodson (2016), describes as 'staggering'. Across the country there are 2346 Aboriginal and Torres Strait Islander prisoners per 100,000 people in the Aboriginal and Torres Strait Islander population. This compares with just 154 prisoners per 100,000 people in the non-Indigenous population. The imprisonment rate for Indigenous people continues to increase in every jurisdiction in Australia, and is highest in Western Australia (3997) and the Northern Territory (2914). These figures mean that the imprisonment rate for Aboriginal and Torres Strait Islander people is thirteen times greater than the imprisonment rate for non-Indigenous people (ABS 2016). In late June 2018 a Northern Territory Estimates Hearing learned that 100 per cent of children in detention in the Territory (a total of 38 young people) were Aboriginal (Allam 2018).

These statistics have only worsened through policies such as the Intervention, discussed in Chapter Five. This is *not* a mark of the effectiveness of such policy in improving safety through incarceration—research shows there has been no discernible increase in prosecutions for family violence or notifications of child abuse in the Northern Territory. Rather, the burgeoning incarceration rates are the result of a significant increase in prosecutions for minor driving-related offences (Anthony and Blagg 2012). One journalist has described Indigenous incarceration as 'colonisation's cruel third act' (Wahlquist 2017a: 1).

Explaining these statistics requires an understanding of the impact of colonial policing on Aboriginal and Torres Strait Islander lives and, more importantly, comprehending the continuities of settler colonialism as they are manifest in the justice system. It is certainly true that Aboriginal and Torres Strait Islander people offend at higher rates than the non-Indigenous population, in part because of the deep poverty and socioeconomic marginalisation that characterise many Indigenous lives. But poverty alone does not explain the extraordinary incarceration rates detailed above, and nor does it explain how criminogenic conditions are created in some Indigenous communities. To understand that we need to understand the ways in which the policing and justice systems continue to embody colonial authority in the lives of Aboriginal and Torres Strait Islander people that unavoidably politicise that relationship. As it has done since colonisation, the settler state continues to assert its sovereignty *over* Indigenous people *through* the power of the criminal justice system, meaning that the system is understood by many Indigenous people as the justice system *of the colonial society* (Cunneen 2001: 4–5). Non-Indigenous criminologist Chris Cunneen (2005: 51) describes the administration of contemporary criminal justice in Australia as 'embedded in practices that maintain the colonised in an inferior position', even as the functioning of the system relies on an appeal to equality and the rule of law. The policing and incarceration of Indigenous people in Australia are shaped by systemic racism that has contributed not just to over incarceration per se, but to the over-representation of Aboriginal people in the justice system who have intellectual disabilities, mental health problems and hearing impairments (see Finlay et al 2016 for discussion).

As in other domains of settler policy, Aboriginal and Torres Strait Islander people are keenly aware of the role that policing and criminal justice has played, and continues to play, in their relationship with the settler state. As Karen Wyld, a writer of Martu descent (2016) has argued, 'one of the longstanding strategies of colonisation has been to criminalise, institutionalise and incarcerate Aboriginal and Torres Strait Islander people.' Larissa Behrendt (1995: 5) has also described the legal system as 'complicit' in the dispossession and ongoing colonisation of Aboriginal and Torres Strait Islander peoples. Noel Pearson (2007: 27–8) attributes some of the breakdown in Indigenous communities to the 'intrusion' of the settler legal system. He argues that the longstanding and 'workable' systems of social order that were maintained through Aboriginal and Torres Strait Islander laws and practices, based on traditional forms of moral and cultural authority, were 'forced to comply with legal authority—and ultimately had to defer to the law.' As a result, the Indigenous forms of authority that gave order and structure to Indigenous lives 'withered away', leaving a void that the settler order was quick to fill. Jiman and Bundjalung trauma scholar Judy Atkinson (2002: 45) suggests that these colonial impacts also made the world 'unsafe' for Aboriginal and Torres Strait Islander people: 'People neither knew how to behave towards others, nor could they understand why the others were behaving towards them in the ways they did.' Despite this, however, the Australian justice system has refused to consider either systemic colonial injustices to Indigenous people in sentencing, or to call into question the legitimacy of its authority over Indigenous lives and nations (Anthony 2016a: 250).

Aboriginal and Torres Strait Islander people are also keenly aware of the different standards applied to their behaviour in comparison to the behaviour of the settler order itself. While Indigenous people are criminalised at an extraordinary rate, the settler state itself is rarely accused, despite the staggering death toll that colonisation left in its wake. Judy Atkinson (2002: 11) has argued that although colonisers disregarded Indigenous peoples' rights and used force to 'dominate, intimidate, subdue, violate, injure, destroy and kill', settler society still does not consider these actions to be violence 'either morally or under the law.' As Henry Reynolds has argued, however, if settlers are unwilling to characterise the first 100 years post-invasion as a long and persistent war, then the only alternative is to understand that thousands of Aboriginal people were murdered in a 'century-long, continent-wide crime wave tolerated by government' (Reynolds 2013: 136). Understood as either war or murder spree, the theft of land and discriminatory legislation inherent in colonisation mean that questions of crime and criminality take on a different perspective for First Nations, and that answers to the questions of 'Who is the criminal?' and 'What is justice?' take on a very different meaning (Roberta Sykes quoted in Cunneen 2001: 4). For the settler state, however, the justice system has been a key institution in its pursuit of the colonial fantasy.

## POLICING AND INCARCERATION

The contemporary criminal justice system in Australia barely resembles its earlier, colonial iterations. British soldiers no longer police the criminality of convicts or the freedom of Indigenous peoples. Nevertheless, colonial continuities are evident in the highly conflictual relations between Aboriginal and Torres Strait Islander peoples and various incarnations of the police force. The policing of First Nations in Australia has been a powerful tool in their colonial subordination and control (Cunneen 2001; Finnane 1994). Colonial policing 'prepared the ground for the implantation of colonial law and sovereignty' by dispossessing and moving Indigenous people off their traditional lands, and 'projecting and communicating white sovereign power' (Blagg and Anthony 2014: 106). Finnane (1994: 111) has argued that what most distinguishes police in Australia from their English and Irish roots is 'their continually changing role in the government of Aborigines.'

The resentment and mistrust that has evolved from this history remains the most notable characteristic of Indigenous–police relations in Australia. For many Aboriginal and Torres Strait Islander people, the criminal justice system is understood primarily as an apparatus of state violence, with the police as a central—and generally oppressive—point of interface between Indigenous people and settler society (Cunneen 2001: 13). As Patrick Dodson has argued:

For the vast bulk of our people, the legal system is not a trusted instrument
of justice—it is a feared and despised processing plant that propels the most
vulnerable and disadvantaged of our people foward to a broken, bleak future
(Dodson 2016: 22).

Anger about police treatment of Aboriginal and Torres Strait Islander
people has sometimes been so intense it has led to significant uprisings,
including in Brewarrina in 1987, in Walgett and Bourke in 1997, on Palm
Island in 2004,[20] in Redfern in 2004 and in Kalgoorlie–Boulder in 2016.
Poor relations between Aboriginal and Torres Strait Islander people and
police forces around Australia have led to local, national and international
criticism of the failure to improve the situation (Cunneen 2001: 1).

The police as an institution did not exist during the first wave of invasion
and dispossession in the south-east of the continent. As police forces were
formed from the 1830s on, however, they added force and capacity to the
colonial authorities that were intent on completing the process of colonisation (Finnane 1994: 111), including through the massacre of Indigenous
groups. Around the continent, First Nations were made subject to colonial
legislatures and courts, bringing Aboriginal and Torres Strait Islander people
under the authority of colonial police who were able to exercise brutal
power without being held to account (Anthony 2016a: 251). The police were
charged with the administration of government policies, including as agents
of a colonial state that perpetuated a range of destructive interventions
under the regime of 'protection' (Chan 1997: 82), regulating Indigenous
movement, maintaining order on reserves, and in many instances enacting
(or ensuring compliance with) child removal policies (Cunneen 2001: 13).
For over 100 years after colonisation began, criminal legislation in the
colonies provided separate punitive provisions solely for Aboriginal and
Torres Strait Islander people, allowing public execution (under the *Capital
Punishment Amendment Act 1871 (WA)*) and corporal punishments (under
the Summary Trial and Punishment of Native Offenders Ordinance 1849
[WA] and the *Aboriginal Offenders Amendment Act 1892 [WA]*), including provisions such as 'whipping of up to two dozen lashes in lieu of or in
addition to imprisonment' in cases where an Indigenous worker objected to
employment conditions or absconded (under the South Australian *Breach*

*of Contract Act 1842* and the *Aboriginal Native Offenders Act 1849* (Anthony 2016a: 251).

In the post-protection period, Aboriginal reserves and settlements were gradually 'deinstitutionalised', but many of the attitudes and practices of colonial policing continued in some form throughout the remainder of the twentieth century and into the present day (Cunneen 2001: 8). In practice, this meant that police and welfare authorities in fact increased their surveillance of Indigenous individuals, families and communities according to the standards and behaviours of the settler society (Anthony 2016a: 252; Cunneen 2001: 8). These new levels of police surveillance and intervention had the effect of producing a 'total institution' within the community (Cunneen 2001: 7), thereby also producing new forms of segregation by increasing levels of penal detention resulting from the prejudicial policing of minor offences (Anthony 2016a: 252). The impact and effects of police prejudice were observed during the Royal Commission into Aboriginal Deaths in Custody (RCIADIC—discussed further below). In the Commission's final report, Commissioner Elliot Johnston observed that

> far too much police intervention in the lives of Aboriginal people through-
> out Australia has been arbitrary, discriminatory, racist and violent. There
> is absolutely no doubt in my mind that the antipathy which so many
> Aboriginal people have towards the police is based not just on historical
> conduct but upon the contemporary experience of contact with many police
> officers (RCIADIC 1991, vol. 2: 195).

The increased criminalisation of Indigenous people is driven by the settler logic of elimination, as the settler state seeks to 'govern through crime' as another means of eliminating Indigenous difference. The criminalisation of Indigenous people transforms Aboriginal and Torres Strait Islander people from a political threat to the legitimacy of the state, into a 'law and order' threat to the stability of the state, thereby legitimating the use of state violence and excessive policing (Cunneen 2001: 10). The increased policing attached to policies such as the Northern Territory Intervention is part of the contemporary settler state's effort to 'normalise' remote Indigenous communities in order to assimilate them into mainstream settler society (Blagg and Anthony 2014: 111). These contemporary interventions also reveal the colonial continuities in the policing of Aboriginal and Torres Strait Islander people, which have become structured into contemporary relations between Indigenous people and police (Cunneen 2001: 13). Aboriginal and Torres Strait Islander people are all too aware of these continuities. Noongar man and chief executive of the Aboriginal Legal Service of Western Australia, Dennis Eggington, sees the over-incarceration of Aboriginal peoples as inextricably linked to colonisation, arguing:

> We've been overrepresented in this prison system since day dot, and it hasn't been about breaking the law, it hasn't been about the criminality of Aboriginal people. It's been about how to deal with the invasion and colonisation of this land. In many ways it's still an occupied country and it's not the soldiers that occupy it any more, it's the police carrying on the occupation (quoted in Wahlquist 2016c: 1–2).

The contemporary impacts of settler colonial policing are keenly felt. Kamilaroi lawyer, and now the first Indigenous magistrate in the Australian Capital Territory, Louise Taylor (2016: 1) describes Aboriginal and Torres Strait Islander people as being 'over-policed, over-incarcerated and over-wrought by the position we still find ourselves in' leaving them 'cynical, frustrated and just plain angry.' Aboriginal and Torres Strait Islander people have found their rights—including rights to racial equality in legal processes and rights designed to protect individuals caught up in the criminal justice system—'routinely ignored' (Cunneen 2001: 2). As a result, Indigenous people hold deep mistrust of the police, which is evident around the country. Murrawarri man Des Jones from the Murdi Paaki Regional Assembly in western New South Wales contends that there is 'entrenched racism in the police force' that combines with practices intended to 'suppress and oppress young people' in order to 'try and get the young people to admit to things that they haven't done' (quoted in Gooch 2017). In Queensland, the Reverend Alex Gater, who has been a long-time prison chaplain, contends that the criminal justice system

> sets up Aboriginal people to fail. There are a lot of Aboriginal people in prison who shouldn't be there. They've ended back in prison because of petty reasons, or failing to meet reporting conditions . . . Aboriginal

people are being targeted, and police are abusing their positions (quoted in Maxwell 2013c: 8).

The over-policing of Aboriginal and Torres Strait Islander people means that they are charged with minor offences for which non-Indigenous people are rarely charged. As noted in the RCIADIC report:

> In many cases, in fact a great majority of cases, Aboriginal people come into custody as a result of relatively trivial and often victimless offences, typically street offences related to alcohol and language. Many of these 'offences' would not occur, or would not be noticed, were it not for the adoption of particular policing policies which concentrate police in certain areas, and police effort on the scrutiny of Aboriginal people (1991: ch 13.2).

Here, settler domination is evident, as the Royal Commission also noted. Most of the conflict between Aboriginal and Torres Strait Islander people and the police relates to 'street offences' legislation (concerning the public consumption of alcohol, noise, language and so on), which 'seeks to impose on Aboriginal people the views of the European culture about the appropriate use of public space' (RCIADIC 1991: ch 13.2). Such concerns are perpetuated today. Peter Collins, director of legal services at the Aboriginal Legal Service of Western Australia (ALSWA) points to charges relating to drinking in public or disorderly conduct for swearing at a police officer as evidence of what he observes to be 'uneven' and 'discriminatory' policing of Indigenous people. Collins lists some of 'the most ridiculous offences' the ALSWA has defended in recent years, including a twelve-year-old boy charged with stealing a Freddo Frog in 2009, who was refused bail and flown thousands of kilometres to Perth; a sixteen-year-old who spent twelve days in custody for attempting to steal an ice-cream; a suicidal boy from Kalgoorlie charged with criminal damage for cracking a windscreen when he threw himself in front of a car; and a man from Meekatharra who was ordered to remove his shoes and socks in the street and was then charged with assault when he threw one of his socks at police. Charges such as these, and other minor offences, often result in incarceration, particularly for young people, who are granted bail with difficult conditions that they subsequently breach. Collins contends that 'the system' is generally 'pretty content' to have Indigenous people incarcerated 'because they're perceived to be a problem, a threat, unsightly, and it's better to have them out of the way' (quoted in Wahlquist 2016c: 4).

For Indigenous people, however, incarceration has often proven to be nothing short of torture. This has been evident from the historical images of Aboriginal men shackled and chained together to the more recent images of young Indigenous people restrained and hooded in the television 'exposé' of the Don Dale Youth Detention Centre in the Northern Territory.

In July 2016, the Australian Broadcasting Corporation program *Four Corners* broadcast a report called 'Australia's shame' (ABC 2016), probably prompted by reporting of the issue in the *Koori Mail*. The broadcast seemed to crystallise Aboriginal and Torres Strait Islander experiences of the criminal justice system, for the first time showing footage of children in the Don Dale Centre being tear gassed, stripped naked, assaulted and physically restrained in chairs, their heads covered in 'spit hoods'. Amy McQuire suggests that the *Four Corners* footage showed:

> The pain of our people, built upon 200 years of trauma, bleeding through each generation, compounding and reproducing in complex ways, suddenly culminated in the CCTV images that slowed a nation down until you could hear the pulsing, hidden heartbeat of Aboriginal Australia (2016: 1).

Indeed, the nation expressed shock and outrage, and by the following morning Prime Minister Malcolm Turnbull had announced a royal commission to investigate youth detention and the child protection system in the Northern Territory. Reporting in November 2017, the Commission—headed by former Aboriginal and Torres Strait Islander Social Justice Commissioner Mick Gooda and retired Supreme Court Justice Margaret White—found that:

- youth detention centres were not fit for accommodating, let alone rehabilitating, children and young people;
- children were subject to verbal abuse, physical control and humiliation, including being denied access to basic human needs such as water, food and the use of toilets;

- children were dared or bribed to carry out degrading and humiliating acts, or to commit acts of violence on each other;
- youth justice officers restrained children using force to their head and neck areas, ground stabilised children by throwing them forcefully onto the ground, and applied pressure or body weight to their 'window of safety', being their torso area; and
- isolation has continued to be used inappropriately, punitively and inconsistently with the *Youth Justice Act (NT)* which has caused suffering to many children and young people and, very likely in some cases, lasting psychological damage (Royal Commission into the Protection and Detention of Children and Young People in the Northern Territory 2017: 5).

The commissioners recommended a sweeping overhaul to the child protection and youth detention systems in the Northern Territory, and a 'paradigm shift' in approaches to youth justice (Royal Commission into the Protection and Detention of Children and Young People in the Northern Territory 2017: 6).

The announcement of the Royal Commission had produced a sceptical response from a battle-weary Indigenous polity. Amy McQuire (2016: 2–3) suggested that the Commission was little more than a convenient way for Prime Minister Turnbull 'to be seen to be doing something, without actually doing it', more about 'placating white outrage, rather than actually providing justice for blackfellas.' Louise Taylor (2016: 1) shared this view, suggesting it was unreasonable to expect Indigenous people

> to see images of their children tied up, stripped naked and brutalised and meekly accept assurances that the government will, this time, find a solution. Our people have been down the royal commission road before and yet here we still are—with the statistics getting worse and the problems seemingly more intractable.

Others pointed out that limiting the Royal Commission's remit to the Northern Territory disguised the fact that the systemic abuse of Indigenous young people in the criminal justice system is a nation-wide concern. Wiradjuri man and New South Wales Aboriginal Land Council chairman,

Roy Ah-See argued that the 'shameful over-representation' of young Indigenous people in detention throughout Australia meant that the federal government should broaden its investigations. Ah-See contended that Indigenous families 'need reassurances' that 'basic human rights are being respected in juvenile justice centres', particularly given that Aboriginal and Torres Strait Islander people have 'little faith in the justice system' (quoted in Caccetta 2016a). In Victoria, Yorta Yorta man and the then Victorian Commissioner for Aboriginal Children and Young People, Andrew Jackamos, pointed to punitive conditions in that state's youth detention centre, including serious injuries to children, the imposition of isolation on young people who were already suffering from trauma, restrictions on soap and toilet paper, and the removal of family photographs. Jackamos suggested that these privations were a reminder 'of how the system treated us at the time of colonisation' and argued that present-day members of the Victorian government should 'hang their heads in shame' (quoted in Hocking 2017b).

Recent history indicates that faith in the politicians, institutions, or even the majority of people in the settler state on this issue would be misplaced, and that the settler logic of elimination will continue to govern the policing and incarceration of Aboriginal and Torres Strait Islander peoples. McQuire suggests that the *Four Corners* program had the potential to be a 'turning point' in the way settler Australia sees Aboriginal and Torres Strait Islander people; 'a concession that finally, First Nations mob could be believed over the lies of the authorities.' Until this point, however, white Australians had found it easier 'to confine the reality of state-sanctioned violence to a memory' (McQuire 2016: 2). Indigenous people participating in the Commission, who hoped it would be transformative, were disappointed. Eddie Cubillo, a Larrakia, Wadjigan and Central Arrernte lawyer who was the Director of Engagement for the Commission, reflected on the toll such work takes on individuals like him, and on the hurt inflicted on Aboriginal and Torres Strait Islander peoples who watch the lessons from such inquiries go unheeded. Just weeks after the Northern Territory Police announced that they would not be laying charges in any of the matters that had been referred to them by the Royal Commission, Cubillo (2018) wrote that he was at the crossroads about where this country is going when we talk about Indigenous people's rights. We all appear to be lost, particularly our mob as we keep hearing promises but no real implementation of those promises to meet our needs . . . there seems no end to this punitive behaviour from governments towards Indigenous people.

Commissioner Gooda suggested there would be a need for ongoing pressure if there was to be any change in the system, suggesting that while the Royal Commission could 'make the bullets' in the form of recommendations, it would have to be the community 'that keeps firing, holding Government to account' (quoted in James 2016). There is little room for optimism on this score. Twenty-five years before the Don Dale Royal Commission, the Royal Commission into Aboriginal Deaths in Custody had handed down its report. In the quarter of a century since, the 'black death toll' (McQuire 2016) had continued to rise along with the incarceration rate, with no evidence of change in either individual or institutional accountability.

DEATHS IN CUSTODY

The Royal Commission into Aboriginal Deaths in Custody was established in 1989 in response to public concern over the deaths in police custody and prisons of 99 Aboriginal people between January 1980 and May 1989. The Commission undertook a rigorous process of inquiry, including the subpoena of the records of all 99 deaths under investigation, from the relevant custodial and police authorities, courts and hospitals, the coroners' records, all departments having specific dealings with Aboriginal people, and where appropriate, from legal aid offices. The Commission's hearings were open to the public, and in many cases, were long and intense, with transcripts running to over one thousand pages. The final report concluded that while there were very few cases in which 'deliberate violence on the part of custodians' could be substantiated (RCIADIC vol. 1, ch. 3), the systemic racism and appalling treatment often endured by Aboriginal and Torres Strait Islander people both before and during their interactions with the police and justice system, along with the gross deficiencies in the standard of care afforded to many of the deceased, were causatively linked to the high rates of death in custody. Although the final report found that the immediate causes of the deaths that had been investigated did not include the 'unlawful, deliberate killing of Aboriginal prisoners by police and prison officers', it painted a shocking picture of the socioeconomic conditions that were contributing to the significant over-representation of Indigenous people in the justice system.

The RCIADIC report emphasised the need for widespread reform in the relationship between First Nations and the Australian settler state, with a focus on land reform, self-determination and improvements in the provision of basic services. As discussed above, the key reasons that Aboriginal and Torres Strait Islander people come into contact with the criminal justice system relate to over-policing, the definition of crime (particularly as that applies to Indigenous people), along with institutionalised practices of placing Indigenous people in custody for their own 'protection' when intoxicated. The Commission sought to explain Indigenous contact with the justice system in terms of 'disadvantage and disempowerment', and concluded that such disadvantage stemmed from:

- prejudicial policing, especially for minor crimes relating to public order;
- the police tendency to caution, charge and arrest Indigenous people, rather than issue warnings or court attendance notices;
- police and courts not granting bail to Indigenous people; and
- courts sentencing Indigenous people to prison rather than handing down non-prison sentences (Anthony 2016b: 2–3).

In 2016, during the twenty-fifth anniversary of the release of the RCIADIC report, it was widely noted that not only had the majority of the Royal Commission's recommendations not been implemented, the number of Aboriginal deaths in custody had not declined and the over-representation of Aboriginal and Torres Strait Islander people in custody had increased. In a 2016 speech to the National Press Club, former commissioner Patrick Dodson pointed out that 'by and large, the problems the Royal Commission was set up to examine and advise governments on, have become worse.' Dodson suggested that this 'raises questions' as to whether 'the issues identified by the Commission are understood or even considered important', saying:

> I don't know for sure, but what I do know is that a quarter of century after
> we handed down our findings the vicious cycle remains the same: Indige-
> nous people are more likely to come to the attention of police. Indigenous
> people who come to the attention of police are more likely to be arrested
> and charged. Indigenous people who are charged are more likely to go to
> court. Indigenous people who appear in court are more likely to go to jail.
> If Indigenous people are being taken into custody at an increasing rate,
> then it stands to reason that our chances of dying in custody also increase
> (Dodson 2016: 22).

As non-Indigenous journalist Paul Daley (2017: 2) points out, 'No state or federal administration since then, conservative or Labor, has adequately explained why the royal commission's recommendations haven't been implemented.'

The release of the 1992–93 cabinet papers revealed that then Minister for Aboriginal Affairs, Robert Tickner, only received about a third of the money he asked for to implement the Commission's recommendations. Many years later Tickner became emotional when asked about the new royal commission into juvenile justice in the Northern Territory, telling a journalist:

> There's two responses—tears or anger: we should all be angry . . . All that
> public money, all those commitments, all those promises, and yet all
> that consequence, of tens of thousands of wasted, damaged lives as a result
> of the failure to implement the recommendations of the royal commission.
> People whose life potential was never fulfilled because governments didn't
> do what they promised (quoted in Damien Murphy 2017a: 4).

It is only the too-frequent, intermittent and high-profile deaths of Indigenous people in custody that keeps public attention on this issue. In 2004, the death in custody of Mulrundji Doomadgee on Palm Island sparked an uprising that led to national and international media attention, and eventually led to a charge of manslaughter against the most senior police officer on the island, Senior Sergeant Chris Hurley. Hurley was subsequently acquitted of the charges although a coronial inquest later found he had in fact caused the fatal injuries. In 2008, Ngaanyatjarra Elder Mr Ward (whose first name is not used in accordance with cultural naming practices for the deceased) was arrested for driving while intoxicated. He subsequently died in the back of a van being driven by a private security company, after being driven 400 kilometres in searing heat without water or air conditioning. A coronial inquest found that Mr Ward had died of heatstroke, with a large full thickness burn to his abdomen from lying on the floor of the van—he had essentially 'cooked' to death. The coroner in the case, Alistair Hope, found Mr Ward's death to be 'wholly unnecessary and avoidable', and suggested that it raised the question of 'how a society, which would like to think of itself as being civilised, could allow a human being to be transported in such circumstances' (Hope 2009: 123). Despite such findings, however, no charges were laid against the two security guards who were driving the van at the time of Mr Ward's death—although one was subsequently given the 'record fine' of $11,000 for her role in the death following a Worksafe prosecution (Wynne 2011). The Western Australian government later made a $3.25 million *ex gratia* compensation payment to the family of Mr Ward in what represented an 'unequivocal apology' for the death (Sonti 2010).

More recently still, Western Australia also saw the death of a 22-year-old Yamatji woman, Ms Dhu (whose first name is also not used for cultural reasons). Ms Dhu died in the Port Hedland lock-up, after being detained for defaulting on the payment of fines. The coronial inquest into her death showed CCTV footage of Ms Dhu's treatment in the hours leading up to her death. As she cried out in pain from the staphylococcal septicaemia and pneumonia that would kill her (an infection resulting from broken ribs suffered during a previous family violence incident), police seemed to determine that she was faking her condition and refused her requests for medical assistance. One officer referred to her as a 'junkie' who was undergoing withdrawal. The CCTV footage also showed police officers dragging an apparently unconscious Ms Dhu along the floor of her cell and into a corridor, from where she was carried by her arms and legs to the back of a police wagon and locked inside. Dhu was eventually taken to the Hedland Health Campus three times during her detention. On the first two occasions she was returned to police cells, and subsequently died on her third visit (Gartry and Trigger 2015). Paraphrasing the comment made by the coroner in relation to the death of Mr Ward, Peter Collins from the Aboriginal Legal Service in Western Australia noted that the question being raised in the case of Ms Dhu's death is also 'how a society which would like to think of itself as being civilised, could allow a human being to die in the circumstances in which Ms Dhu died' (quoted in Wahlquist 2017c: 2). Ms Dhu's uncle, Shaun Harris, expressed frustration that despite being born in 1991, eight months after the conclusion of the Royal Commission into Aboriginal Deaths in Custody, this young woman would die in such circumstances. Harris contended that her death was 'a product of the institutional and systematic problems in the system' (quoted in McQuire 2017b: 1).

In 2017 the Western Australian government announced that it would make a $1.1 million *ex gratia* payment to the family of Ms Dhu, and offered members of her family 'the state's sincerest apologies for the circumstances leading to the death.' Dhu's family did not accept the apology. Shaun Harris argued that his life had been 'shattered' by Ms Dhu's death, and demanded a different kind of justice:

> I cannot accept the State's apology until they hold those responsible account-
> able and ban the practice of jailing fine defaulters. It is premature to suggest
> that this matter has been resolved and that family members are pleased with
> the outcome. We are not pleased at all (quoted in McQuire 2017d: 2).

Harris had previously observed that, 'Every death in custody affects the whole community, they have a massive ripple effect' (quoted in Maxwell 2016a: 5). And yet as Patrick Dodson (2016: 22) has observed, Dhu's story

> could have been plucked at random from almost any moment in the modern
> story of Aboriginal injustice. For our communities, the storyline is all too
> familiar: the minor offence; the innocuous behaviour; the unnecessary
> detention; the failure to uphold the duty of care; the lack of respect for
> human dignity; the lonely death; the grief, loss and pain of the family.

Dodson again questioned the failure to implement the recommendations of the deaths in custody royal commission, suggesting that deaths such as those of Ms Dhu and Mr Ward might have been prevented if the recommendations had been appropriately supported and resourced. Summing up the current state of affairs in the criminal justice system for Aboriginal and Torres Strait Islander people, Dodson argues that the incarceration rates of Indigenous people are 'a complete and utter disgrace' about which there can be no complacency:

> Accepting the status quo permits the criminal justice system to continue to suck us up like a vacuum cleaner and deposit us like waste in custodial institutions. I would hope we are better than that. We must be better than that. There is no choice here.

INJUSTICE IN THE COURTS

Alongside the violence of criminalisation and over-policing, and the profound dangers of incarceration, Aboriginal and Torres Strait Islander people face two further injustices when they come into contact with the settler justice system. On the one hand, settler courts seem lenient towards settler offenders who have committed offences against Indigenous people; on the other hand, settler courts generally ignore First Nations' own laws in their dealings with Indigenous people. Both of these kinds of injustice constitute acts of erasure—of Aboriginal and Torres Strait Islander people both as victims of crime and as makers of law—that are driven by the settler logic of elimination.

The 2016 death of fourteen-year-old Elijah Doughty in the Western Australian Goldfields town of Kalgoorlie is emblematic of the first point. On the day he was killed, Doughty was on the outskirts of town, riding a child's motorbike that may or may not have been stolen. If the bike was in fact stolen, there is no evidence that Doughty had stolen it himself, or that he knew it was stolen—not that such theft would ever justify his death. A non-Indigenous man who had recently had a bike stolen allegedly informed by police that stolen bikes were frequently dumped in a reserve just out of town, and so—angry at the theft of his bike—the man parked his 4WD vehicle near the reserve and waited to see if any young people and bikes would appear. At some point, Doughty rode past, and the man in the 4WD took off in pursuit. What happened next is disputed, but the outcome was that Doughty was run down by the 4WD at high speed and died instantly. The inquest revealed that Doughty's skull had been split in two, his brain stem snapped, his spinal cord severed, and he had suffered a broken pelvis, ribs and a 'mangled' leg (Taylor 2017). The driver denied that he had intentionally run Doughty down, and instead claimed that the child had unexpectedly veered in front of the truck. Amid claims that they had bungled the investigation by driving over tyre tracks at the scene, the police accepted the driver's version of events, and the man was charged with manslaughter rather than murder (Wahlquist 2017g). In court, however, the perpetrator was found guilty of the far lesser offence of 'dangerous driving causing death', and ultimately sentenced to three years' jail (Graham 2017b). In the end, Doughty's killer was released in March 2018, just six months after the conclusion of his trial, and after spending a total of only nineteen months behind bars.

On both the days immediately following Doughty's death, and the day of the perpetrator's sentencing, the Indigenous community in Kalgoorlie–Boulder rose up to protest and keep vigil. Protest erupted outside the courthouse on the day of the first hearing. At rallies following the sentencing, Aboriginal speakers placed Doughty's death in the wider political and historical context of Aboriginal deaths, the history of racial injustice in Australia, colonialism, racism and the broader failings of the justice system (Johnson 2017: 1–2). One participant in the Kalgoorlie–Boulder protests threw red ochre on the steps of the courthouse, screaming, 'This is the blood of Aboriginal people, don't wait for this to be your children's . . . The blood is on the Commonwealth!' (quoted in Thorpe 2017f). Doughty's death was compared to the 2009 death of Kwementyaye Ryder in the dry bed of the Todd River in Alice Springs.[21] One of Doughty's relatives, Meyne Wyatt highlighted the racism involved, arguing:

> Let's not get this twisted, it wasn't manslaughter it was murder. Not manslaughter, not reckless driving. You're treating us like we're animals, we're not animals. We're people, you're killing us! (quoted in Thorpe 2017f).

Kalgoorlie Elder Trevor Donaldson drew connections between the trauma of such deaths and the ongoing scourge of Indigenous suicide (discussed further in Chapter Seven), saying:

> I wish we could just flick the switch and move on, but that doesn't happen . . .
> We'll probably end up with another suicide and they'll be all falling over

themselves to come here, the fly-in fly-out politicians asking 'what's wrong?', 'what's going on?' (quoted in Hamlyn 2017).

Noongar woman and Indigenous human rights lawyer Hannah McGlade pointed out that the verdict had reduced Doughty's death 'to an offence under the *Road Traffic Act*', apparently making it 'open season for vigilantes in Western Australia' (quoted in Thorpe 2017f).

Arrernte writer and unionist Celeste Liddle (2017c: 1) observes, however, that the one response missing from Indigenous people around Australia was any sense of surprise:

> Because we weren't surprised. From one end of the country to the other, Aboriginal community members were expecting this ruling and had been ever since police decided not to charge the 56 year old male driver . . . with murder, instead opting for the lesser charge of manslaughter. We have seen it all happen before and history dictates that, at the end of the day, it is highly unlikely that killing an Aboriginal child, or man, or woman, will attract a sentence at all—if it even goes to court in the first place.

Non-Indigenous psychologist Lissa Johnson (2017: 5) suggests it was entirely predictable that a non-Indigenous jury, such as the one in the Doughty trial, would deliver a lenient sentence to a white offender in the case of an Indigenous death. In such cases, Johnson argues, Indigenous deaths tend to be seen as 'a regrettable accident, devoid of malice, intent or hate. An unfortunate mistake', with the unspoken implication that a white man's property is more valuable than an Aboriginal life. Johnson (2017: 6) observes that the justice system in Australia repeatedly reinforces the suggestion that

> white killers of Aboriginal people in Australia never act with malicious intent. They always kill Aboriginal people accidentally. We white Australians kill Black Australians with the best of intentions. Over and over again.

Muruwuri journalist Allan Clarke (2017) suggests that Australia's failure 'to acknowledge the atrocities of the past committed towards Aboriginal people' has left the nation unable to construct a narrative in which Indigenous people are victims of violence rather than perpetrators of it. Celeste Liddle (2017c: 1) agrees, arguing that a 'reasonable portion' of settler Australia is 'not prepared to acknowledge there is any narrative in which Aboriginal people are the victims of white people, white systems or white governments.'

Compounding the many injustices experienced by Aboriginal and Torres Strait Islander people in the Australian criminal justice system is the inability of this system to recognise First Nations' laws. Before invasion, customary laws—understood to have been laid down by ancestral beings with authority that was external to the community—provided a set of logical rules and norms that both structured the society and maintained community order. The authority of these laws was eroded by the settler state, which sought to replace customary authority with its own. More wide-ranging than Western conceptions of law, Indigenous customary law provides groups and individuals with precise and binding guidelines by which to manage relationships to others, to land and resources, with related rights and obligations. Beyond punitive measures, customary law addresses questions of international relations, border control, trade, and resource management. Patrick Dodson describes customary law as 'an all-encompassing reality' with 'many obligations and responsibilities and structures of accountability.' Dodson regrets the fact that:

> Most people unfortunately have only ever thought of customary law from a punitive position. They've thought about it in terms of punishment, in terms of spearing someone through the leg as a consequence of some violation, or at other extremes of the aberrations that might arise under a promised marriage structure (quoted in KALACC 2006: 15).

From the outset, settler institutions failed to comprehend the broader systems of Indigenous law. The significance of some aspects of customary law in criminal justice systems has, however, been the subject of particular debate. Australian courts have attempted to clarify the use they should make of First Nations' law, including how they should receive evidence about the content of such laws and what impact this should have on issues such as sentencing and the granting of bail (Brennan et al 2005: 57). While these issues may be challenging, they should not excuse contemporary courts and governments from further effort to understand the place of First Nations laws in mainstream political culture. In what Thalia Anthony (2016a: 263) describes as a 'circular rationale', the High Court of Australia has ruled that Aboriginal and Torres Strait Islander people cannot be subjected to their own criminal laws, procedures and punishment processes on the basis that the settler state's criminal law is universal and cannot coexist with other law systems. As Anthony points out, however, in making this determination the High Court did not articulate the basis for the exclusive universal authority assumed by the British Crown and the settler colonial state, despite the fact that Indigenous nations had exercised jurisdiction over their peoples for thousands of years before colonisation. As Yankunytjatjara woman and former Indigenous public administrator Lowitja O'Donoghue has argued:

> The long standing absence of meaningful official recognition of Aboriginal customary law has had a detrimental effect on all facets of Aboriginal community development and has substantially contributed to many of the social problems and varying degrees of lawlessness present today. The failure of successive governments to recognise customary law has resulted in the erosion of Aboriginal cultures (O'Donoghue 1995).

The impacts of this lack of recognition are two-fold. Firstly, as O'Donoghue suggests, the lack of respect afforded to customary law has had the effect of diminishing Aboriginal and Torres Strait Islander cultures, with significant social impacts. For example, Yolŋu independent member of the Northern Territory parliament, Yingiya Mark Guyula (quoted in Watt 2017), suggests that the erosion of customary law, including traditional processes of 'learning to be responsible and preparing for respectful relationships' has contributed to the rise of family violence in some Indigenous communities. Guyula argues that Indigenous peoples' 'rights to maintain justice' has been 'revoked' by settler institutions. The only way to fix this, according to Guyula, is 'with policies of self-determination, self-management, self-governance and ultimately, a treaty'.

Secondly, the failure to recognise First Nations' laws may mean that Aboriginal and Torres Strait Islander people are further disadvantaged in the criminal justice system, particularly with regard to sentencing. In some parts of the country, the recognition of First Nations law may be taken into account in sentencing (Chesterman 2005: 244). Courts in the

Northern Territory, for example, may recognise the continuing operation of Indigenous punishment practices, which are known to take place
alongside or as well as settler criminal proceedings. However, most settler
jurisdictions also choose to outlaw customary practices that are thought
to 'offend non-Indigenous values' (Anthony 2016a: 263). As a result, when
judges fail to take customary law into account, Indigenous people may
find themselves too severely punished, or punished twice, in comparison
to non-Indigenous offenders (Chesterman 2005: 244). Previous research
has shown that Indigenous status does not attract mitigation in sentencing and that Indigenous defendants are as likely—or more likely—than
non-Indigenous defenders to be incarcerated. This suggests a failure to
consider Indigenous offending as a consequence of the impact of colonisation and its attendant trauma and disadvantage which, when combined
with the failure to take customary law into account, exacerbate the injustice of the settler colonial criminal justice system (Anthony et al 2015: 52, 75).

Of course, these issues are far from simple, and not every Indigenous
person supports an approach to criminal justice that would take cultural
context and historical experience into account. Former chair of the
Indigenous Advisory Council, Warren Mundine, suggests that taking
what he calls a 'softy, softy [sic] approach' will lead to 'more broken communities and Indigenous people with broken bones' (quoted on Sky News
2017). Judy Atkinson suggests that it has been settlers who have categorised
much Aboriginal interpersonal violence as 'customary practice' even though
Aboriginal people themselves regard this same behaviour as unacceptable and a transgression of cultural norms (Atkinson 2002: 11–12). This
distortion of Aboriginal customary law has been exacerbated in national
debates in which, in Megan Davis' opinion, settlers mistakenly characterise
the practice of First Nations law as 'Indigenous communities reliving the
halcyon days of Indigenous culture practicing brutal, traditional punishment such as wounding or tribal payback' (Davis 2006: 129).

The point here, however, is not to mount a defence of Aboriginal and
Torres Strait Islander customary law or traditional practices. Determinations
about the merits or otherwise of customary law can and should only be
the business of Aboriginal and Torres Strait Islander people themselves.
Indigenous laws, like legal systems around the world, can and do evolve

all the time. One of the effects of invasion and colonisation, however, has been to disrupt the evolution of Indigenous law, the protection of which has become a defence against an aggressive occupying culture. Acknowledging the sovereignty of First Nations means acknowledging that their systems of law are theirs to develop, change and evolve over time. While Australia is regularly and rightly criticised for its breaches of inter-national human rights law with regard to our system of detaining refugees and asylum seekers in offshore prison camps, we would not countenance a foreign power making a unilateral decision to override our legal system and impose a new order on that basis. Yet that is precisely what the settler state continues to do to Aboriginal and Torres Strait Islander systems of law and justice. Settler legal orders have proved deadly to Aboriginal and Torres Strait Islander people, such that 'real alternatives to the existing court system' are desperately needed (Behrendt 1995: 5). Decolonising the criminal justice system in Australia would mean that space and capacity are afforded to Indigenous clans and nations to determine appropriate justice systems for themselves.

## INDIGENOUS JUSTICE

As previous chapters have made clear, genuine Indigenous self-determination and self-government—the *exercise* of sovereignty—occurs at the clan or nation level. This is also true with regard to the exercise of justice. Aboriginal and Torres Strait Islander clans and nations hold a diversity of definitions of both 'crime' as well as laws, practices and forums for responding to crime. Even where First Nations and government agencies share common objectives (crime reduction, increased community safety, reduced incarceration and so on) they may have 'radically differ-ent' understandings of how to achieve these goals (Blagg and Anthony 2014: 117). As non-Indigenous criminologists Zellerer and Cunneen (2001: 249) argue:

> It is up to Aboriginal peoples to interpret and explain their cultural ways. It is the responsibility of all outsiders, especially those involved in justice, to listen to and understand indigenous approaches within the context of their societies.

Recommendation 188 of the Royal Commission into Aboriginal Deaths in Custody maintained that policy and program delivery for Aboriginal and Torres Strait Islander people must be framed by the principle of self-determination. If alternative approaches are 'initiated and endorsed by the state' they may be 'viewed with suspicion rather than embraced' (Zellerer and Cunneen 2001: 250). Larissa Behrendt (1995: 74) has suggested that with greater community autonomy Aboriginal people would be able to restore traditional laws and dispute resolution processes 'away from the structures of the dominant culture' (1995: 74).

As Kalkadoon man Shane Duffy, former chair of National Aboriginal and Torres Strait Islander Legal Services, and Yuwallarai woman Kirstie Parker, former co-chair of the National Congress of Australia's First Peoples and the Close the Gap campaign, argue, focusing only on the multiple ways that the settler criminal justice system has failed Aboriginal and Torres Strait Islander people 'would be to ignore the significant steps that our people and organisations, and their non-Indigenous counterparts, have taken to achieve change' (Duffy and Parker 2015). There are multiple examples of such initiatives around the continent. The tiny town of Warakurna, on Ngaanyatjarra land in Western Australia, saw a dramatic drop in youth crime after becoming the first town in the state to deploy an all-Indigenous police force. Community Elder Daisy Ward told reporters that people in the community 'used to be scared of the police. Now they see the police are here to help . . . It makes the community feel proud to have an Indigenous person who is the same like us, and it makes a good feeling' (Joyner 2018). Across the border in the Northern Territory, Indigenous night patrols (operating since the 1980s) have developed as 'a uniquely Indigenous Australian form of community self-policing.' Night patrols, often run by women, do not have formal policing powers, but focus on community safety and on combating alcohol-related violence. They are not part of the apparatus of settler state policing and cannot call on coercive state power to ensure compliance. As Blagg and Anthony (2014: 103, 104) argue, the patrols 'demonstrate that Indigenous communities can produce ideas and strategies rather than simply consume those imposed from above by colonial power.'

Other programs are more broadly focused on the education and rehabilitation of Indigenous offenders, often through activities that reconnect them to culture and country. Examples include the Mount Theo program, started by the Yuendumu community for Warlpiri young people, and which has successfully rehabilitated petrol-sniffing teenagers since the 1990s by helping them reconnect to country and culture, or the Yiriman Project based in Fitzroy Crossing in Western Australia, conceived and developed by Elders from the Nyikina, Mangala, Karajarri and Walmajarri language groups, where young people engaging in self-harm and substance abuse are taken out onto country to learn how to become self-sufficient in the bush. There is a strong belief in the power of such programs. Non-Indigenous law scholar Harry Blagg believes they are effective because they treat offending as more than a 'justice issue', instead taking a more holistic approach to understanding that offending is 'an issue about intergenerational trauma, it's an issue about family violence' (quoted in Wahlquist 2017a: 2–3). Noongar woman, Roxanne Moore (2017: 4), a human rights lawyer and Indigenous Rights Campaigner for Amnesty International, describes a conversation she has had in many Indigenous communities, where people protest the incarceration of young people saying:

> Bring our kids back to us. We can heal our kids on country. We can give our kids the support they need, with their families, in their communities. Our kids need to be strong in culture and have opportunities to thrive, not be locked up and bashed. The police need to stop targeting our kids. We say these words again and again. No one listens.

Programs on country may fit within the justice reinvestment model, which is gaining popularity and traction in Aboriginal and Torres Strait Islander communities. The justice reinvestment approach proposes that funds spent on incarcerating people should be diverted—or reinvested—into prevention and early intervention programs that focus on the underlying causes of offending. As Patrick Dodson (2016: 22) has argued

> unproductive expenditure on prisons should instead be invested in programs at the front end that both reduce crime and prevent people entering the criminal justice system. Building more jails and enacting laws that ensure the incarceration of Indigenous peoples is not the solution, and certainly not a good use of taxpayer dollars.

In western New South Wales, the Maranguka Justice Reinvestment Project in Bourke is demonstrating how alternate approaches can reduce prison populations, save money and build stronger communities. The chair of Just Reinvest NSW, Sarah Hopkins, points out that what is happening in Bourke is the result of 'decisions being made on the ground, by community leaders' and with 'broad community input.' While the results have not been a 'magic wand', Hopkins reports 'seeing optimism and a real sense of momentum' that she believes is leading to meaningful change (quoted in *Koori Mail* 2016c: 15). In Western Australia, Dennis Eggington claims he is 'at a loss' as to why the justice reinvestment approach has not been embraced in Australia, given its success internationally. As Eggington points out, 'locking people up in prison doesn't make communities safer, but a justice reinvestment model would create safer communities' (quoted in *Koori Mail* 2013b: 13).

Another approach that has been embraced by Aboriginal and Torres Strait Islander people in some parts of the continent is the development of Indigenous court processes, known as 'Koori courts' or 'Murri courts' depending on what part of the country they are in.[22] These courts involve Elders and other respected community members in the sentencing process for Indigenous offenders, focusing on restorative and reparative justice rather than only on punitive measures. One of the Elders involved in the Victorian Koori Court, Yorta Yorta man Glenn James, says he encourages offenders to respect their Elders and become involved in their communities, 'building up some respect and paying back for the things [they've] done wrong.' Importantly, James says, the court is

> telling kids we love them, and we're here for them and we're on their side and we want them to be part of the team. You see their eyes light up. They haven't been told in a lot of cases that they've been loved and we love them (quoted in Mundy 2014b: 11).

One participant in the Murri Court in Cairns, where offenders have to meet regularly with volunteer Elders for months before they are sentenced by the courts, claims that as a result of the process he 'would never re-offend again. It was my mob, my people. You feel more at ease' (quoted in Terzon 2017).

Yet while these Indigenous sentencing processes may be having a positive impact, they remain subject to the policy determinations of the settler order. In 2012, the Murri Court in Townsville was axed by the Queensland government despite claims by members of the court that it had successfully rehabilitated many offenders (Wilson 2012). And while night patrols may operate autonomously and through the authority of their communities, asserting Indigenous rather than settler law, where they are provided with government funding they must operate in an increasingly restrictive regulatory environment that has reduced local control (Blagg and Anthony 2014: 115, 119). These challenges highlight the fact that most of these reforms, even those that show evident impact, are efforts to 'Indigenise' systems that remain dominated by whiteness and settler colonialism. The hope is that indigenising settler systems will reduce the harms experienced by Aboriginal and Torres Strait Islander people in those systems, but at the end of the day such efforts are a long way from the practice of Indigenous jurisdiction. Nor can issues related to criminal justice be divorced from the other impacts of colonialism, including poverty and violence, which cannot be addressed simply by making existing settler systems more sympathetic or culturally appropriate.

A resurgent, decolonising approach to the criminal justice system requires a deconstruction of the authority of the settler justice system and a reconstitution of jurisdictions that can 'shift power from non-Indigenous appointed judicial officers and legal precedent, towards Indigenous community justice strategies, laws and knowledge systems' (Anthony 2016a: 264–5). As Chris Cunneen (2001: 3) has argued, Indigenous self-determination is 'directly linked to a process of decolonisation: both decolonisation of institutions and decolonisation of the colonial construction of Indigenous people as "criminals".' Or as Patrick Dodson (2016: 22) puts it, if Aboriginal and Torres Strait Islander people are to be 'liberated from the tyranny of the criminal justice system' any discussion must be framed by the philosophy of self-determination: 'If we are to be authors of our own destinies, then governments must stop treating us as passive clients, or as targets of a policy for "mainstreaming".'

Other settler colonial states have developed successful, hybrid systems of justice that are owned by Indigenous communities, using Indigenous instruments of law and governance, while coexisting with state laws and systems[23] (Anthony 2016a: 265). Australia may yet be capable of decentring colonial power and making space for Indigenous resurgence in the justice system, but first it must relinquish the colonial fantasy.

# CHAPTER 7

___

# CLOSING THE GAP

There is perhaps no policy domain that more clearly reveals the colonial fantasy than the policies intent on 'closing the gap' in socioeconomic indicators between Aboriginal and Torres Strait Islander peoples and the settler mainstream. Despite considerable fanfare and substantial expenditure, Aboriginal and Torres Strait Islander peoples continue to fare less well across all statistical indicators than the rest of the population. Life expectancy remains shorter for Indigenous people, and educational outcomes are below those of the non-Indigenous population. For years, prime ministers have reported poor and declining outcomes in health. These poor statistical indicators continue to confound and contradict the settler state's understanding of itself as fundamentally benign and even beneficial to Aboriginal and Torres Strait Islander people. The evidence that this is not so is by now incontrovertible. Despite constant churn in policy, a 'proliferation' of services, and government commitment to throwing 'considerable administrative machinery and public finance at the problem' (Moran 2016: 2–3) the statistical indicators stubbornly refuse to budge.

Yet despite this evidence of policy failure, the Australian settler state continues to pursue broadly the same approach to addressing Indigenous disadvantage, rejecting international evidence suggesting that self-determination and self-government are in fact far more effective in creating change. Poor statistical indicators are framed only as an issue of disadvantage, rather than as a more profound, systemic problem in which the political relationship between Indigenous peoples and the state continues to shape the social determinants of Indigenous health and wellbeing (see Carson et al 2007). This framing directs attention only towards Indigenous lives and behaviour rather than towards their relationship with settlers, and the social environments that relationship has produced. This framing also relies on what Palawa sociology scholar Maggie Walter (2018: 258) describes as '5D Data': data that focuses on difference, disparity, disadvantage, dysfunction and deprivation rather than on engaging with the lived experiences of Aboriginal and Torres Strait Islander peoples' lives. This shapes analysis of the problem to be addressed in policy initiatives. As Taiaiake Alfred (2017a) has argued, contrary to the story told by 5D data, the 'fundamental problem' in Indigenous lives is not the 'symptoms' of poverty and injustice, rather it is 'the dispossession, the continual occupation, the separation of people from their homelands and the fundamental essence of who they are.' The confected consensus on the idea that it is the symptoms (Indigenous disadvantage) rather than the cause (colonisation and political inequality) that requires redress drives the assimilatory view that Aboriginal and Torres Strait Islander lives will somehow be improved by the erasure of Indigenous difference and the completion of the colonial project (Strakosch 2015: 105, 117).

Australia is not alone in this misdirected approach. The 'stark discrepancy' between the socioeconomic indicators for Indigenous populations and other groups in settler societies is a matter of ongoing policy focus in all the former British colonies, which has led to a 'diverse array' of initiatives intended to bring Indigenous indicators more in line with settler society. Sitting among the world's wealthiest nations (with wealth built on land and resources taken from Indigenous peoples) it is a frequent source of embarrassment to settler colonial governments that the Indigenous peoples within their borders remain among their poorest citizens (Cornell 2006: 1). The settler's refusal to come to grips with Indigenous demands for self-determination effectively cripples policies ostensibly designed to overcome Indigenous poverty. This is despite the fact that there is compelling evidence from American Indian nations in the United States that demonstrates that self-determination is, at the very least, a 'necessary element in the struggle against poverty' (Cornell 2006: 12).

As Stephen Cornell (2006: 28) from the Arizona Native Nations Institute and the Harvard Project on American Indian Economic Development has argued

> if central governments wish to perpetuate Indigenous poverty, its attendant ills and bitterness, and its high costs, the best way to do so is to undermine tribal sovereignty and self-determination. But if they want to overcome Indigenous poverty and all that goes with it, then they should support tribal sovereignty and self-determination, and they should invest in helping Indigenous peoples build the governing capacity to back up sovereign powers with effective governments of their own design.

As we saw in chapters Two and Three, however, the Australian settler colony has been unable to advance any meaningful engagement with First Nations' sovereignties, or with Indigenous demands for self-determination and self-government. My contention has been that this inability is fundamentally entwined with the fantasy of colonial completion, which could not survive a confrontation with the foundational illegitimacy of the settler order on sovereign Indigenous territories. Nowhere is the power of this fantasy more evident than in policies and programs seeking to improve socioeconomic parity between settler and Indigenous peoples, despite all evidence that the current approaches are failing, have always failed and will continue to fail in the future.

Of course, not all Aboriginal and Torres Strait Islander people live in poverty. There is a growing Indigenous middle class in Australia that is often overlooked in narratives of Aboriginal and Torres Strait Islander disadvantage, although even wealthier Indigenous people can and do experience systemic racism and other structural barriers that negate the benefits of higher income. Nevertheless, the statistics on socioeconomic inequality do tell us something very significant about the experience of being Indigenous in a settler nation. As Lyndon Murphy and his colleagues (2017) have argued:

> The source of the problem lies in the encounter between two previously discrete peoples, and the dispossession and overrunning of one by the other. Statistics about disadvantage cannot capture that. Instead, they give the mistaken impression that disadvantage can be solved by policy-making on

the terms of those who did the over running. Policy on these terms has been unsatisfactory.

The 2017 Statement from the Heart drew attention to the 'structural nature' of the problem underlying the statistics about Aboriginal and Torres Strait Islander lives. As Aileen Moreton-Robinson (2007: 99) also argues, Indigenous welfare dependency 'has been structured by and in the interests of patriarchal white sovereignty.' Aboriginal and Torres Strait Islander people are impoverished *because* of colonisation, *because* of dispossession, *because* of the loss of an economic base in land and *because* of the loss of the freedom to determine how to live their lives.

Despite this, statistical evidence of socioeconomic disadvantage and a range of associated harms continues to be used to justify paternalistic policies and interventions into Indigenous lives. At one level this is understandable. Indigenous poverty, suffering and deprivation is real and confronting. Images of people without proper housing, living in desperate conditions with lives afflicted by alcohol and violence are hard to ignore, particularly where they involve children. Improving the socioeconomic wellbeing of Aboriginal and Torres Strait Islander peoples remains an urgent task. Yet these issues have become a political football despite Marcia Langton's (2002: 17) warning that Indigenous poverty 'is not the political property of any party but an historical legacy that brings no honour to those who suffer it nor to those who play politics with it.' Focusing only on the 'current calamity' ignores the underlying structural causes of the problem (Bradfield 2006: 81), and the need for a decolonising response that will begin to undo harmful structures and return control to Aboriginal and Torres Strait Islander peoples.

## COMMUNITY CONTROL VS CLOSING THE GAP

The Native Nations Institute and the Harvard Project on American Indian Economic Development have spent decades studying the conditions in which Native Nations in the United States begin to recover from the effects of colonisation. What they have observed is an uneven pattern of development that is not easily explained by 'the usual economic factors' such as location, educational attainment or the capacity to extract (and profit from) natural resources, all of which have in fact produced a wide variation of outcomes. Instead what these researchers have found to be the most consistent predictors of sustainable economic development are not economic factors at all, but three political attributes, specifically:

- *Sovereignty or self-rule*, such that Indigenous peoples have genuine decision-making power that creates accountability for decision-makers who have to own the consequences of their decisions.
- *Capable governing institutions* that enable Indigenous peoples to exercise their decision-making power effectively.
- *Cultural match* between formal governing institutions and Indigenous political culture that supports local clan or nation ideas about how authority should be organised and exercised. Where there is mismatch between Indigenous social and political organisation and an imposed overlay of settler-designed governing institutions, tribal governments have been vulnerable to political opportunism and factional conflict, and subsequently have had difficulty getting things done (Cornell 2006: 13–14).

Stephen Cornell (2006: 18) and his colleagues in this research have found that where tribal leaders stopped asking permission before acting, excluded federal representatives from decision-making processes, and advanced their capacity for self-government by taking the initiative in governmental reorganisation and constitutional reform (including developing alternative funding sources through business enterprises), *and* where they matched these asserted powers with effective and culturally congruent governing institutions, they began to see significant results. Self-governing tribes experienced reduced unemployment and welfare dependency, the emergence of viable and diverse economic enterprises, more effective administration of social services and programs, and improved management of natural resources. In sum, in case after case, these researchers observed that Native Nations 'proved to be much better at running their own affairs and managing their own resources than federal administrators had ever been.'

In Australia, Aboriginal and Torres Strait Islander people have pursued self-government often under the rubric of 'Aboriginal control of Aboriginal affairs' (Land 2015: 40). As discussed in Chapter Two, self-determination has always been intrinsic to an Indigenous politics of decolonisation and resurgence. In the 1970s this politics coalesced around the emergence of Aboriginal community controlled organisations designed to deliver health services, child care and legal services. But while these organisations demonstrated greater success in providing services and meeting the needs of Aboriginal and Torres Strait Islander people, they were less successful in persuading settler governments to hand over the funding for these services. They were also forced to manage and govern themselves according to the practices of the dominant settler culture (Land 2015: 112). Missing these key elements of cultural match in self-government, as outlined by Cornell above, many of these organisations struggled to thrive or even survive over time, often reduced to a reliance on project-based funding that has kept them tied to the goals and aspirations of the settler order. As Jackie Huggins from the National Congress of Australia's First Peoples has argued, even though Aboriginal community-controlled health organisations 'deliver 2.5 million episodes of care a year in their local communities' they continue to endure 'chronic underfunding and an ad-hoc policy approach based on three-year election cycles' (quoted in *Koori Mail* 2017: 5).

The ongoing settler control of organisations providing services to Aboriginal and Torres Strait Islander people contributes to continuing problems on the ground in many communities. There is little trust in government departments to act in the interests of Aboriginal and Torres Strait Islander peoples—and why would there be? As Emma Kowal (2015: 49) points out, the health department in the Northern Territory today is the continuation of that same department in the 1930s that 'participated in stealing children.' More broadly, Kowal argues, 'the authority of Australian governments is continuous with the authority of those who invaded the land.' Patrick Dodson (2017) explains that while many communities 'want help in addressing alcohol abuse and violence' there remains 'a nexus between the situation these communities find themselves in and the policies imposed upon them by governments—policies grounded in a philosophy of institutional control.' Dodson contends that top-down measures focused on the behaviour of vulnerable individuals 'breeds a situation of hopelessness, dependency, and destabilisation in communities' that only exacerbates social problems. In the wake of the findings of the Royal Commission into the Protection and Detention of Young People in the Northern Territory, the chief executive of the National Aboriginal Community Controlled Health Organisation (NACCHO), Pat Turner, insisted that 'white NGOS' need to 'get out of the way and allow Aboriginal community controlled organisations to take over the child protection system.' Turner argues that:

> Those days are over. They need to get out of that space and the Government needs to provide the resources directly to Aboriginal community controlled organisations . . . Our organisations in the NT are the best placed to make sure the reforms that should be in place are in place (quoted in Sorensen 2017).

Chair of the Apunipima Cape York Health Council, Yirrikanji, Umpila, Bindal and Woppaburra man Bernie Singleton, makes a similar point, arguing that 'community control is the way to go in Cape York and in other Aboriginal communities':

> If we ever want to pull ourselves up we've got to be in control of our lives, and that's including health and our social well-being. We've got to be in charge of our own health. We need black community controlled health services. I still remain hopeful that we'll get there, but we've got to realise that no-one else is going to improve health but us. It's about Murri medicine and community control, those are the keys to our health and our future (quoted in Strohfeldt 2012: 21).

Yamatji and Badimia woman and nurse, Banok Rind (2017), is also passionate on this issue, arguing that community control is the only way to improve progress on the government's Closing the Gap targets:

> Government mob need to understand that only community-based interventions and community-controlled organisations will reduce the health, education and employment disparities and finally meet Close the Gap targets. Do not perceive us as people with problems. This isn't an 'Indigenous issue'. It needs national urgency. This is the health of our people. We are people. We are human.

Sustained failure in reaching the Closing the Gap targets has prompted a 'refresh' of the approach, being advanced by the Commonwealth

Department of Prime Minister and Cabinet (DPMC 2017a: 3), which has acknowledged that governments in Australia 'need to work differently with Aboriginal and Torres Strait Islander Australians.' A part of the 'refresh' agenda is a renewed commitment from Australian governments to 'work in genuine partnership with Indigenous leaders, organisations and communities, to identify the priorities that will inform how governments can better design and deliver programs and services, to close the gap.' These are certainly positive commitments, but they are a very long way from a commitment to supporting community control in the provision of services—it is still described as the government's role to 'design and deliver programs and services.' As Megan Davis has argued, First Nations delivered a 'sophisticated roadmap to closing the gap' in the Statement from the Heart. Davis maintains that Indigenous people 'aren't looking for refresh as a priority ... The priority is structural reform' (quoted in Davidson 2018b).

The Closing the Gap policy framework is a set of agreements made by the Council of Australian Governments that addresses seven specific targets that measure health (life expectancy, child mortality), education (early childhood education, school attendance, literacy and numeracy, Year 12 attainment) and participation in paid employment. The framework emerged from the Close the Gap campaign spearheaded by the former Aboriginal and Torres Strait Islander Social Justice Commissioner Tom Calma in 2005, which called on government to take real action towards achieving equal health, education and life expectancy outcomes for Indigenous people within 25 years. Beginning in 2008, the Closing the Gap approach to tracking socioeconomic outcome has become a central plank of Indigenous affairs policy in Australia, and receives considerable public attention when the prime minister presents the annual *Closing the Gap* report to parliament, as he or she has done since 2009. The 2017 *Closing the Gap* report showed some improvement in reading and numeracy for Indigenous children, and reducing infant mortality and smoking rates, but indicated that only one of these targets—to halve the gap in Year 12 attainment by 2020—was on track to be met. The 2018 report again showed some improvement, with three of the seven targets now on track, but with four targets—including the key one to close the ten-year gap in life expectancy between Indigenous and non-Indigenous Australians by 2031—still lagging. The United Nations Special

Rapporteur on the Rights of Indigenous Peoples, Victoria Tauli-Corpuz, has described Australia's lack of progress on these targets as 'woefully inadequate', and particularly unacceptable given that two decades of economic growth in Australia had not improved the level of social disadvantage experienced by many Aboriginal and Torres Strait Islander people (quoted in Brennan 2017b).

What the government distorted in adopting the Closing the Gap approach out of the Close the Gap campaign is that the latter was—and remains—committed to increasing Indigenous ownership of the programs intended to improve their lives. While Closing the Gap uses much of the language and branding of Close the Gap, and reiterates the intention to do things 'with Aboriginal people and not to them', it continues to advance a top-down approach to service delivery (Nicol 2017). Releasing a 2018 report highly critical of government progress in Closing the Gap, the co-chairs of Close the Gap, June Oscar and Rod Little, pointed yet again to the disconnect between government policy and Indigenous control and expertise. Oscar and Little pointed out that the Close the Gap campaign has a level of 'leadership, experience and expertise' in these areas unmatched by any other group. Simply put, they said, 'We have the solutions.'

Yet government is persisting with a 'refresh' strategy that was criticised from the outset for its lack of consultation with Aboriginal and Torres Strait Islander people. More problematically still, the Closing the Gap framework suggests that 'gap-closing' is a 'technical policy matter' rather than an issue of deep political significance (Markham and Biddle 2017: 2). The troubled history of attempts to 'protect' Indigenous children makes this abundantly clear.

CHILDREN

The wellbeing of Aboriginal and Torres Strait Islander children is the focus of four of the seven Closing the Gap targets and yet, as Torres Strait Islander political theorist Sana Nakata (2017: 398) writes, Australia continues to be confronted by 'incomprehensible failure.' Such failure, Nakata suggests, 'troubles the nation' as it represents 'the grief of our history, the demography of our present, and the uncertainty of our future.' Stan Grant (2016a: 1–2) details these failures:

In 2016, the lives of our children are measured in statistics. Indigenous kids make up half of those juveniles behind bars. An Aboriginal or Torres Strait islander boy or girl is nine times more likely to kill themselves. We are failing them and there are many reasons for it.

Regardless of reasons, however, the bottom line for Grant is that 'We bury 10 year-olds who feel Australia has no place for them.'

Melinda Hinkson has argued that the image of the vulnerable and suffering Aboriginal or Islander child has 'an unparalleled potency' in Australian politics, justifying urgent action through the 'essential moral righteousness' of addressing the spectre of child abuse and neglect (Hinkson 2010: 230). Yet, as Nakata (2018: 110) argues, the 'intensive governance' of Aboriginal and Torres Strait Islander families, was undertaken less for their 'own good' (although this was always the justification made by the settler regime), and much more for the good of 'the white imaginary of the Australian nation.' Indigenous children were targeted by colonial regimes for the purpose of disinheriting them of the land to which they belong and which belongs to them. This, again, is the logic of elimination at work, levelled at Indigenous children with 'unmitigated zeal.' Where violence and disease did not eliminate Aboriginal and Torres Strait Islander people, 'the removal of children severed any claims they might come to make as rightful successors' (Conor 2016). And as Nakata (2018: 110) suggests, 'so long as these children ceased to exist, so long as they either died or could be successfully assimilated, the legitimacy of the new white Australian nation-state could remain intact.'

Aboriginal and Torres Strait Islander people know all too well the negative impacts likely to result from settler policies intended to 'help'. The Stolen Generations is the paradigmatic example. The *Bringing Them Home* report from the National Inquiry into the Separation of Aboriginal and Torres Strait Islander Children from Their Families, concluded that, 'between one in three and one in ten Indigenous children were forcibly removed from their families and communities in the period from approximately 1910 until 1970' (HREOC 1997: 36–7). Yet the prime minister at the time, John Howard, rejected these findings by arguing that many Indigenous children 'were taken in circumstances where under today's laws they would be regarded as being properly and lawfully taken from their families in the interests of their own protection' (Parliamentary Debate 2000: 15008).

The impacts of child removal are manifold. Larissa Behrendt (2003: 68) lists the many harms associated with these policies, noting that children who were taken away

> were not taught their own stories by Indigenous Elders. Instead, they were taught the white culture and the white system. They were taught that they were inferior and that their culture was inferior. If children did not have a strong cultural background, they tended to be persuaded by the cultural propaganda preached within the institutions they were confined to, or by the families into which they were adopted.

The Aboriginal and Torres Strait Islander Healing Foundation (ATSIHF 2017: 20) outlines the many ongoing health and social effects for the Stolen Generations and their families. These include significantly poorer physical health and over double the rates of mental illness and alcohol abuse compared to that suffered by Aboriginal and Torres Strait Islander people who were not removed. Members of the Stolen Generations have, on average, received a poorer education and are more likely to be unemployed—a deep irony given that the removal of children was often justified as providing a means for these children to 'succeed' in settler society. Child removal destroyed families and their communities. Members of the Stolen Generations 'no longer belonged to a community, held no memories of belonging to one and were not able to draw on the strengths of a community to help them.' Traumatic impacts have also been experienced by those who were left behind, many of whom have never recovered from the distress of losing their children. As Judy Atkinson (2002: 70) explains, child removal has created

> a group of profoundly hurt people living with multiple layers of traumatic distress, chronic anxiety, physical ill-health, mental distress, fears, depressions, substance abuse, and high imprisonment rates. For many, alcohol and other drugs have become the treatment of choice, because there is no other treatment available.

Natalie Cromb (2018b) suggests the depth of these harms, arguing that it is 'difficult to enunciate a loss as profound as identity and culture and to lose both is an insurmountable loss which embeds upon your DNA.'

Yet although these harms are now widely understood, the removal of Aboriginal and Torres Strait Islander children from their families continues at a staggering rate. In 1993 the *Bringing Them Home* report found that 2 per cent of Aboriginal and Torres Strait Islander children (nationally) were in care, almost 7.5 times the rate for non-Indigenous children. The latest figures (for 2015) show that more than 5 per cent of Aboriginal and Torres Strait Islander children are now in care, almost ten times the rate for non-Indigenous children (ATSIHF 2017: 20). The Royal Commission into the Protection and Detention of Children in the Northern Territory heard evidence that the number of children receiving child protection services in the Northern Territory was at 'epidemic proportions' and could be considered a 'humanitarian crisis', with rates more than doubling since the 2007 Intervention. Research presented to the Commission showed that half of the Indigenous children in the Northern Territory were expected to receive child protection services by the age of ten (5.5 times the rate of non-Indigenous children), and one in twelve would be placed in out-of-home care (Davidson 2017b: 2). As Melinda Hinkson has argued, it is the 'ultimately chilling paradox' of the Intervention policies in the Northern Territory, that although they were justified as a means of ensuring better care of children, 'ten years later child removal and detention have become institutionalised at unprecedented levels' (Hinkson 2017b: 3).

Nationally, the number of Indigenous children in out-of-home care doubled in the ten years following the 2008 apology to the Stolen Generations (discussed further in the following chapter), with Healing Foundation chief executive Richard Weston describing the child protection system as 'punitive, not supportive' (quoted in Wahlquist 2018). That these figures continue to rise a decade after former prime minister Kevin Rudd made the historic apology suggests that the settler state has learned little from this troubled history. On his departure from the role, outgoing Victorian Commissioner for Aboriginal Children and Young People, Andrew Jackomos, described the rising numbers as a 'national disaster' (quoted in Brennan 2018). As Hannah McGlade (2017: 3) argues, more Aboriginal and Torres Strait

Islander children are being removed today 'than they ever were during the Stolen Generations', and these removals are increasing such that if there is no change to policy and practice it is estimated that rates of removal 'will triple by 2030.'

The continuing increase in the rates of removing Aboriginal and Torres Strait Islander children from their families is causing fear and frustration, with advocates warning that the nation is creating 'a new stolen generation.' Andrew Jackomos contends that, 'There would be a national taskforce to fix the crisis in child protection and youth justice if it involved white rather than Aboriginal children' (quoted in *NITV News* 2017d). Stolen Generations advocate Lorraine Peeters describes herself as feeling 'really sick in the stomach' every time she sees the statistics, and asks, 'Who is going to be there for those children in 18 years' time when they enter into trauma and want to know where they come from or who their families are?' (quoted in Chadwick 2013). One Arrernte Elder who gave evidence at the Royal Commission into the Protection and Detention of Children in the Northern Territory, Margaret Kemarre Turner, also compared current child removal rates to the risk of 'another Stolen Generation' and pointed to the risks involved for those children, who

> lose their connection, they lose their parents, they lose their identity. In Aboriginal society you don't usually have one mother or one grandfather or one anything. All of us in the family are responsible for that one child. It's very, very hard for a child to come back (quoted in Campbell 2017).

Andrew Dowadi, a Maningrida Elder and grandfather whose grandson was removed from his family and community at the age of seven, also gave evidence to the Royal Commission about the impact of removal, saying:

> He lost his language. He definitely lost his language. And he was shy to come back. And he was shamed to come back . . . so I have to sit beside him. I say don't worry about it, we go back home now. We're heading home (quoted in Zillman 2017).

The aunt of two boys who had been removed from their family and put into foster care in Darwin more than 1000 kilometres from their home in

Arnhem Land complained that these children 'were asked not to speak their language and weren't called by their Aboriginal names', lamenting that this is 'exactly what happened back then [during the Stolen Generations] and it's happening again now' (quoted in Bardon 2017b).

The implications of continuing to remove Aboriginal and Torres Strait Islander children from their families, communities and culture are well understood. These practices will perpetuate a vicious cycle: traumatised children are more likely to become traumatised adults, the harms done to them cascade to subsequent generations as patterns of substance abuse and violence continue, meaning that more children are again removed. Yet another royal commission—the Royal Commission on Institutionalised Child Sexual Abuse—made only one recommendation specifically concerning Aboriginal people (despite the fact that around 12 per cent of the people who were heard by the Commission were Indigenous), and that concerned the implementation of the Aboriginal Child Placement Principle, which supports children's connection to family and community and their sense of identity and culture. That Commission also found that the child protection system in Australia does not adequately recognise the importance of Aboriginal and Torres Strait Islander culture in keeping children safe, despite laws requiring it to do so (McGlade 2017: 2). While this is disturbing, it is not surprising. As this book has made clear, the colonial fantasy rests on the elimination of Indigenous difference. Raising children in their culture, to sustain their culture, confounds this fantasy. Racist notions about the superior nature of non-Indigenous family life, combined with the settler desire to eliminate cultural difference, makes child 'protection' a dangerous and highly politicised space.

LIVING WITH TRAUMA

The intense focus on children in Australian settler policy history has had disastrous effects. Families that have lost children or experienced other colonial harms can experience a collective, compounding pain that sometimes manifests in abusive and self-abusive behaviours. The frustration or rage that some Aboriginal and Torres Strait Islander people experience is turned inwards (where alcohol and other substances are sometimes used as maladaptive coping strategies), and outwards (where it is expressed in poor relationship skills or antisocial behaviour, including violence), and 'cascades down the generations, growing more complex over time' (Atkinson 2002: 78). Judy Atkinson argues that during the protection era from the 1890s up until the 1950s, binge drinking became a form of self-medication that created an experience of freedom within the traumatising context of total settler control. At the same time, however, binge drinking contributed to violence within the families and groups who were incarcerated under this regime (Atkinson 2002: 67).

These complex symptoms are often represented in mainstream media and politics as the only experiences of Indigenous life, supporting the framing of Aboriginal and Torres Strait Islander people as a problem to be resolved. Not only is this not true but, as should be clear by now, it is not helpful to understand these symptoms as an Indigenous problem. Rather, they are a settler problem and indicative of harmful Indigenous–settler relationships in need of radical transformation.

Not all Aboriginal people accept the view that Indigenous violence, including violence against women and children, stems from the intergenerational traumas of colonialism. Jacinta Price (2017: 2), for example, rejects the suggestion that what she calls a 'family violence epidemic' is 'a result of colonisation and racism.' For Price this idea 'shifts blame' away from perpetrators and 'silences the real victims: the dead or broken women and the children with shattered lives.' Worimi lawyer and member of the Prime Minister's Indigenous Advisory Council, Josephine Cashman, expressed her disappointment with the third National Action Plan to Reduce Violence against Women and their Children, which argues that, 'Responses to family violence in Aboriginal and Torres Strait Islander communities must recognise the impact of past trauma for Indigenous people resulting from colonisation, racism and social disadvantage, and the role of these intersecting factors in perpetuating violence' (DSS 2016: 14). For Cashman, this analysis is little more than 'excuser behaviour for offenders' that does not do enough to protect women and children from violence (quoted in *National Indigenous Times* 2016b).

Nevertheless, the dominant view—and experience—among Aboriginal and Torres Strait Islander peoples connects historical and recent trauma to contemporary experiences of substance abuse, violence and social dysfunction. This is not to suggest that Aboriginal and Torres Strait Islander people are passive victims. For example, many Indigenous people acknowledge the problem that alcohol poses in some communities and have taken self-determining steps to reduce its harms. The current Aboriginal and Torres Strait Islander Social Justice Commissioner, June Oscar, played a pivotal role in her home community of Fitzroy Crossing in the Kimberley where, as CEO of the Marninwarntikura Fitzroy Women's Resource Centre, she led a campaign for alcohol restrictions in the town. Oscar had attended 50 funerals in eighteen months, including a spate of 22 self-harm deaths (both suicides and alcohol-related deaths) over thirteen months, and observed the related impacts of family violence and child abuse along with an alarming increase in the number of children being born with Foetal Alcohol Spectrum Disorder (FASD) as a result of their mothers drinking while pregnant. For Oscar and the other women in the organisation, 'enough was enough':

> Alcohol was destroying our community and it was affecting every aspect of life. It was being consumed to a level where everyone's quality of life in Fitzroy Crossing was shocking. We had to stand up and fight for our future—our children's future . . . Alcohol was playing a big part in the level of domestic violence, and it was tearing families apart. We could not tackle educating people about their violent behaviours and their emotional triggers until we had restricted their access to alcohol (Oscar and Pedersen 2011: 83).

Oscar's fight against alcohol was not new. Fitzroy Crossing had an Anti-Grog Committee in the late 1970s, and through much of the 1980s Aboriginal people in the Kimberley pursued the potential of the Aboriginal Communities Act 1979 as a way of managing alcohol and social disorder in their communities. However, a lack of resourcing and support from the state government frustrated those efforts (Oscar and Pedersen 2011). It was not until 2007, after a long battle with alcohol retailers and others in the town, that the women won approval for bans that would restrict the sale of all but light-strength takeaway alcohol. Within six months, the results of the restrictions were evident, with alcohol-related injuries falling from 85 per cent to below 20 per cent of hospital presentations, and alcohol-fuelled domestic violence incidents also falling by 43 per cent. Police reported a decline in sexual assaults and street violence, while children were going to school more (Clarke 2016). These changes were sustained in the following years. And the women did not stop there. Shortly after the alcohol ban took effect, Oscar and her colleagues convened a meeting of women from four language groups that took the decision to ask leading paediatricians and researchers from the George Institute and Sydney University to help quantify the FASD problem in the community so that they could lobby for additional supports for affected children. This led to the Lililwan study, meaning 'all the little children', which involved more than 120 eight-year-old children in the first ever prevalence study of FASD in Australia, and possibly the world. As further evidence of the effectiveness of such self-determining strategies, the Lililwan study involves local women in every stage of the research, which resulted in an unheard of participation rate of 95 per cent (Power 2014).

Other forms of alcohol management or restriction continue to cause controversy, however, particularly where they are experienced as top-down rather than community-owned and led. For example, in 2011 the Northern Territory introduced the Banned Drinker Register (BDR), which identified people banned from purchasing, consuming or possessing alcohol and prevented their purchase of takeaway alcohol. The program, which was never properly evaluated, was abandoned after a change of government in 2012. Former senator, Nova Peris, defended the program after it was suspended, and argued for its return:

> Every night our hospitals overflow with the victims of alcohol violence . . .
> The BDR meant that every person on an alcohol-related Domestic Violence
> Order was banned from purchasing alcohol at every alcohol takeaway venue
> in the NT at every hour of the day. Nothing in the recent alcohol initia-
> tives from the NT Government provides this level of protection for women
> (quoted in *Koori Mail* 2014a: 18).

The register was in fact returned in 2017, but not everyone was happy. In the Arnhem Land community of Yirrkala there was concern that the reinstated BDR would conflict with the community's own drinking permit system, which is seen as a community-controlled success. The local system, developed in 2002 by the Mawal Harmony women's group in collaboration with the thirteen clans in the area, requires anyone buying alcohol across the five communities to have a permit. Restrictions are determined by each community's committee. The reinstatement of the BDR created anxiety about whether the register would work to complement their permits, or reduce their control over a locally led system (Davidson 2017c).

Aside from the obvious health-related consequences of problem drinking in Indigenous communities, there is national concern with alcohol-related violence, and particularly violence against women. Pyemairrenner man Ian Anderson—now Deputy Secretary in the Commonwealth Department of Prime Minister and Cabinet and responsible for the 'refresh' to Closing the Gap outlined above—has argued for the importance of understanding contemporary violence in the context of 'the violent history of Australian colonialism', which he argues is essential to understanding the 'trans-generational processes' that produce such problems. Without this context, policy becomes focused only on 'what is happening internally within Indigenous communities', rather than on the relationship with the settler state (Anderson 2002: 409). Renee Leslie, an Indigenous social worker from the New South Wales town of Nowra, contends that 'intergenerational trauma is a significant factor in why this is happening in communities' and maintains that a better understanding of these impacts will 'minimise future domestic and family violence in communities' (quoted in Caccetta 2016b). Chief executive of the Ngaanyatjarra Pitjantjatjara Yankunytjatjara (NPY) Women's Council Andrea Mason also suggests that there has not been a 'structure' to manage 'the depth of trauma in our communities.' For Mason the answers lie in strengthening 'cultural governance' that will allow communities to take better leadership on this issue (quoted in Caccetta 2016c).

Examples of this type of First Nations governance might include the plan to deal with family violence developed by more than 90 Indigenous men and women in the community of Galiwin'ku on Elcho Island. The plan, which focuses on legal education (including educating police about Yolŋu law), proposes that when police respond to an incident of violence, they first contact the Yolŋu community authority, which Yirrininba Dhurrkay, who worked on the plan, describes as functioning 'like the old village councils of the past' and would ensure that the correct clan and kin of both offenders and victims would be a part of the response. Dhurrkay contends that the Yolŋu authority could

> oversee alternative punishments for Yolŋu offenders that bring them back to their foundations and remind them that we must all live together. In many instances, jail makes the problems worse and young people come out and return to causing problems (quoted in James 2017b).

These cultural governance models do not allow the settler state off the hook. Substantial resources will still be required. Tasmanian Aboriginal woman of the Trawlwoolway nation, family violence educator Fiona Hamilton (2017b), who works in the Barkly region in the Northern Territory, suggests that these resources should support the provision of appropriate long-term safe-housing, along with a 'hub for the many services required to support Aboriginal women and children through coordinated approaches, and towards a safer future.' What needs to be avoided, however, are further paternalistic incursions into Indigenous community control. Researcher Elise Klein obtained police data under freedom of information laws that shows an increase in domestic violence in the East Kimberley since the introduction of the cashless debit card in the region. Klein suggests that there is a causal link between financial hardship, the lack of autonomy associated with the card, and family violence (in Knaus 2018).

A lack of autonomy is also one of the factors related to the scourge of Indigenous suicide—an immense topic that cannot be given an adequate place here. Across the continent, suicide is the second-leading cause of death for Aboriginal and Torres Strait Islander children aged five to fourteen years old, and the leading cause of death among Aboriginal and Torres Strait Islander young people aged fifteen to 34 years—truly staggering statistics that have never been the subject of urgent national inquiry.

There has been some recent effort to understand the problem. In 2016 the Aboriginal and Torres Strait Islander Suicide Prevention Evaluation Project report made a series of comprehensive recommendations for addressing the high incidence of suicide among Indigenous people. The report, which notes that suicide among Aboriginal and Torres Strait Islander people was virtually unheard of prior to the 1960s, emphasised that the most common success factor in community-based responses to Indigenous suicide was their development and implementation through Indigenous leadership and in partnership with Indigenous communities (Dudgeon et al 2016: 2). Almost twenty years after Colin Tatz (1999) reported that 'Aboriginal suicide is different', the Australian settler state seems perhaps slightly closer to understanding or responding to this difference.

First Nations people articulate a complex range of factors that contribute to Indigenous suicide, including the complex interplay of mental health issues, systemic racism and societal-rejection, which often leave young people unable to see a future for themselves. Government control and intervention fuel the sense of a lack of agency, too often compounded by a lack of opportunities for employment; lack of accessible, culturally safe health services; and a lack of access to addiction treatment services and social and emotional wellbeing programs, including when such services are defunded. Feelings of powerlessness and experiences of persistent systemic and everyday racism are also significant contributors to the decisions Indigenous people make to end their lives. James Gaykamangu, a senior leader from Gapapuyngu in north-east Arnhem Land, and co-author of *The Elders' Report into Preventing Indigenous Self-Harm and Youth Suicide*, suggests that one of the problems is the way that settler services 'stand over' Indigenous families and undermine their parental responsibility. Another co-author of this report, Lorna Hudson from Derby, suggests that many Indigenous people feel 'cast aside from the mainstream' and so 'see themselves as no good.' A third co-author, Joe Brown from Fitzroy Crossing, suggests that when Indigenous people 'lose language and connection to culture they become a nobody inside and that's enough to put them over the edge' (all quoted in Zillman 2016).

Others draw more direct connections to the impacts of colonisation. Wakka Wakka woman Julie Turner, a Darwin-based teacher who flies in to remote Indigenous schools, and who has spoken about Australia's epidemic of Indigenous self-harm and suicide to the United Nations Permanent Forum on Indigenous Issues, suggests there are 'lots of reasons' behind Indigenous suicide:

There's the history of colonisation and inter-generational trauma left by the Stolen Generation policies, ongoing racism, poverty, unemployment, marginalisation . . . To escape the pain people turn to drugs and alcohol, and too many take their lives, to escape the pain.

Turner also suggests, however, that the problem has been exacerbated by 'so many years of top-down policy-making', which has been profoundly ineffective. Turner argues that 'Indigenous people are crying out to be heard. They want to give young Indigenous people their inheritance of cultural knowledge, identity and strength' (quoted in Fischer 2014b: 12). Tom Calma agrees with this argument, suggesting that in 'report after report' Aboriginal and Torres Strait Islander people have told the government, 'It's not us, it's you, the way you develop policy, the way you change policies and programs at the drop of a hat, the total inconsistency in your approach—that's what's causing the problems' (quoted in *Koori Mail* 2015e: 8).

What many in the field advocate as the most effective response to Indigenous suicide has its basis in ideas of resurgence. Chief executive of the Healing Foundation, Meriam man Richard Weston, believes culture is the key to effective healing projects. Culture is 'providing a place people can find strength, they can find support for the issues and challenges they face', it creates 'a sense of purpose, a sense of connection to their past, and those are things that build resilience and safety.' Bardi woman and Indigenous Studies academic, Pat Dudgeon also advances this view, contending that solutions lie in Aboriginal and Torres Strait Islander peoples'

> cultural strength, our connection to our culture and understanding our histories. For Australian Aboriginal and Torres Strait Islander people, it's not about trying to have a debate in this country about blame or guilt for non-Aboriginal people, it's really just trying to understand how we got to where we are. So if we understand how we got to where we are, we can create solutions that can change the situation (both quoted in Noonan 2017).

At least one school is advancing a cultural approach to the issue of Indigenous suicide. At the Yirrkala School in Arnhem Land, Yolŋu ideas about wellbeing are a part of a curriculum designed to improve student mental health; connecting the idea of *gapu* (water) with student's changing emotions. Co-principal Merrkiyawuy Ganambarr-Stubbs, explains:

Sometimes older people say, 'I'm feeling like this body of water' and we know that this body of water can be really rough and fast, like a tidal sort of wave or current, that can sweep people out to sea. They tend to talk about that particular water, but really they are talking about themselves and how they are feeling. They also learn, 'hey that's my country, I am the person that belongs to that water' (quoted in James 2017a).

This is just one example of the role that education might play in a resurgent politics of decolonisation, with far-reaching social benefits.

EDUCATION
Education sits at a crossroads in contemporary Aboriginal and Torres Strait Islander politics. It holds potential both for advancing Indigenous success in the settler world, and for providing new forms of cultural transmission following the loss of fully initiated Elders in many parts of the continent—yet another consequence of colonisation. As we have seen, the settler education system is deeply implicated in the breakdown of traditional authority structures, and has 'interrupted the natural course of traditional education' (KALACC 2006: 43). Indeed, in its mainstream forms, settler education cannot meet the cultural learning needs of young Indigenous people, who often also experience racism and bullying within the mainstream education system.

Despite its many shortcomings, many Aboriginal and Torres Strait Islander people understand the importance of education for survival in settler Australia. Sue-Anne Hunter from the Victorian Aboriginal Child Care Agency, observes that 'Aboriginal people have been in survival mode for a very long time' such that it is 'only recently that we've understood that education is power' (quoted in Brennan 2016). The late R. Marika, a renowned Yolŋu educator and scholar, made a similar point in relation to education and curriculum development, which she says is 'all about power' and can be used to strengthen Yolŋu culture and avoid 'an intellectual terra nullius' (1999: 7, 9). Bardi and Gija woman and teacher Sharon Davis (2016: 2) sees education as 'essential to our freedom and self-determination.' For Davis, and for many other Aboriginal and Torres Strait Islander people, education has been a source of confidence and a pathway into a professional career. Yet Davis remains keenly aware of problems in the settler education system—what she calls 'unresolved education issues that have stemmed from the colonial hangover' (Davis 2016: 4)—and suggests there is no easy way to resolve them:

> Throwing funding at education programs that attempt to 'fix the Aboriginal problem' by focusing narrowly on attendance, or correct parenting courses, or one-off scholarships lays blame exclusively with Aboriginal people. It is like saying to Aboriginal families, 'If you only made your kids go to school, or knew how to parent properly, or weren't so poor, then you would succeed. Just try harder'.
>
> Comparably, force-feeding school staff with umpteen cultural aware-ness courses, or raising the Aboriginal flag once a year, or having kids paint coloured hands in the school quad and posting pictures in the school newsletter are also not solutions. As far as I am concerned, educational outcome parity is not solved with deficit-based programs, an open cheque-book, or token Aboriginal events (Davis 2016: 2).

There are many established and emerging initiatives in education that are beginning to address these concerns. At the Murri School in Brisbane, for example, a holistic approach developed in collaboration with the Aboriginal and Torres Strait Islander Healing Foundation (ATSIHF) is showing results. The program, designed for Indigenous children and young people who have faced issues such as trauma, grief and loss, cultural dislocation and social disadvantage, takes a whole-of-school approach to these issues and brings together family support workers, psychologists, health professionals and trauma-informed teachers to create a culturally appropriate, supportive environment. Richard Weston from the Healing Foundation explains that the program 'addresses the intergenerational trauma experienced by so many Indigenous children and young people by creating a safe environment where students feel comfortable seeking support, and adopting a trauma-informed, holistic approach' (quoted in *Koori Mail* 2015b: 18). Its success has seen the approach adopted in the New South Wales state school system.

At the Yirrkala School, Yolŋu culture is blended with settler education through a Learning on Country framework that has seen attendance rates rise. Yolŋu culture and ways of knowing are being used to teach Western subjects in the school, where students are also taught ceremony by

Langani Marika, the oldest living traditional owner for the Rirratjingu clan. Co-principal Merrkiyawuy Ganambarr-Stubbs explains that starting with Yolŋu culture helps children in the school learn:

> It is much easier for children to think into the western world if they've got their own way of thinking first. The children learn in both ways, they learn both curricula . . . Teaching through our culture makes it much easier to learn western maths, or western geography, or western history (quoted in Dias 2017).

Beyond reforms to the settler system, however, there is an evident need to create alternative—or at least parallel—modes of education that focus on Indigenous knowledges. There are emerging models for this type of education. Rosalie Kunoth-Monks is working with her daughter Ngarla to set-up an 'immersion school', where culture comes first and children will not study English until Year 7. In the school, Kunoth-Monks says children will, 'Not just be speaking language. But reading and writing, and knowing why they are putting the body paint on' (quoted in Hocking 2017b). The project to open the Jedda Academy for the Education of Young Girls on the Utopia homelands is supported by Sydney private school Barker College in what Kunoth-Monks hopes will be 'the beginning of really growing two diverse cultures to come together in a way without destroying the other, or without being disengaged from the other.' Kunoth-Monks argues that teaching Indigenous culture first is important for building confidence in Aboriginal and Torres Strait Islander children:

> We have a right to retain our identity. In that identity comes your stability, your belongingness and the capacity [for children] to comprehend in their earlier years. There's many of my people in the Top End of Australia that are also querying that shoving down your throat of a foreign ideal and so forth; that is wrong [. . .] You've got to first of all get that child to accept itself and have confidence in that little body to say, 'This is who I am. Now I want to know further, I want to know what it is in that big wide world' (quoted in Vanovac 2017).

Making the decision to develop schools and teaching programs of this kind is an exercise of sovereignty. Noongar woman and academic Colleen

Hayward argues that First Nations have a sovereign right to see education delivered in culturally appropriate ways that may differ from community to community, nation to nation. Decisions about education belong to each nation. As Hayward argues:

> This community might say that's fine, but we want our kids to be literate and numerate in *our* language as well . . . What then varies from community to community is that [some will say], 'We want that to happen while the kids are at school, so we want some of our elders to come in and teach that', and others will say, 'Well our kids are going to do it too, but it's got nothing to do with you, that's our business. We're going to do it out bush' (quoted in Maddison 2009: 57).

Narungga, Kaurna and Ngarrindjeri education scholar Lester Irabinna Rigney also suggests a link between sovereignty and education, arguing for Indigenous jurisdiction and control rather than a view of Indigenous people as merely 'consumers' (2003: 77).

Learning in First Nations languages is essential to these programs if they are to see Indigenous children thrive. This is challenging in the settler Australian context where Indigenous languages continue to be lost at an alarming rate. Protecting and revitalising languages is seen as an urgent task. Cherry Wulumirr Daniels, who is the last fluent speaker of the Ngandi language, works at the Ngukurr Language Centre, a not-for-profit organisation trying to revitalise languages. Daniels admits to being tired, saying, 'Sometimes I feel I can't teach anymore', but says she worries about the future—'what will happen when I go?' (quoted in James 2017c). Her commitment is certainly valued. Grant Mathumba Thompson, who also works at the Ngukurr Language Centre, has been learning Ngandi, and says it has changed his life:

> Knowing, learning the languages has saved my life in a way I couldn't think of. It's given me responsibility. It's given me so much to look forward to. You find yourself in the deep ocean and to get to the bottom, language, my Ngandi, is like an oxygen. Before you get to the bottom, you realise how beautiful the ocean is—it's full of beautiful creatures, that's how beautiful Ngandi is to me, learning my language (quoted in James 2017c).

The ways in which language teaching occurs, however, is also a question to be determined by Indigenous nations rather than the settler state. This is not the case in New South Wales where the Department of Education operates five Aboriginal Language and Culture Nests across the state. Each 'Nest' is a network of communities that shares a connection to an Aboriginal language, and is intended to 'provide communities with opportunities to revitalise, reclaim and maintain their traditional languages' by involving communities, schools, universities and other community language programs or groups (NSW Department of Education n.d.). For some Indigenous educators, however, this approach takes away their right to determine for themselves how language revitalisation occurs. Gumbaynggirr man Clark Webb, an educator and the executive officer of the Bularri Muurlay Nyanggan Aboriginal Corporation, argues that:

> We feel it is our community that needs to drive the direction of our language and how they are taught and learnt, not the department. Rather than having an emphasis on reading and writing we need to have a greater emphasis on hearing, responding and speaking, because that's how we revitalise the language. I have zero confidence that the Department of Education is able to produce proficient speakers but through the community we can produce people who speak the language very well.

Gumbaynggirr Elder Uncle Barry Hoskins underscores the reasons for a lack of trust in a government department, saying:

> Aboriginal kids were actually punished for speaking language when I was at school, so how can the Department of Education now decide how my children and grandchildren learn our language? (both quoted in Mascarenhas 2016).

A further concern about education relates to the place of Aboriginal and Torres Strait Islander peoples and histories in the national education curriculum. Changes to the curriculum in 2015, intended to place greater emphasis on Australia's 'Christian heritage' and remove specific reference to Indigenous people from sections of the curriculum focused on 'Contributions to our society', drew the ire of Indigenous commentators. In reflecting on the changes, Murri consultant in creative industries and learning resources, Leesa Watego noted that in the new curriculum, Indigenous references were to be contained in history, geography and art. For Watego, such an approach

> flies in the face of our children's humanity, failing to see Aboriginal and Torres Strait Islander people as fully human. 'Aboriginal' thus becomes an historical issue, a geographical phenomena or an artistic approach. There is no science, economics, mathematics, political or legal dimension to Indigenous knowledges.

This, for Watego, was 'another slap in the face reminder that the way that Aboriginal and Torres Strait Islander peoples' stories, histories and voices are presented to the next generation of Australians is under the control of another' (quoted in Luke Pearson 2015b). Noonuccal man Chris Matthews from the Aboriginal and Torres Strait Islander Mathematics Alliance agrees, suggesting that the Australian government and the Australian Curriculum Authority 'simply do not understand the significance and importance of Indigenous content in the curriculum':

> Including Indigenous content in the national curriculum is for ALL students. It provides a platform for Indigenous people to see their culture, their language and their way of life valued by the education system. It provides a mechanism for having bilingual education, to support language and culture revival and, consequently supporting the identity, and health and wellbeing of Indigenous students ... It provides an opportunity for non-Indigenous people to learn our languages, to dance with us, sing with us, hear our stories and gain insight into our ancient and contemporary knowledges. It is about respectful relationships with clear benefits for us as a nation (quoted in Luke Pearson 2015b).

For Luke Pearson (2015b), the curriculum changes were further evidence of the colonial fantasy at work. For him, the changes were blatantly racist, driven by 'ideology, not best practice':

> These changes ignore that the invasion and colonisation of Australia is a part of a much larger story of colonialism, colonisation, and empire building ... It is about fighting to create an image of a peacefully 'settled' democratic White Australian history, in order to better justify a White Australian dominated future.

## RESURGENT WELLBEING

Resurgence is an idea and a set of practices that has been developed by Indigenous scholars in a different settler colonial context (Canada). Aboriginal and Torres Strait Islander peoples must decide for themselves if it is a concept that resonates and has meaning for them, just as measures of 'success' or 'progress' for the Aboriginal and Torres Strait Islander peoples can only be defined by Indigenous people themselves (Markham and Biddle 2017: 5). As many of the examples in this chapter (and earlier chapters) suggest, however, there are practices emerging all over the continent that we might call resurgence, which are both based in Aboriginal and Torres Strait Islander cultures and are directed towards Aboriginal and Torres Strait Islander self-determination and self-government. Almost 30 years ago, the late Yorta Yorta artist and activist Lin Onus (2003 [1990]: 94) observed the beginning of this movement:

> Dispossessed Aboriginal people throughout the country are presently engaged in the most extraordinary salvage operation. Strangely, very few non-Aboriginal experts seem to have noticed this phenomenon. Young people who had formerly been given up as 'lost' are enrolling in courses to speak Pitjantjatjara or Banjalong; not their original languages to be sure, but as an expression of desire for knowledge and cultural awareness this process is extremely significant. Language is the foundation upon which a cultural revival can be built . . .

Regardless of the language being used, it seems clear that more and more Aboriginal and Torres Strait Islander people are articulating the idea that resurgence and cultural revitalisation are deeply connected to social, physical and emotional wellbeing—ideas that First Nations have been researching and practising for decades. Arrernte Elder William Tilmouth suggests that:

> The right for Aboriginal people to *be* Aboriginal people is a key to 'Closing the Gap.' You won't 'close the gap' in quality of life by trying to 'fix' Aboriginal people. You need instead to fix the system of solutions which are repeatedly imposed on all our people (quoted in Children's Ground 2017).

Art, and its ties to culture and identity, is one important element of resurgence. Yindjibarndi artist Katie West (2016), who 'missed out on being born into Yindjibarndi society', describes this process as one of 'personal decolonisation.' For West, this process is one of 'shedding beliefs that provide no nourishment and seeking out ones that do':

> When I am walking to collect native plants for sculptures and bush dyeing,
> this is a chance to just focus on the task at hand. As I walk and gather
> I try to imagine how the landscape has morphed over the centuries. When I
> sew together fresh gum leaves and gum blossoms I wonder what other uses
> people had for these plants . . . In these moments of uncomplicated contem-
> plation I simply exist. I have no trauma. I have no anxiety.

Through her work West sees herself as sharing her 'personal antidote for the effects of colonisation' through 'an identity that both understands the legacy of colonisation and seeks to privilege Indigenous world views, philosophies and culture.'

Art is also being used to support the rehabilitation of Indigenous women and men who are incarcerated, such as through the Indigenous Arts in Prisons and Community Program run by Victorian organisation The Torch. Barkandji man and chief executive of The Torch, Kent Morris, describes art as the end of a process of cultural learning focused on the healing of intergenerational trauma. Morris suggests that people need to know where they are from, their stories, and their family histories and 'what the culture is', because

> what do you paint about if you don't really know who you are? It's a cultural
> vacuum in there and, for a lot of the men and women, part of the reason that
> they've ended up where they are is due to the impacts of colonisation and
> that removal of connection to country and culture and understanding your
> identity . . . That's why I reckon when we've got our own programs we know
> what's going on, because we've lived through it . . . If we put our fellas back
> together culturally with their identity, you don't know what that person's
> capable of (quoted in Mundy 2017: 8).

Traditional healing practices are also a part of Indigenous resurgence. The Ngaanyatjarra Pitjantjatjara Yankunytjatjara (NPY) Women's Council in Alice Springs employs traditional healers known as *ngangkari*, who use complex methods of touch, breath and spiritual healing in their work with mainstream health professionals. One of these *ngangkari*, Pitjantjatjara man Andy Tjilari, learned from his father 'how to work on the head and the body and give treatments and take away pain and make people feel well again.' In Tjilari's experience, Western and traditional medicine 'work incredibly well together' often at the request of Western doctors who show 'a lot of cooperation these days and respect' (quoted in Sleath 2013). Some of these traditional methods have travelled to the city, where the original local practices may have been lost. Kubbi Kubbi man Ken Zulumovski co-founded Gamarada, a not-for-profit community organisation that addresses issues contributing to suicide, self-harm, family violence, incarceration, addiction and homelessness. Zulumovski runs weekly sessions in Redfern in Sydney, where he teaches the ancient meditation tradition of *Dadirri*—'deep listening and quiet stillness'—which was passed to him from Ngangiwumirr Elder Miriam Rose Ungunmerr Baumann, from Daly River in the Northern Territory. Zulumovski, who has long worked in community-controlled health services, sees teaching this practice through organisations like Gamarada as 'an opportunity for me and others like me who've made positive change to come together with others who are more vulnerable or at risk' (quoted in Jenkins 2016b: 21).

Yuragmana munda–Jarm is a 25-year healing strategy developed at the Yura Yungi Medical Services in Halls Creek. Yura Yungi is an Aboriginal community-controlled health service that provides holistic, culturally appropriate services with integrated preventative programs. The Yuragmana munda–Jarm strategy combines modern and traditional healing practices. Wunmulla man Darrell Henry, who has worked as a psychologist in Aboriginal communities, wrote the strategy in consultation with the community. He explains that *Yuragmana munda* means 'your deepest inner spirit' in Djaru, and *Jarm* means the same in Kiga, the two language groups from the area. Henry says:

These are powerful words. And we're using them in this healing strategy because that's where the deepest social changes come from, spiritual regeneration . . . Our focus is on social change through healing, not coercion (quoted in Mundy 2013: 12).

Traditional and hybrid health strategies are not only being practised in remote areas like Halls Creek. The Winnunga Nimmityjah Aboriginal Health Service in Narrabundah in the Australian Capital Territory is the only Indigenous-run health service in the Territory and works with complex problems of comorbidity, mental and physical health issues and drug dependence. The service cares for 74 per cent of the ACT's Aboriginal and Torres Strait Islander residents and is trying to deal with the ongoing impact of the Stolen Generations on these communities. Ngiare Brown, a Yuin woman and medical specialist working with the service, articulates the challenge:

> When you are disconnected, when you do not know who you are, where you are from, what your language is or who your family is, then you are dysfunctional, you are lost and you are less resilient than you could be. When you are disconnected, outcomes in education, employment, economic stability, physical and mental health are all affected. I see all of these things impact on people's behaviour, mental health issues, post traumatic stress disorders, anxiety and depression, psychotic illness and in the early onset of chronic disease. I'm conscious that the environment of grandparents and great grandparents [who] experienced racism, discrimination and removal . . . has affected subsequent generations.

In light of these challenges, Brown advocates 'protecting and promoting cultural practice and cultural integrity', arguing that, 'If we can't get all their pieces back together, we will never have a whole person, we will never be well and we will never be able to pass [wellbeing] on to our children and their children' (quoted in Jacobs and Walmsley 2015).

The work of resurgence, of putting all the pieces back together, can only ever be effective if it is owned and controlled by Aboriginal and Torres Strait Islander peoples. As CEO of the National Institute for Aboriginal and Torres Strait Islander Health Research, Djugun and Yawuru man Romlie Mokak (2018: 301) has argued, 'to improve health and wellbeing outcomes, Aboriginal and Torres Strait Islander people—organisations, communities, individuals—must exercise agency, take control. And governments at all levels must let go.'

Years of settler control have only caused more harm and damage. Community-controlled organisations, working in self-determining and self-governing nations, are the only viable way that the 'gaps' will be closed.

# CHAPTER 8

# RECONCILIATION

In May 2000, an estimated 250,000 people walked across the Sydney Harbour Bridge to demonstrate their support for reconciliation between Aboriginal and Torres Strait Islander peoples and the Australian settler state. Over five-and-a-half hours, as a skywriter scrawled a giant 'SORRY' in the sky overhead, Indigenous and non-Indigenous Australians streamed towards the Sydney Opera House, where the event Corroboree 2000 was being held to mark the end of the formal Decade of Reconciliation. After years of turmoil in the relationship between Aboriginal and Torres Strait Islander people and settler society, this event was meant to be a turning point. The formal Australian reconciliation process had asked settler Australia to take a look in the mirror, a process made all the more confronting by the release of the reports from the Royal Commission into Aboriginal Deaths in Custody and the *Bringing Them Home* Inquiry. Not for the first time, settler Australia had been asked to reckon with the brutality of the nation's colonial foundations, and to make amends for past wrongs. For many people, the bridge walk—by any measure an extraordinary and beautiful event—symbolised a turning point in relations, a growing up of a settler state at last ready to confront its history and make some fundamental changes to this foundational relationship.

Such ambition was not to be realised. A different political reality was evident even as the marchers left the Harbour Bridge and walked towards the Opera House. Here they were greeted by First Nations groups protesting the limitations of a reconciliation process that they saw as providing no redress for colonial injustice, holding placards claiming 'No Reconciliation Without Justice,' 'Restore Land Rights Now' and 'Recognise Aboriginal Sovereignty' (Short 2008: 7). Inside, Prime Minister John Howard, who had refused to join the bridge walk, was jeered by a crowd angry at his continued refusal to make a formal apology to the Stolen Generations. The document presented at Corroboree 2000 was meant to be a Declaration *for* Reconciliation but had instead become a Declaration *Towards* Reconciliation. The inaugural chairman of the Council for Aboriginal Reconciliation, Patrick Dodson, (who had resigned in 1997 in protest at Howard's attitude to the reconciliation process) boycotted the ceremony, saying, 'I think it's appalling that you end a 10-year process with one quarto-size piece of paper with words on it. It's not going to go anywhere' (quoted in Davis 2010). Both before and after the event, Howard (2000) had taken to the media to reaffirm his opposition to a treaty between Aboriginal and Torres Strait Islander peoples and the state, declaring that 'an undivided united nation does not make a treaty with itself. I mean to talk about one part of Australia making a treaty with another part is to accept that we are in effect two nations.' In the end, settler aspirations for reconciliation with First Nations fell short.

Disappointment in reconciliation is not unique to Australia. Reconciliation as an idea, and as a practice, developed in societies emerging from periods of authoritarian rule or civil war and subsequently 'migrated' to established democracies like Australia and Canada as a framework for addressing historical injustice (Bashir and Kymlicka 2008: 4). Yet observing countries around the world that have attempted processes of reconciliation, non-Indigenous (and non-Australian) legal scholars Erin Daly and Jeremy Sarkin (2007: 146) contend that Australia presented

> the best possible conditions for the promotion of reconciliation—a generally liberal public, a tiny minority of people in the (therefore non-threatening) victim class, few perpetrators still alive to be punished or shamed (and therefore few people with a large stake in resisting the dissemination of the truth) and a prevalent morality that soundly rejects legalized racial oppression. Almost no one in Australia now maintains that the policies of the past were good, and few would argue publicly that they were justified even at the time they were promulgated and enforced.

Yet even with what were perceived to be such favourable conditions, the Australian reconciliation process is still widely considered to have failed. While the formal reconciliation process in Australia did introduce a new 'moral language' with which to speak about issues of colonial injustice, it did not resolve any of the questions that were raised by these issues (Pratt 2005: 157). There were no reparations, no significant improvements in socio-economic inequity between Indigenous and non-Indigenous people, and no treaty or 'document of reconciliation' that addressed the political grievances of Aboriginal and Torres Strait Islander peoples (Gunstone 2009: 147). It seems perhaps that Daly and Sarkin underestimate what is at stake for reconciliation in a settler colonial society.

Like each of the other policy areas that have been examined in this book, reconciliation in Australia proved itself vulnerable to the colonial fantasy in multiple ways. For settler societies, reconciliation is thought to present a unique opportunity to confront an unjust colonial history, resolve destructive colonial relationships, and enter a unified future—not through treaty but through rational agreement that leaves colonialism behind and 'completes' the post-colonial nation. Settler structures become 'newly legitimate, consolidated by consent and consensus' (Strakosch and Macoun 2012: 55–6). As Alissa Macoun (2016: 85) has argued, in settler societies, 'Reconciliation is about rescuing settler normalcy, about rescuing a settler future.' This fantasised future conceals the persistent assimilationist agenda contained within reconciliation's premises. Cloaked in the language of unity and nation building, reconciliation in Australia provided Aboriginal and Torres Strait Islander peoples with 'a right to be incorporated into the Australian nation but not a right to refuse' (Short 2005: 274). Megan Davis (2016b) points out the exceptionalism of Australia's reconciliation process has eschewed the 'twin pillars of truth and justice' that have been the bedrock of reconciliation processes elsewhere in the world. Absent from the reconciliation agenda has been any serious discussion about white-ness, systemic racism, decolonisation, self-determination, sovereignty or self-government. Aboriginal and Torres Strait Islander peoples have been denied the opportunity to pursue their claims regarding colonial injustice, and instead exhorted to focus only on future relations with settlers and the settler state.

What this suggests is that Indigenous peoples and settler states may participate in 'reconciliation' activities for quite different ends. Indigenous people want to see the truth about past harms generate a wider debate about contested sovereignty and collective rights in the present. For them, reconciliation is about building 'not a wall but a bridge', enabling them to 'draw history into the present' by highlighting the complex ways in which contemporary policy regimes perpetuate and reinscribe colonial injustices (Jung 2011: 231). Settler governments, however, address these same issues as a means of drawing a line under the past, driven by the desire to say to the nation that colonial injustices and abuses are a part of the nation's history and that present-day governments and settler citizens can no longer be held accountable. This, again, is the colonial fantasy at work, fostering the view among settler society that such issues have been resolved and the colonial project is complete.

RECONCILIATION AS PROMISE, RECONCILIATION IN PRACTICE

The formal Australian reconciliation process originally developed from a recommendation made by the Royal Commission into Aboriginal Deaths in Custody. The Commission's final recommendation argued that, 'reconciliation between the Aboriginal and non-Aboriginal communities in Australia must be achieved if community division, discord and injustice to Aboriginal people are to be avoided' (RCIADIC 1991: 65). After reneging on their promise to negotiate a national treaty and legislate for national land rights, the Hawke government announced a ten-year reconciliation process (1991–2000) and created the Council for Aboriginal Reconciliation (CAR) as, what they hoped would be, a political panacea. The Minister for Aboriginal Affairs at this time, Robert Tickner (2001: 29), later outlined what he saw as the three objectives for reconciliation in Australia. First, the need to educate non-Indigenous Australians about Aboriginal and Torres Strait Islander culture and the extent of disadvantage still experienced by Indigenous people. Second, the process needed to get onto the public agenda what Tickner—in an attempt to get away from the apparently polarising language of 'treaty'—described as a 'document of reconciliation.' Finally, Tickner envisaged that the reconciliation process would build a social movement that would drive the nation to 'address Indigenous aspirations, human rights and social justice.' The Council for Aboriginal Reconciliation echoed these ambitions, outlining 'eight key issues' as essential to assessing the process of reconciliation:

- a greater understanding of the importance of *land and sea* in Aboriginal and Torres Strait Islander societies;
- *better relationships* between Aboriginal and Torres Strait Islander peoples and the wider community;
- recognition that Aboriginal and Torres Strait Islander *culture and heritage* are a valued part of the Australian heritage;
- a sense for all Australians of a shared ownership of our *history*;
- a greater awareness of the causes of *disadvantage* that prevent Aboriginal and Torres Strait Islander peoples from achieving fair and proper standards in health, housing, employment and education;
- a greater community response to addressing the underlying causes of the unacceptably high *levels of custody* for Aboriginal and Torres Strait Islander peoples;
- greater opportunities for Aboriginal and Torres Strait Islander peoples to *control their destinies*; and
- agreement on whether the process of reconciliation would be advanced by a *document or documents* of reconciliation (CAR 2000: 13, emphasis in the original).

The education of non-Indigenous peoples in order to 'change their hearts and minds' was at the core of the Council's strategy and absorbed considerable effort and expenditure. Facilitating a deeper understanding of the nation's colonial history and its impact on Indigenous peoples was seen as crucial if any further structural or institutional change was to be possible. The Council actively encouraged changes in non-Indigenous attitudes through the development of learning materials such as the Australians for Reconciliation Study Circle Kit released in 1993, which was designed to enable small, self-directed groups to undertake an eight-week learning program exploring reconciliation and a range of Aboriginal and Torres Strait Islander issues (Gunstone 2009: 96; Maddison and Stastny 2016).

The Council for Aboriginal Reconciliation pursued this kind of 'bottom up' reconciliation process in the belief that social change would be inevitable once the non-Indigenous population was adequately educated about the needs and aspirations of Aboriginal and Torres Strait Islander people. Rather than prioritising Indigenous distinctiveness and difference, however, the CAR pursued a program focused on the overarching goal of national unity and identity (de Costa 2016: 55). Developing a formal agreement or treaty was not part of CAR's mandate.

In general terms, the CAR and its associated groups and organisations adopted very moderate, unthreatening language that would not 'offend the sensibilities of non-indigenous Australians' (Short 2008: 116), and pursued this agenda through the creation of new networks in civil society. What became known as 'the people's movement for reconciliation' drew in local councils, community groups, service clubs, churches, ethnic groups, conservation, youth, sporting and women's organisations. In its final report, the CAR (2000: 61) described the so-called 'people's movement' as 'one of the most celebrated outcomes of the work of the Council' contending that, 'Reconciliation has not ended with the finishing of the Council. The people's movement will take it forward.' The Declaration Towards Reconciliation, presented at Corroboree 2000, asked all Australians to 'make a commitment to go on together in a spirit of reconciliation.'

Since the end of the CAR, however, the momentum of the 'reconciliation movement' has dissipated. Reconciliation Australia (RA), the body established by the federal government to replace the CAR at the end of the Decade of Reconciliation, has been criticised for its strong focus on the corporate sector and relative neglect of smaller groups and grassroots activity. This approach has seen former CAR member (now federal MP) Linda Burney 'stepping away from the formal reconciliation process' because it

> didn't support the thing that will make reconciliation in the minds and actions of Australians a reality, and that is the grassroots movement. If you don't have that and if you're not engaging at a local level between Aboriginal and non-Aboriginal Australians, then I'm not quite sure what the point is (quoted in Maddison 2015: 191).

Reconciliation Australia's flagship program involves the development of Reconciliation Action Plans (RAPs), which support private and public organisations to 'identify clear actions with realistic targets that they can take to improve the relationship between Indigenous people and other Australians both within the organisation and more widely.' Actions might include cultural awareness training or targets relating to Indigenous employment and training. A 2012 evaluation of the program, undertaken by RA, concluded that RAPs have had a generally positive impact on employees in organisations that have developed them. For example, 75 per cent of employees in RAP organisations view the relationship between Indigenous people and other Australians as very important for Australia as a nation (Auspoll 2012). Nevertheless, a program such as this is about as far from structural reform as one could imagine, and the program has many critics who fail to see how individual plans will advance substantive change. One Indigenous community worker sees RAPs as reinforcing a 'colonisation mentality' in which the 'driving force [is] to lift Aboriginal people out of their mire' rather than acknowledge the colonial history that has produced contemporary Indigenous disadvantage. The former convenor of the New South Wales Reconciliation Council, Leanne Townsend, describes RAPs as little more than 'HR equity statements for corporations and businesses', which 'suits the government' because they create an impression of national action on Indigenous employment. Townsend asks, however, 'What are the real outcomes?' (both quoted in Maddison 2015: 158). The focus on RAPs has produced what Davis (2016b) describes as a hyper-optimistic form of 'philanthrocapitalism' underpinned by Indigenous success stories intended to satiate 'the constant thirst for upbeat, optimistic stories that give *white Australia* hope.' For Davis the avoidance of any formal reckoning with the truth of Australia's history suggests that Australia 'would like to skip the difficult part of reconciliation' and instead 'move immediately to recovery and a peaceful co-existence.' The desire for colonial completion has undermined the roots of Australian reconciliation.

Strategies such as community education and Reconciliation Action Plans suggest that Australia has not pursued reconciliation as a path towards decolonising relationships between First Nations and the settler state. Yet even this very modest and unthreatening approach still met with intense resistance from conservative forces in Australian politics. As early as the mid-1990s public discussion about reconciliation had become dominated by a heated debate about Australian colonial history, with renewed assertions of the modern-day economic, social and political benefits accruing to *all* Australians (including Aboriginal and Torres Strait Islander peoples) as a result of colonisation. The election of the Howard government saw a significant change in official attitudes towards the reconciliation process, with the rejection of anything thought to be merely 'symbolic' (discussions of sovereignty or treaty) and a new focus on the need to adopt 'practical measures' to address Indigenous disadvantage—a forerunner of the Closing the Gap policy discussed in Chapter Seven. This subversion of the Australian process was seen by many as the Howard government's attempt to divert reconciliation away from discussion of the need for structural changes in the relationship between Aboriginal and Torres Strait Islander peoples and the settler state, and towards a focus on socioeconomic disadvantage (Gunstone 2009: 145).

The change in strategy advanced by Howard confirmed the fears that many Aboriginal and Torres Strait Islander people had held about the formal reconciliation process from the outset, namely that it was an attempt to avoid a political settlement. As in other settler colonial societies, reconciliation in Australia became a means of justifying colonial domination rather than transforming the relationship between Indigenous peoples and the settler state. As Short (2008: 111) points out, this vision was 'a far cry from the restitution, compensation and acknowledgment demands made by the Treaty campaign from which the reconciliation process eventually emerged.' For many Aboriginal and Torres Strait Islander people, the process seemed to be little more than an exercise in colonial obfuscation of their ongoing dispossession and the persistence of settler colonial structures (Short 2008: 8). As the late poet and activist Kevin Gilbert expressed with force:

> What are we to reconcile ourselves to? To a holocaust, to massacre, to the removal of us from our land, from the taking of our land? The reconciliation process can achieve nothing because it does not at the end of the day promise justice (quoted in Mudrooroo 1995: 228).

By emphasising nation-building and national unity above all else, the formal Australian reconciliation process placed a 'colonial ceiling' on Indigenous aspirations towards decolonisation and political autonomy (Short 2008: 162). As in other settler states, reconciliation in Australia focused less on addressing colonial harms and more on the legitimacy of the settler order. By pursuing a strategy focused on the inclusion of Aboriginal and Torres Strait Islander peoples within the settler state, rather than advancing Indigenous demands for greater self-determination and self-government, the Australian reconciliation process merely perpetuated colonialism. As Henry Reynolds (2013: 237) has argued, reconciliation came down to white Australia saying to Indigenous Australia, 'we want to be reconciled':

> After living together on the same continent for so long we would like you to become fully incorporated into the nation. So come along now. But don't mention the war and don't expect us to honour your countrymen and women who died while resisting our invasion.

Yet despite these evident limitations to reconciliation in Australia, many Aboriginal and Torres Strait Islander people still support it as both a concept and a practice. For some this is a purely pragmatic belief. Aboriginal and Torres Strait Islander people make up only around 3 per cent of the total population, meaning that the attitudes of the non-Indigenous majority to Indigenous claims may effectively shape the political response. Others, however, remain committed to the ideal that a transformation in the relationship will be a valuable end in itself. A 2012 report, Yarn about Youth, co-authored by Reconciliation Australia (RA) and the Australian Youth Affairs Coalition (AYAC), found that the young people who participated in their survey and roundtable believe that 'stronger relationships between Aboriginal and Torres Strait Islander and non-Indigenous Australians are essential to achieving lasting change as well as genuine recognition of the effects of colonisation.' Young Wiradjuri and Dunghutti man, Blake Tatafu—the then AYAC Indigenous projects officer—described reconciliation as important because he wants to 'live in an Australia free from racism . . . where there is compassion and love and respect between every member of the Australian family.' For Tatafu, 'There's no single strand to reconciliation. It takes lots of people doing lots of different things sharing a common goal' (quoted in Koori Mail 2012b: 17). Some older Aboriginal and Torres Strait Islander people also retain a commitment to the process. The man known as the 'Father of Reconciliation', and the first chair of the Council for Aboriginal Reconciliation, Patrick Dodson, still believes that Australia 'can transcend the politics of fear and guilt as a nation and work towards a reconciliation based on truth-telling, healing and justice—wrongs can be righted' (quoted in Osborn 2017).

Others, however, remain unconvinced. Pakana woman Heather Sculthorpe, chief executive of the Tasmanian Aboriginal Centre, maintains that groups like Reconciliation Australia 'have been funded for a lot of years' but that she 'can't see that they've made enough change' to warrant a similar organisation being established in Tasmania. Instead, Sculthorpe argues, there needs to be 'financing of the Aboriginal community to find its own solutions' (quoted in Shine 2017). For Irene Watson (2002), reconciliation cannot even begin to occur 'until there is a return of what has been stolen from us.' As Tony Birch (2007: 112) observes, however, discussion of sovereignty and land justice was 'left behind in 2000' as discussion of material and structural reform would have 'taken the reconciliation pageantry beyond symbolism into fraught political territory.'

At the end of the formal decade of reconciliation, the Final Report of the Council for Aboriginal Reconciliation made a series of broad recommendations intended to advance the reconciliation project. These recommendations focused on overcoming Indigenous disadvantage; legislating to enshrine the principles of reconciliation; committing to supporting reconciliation including through the creation of Reconciliation Australia; initiating a referendum that would recognise Aboriginal and Torres Strait Islander peoples in the Australian Constitution; and pursuing the negotiation of a treaty or agreement that would protect the political, legal, cultural and economic position of Aboriginal and Torres Strait Islander peoples. The Council asserted that if these recommendations and strategies were acted upon, then Australia would have 'a solid claim to asserting itself as a reconciled nation' (CAR 2000: ix). Almost two decades later, however, such ambition has clearly not been achieved. The quest for reconciliation continues to elude settler Australia. As Galarrwuy Yunupingu (2016) writes:

The Australian people know that their success is built on the taking of the land, in making the country their own, which they did at the expense of so many languages and ceremonies and songlines—and people— now destroyed. They worry about what has been done for them and on their behalf, and they know that reconciliation requires much more than just words.

Yet despite this knowledge, settler Australia continues to evade and contest the truth of their very existence.

## APOLOGY AND THE ONGOING QUEST FOR TRUTH

> Listen! Can't you hear country keeping its peoples' memories beating strongly, everybody heard? It's the pulse of all our broken hearts crying for families lost in the war we keep having, the children we keeps losing (Wright 2018: 46).

On 13 February 2008, during the first sitting of the new parliament, the newly elected prime minister, Kevin Rudd, made a moving speech in the House of Representatives. In a moment that had been long anticipated, Rudd acknowledged that:

> The time has now come for the nation to turn a new page in Australia's history by righting the wrongs of the past and so moving forward with confidence to the future. We apologise for the laws and policies of suc- cessive Parliaments and governments that have inflicted profound grief, suffering and loss on these our fellow Australians. We apologise especially for the removal of Aboriginal and Torres Strait Islander children from their families, their communities and their country. For the pain, suffering and hurt of these Stolen Generations, their descendants and for their families left behind, we say sorry. To the mothers and the fathers, the brothers and the sisters, for the breaking up of families and communities, we say sorry. And for the indignity and degradation thus inflicted on a proud people and a proud culture, we say sorry (Rudd 2008).

Public events around the country enabled many thousands of Indigenous and non-Indigenous people to watch the national apology to the Stolen

Generations via live stream. In response, there was an outpouring of
emotion; feelings of joy, relief and gratitude that a wrong had at last been
acknowledged and that the nation was perhaps better for having done so.

In many ways, Kevin Rudd's apology was seen as the belated conclusion
to the Australian reconciliation process—the conclusion that Howard had
so vociferously resisted. An apology to the Stolen Generations was first recommended in the *Bringing Them Home* report in 1997, which documented
the forcible removal of Indigenous children from their families under past
policies of protection and assimilation, which the authors charged constituted an act of genocide contrary to the UN Convention on Genocide.
The report recommended that all Australian governments should officially
and publicly apologise to the Stolen Generations and their families for the
harms done. The Howard government contested the findings of the report
and ruled out any formal apology to the individuals and families that had
been devastated by practices of child removal and institutionalisation. The
debates that followed focused on the fundamental question of whether
past injustice should be judged by contemporary moral standards, with
many Aboriginal and Torres Strait Islander people insisting that coming to
terms with the wrongs of Australia's history was a vital prelude to genuine
reconciliation (Reynolds, 2013: 31). Howard's refusal to apologise sparked
a decade-long movement, beginning with the first Sorry Day held on the
anniversary of the release of the *Bringing Them Home* report. The movement
eventually collected hundreds of thousands of signatures in Sorry Books,
all calling for a national apology. Without an apology, reconciliation was
considered impossible.

Apologies of the kind made in Australia are a deeply symbolic means of
publicly expressing responsibility and regret for past wrongs, particularly by
political elites who are seeking to rebuild damaged relationships (Verdeja
2009: 79, 83). Perhaps unsurprisingly, however, the eventual apology from
the Australian settler state fell short of expectations in multiple ways.
Without questioning the intentions of any individual or group involved
in seeing the apology made, the event itself can also be understood as a
prime example of a settler state *appearing* to respond to First Nations' claims
without in fact changing any of the structures that continue to contain and
oppress Indigenous peoples (Simpson 2017: 46). Indeed, despite significant

consultation with Aboriginal and Torres Strait Islander peoples around the continent, the eventual text of the apology was overtly nation-building and assimilatory in tone. In his speech Rudd addressed Aboriginal and Torres Strait Islander people as 'fellow Australians' rather than acknowledging their sovereignty. The apology omitted any reference to the genocidal nature of child removal outlined in the *Bringing Them Home* report, thereby failing to place this atrocity in the wider context of the settler drive to eliminate Indigenous peoples (Muldoon and Schaap 2012: 184, 188). In ruling out any discussion of compensation or reparation (beyond the establishment of the Healing Foundation) before the speech was even made, the state maintained its authority to determine which Indigenous claims may be recognised and what reparation would or would not be made in response to these claims (Balint et al 2014: 209–10). The racialised, colonial nature of this authority was only underscored when, a decade later, Malcolm Turnbull announced that his government *would* pay compensation to victims of institutionalised child sexual abuse (see Graham 2018 for discussion). Thus, in an important sense, the apology was used to strengthen rather than challenge the legitimacy of the settler state, leaving settler domination untroubled. Such an apology is imagined as a moment of colonial completion. As Elizabeth Strakosch (2016: 29–30) argues, by apologising it is imagined that 'we enter into a completely new phase. We are released from a past that has captured us in the present and finally enter into a delayed and non-colonial future'— the colonial fantasy writ large.

This critique does not override the fact that the apology was an important moment in which Aboriginal and Torres Strait Islander counter-narratives to settler versions of history could be heard and—however briefly—acknowledged. The stories that had been recounted in the *Bringing Them Home* report—stories of trauma and grief and loss—which had been diminished and disregarded by previous governments, were at last acknowledged as real, as horrific, and as inexcusably wrong. The tears shed that day were for children lost, for families broken, and for cultures destroyed in the pursuit of colonial completion. As Harvard law professor Martha Minow (2000: 244) suggests, 'Tears in public will not be the last tears, but knowing that one's tears are *seen* may grant a sense of acknowledgment that makes grief less lonely and terrifying.' For many of the Aboriginal and Torres Strait

Islander people who heard Rudd's apology, having their tears finally seen and honoured was a moment of relief and of hope.

In part the hope that flowed from the apology rests in a deeper belief about the role of truth in transforming relationships. There is a sustained view among both Aboriginal and Torres Strait Islander people *and* settlers that knowing the truth about Australia's colonial history will in itself prove transformative of the relationship between Indigenous peoples and settler society. Contesting the heroic settler narratives of Australian colonialism has been an important project advanced by Indigenous historians and other scholars. These critical histories have refused to allow colonial injustice to be excused as incidental to the nation-building agenda. As we have seen in previous chapters, the past lives on in Aboriginal and Torres Strait Islander lives, and the consequences of colonialism are experienced as a daily, embodied reality. Forgetting the past—'moving on' as Indigenous people are so often exhorted to do—is simply not a possibility. As Tony Birch (2007: 112) has argued, 'While governments, populist conservatives and some self-proclaimed Indigenous "leaders" promote versions of forgetting in order to facilitate "progress," other Indigenous people have refused the offer of a future without an identity.'

This desire for truth was evident again in the Statement from the Heart's call for a process of 'truth-telling about our history', which is deemed necessary before agreements can be negotiated (Referendum Council 2017a). In Australia to date there has been no process officially labelled a truth commission, although three processes—the Royal Commission into Aboriginal Deaths in Custody (RCIADIC), the Inquiry into the Separation of Aboriginal and Torres Strait Islander Children from their Families, and the work of the CAR—have each contributed to efforts to deal with the past by investigating forms of historic and ongoing violence (Read 2010: 286–7). The Inquiry into the Separation of Aboriginal Children from their Families, for example, received written submissions and oral evidence from Indigenous organisations, government representatives and former govern-ment employees, church representatives and NGOs, including confidential evidence taken in private from Aboriginal and Torres Strait Islander people affected by the policies and from adoptive and foster parents. The *Bringing Them Home* report included harrowing evidence of the forcible removal of

Indigenous children that it charged constituted an act of genocide contrary to the United Nations Convention on Genocide (Short 2008: 93, 98). Peter Read (2010: 288) describes the accusation of genocide as opening a 'hornet's nest.'

And herein lies one significant problem with the idea that knowing the 'truth' will transform political relationships. On the one hand, it is clear that the *Bringing Them Home* findings did indeed influence efforts to transform Indigenous–settler relations. Although the issue of child removal had not been seen as significant enough to warrant mention in the preamble to the Australian reconciliation legislation, following the release of the report it became central to the reconciliation process, opening a new space for Aboriginal and Torres Strait Islander experiences of abuse and suffering to enter the public domain (Short 2008: 99). As discussed above, the 2008 apology was an eventual acknowledgement that these experiences had been heard and believed; indeed, knowledge of the Stolen Generations is the only publicly accepted (although certainly not by everyone) narrative of significant wrongdoing towards Aboriginal and Torres Strait Islander peoples (Read 2010: 288). On the other hand, however, the process of truth-telling that produced the *Bringing Them Home* report also unleashed the 'history wars.' Critical historians met 'sharp resistance' from a public that had been schooled in a 'comforting and deeply ideological story' that downplayed the violence of colonisation (Reynolds 2013: 27). Conservative historians found a new platform from which to argue that critics of Australian colonial history were doing nothing more than advancing a 'black armband view of history.' This view was taken up by John Howard (1996) when he argued that, in contrast to the 'black armband' view, by his reckoning the 'balance sheet' of Australian history was dominated by 'heroic achievement.' Howard's intransigence ensured that the impact of Australia's most concerted effort at truth-telling was contained to the symbolic recognition in the eventual apology to the Stolen Generations.

As the chapters in this book make clear, little has changed for Aboriginal and Torres Strait Islander people in the decade since the apology was made. Commemorating the anniversary of the apology has become a public relations exercise in 'soft reconciliation' when, as Goori writer Jack Latimore (2018a) suggests, it should be 'the sharpest spur to the side of government' that 'should stand principally as a day of shame and accountability'. Yet it seems hard to imagine that any future exercise in truth-telling would be any more successful in debunking the colonial fantasy, or indeed more substantively transformative in the way that so many Aboriginal and Torres Strait Islander people desire.

Nevertheless, a need for truth-telling is seen as a necessary step 'prior to a constitutional reform or as part of a Treaty negotiation' (Referendum Council 2017b: 32). Megan Davis (2017a: 4) reports that during the Referendum Council dialogues, in 'region after region'

> this word 'truth' came to the fore. The dialogues spoke of the wound caused by the silencing of the Aboriginal experience after the arrival. In North Queensland they spoke about how their ancestors saw Cook, telling one another with smoke, yet the history books still say he 'discovered' us. Frontier wars, massacres and forced racial segregation on reserves and missions are not commonly known by fellow Australians. Some spoke of statues being erected to honour early Australian explorers, one in north Australia holding a gun to commemorate the opening up of the frontier for the telegraph line, while the descendants of the massacred families suffer only sadness and hurt at having to see it. They spoke of the sensitivity of these 'one way' commemorations of Australian history.

Stan Grant has echoed this call for truth-telling, suggesting that while in the past he was cautious about such initiatives, concerned that they might 'harden division', today he is of the view that Australia needs 'this mirror into our soul . . . a full reckoning of our nation's past, that may set loose the chains of history that bind this country's first and, today, most miserably impoverished people' (quoted in Mitchell 2016: 3–4). For Davis (2017a: 4), this is the only way to restart a meaningful reconciliation process. She suggests that reconciliation in Australia 'has stalled because it failed to do what reconciliation should do: talk about the truth.' Recent debate suggests that settler Australia is still eager to avoid this conversation.

TEAR DOWN THE STATUES? CHANGE THE DATE?
Two contemporary debates about the ways in which settler Australia memorialises its history lend weight to questions about the capacity for truth to be transformative. The generic facts of the invasion and colonisation of this

continent are widely known, at least on the east coast where invasion began. In August 1770 Captain James Cook declared possession of the east coast of what is now known as Australia in the name of the King of Great Britain. Despite instructions from the King that he should take possession of the land 'with the consent of the natives' Cook acted contrary to this order and sought no such consent or agreement. When Captain Arthur Phillip raised the British flag at Sydney Cove on 26 January 1788, creating the colony of New South Wales, he also ignored instructions from the King by failing to 'open an intercourse with the natives, and to conciliate their affections, enjoining all our subjects to live in amity and kindness with them.' The land these men colonised was clearly populated by Indigenous nations, as it had been for some 60,000 years prior to the arrival of the British. As colonialism was unfurled across the continent over subsequent years, nation after nation after nation was invaded, brutalised, massacred and dispossessed.

These broad facts are not disputed. At a fundamental level the truth is known. Nevertheless, despite these well-known facts, today both Cook and Phillip are memorialised in statues around the country, including Cook in Sydney's Hyde Park and Phillip nearby in the Botanical Gardens. On the base of Cook's statue, erected in 1879, is an inscription that reads 'Discovered this territory 1770.' Phillip's statue is more technically accurate, inscribed only 'First Governor of New South Wales 1788–1792.' Elsewhere in Hyde Park, there is also a statue of Governor Lachlan Macquarie, the fifth Governor of New South Wales and the last to oversee it as a penal colony before it became a 'free settlement.' The inscription on Macquarie's statue is particularly prosaic, beginning with the words, 'He was a perfect gentleman, a Christian and supreme legislator of the human heart.' Macquarie's mausoleum on a remote Scottish island is maintained by the National Trust of Australia and is inscribed 'the Father of Australia.'

In a settler colonial context, where truth allegedly has some currency, each of these monuments is problematic. Following from the Rhodes Must Fall movement, which migrated from Cape Town to Oxford, and campaigns to remove Confederate monuments and statues of Columbus and other colonists in the United States, there has been renewed debate on the appropriateness of publicly memorialising historical figures known to be responsible for atrocities and injustice. As Tony Birch (2017: 2) observes, in Australia these monuments represent a mythical history that ignores the brutal reality of colonialism:

> At present, these bronzed heroes stand unchallenged, representing either a fictional history of terra nullius or the passive conquest of a land inhabited by unproductive 'savages' awaiting British ingenuity and capitalist exploitation. Such histories do not venture beyond myth. Aboriginal nations were invaded. Many people suffered horrific violence. And in the decades and centuries following the original killing fields of the frontier, communities continued (and continue) to suffer government policies, such as the forced removal of children, dedicated to the extinction of Aboriginal people.

Public debate about these kinds of monuments was reignited in 2017 when Stan Grant (2017a) wrote of his discomfort over the Cook statue in Hyde Park. Grant wrote that when 60,000 people turned out to see the statue unveiled in 1879, 'No-one present then questioned that this was the man who founded the nation.' But, he suggested, 'think about that today. Think of those words: "Discovered this territory":

> My ancestors were here when Cook dropped anchor. We know now that the first peoples of this continent had been here for at least 65,000 years, for us the beginning of human time. Yet this statue speaks to emptiness, it speaks to our invisibility; it says that nothing truly mattered, nothing truly counted until a white sailor first walked on these shores. The statue speaks still to *terra nullius* and the violent rupture of Aboriginal society and a legacy of pain and suffering that endures today.

Grant pointed out that while there are monuments across Australia that honour 'those who drove Aboriginal people from their lands', the Australian War Memorial still has no place on its wall of remembrance 'for those Aboriginal people who died on our soil fighting to defend their country.'

Grant's article sparked an extraordinary response from both supporters and detractors. In Melbourne, non-Indigenous artist Ben Quilty advanced a similar call, arguing that John Batman's statue should be removed from Melbourne's CBD. Quilty described Batman, one of the so-called 'founding fathers' of the city of Melbourne, as a 'mass murderer' who 'makes the American Confederates look friendly' (quoted in Hinchliffe 2017).

In Sydney, protestors who also apparently agreed with Grant's position made their own statements on the statues, spray-painting 'no pride in genocide' and 'change the date' (a reference to the campaign to change the date of Australia Day, discussed further below) on Cook's statue, and similar statements on the statues of Lachlan Macquarie and Queen Victoria. Grant himself was critical of these actions.

The conservative response, however, was much more vicious. Although Grant had not suggested that Cook's statue be torn down, merely that the inscription be changed to acknowledge the Indigenous presence before his arrival, Prime Minister Malcolm Turnbull described this suggestion as 'Stalinist' and declared that:

> Trying to edit our history is wrong. All of those statues, all of those monuments, are part of our history and we should respect them and preserve them—and by all means, put up other monuments, other statues and signs and sights that explain our history (quoted in K. Murphy 2017b).

Others were more vicious still. Right-wing columnist Andrew Bolt (2017) described Grant as part of something he called the 'Taliban Left', prosecuting the idea that a call for more truthful historical monuments is somehow akin to the actions of a violent, totalitarian regime. Unpersuaded, Grant (2017b) responded by noting that:

> It seems to have taken some people by surprise, the idea that people were here for more than 60,000 years before the Endeavour dropped anchor. What were we doing all that time, just waiting for white people to find us? And to dare challenge this 'discovery'; how impertinent. I can hear someone saying, 'know your place.'

Aboriginal and Torres Strait Islander people express a range of views about the place of these statues in contemporary society. Speaking of Melbourne's Batman statue, Wemba Wemba and Wergaia historian Dean Stewart suggests that Batman's story was unknown to many Melburnians and should be told rather than buried. Stewart describes Batman, whose own diary discussed leading a massacre of a sleeping village and executing the injured, as a young guy who made his name as a bounty hunter killing Tasmanian Aboriginal people. He was a major player in the 'black wars' of the 1820s, which was a government-sanctioned genocide of the Palawa people. That's how he made his name, that's how he built his massive estate over in Kingston, and that's how he got his wealth (quoted in Hinchliffe 2017).

But Stewart also suggests there was some kind of 'karma' to Batman's story, pointing out that after investing his wealth in the Port Phillip Association only for the other 'founding fathers' to 'rip him off', Batman was afflicted with syphilis, which rotted off his nose, and was ostracised by the white community, eventually being wheeled around the town in a barrow by two Aboriginal men who were among the few people who would still acknowledge him. Stewart says this story is one that leaves him only with 'pity' for Batman, and maintains that while, 'Most Melburnians don't know this history' it is a story that 'shouldn't be lost' (quoted in Hinchliffe 2017).

Even statues such as those of Lachlan Macquarie, which causes particular offence due to the incontrovertible record of his violence towards Indigenous peoples, is thought to hold some educative value. Indigenous artist and curator Tess Allas believes that Macquarie—who ordered the massacre of Indigenous people in western Sydney and instructed his troops to hang the victims from trees in order to terrorise the survivors—should not be 'honoured' through his statue, asking, 'How is it possible to honour such a fellow and still believe our society is a just society?' But rather than seeing the statue removed, Allas suggests that providing more accurate information about Macquarie's role in the violent dispossession of the Eora nation would be more appropriate—'The full story of Macquarie's governorship should be added to reflect his whole story' (quoted in A. Taylor 2017). Bronwyn Carlson, an Aboriginal woman born on D'harawal country and head of the Department of Indigenous Studies at Macquarie University, agrees, suggesting that Australia needs to 'mature' and 'come to terms with its brutal colonial history'; to learn how to teach history 'without celebrating those who ordered and participated in massacres' (quoted in A. Taylor 2017).

Non-Indigenous genocide historian Dirk Moses (2017: 1–2) argues that ignoring Aboriginal and Torres Strait Islander claims for a more accurate representation of history is merely 'repeating the silences that led to the erection of these monuments in the first place, and concealing a truth that dare not speak its name.' But, Moses argues, 'repressing the ugly colonial past' will not change the historical record. He suggests that if settler Australians 'wish no longer to be haunted by the past' they will need to 'negotiate national symbols that don't symbolically repeat the violence.' Yet settler Australia seems determined to cling to its old symbols, whatever the facts. Not only did the Turnbull government announce in April 2018 that they would build a new $3 million memorial to Cook at Botany Bay, but new symbols, such as those acknowledging massacres and other traumatic events seem to remain intolerable. Indeed, in contrast to the reverence shown towards statues of white colonists, the few public memorials to Aboriginal and Torres Strait Islander history have been repeatedly vandalised. In Perth, the bronze statue of the Noongar resistance fighter Yagan, whose head was sent to England after he was killed by white settlers in 1833, was itself beheaded when vandals took to it with an angle grinder in 1997. The statue was repaired, but later beheaded again. And in New South Wales the Myall Creek Massacre and Memorial Site was subject to vandalism when in 2005, the words 'murder' and 'women and children' were hammered out of the metal plaques (Dovey 2017). In a country that has four or five thousand war memorials honouring soldiers who died in overseas combat, these van-dalised monuments are among only a handful commemorating frontier conflict (Reynolds 2013: 237).

The other contemporary—and recurrent—debate about the 'truth' of Australia's colonial history concerns the date of settler society's national day of celebration: Australia Day. As noted in the opening of this book, this is a day that produces strong sentiment among many Aboriginal and Torres Strait Islander people. Indeed, each year there is both heated debate and passionate protest about the continuing celebration of the day that formally began the invasion of First Nations' territories. As Jack Latimore (2018b) argues, the 'overwhelming sentiment' about Australia Day among Aboriginal and Torres Strait Islander peoples is 'an uneasy blend of melancholy approaching outright grief, of profound despair, of opposition and antipathy, and always of staunch defiance.' For First Nations, Latimore points out, 'The day and date is steeped in the blood of violent dispossession, of attempted genocide, of enduring trauma', leading to a shared understanding among Aboriginal and Torres Strait Islander peoples 'that there has been no conclusion of the white colonial project when it comes to the commonwealth's approach to Indigenous people'. Such views are widely expressed. Bundjalung woman and CEO of Reconciliation Australia, Karen Mundine suggests that, 'Asking Indigenous people to celebrate on January 26 is like asking them to dance on their ancestors' graves'. Richard Weston contends that for most Aboriginal and Torres Strait Islander people, 'It is impossible to celebrate when it brings to mind the deep hurt borne by our ancestors and how that suffering continues to impact today' (both quoted in Wahlquist and Karp 2018). In a speech in the Senate, Patrick Dodson acknowledged that although his party (the Australian Labor Party) does not support changing the date, he understands that for many Aboriginal and Torres Strait Islander people 26 January continues to represent 'dispossession and sadness—a legacy we struggle with in this nation and in this place, constantly . . .' (quoted in Wahlquist and Karp 2018).

This is a truth that is surely hard to avoid. While settler Australia seeks to celebrate the glory of this colonial founding moment, Karen Wyld (2018) points out that 'there are other versions of this story':

> Truths that many have tried to erase from both books and memories, and even the tongues of First Peoples. Accounts of invasion, waves of violence, loss and grief, and culturally-biased control—as well as resistance, self-determination, strength and survival.

Henry Reynolds (2017), like many others, ask why so many Australians want to 'commemorate an act of egregious injustice? And why fail to recognise that it predetermined the great tragedy that unfolded over the whole continent for generations to come?' More simply, Irene Watson (2018) asks, 'Why celebrate this violent colonial history of genocide? Who does this?'

Yet the vitriol that attends the annual debate about changing or abolishing the date of Australia Day suggests that many settlers do indeed want to commemorate these events, or at the very least not have their January long weekend disrupted by historical reflection. Others continue to deny that colonisation is in fact problematic at all. Former prime minister, Tony Abbott declared in a radio interview that:

What happened on the 26th of January 1788 was on balance, for everyone—
Aboriginal people included—a good thing because it brought Western
civilisation to this country, it brought Australia into the modern world
(quoted in SBS 2018a).

More recently, Malcolm Turnbull's replacement as prime minister, Scott
Morrison, weighed into the conversation by tweeting on 23 September
2018 that:

Indulgent self-loathing doesn't make Australia stronger. Being honest about
the past does. Our modern Aus nation began on January 26, 1788. That's the
day to reflect on what we've accomplished, become, still to achieve. We can
do this sensitively, respectfully, proudly, together.

Two days later Morrison dismissed the trauma of colonisation as 'a few
scars' while proposing that 26 January should remain the national day, but
suggesting that a new day for recognising and celebrating Aboriginal and
Torres Strait Islander people and culture might be found. This, for many
Indigenous people, profoundly missed the point of their protests about
26 January. As the Wirlomin Noongar author Claire Coleman (2018)
pointed out, First Nations 'don't want a celebration of how we "contributed" to Australia ... we want white people to stop celebrating the day they
invaded us.'

Views such as Abbott's and Morrison's fly in the face of Australia's historical truth and perpetuate the colonial fantasy. Luke Pearson (2017d) argues
that despite 'overwhelming evidence to the contrary', the attitudes expressed
by Australian politicians suggest that

white people know best and that the theft of land and resources and the
attempted destruction of Aboriginal lives, families, communities, languages,
and sacred sites is so much in the best interests of Aboriginal people that
they should actually be thankful for it. Such is the pathological paternalism
of colonial oppression.

Arrernte writer and unionist Celeste Liddle (2017a) suggests that
references to 'Amnesia Day' might be more appropriate given the 'deeply
embedded amnesia' that affects those seemingly unable to remember

injustices such as massacres or the Stolen Generations. These amnesiacs also seem to forget the annual conversation about these issues only to again 'expect Indigenous people to happily assimilate into the festivities' the following year. The comedian Steven Oliver (2018), who is of Kuku-Yalanji, Waanyi, Gangalidda, Woppaburra, Bundjalung and Biripi descent, suggests that even those settler Australians who do not see the politics of the day could

> spare a thought for the thousands of Aboriginal lives that were taken and that have been affected and think of what it must have been and continues to be like. I'm not asking you to dwell on it, just think about it in the way you would Gallipoli. You don't need to feel guilty because you didn't actually take anyone's life but it is because of the price they paid that you enjoy the benefits you do and that at its very least, deserves consideration.

Not all Aboriginal and Torres Strait Islander people support the campaign to change the date. Some, like Alice Springs town councillor Jacinta Nampijinpa Price, daughter of former Country Liberal Party minister Bess Price, contend that a focus on Indigenous disadvantage is more important than an analysis of history, which she sees as an agenda important only to privileged, middle-class Indigenous people. While pointing out that the 2008 apology to the Stolen Generations 'had not changed things for the better,' Price insists that:

> Our future is where we should be focused, so that the most marginalised Aboriginal people of this country whose first language is usually not English, who do not have access to media, whose lives are affected at alarming rates by family violence can have the same opportunities as those who claim to feel pain because a country celebrates how lucky we are on a date that marks the arrival of the First Fleet (quoted in Gorey 2017).

In 2018 Price joined forces with the former federal Labor leader turned conservative commentator Mark Latham to appear in a bizarre 'Save Australia Day' advertising campaign depicting a dystopian future in which Australians were frightened to openly celebrate the national holiday. Despite strong criticism of her involvement in the campaign, Price maintained that she was tired of Indigenous voices being 'lumped together', saying:

We've got to stop painting each other with the same brush . . . not all white
people are racists and not all Aboriginal people are feeling like they are
victims of our country's history (quoted in SBS News 2018b).

Other Aboriginal and Torres Strait Islander people, however, are opposed
to changing the national holiday for very different reasons. For some,
changing the date would not go far enough to address colonial injustice.
Tiwi, Larrakia Chinese and Muslim woman Eugenia Flynn (2018) suggests
that 'soft entreaties' to change the date

> only moves the celebration of unfinished business to another date. Another
> date on which to celebrate 'the country we are now' and 'how lucky' we all
> are will only continue Australia Day's tradition of denial . . . Such tools of
> nationalism are soft in nature, smoothing over racial inequities in order to
> present a 'great country', one that is then worthy of celebration—just on a
> different date.

Celeste Liddle (2017a) agrees, suggesting that 'changing the date would
be little more than celebrating the invasion and genocide of Indigenous
people on another day.' Karen Wyld (2018) also thinks that it is the day itself
that needs to change, not just the date:

> Change the day to tell the real stories of Australia. If we cannot even manage
> to tell truthful stories, we cannot address the ongoing injustices caused by
> colonisation. If we continue to give preference to a whitewashed history,
> then what are settler-colonists really celebrating every Australia Day, regard-
> less of the date? Attempted conquest.

As Natalie Cromb (2018a) points out, protests about the date of Australia
Day are not about the day itself. The day, Cromb suggests, is 'a symbol of a
much larger problem that pervades Australian society' in which 'Indigenous
issues are debated by the majority, decided by the majority and policies are
drafted and implemented by the majority.' Continuing a national celebration on a date that many Aboriginal and Torres Strait Islander people clearly
find painful and offensive serves to perpetuate the gross power imbalances
inherent to colonial relations. As Eugenia Flynn (2018) points out, for many
Aboriginal and Torres Strait Islander people, January 26 is a day with a

different history and a different set of meanings. A history of Indigenous protest on this date means that rather than being a day consumed only by 'offence and hurt', January 26 is also 'used by First Nations activists to mourn ongoing oppression, assert sovereignty and demand Land Rights.' These protests will not stop if the date of Australia's national day should change, because they point to the far more substantive and structural problems that continue to form the bedrock of relations between Aboriginal and Torres Strait Islander peoples and settler Australia.

IS A DIFFERENT RELATIONSHIP POSSIBLE?
In the Introduction to this book I noted a list of anniversaries that were marked in 2017—anniversaries of events that each, in their time, had the potential to transform the relationship between Aboriginal and Torres Strait Islander peoples and the settler state. In 2018 several other anniversaries were marked that were of equal significance, if for very different reasons. 26 January 2018 was the eightieth anniversary of the Day of Mourning march in 1938, in which Indigenous campaigners including Doug Nicholls, Jack Patten, Bill Cooper, Pearl Gibbs and Margaret Tucker gathered around 100 supporters to protest Australia's sesquicentenary, despite the existence of 'protection' laws that restricted Aboriginal and Torres Strait Islander peoples' freedom of movement. 26 January 2018 was also the thirtieth anniversary of the 1988 March for Freedom, Hope and Justice, which saw more than 40,000 people, including First Nations representatives from all over the country, converge in Sydney to disrupt settler celebrations of the bicentennial of the arrival of Phillip and the First Fleet (Latimore 2018b).

Many Aboriginal and Torres Strait Islander people are still seeking transformation of their relationship with the Australian settler state, based on truth and justice. What is clear, however, is that what settlers want from reconciliation, and what Indigenous peoples want in a transformed relationship with the settler, are profoundly, perhaps incommensurably different. There is a strong sentiment, although not universally or constantly held, that many First Nations people want, as Stan Grant (2016a: 2) has argued, for settler Australians to 'get out of our lives! The ignorant, the racist, the well intentioned, whoever: just stop.' Yingiya Mark Guyula (2016) puts it slightly differently when he writes:

We want our power back we want to do our own justice, we want to do
our own discipline, we want to be who we are, who we have been for over
40,000 years of culture that has been here and survived. We want our system
of law to be recognised. I will speak for my people, what the voices are saying;
'Give us our power back, give us our freedom back, give us our life back.' We
want treaty. We want a partnership. We want a dialogue in decision-making.
We want diplomatic discussions with the government, the Yolŋu government and the balanda government working together, making decisions for
our people together.

There is no way to answer the question 'what do Indigenous people
want?' without asking that question of every Aboriginal and Torres Strait
Islander person on the continent. It may not be possible to know precisely
who or what to ask until the necessary work has been done to revive and
restore Indigenous nationhood where it has been damaged. There will
be some Indigenous nations that want only the most minimal relationship with the settler state—seeking only reparations, support to establish
their own governance structures, and then to be left alone. Tony Birch
(2017) looks to a new generation of Indigenous activists who have learned
from the activists before them, but who have 'found their own voice'; a
voice that is 'rowdy and at times, justifiably angry.' The pathways for these
young activists, according to Birch 'will be forged in action and a call for
self-determination rather than hollow symbolism and a patronising call
to display patience.'
      There will be others that seek to negotiate a closer relationship between
settler and Indigenous nations, and these negotiations will vary as much as
Indigenous nations vary. Gumatj clan leader Galarrwuy Yunupingu bridges
both of these approaches when he writes of a need for a new approach to
reconciliation. Trying to change Aboriginal and Torres Strait Islander people
will not work, Yunupingu maintains. For Yolŋu, there is 'a law of another
kind and that law is lasting and alive, the law of the land, *rom watangu*—my
backbone.' But the pressure from the settler state is relentless:

There is always something wanted by someone who knows nothing of our
land or its people. There is always someone who wants us to be like them, to
give up our knowledge and our laws, or our land. There is always someone
who wants to take something from us. I disapprove of that person, whoever

he or she is. There is no other way for us. Our laws tell us how to live and
lead in the proper way. Others will always seek to interrupt my thinking,
but I will tell the difference between their ways and my laws, which are the
only ones to live by. I am mindful of the continuing attempts to change
all that is in us, and I know that it is not workable at all. It cannot work
(Yunupingu 2016).

It cannot work. Surely this is evident, from whatever viewpoint one might
take. But this knowledge leaves the settler state with a conundrum and a
challenge. The conundrum is: how will the settler state know itself if it lets
go of the fantasy of colonial completion? The challenge is: will it be able to
relinquish this fantasy enough to enable and support First Nations' aspirations and self-government without the need to intervene and control?

Determining a way forward will be slow, painstaking, and complicated.
It can only, in any meaningful way, be the work of Aboriginal and Torres
Strait Islander peoples. The settler state has a role to play in ensuring that
this work is adequately resourced, but it must otherwise get out of the way.
Settler Australia must relinquish the colonial fantasy and embrace the fact
that there can never be a moment of colonial completion in which the
Indigenous presence is eliminated. The future is something altogether
different. As Irene Watson (2018) argues, Indigenous futures on this continent 'lie in the acknowledgement of the standing sovereign position of the
Aboriginal peoples of Australia, whose lands have been unlawfully entered,
stolen and governed without our consent.'

Educator Sharon Davis (2016) writes that one day:

A day will come when the word 'decolonise' is clearly understood, not as an
attack on non-Aboriginal Australians, but as a crucially important process
to ensure an equitable education for Aboriginal Australian children, which
will benefit everyone.

This point might be made not just about education, but about any of the
policy issues discussed in this book. Decolonisation means accepting that
white Australia cannot solve black problems because white Australia is
the problem. Reconciliation, recognition, justice—achieving any of these
aspirations means accepting that white Australia itself is the problem.

Australia does not have an Indigenous problem, it has a settler problem. There is a groundswell of Indigenous resurgence taking place all over this continent. It is time for settler Australia to get out of the way and let Aboriginal and Torres Strait Islander peoples solve their own problems and govern their own lives.

# APPENDIX:

# UNDERSTANDING AUSTRALIAN SETTLER COLONIALISM

This book has argued that even the most progressive-seeming policies—like reconciliation or recognition—are tripped up by the settler colonial logic of elimination and the desire to complete the colonial project. Racialised and racist politics are also deeply bound up in these colonial logics. And yet, for the most part, settler colonial structures and practices have been normalised to the point of invisibility—or perhaps one should say wilful blindness—on the part of the dominant society.

Settler colonialism has never been invisible to Indigenous peoples, who have lived with its consequences since the moment of invasion of their territories. Aboriginal and Torres Strait Islander peoples, as the targets of colonial elimination, are—unsurprisingly—acutely aware that this has always been the settler's intention. Stan Grant (2016c: 25-6) sets out this view with brutal honesty:

Here is how we—Indigenous people—see the Australian dream: here's the worst of it. Aborigines rounded up and shot, babies buried in the sand and decapitated, women raped, men killed as they hid in the forks of trees, waterholes poisoned, flour laced with arsenic. The Australian dream abandoned us to rot on government missions, tore families apart, condemned us to poverty. There was no place for us in this modern country and everything we have won has come from dissent, it has been torn from the reluctant grasp of a nation that for far too much of its history hoped that we would disappear.

Settler colonial studies is a relatively new field of academic scholarship and so much of its terminology has yet to appear in everyday parlance. Yet if we are to imagine a radically different set of relations between Indigenous peoples and settlers in Australia—as I think we must—then we must also bring new conceptual tools to this task. If there is to be any genuine possibility of decolonising a settler society like Australia it must begin with developing the capacity to make the invisibility of 'settler common sense' visible to all (Veracini 2015: 8). In this Appendix I outline what I see as the three key elements that support the maintenance of the Australian colonial fantasy:

1. The logic of elimination and the desire for colonial completion.
2. The practices and structures of race and racism that continue to shape settler–Indigenous relationships.
3. The misplaced belief that public policy will provide a means of resolving the colonial problem.

Understanding these political dynamics helps us understand the ways in which the colonial fantasy has been structured into the very bones of Australian society.

THE LOGIC OF ELIMINATION, THE DESIRE FOR COMPLETION
Colonialism is generally understood as a set of social and political institutions and practices that maintains significant inequalities between coloniser and colonised (Veracini 2017: 3). *Settler* colonial societies structure these forms of domination and inequality into relatively stable social relations that enable the ongoing dispossession of Indigenous peoples from their lands, and the denial of their sovereign authority and political difference (Coulthard 2014: 7). Maintaining these social relations requires the ongoing and forceful domination of Indigenous peoples through the repression of their culture, identity and history, the persistence of which challenges the legitimacy of the colonial mission (Rouhana 2008: 73). Where this

repression is acknowledged it is justified as being only temporary, as the settler society is understood as moving inevitably towards a post-colonial state in which the nation will be experienced as united and fair. This belief in the inevitable completion of the colonial project obscures the intent to permanently displace the Indigenous populations within the acquired territories, without any intention that the nation might one day undertake a process of structural decolonisation (Strakosch and Macoun 2012: 41; see also Veracini 2010).

Non-Indigenous Australian historian Patrick Wolfe's seminal formulation of settler colonialism rests on the central insight that settler colonies were and are premised on the *elimination* of Indigenous societies (Wolfe 1999: 2), whether by their physical obliteration or by absorbing them into the wider population. This is what is referred to as the 'logic of elimination' that is constitutive of settler colonial societies. Through physical elimination, coercive 'consent', physical removal and confinement, and assimilation, settler societies seek to neutralise the fact that Indigenous peoples have (still) existing sovereignty over the land (Wolfe 2016: 35–6).

The logic of elimination is driven by the desire for territory, for sole possession of the land; a desire that cannot be achieved with any legitimacy so long as Indigenous peoples persist to disrupt it (Strakosch 2015: 40). The coexistence of Indigenous and settler sovereignty is seen as impossible, meaning that the survival and persistence of Indigenous peoples is a problem for settlers. Under the logic of elimination, Indigenous sovereignties, creation stories and relationships to land cannot be allowed to survive, cannot be allowed to compete with narratives of frontier heroism, or to undermine colonial claims to territory. As Patrick Dodson (1997: 145) has observed, once the lie of *terra nullius* was laid bare by the fact that 'the natives were still out in the scrub' there could be 'no hiding' from the 'systemic sustained, and deliberate' ways in which Aboriginal and Torres Strait Islander peoples 'had to be removed.' Thus, although a settler state may not continue to pursue the physical death of Indigenous people *per se* (although violent death is intrinsic to colonialism in the past and present), it will continue to seek the social and political death of Indigenous peoples *as such* (Battell Lowman and Barker 2015: 30). Elimination is not then some kind of one-off occurrence that may later be overcome or superseded, but is, more fundamentally, an organising principle of the settler state (Wolfe 2016: 33).

The different modes of elimination—through violence or through assimilation—are important, as they demonstrate the persistence of the colonial fantasy over time. It is now generally understood that the violence of frontier warfare was cruel and unjust—although Henry Reynolds (2013: 16) notes that this violence is still often cast as a 'struggle *with* the land, rather than a fight for possession *of* it.' There is more debate about the rights and wrongs of more recent policies such as assimilation or (more recently still) reconciliation or recognition. As non-Indigenous Australian political theorists Elizabeth Strakosch and Alissa Macoun (2012: 45) have argued, there are several ways to eliminate Indigenous political difference, some of which may appear more benign or progressive than others. The most obvious strategy is the physical elimination of Indigenous peoples through massacres and other forms of frontier violence. Over time, however, governments have pursued other strategies of elimination, including the dispossession of Indigenous peoples from the lands that are central to their political systems, identities and spiritual lives; the destruction of Indigenous families and communities through policies of containment and child removal; the inclusion or recognition of Indigenous polities within the settler state; and even the negotiation of treaties or other agreements. Indeed, as Wolfe (2006: 402) has argued, these other modes of elimination—such as assimilation—may be more effective for the settler than killing as they do not disrupt the conventional rule of law.

Pursuing the elimination of Indigenous people has always created some anxiety within settler societies. From the outset, not all settlers endorsed the dominant, racialised view of Indigenous people as primitive or 'subhuman' that was used to justify their inhumane and unjust treatment. Many settlers experienced the 'whispering in our hearts' (Reynolds 1998) that arose from troubled consciences and the evidence of ongoing Indigenous family and community life. The public debate that arose from such anxiety could only be appeased through the argument that colonialism was something sad but inevitable, a nation-building process through which all Australians, including Aboriginal and Torres Strait Islander peoples, would inevitably benefit over time. This belief in the transience and general benevolence of colonialism was fed by a desire for colonial 'completion'—a process through which colonialism would come to be supplanted by a modern, unified nation. The persistence and survival of Aboriginal and Torres Strait Islander people frustrated the completion of the colonial project, but the desire continues just the same.

We can hear this desire for completion reflected, for example, in Kevin Rudd's apology to the Stolen Generations, in which he invokes the nation to 'turn a new page in Australia's history' (Rudd 2008). This new page that Rudd imagines turning is the fantasised moment of colonial completion, where the nation can indulge a belief that it has left the wrongs of colonialism behind *and* been forgiven by Indigenous people. 'There', the nation says. 'That's done. Let's move on.' But there can be no moving on while Indigenous people survive, and so this desire for colonial completion—a moment that is always only just around the corner, so close that present-day Australia can already re-imagine itself as post-colonial (Strakosch 2015: 45; Short 2008: 160)—remains only an aspiration. Its effect, however, is to derail apparently progressive initiatives. The desire for completion is lived out in attainable, symbolic moments, like the apology, rather than structural reforms that seem to push colonial completion out of reach.

In the absence of genuine, structural decolonisation, the trajectory of colonisation–decolonisation–post-colonialism that has occurred in some parts of Asia, Africa and Latin America is simply not evident in settler colonial states like Australia. As Reynolds (2013: 248) notes, 'The wave of decolonisation passed Australia by . . . There was no return of sovereignty, no lowering of the imperial flag.' Settler colonial states, by definition, have not decolonised. Even as the colonial fantasy imagines the nation moving towards a more peaceful, equitable, and reconciled future, the reality is that settler colonialism persists in structure and policy. As Wolfe has argued, invasion is a structure not an event (1999: 2). Founded on violence, the settler state invests in sustaining the colonial order, structuring institutions and practices that maintain inequalities and injustice 'for the purpose of sustaining the life and continuity of the state' (Watson 2009: 45).

Canadian settler scholars Emma Battell Lowman and Adam Barker (2015: 32–3) suggest that the structures of settler colonialism shape our contemporary *spaces, systems and stories.* These structures displace Indigenous peoples from *their* spaces, which are recreated as settler spaces; they develop political, legal, economic and educational systems that further disempower and displace Indigenous peoples; and they create stories that recast the violence of colonisation as narratives of frontier bravery in a savage land. In Australia, these narratives are all too familiar, articulating the desires, fantasies and needs of settlers, as outlined by Macoun and Strakosch (2013: 433), who include in their extensive list the ideas that:

- Aboriginal society exists only in 'the past', and is unable to survive;
- Aboriginal society is inferior, in deficit and in need of help;
- Aboriginal society is non-existent or has been destroyed;
- the settler state is universal and inclusive;
- the settler state is beneficial and/or benevolent;
- colonialism is in the interests of Aboriginal people;
- colonialism does not exist or has ended: with continual varied repetitions of 'it's over'; and
- the settler colonial future is seen as inevitable and therefore there is a need for everyone to accept this future.

The emphasis on the structural nature of colonialism has attracted criticism. There is concern that the emphasis on structure may suggest that existing relationships between Indigenous peoples and the settler state are inevitable, effectively letting the settler off the hook. As discussed in the Introduction to this book, colonising white innocence imagines a 'good settler' who might work with or for First Nations in their efforts to create more just and equitable relations. Many iterations of settler colonial policy have been advanced by such 'good settlers', who generate authoritative accounts of all that is wrong in Indigenous lives and represent their policy 'solutions' as benign and progressive (Macoun 2016: 93). Yet in each of the policy regimes that this book considers, the settler logic of elimination, combined with the settler desire for colonial completion, have undercut the policy's potential.

Debates about the 'recognition' of Aboriginal and Torres Strait Islander peoples are a key example. There are a number of problematic assumptions that underpin the idea that settler states might recognise Indigenous peoples. Key among these is the assumption of the settler state's *right* to bestow such recognition. Settler states tend to think of recognition as a demand that the state modify itself (for example, by changing its constitution) so as to more appropriately recognise the distinct place of Indigenous peoples within contemporary society. In reality, however, this relies on the presumption that the settler state *already possesses* the legitimate power to recognise (Elliott 2016: 414). This view is like gazing in a mirror. When the settler state tries to see Indigenous peoples in order to recognise them, what gazes back is its own colonial authority. More than this, the desire to recognise Indigenous peoples is fed by the desire for colonial completion. The hope is that when Indigenous people have been included as equal members in the society (again, for example, by recognition in a constitution) the settler state can imagine that the elimination/assimilation of Indigenous people is complete and therefore that colonialism has ended.

This is precisely what First Nations are refusing when they contest the idea of recognition. Indigenous peoples do not seek recognition only as subjects or citizens of the settler state but instead, as peoples who have never willingly ceded their lands or political autonomy, they seek recognition of their distinct moral claims as *dispossessed First Nations* (Short 2005: 272). Indigenous peoples seek to have their status as sovereign peoples acknowledged as the basis for their relationship with the settler order. In lieu of this sovereign recognition, Dene scholar Glen Coulthard (2014: 3) argues that settler recognition (such as has been on offer in Australia in recent years) can only reproduce the kinds of racist, colonialist power that Indigenous demands for recognition are in fact seeking to transcend. Rather than transforming the Indigenous–settler relationship, recognition reaffirms settler authority over Indigenous peoples and their lands.

This then is the reality of settler colonialism, in which a move towards constitutional recognition can be understood not as a long overdue redress for nonrecognition or misrecognition, but as a further attempt to eliminate Aboriginal and Torres Strait Islander peoples by drawing them into the settler state. Thus, as Audra Simpson (2014: 20) notes, while the more modest regimes of recognition that have recently been debated in Australia are invariably understood as virtuous, they are in fact a practice of settler governance that may 'salve the wounds of settler colonialism' but will never deliver benefits to Indigenous peoples.

Racism also plays a part here. As long as Indigenous identity is perceived as inferior, deficient or even dangerous, there is no room for the possibility that what Aboriginal and Torres Strait Islander people actually want is recognition for specific forms of Indigenous identity and belonging.

RACE, RACISM AND IDENTITY

Prior to colonisation, 'Aboriginal' or 'Indigenous' people did not exist in those terms, there was no 'Indigeneity' or 'Aboriginality' in the sense that there is today (Langton 2003: 118). As Irene Watson (2009: 49) has argued, the categories of Indigenous or non-Indigenous were 'imposed by the colonial project' and the definition of Indigenous peoples has remained a powerful settler colonial tool. Overtly racist classificatory distinctions (for example, between 'primitive' and 'civilised' people) were used to justify colonialism, structuring colonial ideology into all manner of social institutions. At the same time, however, whiteness and white privilege remained invisible. Discussing colonialism without also discussing race hides the fact that those of us who are white also accrue greater benefit from colonial structures and institutions and facilitates the view that the state is benign or neutral (Macoun 2016: 88).

The links between race/racism and settler colonialism are important. These ideas are certainly not synonymous but they do articulate with one another in some complicated and powerful ways (Strakosch 2015: 45). As Wolfe (2016: 5) has suggested, 'race is colonialism speaking.' Wolfe (2006: 388) also draws a distinction between the racialisation of enslaved people, (who are required to reproduce as a means of increasing the wealth and labour force of their 'owners'), and the racial classification of Indigenous peoples (whose elimination is sought as a means of gaining unfettered access to their territories). Constructions of 'race' and associated racial prejudice have been used to justify colonial actions including the expansion of European settlement, violence and Indigenous dispossession (Battell Lowman and Barker 2015: 42). As Aileen Moreton-Robinson (2007: 87) has argued, 'race' has indelibly marked the formation of settler states and the development of national identity in former British colonies including

Australia. Settler colonialism has used the 'organising grammar of race' (Wolfe 2006: 387) to advance its nationalist projects and justify its logic of elimination. The deep racism that is generally constitutive of settler colonial societies is, at least in part, motivated by that logic (Macoun and Strakosch 2013: 432).

After the first violent confrontations of the colonial encounter, efforts at elimination became focused less on an attempt to eradicate the *bodies* of Indigenous peoples than they were on trying to erase their histories and geographies, thereby eradicating their existence *as peoples* (Alfred and Corntassel 2005: 598). What Yiman and Bidjara academic Marcia Langton (2003: 118) describes as a 'fixation on classification' was part of the intensification of colonial administration of Indigenous lives after 1788. As in other colonial territories, complex systems of classification and control became an intrinsic part of the colonial administration, intended to 'exterminate' one type of Aboriginality and replace it with a more acceptable, 'sanitised' version (Langton 2003: 116). Colonialism subjected Aboriginal and Torres Strait Islander people to imposed and racialised identity categories based on 'degrees of blood', labelling individual people as 'full blood', 'half caste', 'quarter caste', 'octoroon' and so on—labels that were then used to assess an Aboriginal person's character and employability, and were the foundation of policies such as child removal. Lighter-skinned children, with 'less Aboriginal blood' were, for example, considered more likely to assimilate and were therefore at greater risk of removal from their families to be placed with a white family or institution. The categorisation of 'degrees' of Aboriginality also fragmented Indigenous resistance to colonial domination and further denigrated Indigeneity by giving higher status to those considered to have a greater percentage of 'white' blood. At the same time, those categorised as 'less' Indigenous, particularly lighter-skinned or urban Aboriginal people whose 'authenticity' was (and is) called into question, were likely to see the legitimacy of their political claims diminished (Burgmann 2003: 51).

The elimination of Indigenous peoples is the self-evident driver of these practices of regulating Indigenous identity. As Indigenous peoples became less and less Indigenous (according to the categories through which settlers intended to 'breed out the black'), they would simultaneously be absorbed further and more completely into the settler population.

These policies were explicitly intended to erase the Indigenous presence by blending Aboriginal and Torres Strait Islander peoples into invisibility within the colonial population. Aboriginal and Torres Strait Islander peoples were reassured of their 'potential to become white', with the ultimate absorption of the Indigenous population proposed by the settler state as 'a supposedly humane answer to the destruction and extermination of the early days of settlement' (Grant 2016c: 89–90). This was used to justify the infliction of a myriad of harms on Indigenous people, including the removal of Indigenous children from their families, and these views have ensured that such harms continue to be perpetrated, justified and denied (McMillan and Rigney 2018: 759). As Stan Grant argues (2016c: 213), 'Racism isn't killing the Australian dream. The Australian dream was founded on racism. From the first time a British flag was planted in this soil, the rules have been different for us.'

At the same time, the privileging of whiteness also remains intrinsic to settler colonialism. Australian settler colonialism can be understood as 'a system built on white privilege' (Grant 2016c: 68). From the earliest days of colonisation, the privileging of whiteness simultaneously animated views of Australia as 'civilised' and 'at the forefront of progress' while also connecting the relative newness of settler culture to 'the heritage, history, and culture' of its British settler roots (McGregor 2011: xx). Whiteness indicated that settler Australians were 'drawn from common stock', a condition deemed necessary for nationhood, equality and democracy to flourish (McGregor 2011: xxi). Even as Australian society has become increasingly multicultural and ethnically diverse, whiteness, and its alignment with Britishness, has remained a 'treasured quality' for settler Australians.

Whiteness also conveys a degree of entitlement that Indigenous people continue to observe. As Nayuka Gorrie (2017: 20) argues, Aboriginal people see 'the entitlement of white settlers'

in statements about what Australian values are. We see it in discussions around who white Australia allows to come to this country and how they get here. The entitlement to country that their ancestors stole and continue to steal is truly mind boggling. The wilful historical amnesia of forgetting the very boats your ancestors came on while denying the rights of other people on boats is breathtaking.

Gorrie, like many Aboriginal and Torres Strait Islander people, recognises the logic of elimination in these practices, arguing that, 'To the white settler who feels entitled to this country, Aboriginal people are inconvenient. Our existence is a reminder of the cost of their existence that they would prefer to ignore' (Gorrie 2017: 2).

Aboriginal and Torres Strait Islander people are—of course—also alert to the racialised modes of elimination advanced by the settler state. As Tony Birch has argued, settler Australia 'attempted to exterminate both the physical and social body of Indigenous people from national historical memory within what would become a homogenised pure white nation' (Birch 2007: 110). As Chelsea Bond (2017a: 4) has argued, Indigenous people understand that race has been used to maintain a relationship of power over them 'physically, morally, intellectually, politically and legislatively'. Bond understands racism to be both intrinsic to settler society and as 'enshrined' in state institutions and legislation, while race itself has been 'central to the colonial project' and today remains inescapable in settler society. As Amy McQuire (2016: 2) writes

> racism is not some aberration confined to the jurisdiction of redneck areas like the Northern Territory. It is not a problem of the individual, but deeply engrained in Australia's institutions and propped up by power.

Yet as Luke Pearson (2018) argues, the racism that is structured into Australian institutions continues to be ignored or denied:

> We look at Aboriginal prison rates and label Aboriginal people as criminals rather than looking at racism in policing or in sentencing. We see Aboriginal suspension rates, or low attendance rates, in school and blame Aboriginal children and parents instead of looking at our curriculum, pedagogy, and how and when school policies are enforced.

Aboriginal and Torres Strait Islander peoples continue to refuse the power of the settler order to name and contain them. As Chelsea Bond (2017b: 6) has argued:

> Our being as Aborigines is a racial classification of white imagining which insists that inferiority frames every aspect of our being. But we are not their

Aborigines—we are First Nations peoples. Our very being is not determined on the basis of our being placed last on the evolutionary or economic ladder—it is on the basis of us being located here first. Our presence as First Nations peoples is not on the premise or promise of equity. It is on the basis of sovereignty that we articulate our place in relation to this place—and we will not disappear once we become statistically more like them.

Since the arrival of the British, Aboriginal and Torres Strait Islander people have had to fight to regain the right to name themselves and reclaim the political identities associated with the hundreds of Indigenous nations that were usurped by the colonial presence. This struggle has been crucial to the survival of Aboriginal and Torres Strait Islander peoples, who have resisted the idea of their socialisation as 'Australians' (Ridgeway 2000: 13). Indeed, as Celeste Liddle (2017b: 2) has argued, any assumption that Indigenous people are 'okay with being assimilated into this Australian narrative' is nothing but 'colonial arrogance.' As Mick Dodson (2003: 38) argues:

We have never totally lost ourselves within the other's reality. We have never fallen into the hypnosis of believing that those representations were our essence. We have never forgotten that we have an identity that cannot be reduced to a relation, and cannot be destroyed by misconception.

It is yet another aspect of the colonial fantasy to assume that settler representation and regulation of Indigenous identity might overwhelm Indigenous peoples' knowledge of themselves. In fact, the struggle to regain control of Indigenous identity is central to a politics of refusal and resurgence. Dodson (2003: 31) foregrounds the importance of

the right to inherit the collective identity of one's people, and to transform that identity creatively according to the self-defined aspirations of one's people and one's generation. It must include the right to live outside the cage created by other people's images and projections.

Stan Grant (2016c: 55) agrees, arguing that, 'Being black—being Aboriginal— was always intensely political', asserting an Aboriginal identity in this context was (and remains) 'a political statement.'

First Nations' refusal of settler efforts to control Indigenous identities should not obscure the harms that Aboriginal and Torres Strait Islander peoples continue to endure. Settler colonial policies and institutions remain blind to their whiteness and refuse to acknowledge the ways in which they marginalise and discriminate against Indigenous peoples. Yet racist settler structures continue to be deeply harmful to Indigenous people. Mick Dodson (2003: 33) has written of the ways in which both Indigenous and non-Indigenous constructions of Aboriginality provide a context for Indigenous lived experiences that can also become 'the enemy within.' The impact of these experiences is profound. In relation to the extraordinarily high rate of Indigenous suicide (which claims 5.2 per cent of the Indigenous population each year), which he describes as a 'humanitarian crisis', Dameyon Bonson (2016: 1) argues that, 'It is not our indigeneity that causes us distress. It is the drivers of racism, whiteness and social exclusion.'

The earlier violence against Indigenous identity in Australia has ameliorated somewhat over time. Since the 1970s the three-part, government-endorsed definition of Indigeneity has accepted that an Aboriginal or Torres Strait Islander person is any person of Aboriginal or Torres Strait Islander *descent*, who *identifies* as an Aboriginal or Torres Strait Islander person and is *accepted as such by the community* in which they live (for a discussion of this see Gardiner-Garden 2000). Although conservative opponents of the idea of self-definition considered the new policy to be dangerous precisely because it took the power of definition away from white bureaucrats and gave it to Aboriginal people themselves (Bennett 1989: 59) this definition is, unsurprisingly, preferred by the 'vast majority' of Indigenous Australians (Gardiner and Bourke 2000: 44). What Dodson calls 'self-representations of Aboriginality' can always be understood as 'an act of freedom.' Stan Grant (2016c: 91) makes a similar point, arguing that Aboriginal and Torres Strait Islander people

> baffled governments who tried to place us on a trajectory towards white-
> ness. They failed to see we were human. We kept our culture alive and our
> people together. We married each other and reinforced our visible identities.
> Sometimes we married white people and in their own way they too became
> black. Not just to us, also to a white world so puzzled at why they would
> choose us that they would have them punished for it.

Yet despite the resistance evident in Indigenous peoples' reclamation of their self-representations, the racism inherent to the logic of settler colonialism persists. The more successful the logic of elimination appears to have been—that is, the more assimilated, colonised, urbanised or educated an Indigenous person seems to be—the more likely it is that they will be called upon to justify their Aboriginality (Taylor 2003: 91–2). The high-profile legal case of *Eatock vs Bolt* (often referred to as 'the Bolt case') revealed precisely this dynamic, after the well-known conservative commentator Andrew Bolt criticised so-called 'political aborigines' who he claimed had chosen to emphasise their Indigenous heritage for material and professional gain despite their lighter skin (see Maddison 2013 for more). This commentator was eventually found to have committed an act of racial discrimination, but this decision only served to unleash the anger of conservative politicians and commentators, with new calls for the *Racial Discrimination Act* itself to be amended to ensure that other racists would not be held to account.

Race continues to structure settler colonial society (Bond 2017b: 4), but settler society refuses to see its systemic racism, focusing instead on 'individual acts committed by the ignorant' (Liddle 2016: 3). These systemic issues cannot be resolved by policy alone—the system itself needs to change.

BETTER POLICY IS NOT THE ANSWER

There is a particularly Australian habit of looking to government for answers to complex social and political problems. This is nowhere more evident than in Indigenous affairs, where faith in government to 'improve' the lives of Aboriginal and Torres Strait Islander peoples persists despite all evidence to the contrary. The majority of settlers tend not to see the state's role in the lives of Indigenous peoples as a problem, and even some Aboriginal and Torres Strait Islander people continue to focus their reform efforts on government policy and service delivery. But while policy remains a crucially important site of political encounter and engagement between Indigenous peoples and the settler state (Strakosch 2015: 2), it is not a site through which Aboriginal and Torres Strait Islander peoples are likely to develop the autonomy they seek. The state and its agents (government departments and services) are not neutral or benign, and cannot be the 'heroic protagonists' they are imagined to be (Macoun 2016: 93). Yet the legitimacy of settler state jurisdiction over Indigenous people is rarely questioned (by non-Indigenous people). By operating through the familiarity of state bureaucracy, colonial authority over Indigenous lives has been naturalised, and the assumption that Indigenous peoples have already been incorporated within the settler regime remains unquestioned (Strakosch 2015: 9, 51). This is also further evidence of the desire for colonial completion, as by framing Indigenous peoples as the legitimate subjects of domestic policy, the settler state is asserting that the political independence of these groups is in the past.

In its desire for colonial completion, Australian Indigenous policy has undergone endless overhaul as it has become evident, time and again, that the Indigenous population would not be quietly eliminated. For Aboriginal and Torres Strait Islander people, the experience of constant policy change has been frustrating, destabilising and disempowering, underscoring settler disregard for Indigenous sovereignty and autonomy. Yorta Yorta and Dja Dja Wurrung woman Muriel Bamblett has described this experience as like being 'caught in a big washing machine':

> You've got change all the time; every time we just get used to something you move to another cycle and the cycle keeps changing and we keep moving and we haven't got used to the last cycle before we're moving on to the next cycle (quoted in Maddison 2009: 3).

The constant turmoil in Indigenous affairs lends weight to Wolfe's (2016: 37–8) observation that settler colonial societies direct a disproportionate amount of energy and effort towards administering the lives of Indigenous peoples, who are generally very statistically small groups in the society. In Australia, during the last 50 years there have been 21 different ministers in the Indigenous portfolio, and ten different organisational structures, nine of which have been created/dismantled within the past 30 years. These endless changes have only worsened already complex problems in the Indigenous policy domain, embedding uncertainty and scepticism, and fracturing fragile relationships that have often taken years to establish (Patterson 2017: 15–16).

The last 50 years have also seen some extreme ideological swings in the Indigenous policy domain. Up until around the middle of the twentieth century Aboriginal and Torres Strait Islander people were still considered a 'fleeting problem' with no conceivable future. At the time of Federation it was deemed barely necessary to even consider Indigenous people in the new Australian Constitution because the nation foresaw a future in which Aboriginal and Torres Strait Islander people simply did not exist (McGregor 2011: xx). This was the policy era framed as 'protection', during which Aboriginal and Torres Strait Islander peoples were removed from their lands to live on reserves and missions, kept separate from white society and denied any rights to the land on which they were contained (Burgmann 2003: 70). Between 1901 and 1946 all Australian states passed legislation that would 'protect' Indigenous people by controlling their independence of movement, marriage, employment and association and that authorised the removal of Aboriginal children from their families. Protection policies assumed that Aboriginal people were merely an ancient remnant who would inevitably die out. As colonial governments attempted to 'smooth the dying pillow' of a culture apparently destined for extinction, Aboriginal and Torres Strait Islander people experienced further threats to their spiritual beliefs and traditional ways of life while becoming newly dependent on rations and handouts. Ostensibly intended to create safer environments for people who had been traumatised by invasion and frontier warfare, instead protection policies tore families apart by relocating individuals and groups to missions and reserves; destroyed feelings of individual self-worth; and damaged culture through outlawing ceremony and language (Atkinson 2002: 67). These harms would continue to reverberate through generations to come. In the wake of frontier violence, here was the next stage of the settler colonial logic of elimination at work. The belief that Aboriginal people were a 'dying race' was fuelled by the colonial fantasy and the dream of colonial completion.

The 1930s brought a reassessment of government responsibility to Indigenous people. As it became evident that Aboriginal people were not dying out, national policy changed again and by 1951 the state had adopted a policy of 'assimilation'. The underlying assumption this time was that, rather than dying out, Aboriginal people would be absorbed into the white population to live like other Australian citizens. Many non-Indigenous people at the time believed that assimilation and advancement meant the same thing, and that full engagement and participation in white society would offer Aboriginal people the best way out of poverty and social marginalisation. During the assimilation era, citizenship was offered as a 'reward' to Aboriginal people prepared to renounce their Aboriginality and embrace the dominant culture. Many such assimilatory policies were justified as being 'for the good' of Indigenous people, an exercise in colonial fantasy that masked their eliminatory intent.

By the 1970s, however, there was growing optimism among many Aboriginal and Torres Strait Islander people that yet another policy reorientation might see the Australian settler state at last begin to recognise their status as First Nations peoples and make policy accordingly. In 1972 the newly elected Whitlam government introduced the formal policy of self-determination, which was endorsed and further developed by the successor Fraser government. Subsequent decades—and governments— saw further change. Under Hawke and Keating there was talk of a treaty (which never eventuated); native title became enshrined in legislation (although the promised social justice package component was never developed); the creation of the Aboriginal and Torres Strait Islander Commission (ATSIC) meant that Aboriginal people had elected representation for the first time; and the official decade of reconciliation was initiated. Yet each of these apparently decolonising policies was rapidly undermined by the eliminatory logic that lurked within them. The version of self-determination that was introduced in Australia had weak and compromised philosophical underpinnings. Australian governments have never dealt with Aboriginal people 'government-to-government' instead maintaining a 'top-down approach' to self-determination (Brennan et al 2005: 32) that was clearly a contradiction in terms. This approach meant that aspirations for autonomy were buried in assimilationist practices (Young 2005: 120). Each of these apparently decolonising policy developments in fact perpetuated the settler logic of elimination.

The election of John Howard as prime minister in 1996 signalled yet another drastic change in policy orientation. Abolishing the Aboriginal and Torres Strait Islander Commission (ATSIC), and announcing that the 'failed experiment' in separate representation was over, Howard introduced a set of so-called 'new arrangements' in Indigenous affairs that centred on the mainstreaming of Indigenous policy and programs with a broadly paternalistic approach. The new policy regime—which continues into the present—focused on enforced behavioural change in Aboriginal people with strict controls and penalties for non-compliance. Many Aboriginal and Torres Strait Islander people described the Howard years as a 'living nightmare' (Graham 2007) during which many of the hard-won rights achieved in political struggle over the previous 30 years seemed to slip from their grasp. Perhaps more than any other prime minister in living memory, Howard overtly articulated the settler logic of elimination, demanding the 'normalisation' of Indigenous lives in ways that have been critiqued as 're-coded assimilation' with a specific intent of eliminating Indigenous difference (Sullivan 2011: 47). All reference to self-determination and culture have been removed from government policy, to be replaced with an emphasis on 'responsibility', 'engagement' and 'capacity building' (Kowal 2015: 162).

Today, the logic of elimination is still seeking to 'normalise' Aboriginal and Torres Strait Islander peoples such that they no longer disrupt the colonial fantasy. But as this very brief policy history makes clear, no matter what the policy orientation, the very fact of acting *upon* Indigenous people as subjects of domestic policy allows the settler state to demonstrate its colonial sovereign authority. As Wolfe (2016: 37-8) has argued, it is a common strategy for the settler state to conflate Indigenous affairs with concerns about crime, delinquency and neglect. Political debate focuses on Indigenous wellbeing (or lack thereof), with government policy represented as settler goodwill and benevolence (Strakosch 2015: 52).

Unsurprisingly, such policy has done nothing to change the life circumstances of Aboriginal and Torres Strait Islander people, although it has done much to further pathologise them in the eyes of settler society. As settler scholar Elise Klein (2016: 2) notes of the Productivity Commission's 2016 *Overcoming Indigenous Disadvantage* report, not only does the focus of analysis remain centred on Indigenous 'deficit' and on 'gaps' in socioeconomic outcomes, it also fails to 'look up' and consider either the impact of government ideology or 'the enduring will of settler society to continue to colonise.' Stan Grant echoes the frustration of many Indigenous people when he argues that while to 'outside eyes', this lack of change is understood as 'a failure of the people themselves', Indigenous people 'know that this is the legacy of history and generations of poor government policies':

Money is spent, houses are built, new programs are devised, and the malaise deepens. With each new era of policy—protection, integration, assimilation, or self-determination—the problem remains the same; communities themselves are rendered powerless with limited input into how they run their lives (Grant 2016c: 185).

Indeed, despite relentless change in focus and ideology, the underlying logic of elimination has remained abundantly clear to Indigenous people, who have never been fooled by policy dressed up as 'good intentions.' For Aboriginal and Torres Strait Islander Social Justice Commissioner June Oscar, dealing with government has

always been a struggle and it's always been a fight for survival but I think this particular time in our history we see government being just so sneaky in trying to erode the strength within the Aboriginal community. Their tactics and their strategies have been covered up. On the surfaces of it their approaches mightn't appear to be for the wrong reasons, but underlying that they've been very clear in what their intent has been: to try and diminish Aboriginal people . . . *As if they want to try and remove us from the face of the earth, from this country* (quoted in KALACC 2006: 129–30 my emphasis).

None of the recent iterations of Indigenous policy have broken out of the settler colonial frame—by definition they cannot. Both progressive and conservative approaches to Indigenous policy are contained within the settler colonial logic of elimination, pursuing colonial completion through the dissolution of Indigenous difference. While Indigenous policy is usually framed as progressing from exclusion to inclusion, in reality these are 'twin strategies of settler colonialism' that effectively trap Indigenous resistance in the continual oscillation between the two (Macoun and Strakosch 2013: 429). The advent of neoliberalism has only intensified these dynamics, and Aboriginal and Torres Strait Islander people are represented as having failed to engage effectively with modernity and the free market. Indigenous disadvantage is now routinely used to justify paternalistic interventions that further assimilate Aboriginal and Torres Strait Islander people into the settler state (Howard-Wagner 2017: 3).

What this means in the lives of First Nations is that none of these policies, even those considered most 'decolonising' in intent, have put control in the hands of Aboriginal and Torres Strait Islander peoples. Indigenous people have long recognised and articulated the harms inflicted upon them by settler policy regimes. The late Aboriginal activist Isabel Flick recognised the protection era policies, and the constant changes in policy orientation, as designed to 'keep us from ruling our own lives' (in Flick and Goodall 2004: 30). In a 1994 speech, the late Western Australian Aboriginal activist Rob Riley also argued that:

> Historically, the truth is that the Indigenous people of Australia have been subjected to more intense social engineering, and social and cultural genocide, than people from any other former British colony. The legacy of the policies of indentured labour, assimilation and integration will continue to manifest itself for many years to come (quoted in Beresford 2006: 5).

Today, Indigenous policy seems to barely require any input at all from Indigenous people. Critical feedback and complaints about the impact of policy in Indigenous communities is rejected or ignored. Indigenous participation is now seen as a 'distraction', even an 'indulgence', often met with the argument that settler governments 'tried that and it didn't work' (Davis 2016: 1–2).

What all of this tells us is that, despite the ambitions of progressive activists and well-meaning bureaucrats, answers to the dilemmas of settler colonialism cannot be found *within* the settler state. If there are answers to these seemingly entrenched issues—and I believe there are—they can only be located outside of settler control in the hands of Aboriginal and Torres Strait Islander people themselves.

# ACKNOWLEDGMENTS

Even a book with just one author's name on the cover involves the labour and love of many people. In the course of writing this book I've been supported by colleagues, friends, and interlocutors who have helped to both challenge and sustain me when the work got tricky.

My first and most significant debt is to the Wurundjeri-Woiwurrung people. I live and work on Wurundjeri-Woiwurrung lands, beautiful Country threatened by colonial settlement and development from the earliest days of invasion. Nonetheless, the Wurundjeri-Woiwurrung people have preserved and protected their Country, sustaining important cultural practices that look after the land and the waters of the Birrarung (Yarra River), preserving sacred places, generously sharing their knowledge with the community, and sustaining and revitalising their traditional language—Woiwurrung. Living on unceded Wurundjeri-Woiwurrung territory is a privilege. In my personal and professional life I am engaged in developing relations with Wurundjeri-Woiwurrung people that are more just and ethical, and that centre Wurundjeri-Woiwurrung authority and power in the way we go about our business on this territory. This is ongoing work and I am deeply grateful to Wurundjeri-Woiwurrung Elders and their representative peak body, the Wurundjeri-Woiwurrung Cultural Heritage Aboriginal Corporation, for their patience, encouragement and support.

My second debt is to my wonderful colleagues in the Indigenous Settler Relations Collaboration at the University of Melbourne, and particularly my co-director Dr Sana Nakata who made time and space for me to complete this book. Sana is often the other half of my brain, and although our ideas and orientations can be quite different we share a vision of the ways in which academic institutions can be made to work harder in the transformation of Indigenous-settler relations. My collaborators are a wonderful and generous group of Indigenous and non-Indigenous scholars who both support and challenge my work every day. Our research unit explores the challenges that lie at the heart of relations between Indigenous and settler Australians, engaging in work that we hope will inform, shape and give life to more just relations between Indigenous and non-Indigenous peoples. Special thanks to collaborator Dr Elise Klein, who read this manuscript in an early stage and provided valuable feedback.

My editors at Allen & Unwin have again been brilliant. Elizabeth Weiss is the commissioning editor of any writer's dreams—both encouraging of what she calls 'big, crunchy ideas' while also willing to pull me back into line when those ideas have become dense and inaccessible. Elizabeth has shared my hope that this book will be read by many progressive Australians who genuinely want to shake up the current state of First Nations Politics in this country, and she has helped me write a book intended to engage that readership. It was also a delight to work with in-house editor Rebecca Kaiser once again. Rebecca is the kind of professional, conscientious, and encouraging editor that everyone hopes to have in their corner.

Other friends and colleagues from various walks of life read drafts of this book, and for their critical feedback I am particularly grateful to Elizabeth Strakosch, Karen Wyld, and Chris Graham, along with participants and discussants at various conferences and seminars where some of these ideas have been shared.

I had excellent research assistance from my doctoral students Angelique Stastny (now Dr Stastny) and Lucas Grainger-Brown. Angelique did some outstanding work compiling the media sources that have brought so many First Nations voices into this book, and Lucas helped me compile a somewhat epic list of references. I am grateful for the financial and institutional support I received from the Faculty of Arts at the University of Melbourne, which provided me with the funds to complete this research. The ideas that stimulated my thinking for this book emerged through focus group research with non-Indigenous Australians funded by the Australian Research Council Discovery Project DP140102143.

Finally, my deepest love and gratitude to my partner and my great love, Hayley Conway. Hayley has never grown tired of this project despite hours and hours of conversation, and she has helped me to really understand what it meant to be writing for an audience of 'progressive non-Indigenous Australians'. Hayley read multiple drafts and helped refine many an idea. Probably more importantly she talked me through the crises of confidence that inevitably accompany putting ideas out into the world. Words will never convey the depth of my love for her, but she knows.

# NOTES

1   Whiteness refers to more than just skin colour, and instead draws attention to a system of power and privilege that tends to be invisible to white people—a norm against which 'other' people are understood. There is more on whiteness, privilege and racism in the Appendix.

2   For anyone interested to read more about the ideas and structures of settler colonialism I have included an Appendix with an extended discussion of key issues.

3   The terms 'native' and 'Native Nations' are used in a similar way in the United States to the use of the term 'Indigenous' in Australia. In Australia the term 'native' is generally considered offensive by Aboriginal and Torres Strait Islander people.

4   From the 1890s to around the 1950s, the lives of most Aboriginal and Torres Strait Islander people were governed and controlled by state- or territory-based 'Protectors' and Protection Boards that controlled almost every aspect of Indigenous lives. Protectors could determine where people lived (often removing people to reserves and missions), where they worked, who they could associate with or marry, and usually maintained strict control over Indigenous wages and Aboriginal and Torres Strait Islander peoples' freedom of movement.

5   *Coe vs Commonwealth* failed when a majority of the High Court found that the Australian colonies had become British possessions 'by settlement and not by conquest.'

6   Naming a statement after the place at which it was made has a long history in Aboriginal and Torres Strait Islander politics—the Barunga Statement, the Eva Valley Statement and the Redfern Statement being some examples. Nevertheless, Anangu traditional owners have asked the Referendum Council not to use the word 'Uluru' in relation to the statement from 26 May 2017, citing a lack of proper protocol and consultation with Anangu during the convention. At the time of writing the Referendum Council had not responded to this request (see Lindsay 2017 for more).

7   Non-Indigenous journalist Bob Gosford at Crikey has produced a useful set of backgrounders on some of these key statements. You can find the first one, on the Yirrkala Bark Petitions, at https://blogs.crikey.com.au/northern/2017/06/04/four-essential-documents-aboriginal-australia-part-one-1963-yirrkala-bark-petitions/>

8  In February 2018 the Opposition leader, Bill Shorten, announced that Labor would begin work on legislating the Voice to Parliament without government support.

9  In June 2018 the *Advancing the Treaty Process with Aboriginal Victorians Act* was passed in the Parliament of Victoria. This historic legislation, the first of its kind in Australia, commits the Victorian government to creating and working with an Aboriginal Representative Body made up of traditional owners. The Representative Body will determine who in Victoria can negotiate a treaty or treaties and what will be on the table for negotiation.

10 Indigenous self-determination is recognised in international law, notably in Article 1 of both the International Covenant on Civil and Political Rights and the International Covenant on Economic, Social and Cultural Rights. Article 3 of the UN Declaration on the Rights of Indigenous Peoples specifies that 'Indigenous peoples have the right of self-determination. By virtue of that right they freely determine their political status and freely pursue their economic, social and cultural development', and Article 4 confirms that 'in exercising their right to self-determination, [Indigenous people] have the right to autonomy or self-government in matters relating to their internal and local affairs, as well as ways and means for financing their autonomous functions.'

11 At least three other members of the federal parliament have acknowledged Indigenous ancestry, but are or were not generally regarded as Indigenous according to the accepted three-part definition of descent, self-identification and community acceptance. They are David Kennedy (1967–1972), Mal Brough (1996–2007 and 2013–2016), both in the House of Representatives, and Senator Jackie Lambie (2014–2017). By the time of Lambie's resignation from the Senate during the Section 44 constitutional crisis of 2017, it appeared she had been accepted as Indigenous, at least by her parliamentary colleagues—if not the wider Indigenous or non-Indigenous community.

12 Farrer highlighted the significance of this in her speech, pointing out that, 'To speak in my own Indigenous language I had to get permission because no language other than English had ever been spoken in Parliament, so for me to ask for permission, it made people stop and think because this is my first language. It comes from this country and it belongs to this country' (quoted in Maxwell 2013a).

13 The exception to this might be Australia's First Nations Political Party (AFNPP), which was founded by Maurie Japarta Ryan (grandson of the famed Gurindji leader Vincent Lingiari) in the Northern Territory in 2011. It lost its federally registered party status in 2015 when it failed to demonstrate evidence of the required 500 party members to the Australian Electoral Commission. The party is also no longer registered at a territory level. The AFNPP fielded candidates in the 2012 Northern Territory election and the 2013 federal election.

14 Balanda is a Yolŋu word for white or non-Indigenous people.

15 *Terra nullius* did not in fact become a doctrine of Australian law until the *Mabo* judgment of 1992 when the High Court attributed it as legal doctrine (evidenced by Crown actions of the past) in order to refute it.

16 Indigenous Land Use Agreements (ILUAs) are agreements that enable traditional owners to negotiate and agree to the terms and conditions for economic activity on their land. Benefits may include payments, employment opportunities and other financial benefits.

17 This deal was especially problematic as it was arrived at after secret meetings between Galarrwuy Yunupingu, Noel Pearson and government representatives, which were designed to counter Yunupingu's opposition to the Northern Territory Intervention.

18  Songlines—which are recorded in traditional art forms including song, dance, painting
    and storytelling—are the paths across the land, water and sky that mark the tracks of the
    'creator beings' intrinsic to Indigenous cosmology. They may also be known as 'dreaming
    tracks'.
19  The ABC, and particularly the now defunct program *Lateline*, had a particular role to
    play in establishing the 'crisis' that led to the Intervention. In 2006 *Lateline* broadcast a
    scandalous interview with an incognito subject who claimed to be a former youth worker
    from the community of Mutitjulu. It was later revealed that this interviewee was in fact
    Gregory Andrews, an adviser working in the office of the then Minister for Indigenous
    Affairs, Mal Brough. The claims made by the 'youth worker' during the interview, who
    alleged the existence of 'paedophile rings' in Mutitjulu, were found to have no basis (see
    Graham 2017a for more).
20  In May 2018, after three days of court-ordered mediation between the state government,
    Queensland Police and the Palm Island community, the Queensland government agreed
    to pay $30 million to 447 claimants and deliver a formal apology to Palm Island residents
    to settle a landmark class action in the federal court. The $30 million settlement includes
    interest, applicants' legal costs and administrative costs, and the delivery of an apology
    (made in June 2018), leaving payments of between $5000 and $80,000 to individuals. The
    class action related to events following the death in custody of Mulrunji Doomadgee in
    2004. Palm Island man Lex Wotton was convicted of inciting the riots that followed the
    death, but Mr Wotton launched legal action on behalf of the community in 2014 accusing
    the Queensland government and police of being racist in their response to the incident.
    In December 2016, Mr Wotton was awarded $220,000 in damages in a judgment that
    determined police had violated the *Racial Discrimination Act*, opening the door for com-
    pensation in the class action.
21  Ryder was deliberately run down by a group of five white men in what the court found
    was a racially motivated crime. Despite the apparently intentional nature of the killing,
    however, the perpetrators were convicted only of manslaughter and sentenced to
    between five and six years' jail each (Wahlquist 2016d). They received non-parole periods
    of between twelve months and four years.
22  Terms like 'Koori' and 'Murri' are Indigenous language 'people words' that refer to the
    people from a large area or region. Koori is used by people living in New South Wales
    and Victoria, and Murri is used by people from Queensland and far northern New South
    Wales.
23  For example, in the United States, the Navajo Nation has its own court system, which
    processes thousands of cases a year and exercises considerable civil and some criminal
    jurisdiction within Navajo lands. The Navajo system uses two very different judicial
    approaches: one that is modelled on the adversarial Western system; the other—the
    peacemaking process—built on traditional Navajo methods of dispute resolution that
    focus on the restoration of harmony in relationships. The structure and organisation
    of the Navajo Nation Court resembles other American court systems, while it practices
    Navajo law, including common law rooted in ancient Navajo culture (Cornell 2015: 16).

# BIBLIOGRAPHY

AAP see Australian Associated Press

ABC see Australian Broadcasting Corporation

ABS see Australian Bureau of Statistics

Aboriginal and Torres Strait Islander Commission (ATSIC), 1995, 'The final report of the evaluation of the effectiveness of ATSIC programs in meeting the needs of Aboriginal women and Torres Strait Islander women', Canberra: Office of Evaluation and Audit.

Aboriginal and Torres Strait Islander Healing Foundation (ATSIHF), 2017, *Bringing them home 20 years on: An action plan for healing*, Canberra: Aboriginal and Torres Strait Islander Healing Foundation

Aboriginal and Torres Strait Islander Peak Organisations, 2016, *The Redfern Statement*, <http://nationalcongress.com.au/about-us/redfern-statement/>

Aboriginal and Torres Strait Islander Social Justice Commissioner (ATSISJC), 2006a, *Submission to the Australian Senate Community Affairs Legislation Committee on the Aboriginal Land Rights (Northern Territory) Amendment Bill 2006 (Cth)*, 13 July

——2006b, *Ending family violence and abuse in Aboriginal and Torres Strait Islander communities—Key issues*, Sydney: Human Rights and Equal Opportunity Commission

——2007a, *Native Title Report 2006*, Sydney: Human Rights and Equal Opportunity Commission

——2007b, *Social Justice Report 2006*, Sydney: Human Rights and Equal Opportunity Commission

Alfred, Taiaiake, 2013a, 'What does the land mean to us?', *Nations Rising*, 19 November, <http://nationsrising.org/what-does-the-land-mean-to-us/>

——2013b, 'Being and becoming Indigenous: Resurgence against contemporary colonialism', Naarm Oration, University of Melbourne, 13 December, <https://taiaiake.net/2013/12/13/being-and-becoming-indigenous-resurgence-against-contemporary-colonialism/>

——2017a, 'The great unlearning', *Taiaiake*, 28 February, <https://taiaiake.net/2017/02/28/the-great-unlearning/>

——2017b, 'For Indigenous nations to live, colonial mentalities must die', *Policy Options*, 13 October, <http://policyoptions.irpp.org/magazines/october-2017/for-indigenous-nations-to-live-colonial-mentalities-must-die/>

Alfred, Taiaiake & Corntassel, Jeff, 2005, 'Being Indigenous: Resurgences against contemporary colonialism', *Government and Opposition*, vol. 40, no. 4, pp. 597–614

Allam, Lorena, 2018, 'All children in detention in the Northern Territory are Indigenous', *The Guardian*, 26 June, <https://www.theguardian.com/australia-news/2018/jun/25/all-children-in-detention-in-the-northern-territory-are-indigenous>

Altman, Jon, 2017a, 'The debilitating aftermath of 10 years of NT Intervention', *New Matilda*, 28 July, <https://newmatilda.com/2017/07/28/the-debilitating-aftermath-of-10-years-of-nt-intervention/>

——2017b, 'Modern slavery in remote Australia', *Arena Magazine*, no. 150, pp. 12–15

Altman, Jon & Klein, Elise, 2017, 'Lessons from a basic income programme for Indigenous Australians', *Oxford Development Studies*, vol. 46, no. 1, pp. 132–146

Altman, Jon, Linkhorn, Craig & Clarke, Jennifer, 2005, *Land rights and development reform in remote Australia*, Working Paper no. 276/2005, Centre for Aboriginal Economic Policy Research, Canberra: Australian National University

ANAO see Australian National Audit Office

Anaya, James, 2010, *Observations on the Northern Territory Emergency Response in Australia*, National Council of Churches in Australia, <http://www.ncca.org.au/files/Natsiec/NTER_Observations_FINAL_by_SR_Anaya_.pdf>

Anderson, Ghillar Michael, 2013, 'Sovereign union will revive nationhood', *Koori Mail*, 6 November, p. 25

——2014a, 'Sovereignty is still ours', *Koori Mail*, 4 June, p. 25

——2014b, 'Ball is in our court', *Koori Mail*, 17 December, p. 24

Anderson, Ian, 2002, 'Understanding Indigenous violence', *Australian and New Zealand Journal of Public Health*, vol. 26, no. 5, pp. 408–409

Anderson, Pat, 2007, The Douglas Gordon Oration, Public Health Association of Australia Annual Conference, 25 September

Anthony, Thalia, 2016a, 'The limits of reconciliation in criminal sentencing', in S. Maddison, T. Clark & R. de Costa (eds), *The Limits of Settler Colonial Reconciliation*, Melbourne: Springer, pp. 249–269

——2016b, 'Deaths in custody: 25 years after the royal commission, we've gone backwards', *The Conversation*, 13 April, <https://theconversation.com/deaths-in-custody-25-years-after-the-royal-commission-weve-gone-backwards-57109>

——2017, 'FactCheck Q&A: are Indigenous Australians the most incarcerated people on Earth?', *The Conversation*, 6 June, <https://theconversation.com/factcheck-qanda-are-indigenous-australians-the-most-incarcerated-people-on-earth-78528>

Anthony, Thalia, Bartels, Lorna & Hopkins, Anthony, 2015, 'Lessons lost in sentencing: Welding individualised justice to Indigenous justice', *Melbourne University Law Review*, vol. 39, no. 3 pp. 47–76

Anthony, Thalia & Blagg, Harry, 2012, *Addressing the 'crime problem' of the Northern Territory Intervention: Alternate paths to regulating minor driving offences in remote Indigenous communities*, Report to the Criminology Research Advisory Council Grant: CRG 38/09-10, <http://www.criminologyresearchcouncil.gov.au/reports/CRG_38-0910_Final Report.pdf>

Appleby, Gabrielle, 2017, 'Power, treaty and truth', *Inside Story*, 29 May, <http://insidestory. org.au/power-treaty-and-truth/>

Appleby, Gabrielle & Brennan, Sean, 2017, 'The long road to recognition', *Inside Story*, 19 May, <http://insidestory.org.au/the-long-road-to-recognition>

Arabena, Kerry, 2005, *Not fit for modern Australian society: Aboriginal and Torres Strait Islander people and the new arrangements for the administration of Indigenous affairs*, Research Discussion Paper No. 16, Canberra: Australian Institute of Aboriginal and Torres Strait Islander Studies

Araluen, Evelyn, 2018, 'Finding ways home', in A. Heiss (ed), *Growing up Aboriginal in Australia*, Melbourne: Black Inc., pp. 12–15

Archibald-Binge, Ella, 2017, 'Did we miss a chance for a treaty? Charles Passi reflects on the Mabo verdict', *NITV News*, June 1, <http://www.sbs.com.au/nitv/nitv-news/ article/2017/05/31/did-we-miss-chance-treaty-charles-passi-reflects-mabo-verdict>

Atkinson, Judy, 2002, *Trauma trails, recreating song lines: The transgenerational effects of trauma in Indigenous Australia*, Melbourne: Spinifex Press

Atkinson, Wayne, 2008, 'Ngariarty: Speaking strong. The schools of human experience', in R. Perkins & M. Langton (eds), *First Australians: An illustrated history*, Melbourne: The Miegunyah Press, pp. 285–329

ATSIC see Aboriginal and Torres Strait Islander Commission

ATSIHF see Aboriginal and Torres Strait Islander Healing Foundation

ATSISJC see Aboriginal and Torres Strait Islander Social Justice Commissioner

Attwood, Bain, 2003, *Rights for Aborigines*, Sydney: Allen & Unwin

——2005, *Telling the truth about Aboriginal history*, Sydney: Allen & Unwin

Attwood, Bain & Foster, Stephen (eds), 2003, *Frontier conflict: The Australian experience*, Canberra: National Museum of Australia

Attwood, Bain & Markus, Andrew, 1999, *The struggle for Aboriginal rights: A documentary history*, Sydney: Allen & Unwin

——2004, *Thinking Black: William Cooper and the Australian Aborigines' League*, Canberra: Aboriginal Studies Press

Auspoll, 2012, *Evaluating the effectiveness of Reconciliation Action Plans*, Canberra: Reconciliation Australia

Australian Associated Press (AAP), 2009, 'Indigenous poverty "outrageous": Amnesty', *Sydney Morning Herald*, 18 November, <http://news.smh.com.au/breaking-news-national/indigenous-poverty-outrageous-amnesty-20091118-imnr.html>

——2017a, 'Indigenous groups protest title law change', *Nine News*, 2 March, <https://www. 9news.com.au/national/2017/03/02/13/43/indigenous-groups-protest-title-law-change>

——2017b, 'NT Intervention seen as "act of war" on Aboriginal people, Nova Peris says', *The Guardian*, 26 June, <https://www.theguardian.com/australia-news/2017/jun/26/ nt-intervention-seen-as-act-of-war-on-aboriginal-people-nova-peris-says>

Australian Broadcasting Corporation (ABC), 2003, 'Interview with Gary Foley', *Late Night Live*, 28 August, <http://www.abc.net.au/rn/latenightlive/stories/2003/927329.htm>

——2006, 'Crown prosecutor speaks out about abuse in central Australia', *Lateline*, 15 May, <http://www.abc.net.au/lateline/content/2006/s1639127.htm>

——2007a, 'McArthur River mine court ruling sidestepped', *ABC online*, 1 May, <http:// www.abc.net.au/news/2007-05-02/mcarthur-river-mine-court-ruling-sidestepped/ 2537932>

——2007b, 'Noel Pearson discusses the issues faced by Indigenous communities', *Lateline*, 26 June, <http://www.abc.net.au/lateline/content/2007/s1962844.htm>

——2016, 'Australia's shame', *Four Corners*, 25 July, <http://www.abc.net.au/4corners/australias-shame-promo/7649462>

——2017a, 'Q&A from Garma Festival 2017', ABC Television, 7 August, <http://www.abc.net.au/tv/qanda/txt/s4692070.htm>

——2017b, 'Western Bundjalung native title granted as Federal Court judge criticises process as too slow', *ABC News*, 13 September, <http://www.abc.net.au/news/2017-08-29/western-bundjalung-native-title-granted-criticises-slow-process/8851752>

——2017c, '1967 and Mabo: Moving forward', *Q&A*, ABC Television, 29 May, <http://www.abc.net.au/tv/qanda/txt/s4655309.htm>

Australian Bureau of Statistics (ABS), 2016, *Prisoners in Australia*, cat. no. 4517.0, <http://www.abs.gov.au/ausstats/abs@.nsf/Lookup/bySubject/4517.0~2016~Main Features~Imprisonment rates~12>

Australian National Audit Office (ANAO), 2017, *Indigenous Advancement Strategy*, Canberra: Department of the Prime Minister and Cabinet, Commonwealth of Australia

Balint, Jennifer, Evans, Julie & McMillan, Nesam, 2014, 'Rethinking transitional justice, redressing Indigenous harm: A new conceptual approach', *International Journal of Transitional Justice*, vol. 8, no. 2, pp. 194–216

Bamford, Matthew, 2017, 'WA election: Aboriginal candidates for both major parties in first for WA seat of Kimberley', *ABC News*, 26 February, <http://www.abc.net.au/news/2017-02-26/wa-election-kimberley-seat-profile-aboriginal-candidates/8302502>

Bardon, Jane, 2017a, 'Expansion plans for NT's McArthur River Mine dividing Indigenous families', *ABC News*, 9 June, <http://www.abc.net.au/news/2017-06-09/sacred-site-dispute-could-block-mcarthur-river-mine-expansion/8600614>

——2017b, 'Indigenous families battling against becoming second Stolen Generation in Northern Territory', *ABC News*, 20 March, <http://www.abc.net.au/news/2017-03-20/indigenous-families-battling-second-stolen-generation/8365072>

Barker, Joanne, 2017, 'The analytic constraints of settler colonialism', *Tequila Sovereign*, 2 February, <https://tequilasovereign.com/2017/02/02/the-analytic-constraints-of-settler-colonialism/>

Bashir, Bashir & Kymlicka, Will, 2008, 'Introduction: Struggles for inclusion and reconciliation in modern democracies', in B. Bashir & W. Kymlicka (eds), *The politics of reconciliation in multicultural societies*, Oxford: Oxford University Press, pp. 1–24

Bates, William 'Badger', 2017, 'When they take the water from a Barkandji person, they take our blood', *The Guardian*, 26 July, <https://www.theguardian.com/commentisfree/2017/jul/26/when-they-take-the-water-from-a-barkandji-person-they-take-our-blood>

Battell Lowman, Emma & Barker, Adam J., 2015, *Settler: Identity and colonialism in 21st century Canada*, Halifax: Fernwood Publishing

Behrendt, Larissa, 1995, *Aboriginal dispute resolution*, Sydney: The Federation Press

——2003, *Achieving social justice: Indigenous rights and Australia's future*, Sydney: The Federation Press

——2004, 'Election 2004: Indigenous rights and institutions', *Australian Review of Public Affairs*, 16 August, <http://www.australianreview.net/digest/2004/08/behrendt.html>

——2007, 'The emergency we had to have', in J. Altman & M. Hinkson (eds), *Coercive reconciliation: Stabilise, normalise, exit Aboriginal Australia*, Melbourne: Arena Publications, pp. 15–20

Benjamin, Clinton, 2017, 'An Indigenous treaty would create a virtuous circle of self-determination', *The Guardian*, 8 February, <https://www.theguardian.com/commentisfree/2017/feb/08/an-indigenous-treaty-would-create-a-virtuous-circle-of-self-determination>

Bennett, Scott, 1989, *Aborigines and political power*, Sydney: Allen & Unwin

Beresford, Quentin, 2006, *Rob Riley: An Aboriginal leader's quest for justice*, Canberra: Aboriginal Studies Press

Bern, John & Dodds, Susan, 2002, 'On the plurality of interests: Aboriginal self-government and land rights', in D. Ivison, P. Patton & W. Sanders (eds), *Political theory and the rights of Indigenous peoples*, New York: Cambridge University Press, pp. 163–179

Biddle, Nicholas, 2017, 'Government spending on Indigenous people is rising, so why do so many still live in poverty?', *The Conversation*, 26 October, <https://theconversation.com/government-spending-on-indigenous-people-is-rising-so-why-do-so-many-still-live-in-poverty-86210>

Billings, Peter, 2010, 'Social welfare experiments in Australia: More trials for Aboriginal families?', *Journal of Social Security Law*, vol. 17, no. 3, pp. 164–197

Birch, Tony, 2007, 'The "invisible fire": Indigenous sovereignty, history and responsibility', in A. Moreton-Robinson (ed), *Sovereign subjects: Indigenous sovereignty matters*, Sydney: Allen & Unwin, pp. 105–117

——2017, 'If we are to recognise heroes, where are the stories of Aboriginal courage?', *The Guardian*, 8 September, <https://www.theguardian.com/commentisfree/2017/sep/08/if-we-are-to-recognise-heroes-where-are-the-stories-of-aboriginal-courage?>

——2018, 'A change of date will do nothing to shake Australia from its colonial-settler triumphalism', *IndigenousX*, 21 January, <https://indigenousx.com.au/tony-birch-a-change-of-date-will-do-nothing-to-shake-australia-from-its-colonial-settler-triumphalism/>

Blagg, Harry & Anthony, Thalia, 2014, '"If those old women catch you, you're going to cop it": Night patrols, Indigenous women, and place based sovereignty in outback Australia', *African Journal Of Criminology & Justice Studies*, vol. 8, no. 1, pp. 103–124

Blanco, Claudianna, 2017, 'Racism puts Indigenous kids at abuse risk, while culture protects them, royal commission finds', *NITV News*, 12 July, <http://www.sbs.com.au/nitv/nitv-news/article/2017/07/12/racism-puts-indigenous-kids-abuse-risk-while-culture-protects-them-royal>

Bolt, Andrew, 2017, 'Stan Grant and the Taliban Left: At war with Statues', *Herald Sun*, 24 August, <http://www.heraldsun.com.au/blogs/andrew-bolt/stan-grant-and-the-taliban-left-at-war-with-statues/news-story/1d8159473585cf6080a3d198dd1b8ea1>

Bond, Chelsea, 2016, 'Refusing to play the race game', *The Conversation*, 29 September, <https://theconversation.com/refusing-to-play-the-race-game-66043>

——2017a, 'Fifty years on from the 1967 referendum, it's time to tell the truth about race', *The Conversation*, 30 May, <https://theconversation.com/fifty-years-on-from-the-1967-referendum-its-time-to-tell-the-truth-about-race-78403>

——2017b, 'Class is the new black: The dangers of an obsession with the "Aboriginal middle class"', *ABC News online*, 28 June, <http://mobile.abc.net.au/news/2017-06-28/opinion-class-is-the-new-black-chelsea-bond/8655544?pfmredir=sm>

——2018, 'Victims and vultures: The profitability of problematising the Aborigine', *IndigenousX*, 15 January, <http://indigenousx.com.au/chelsea-bond-victims-and-vultures-the-profitability-of-problematising-the-aborigine/>

Bonson, Dameyon, 2016, 'Indigenous suicide is a humanitarian crisis. We need a royal commission', *The Guardian*, 25 July, <https://www.theguardian.com/commentisfree/2016/jul/25/indigenous-suicide-is-a-humanitarian-crisis-we-need-a-royal-commission>

Bradfield, Stuart, 2004, 'Citizenship, history and Indigenous status in Australia: Back to the future or towards treaty?', *Journal of Australian Studies*, vol. 27, no. 80, pp. 165–176

——2006, 'Separatism or status quo?: Indigenous affairs from the birth of land rights to the death of ATSIC', *Australian Journal of Politics and History*, vol. 52, no. 1, pp. 80–97

Bradley, John & Seton, Kathryn, 2005, 'Self-determination or "deep colonising": Land claims, colonial authority and Indigenous representation', in B.A. Hocking (ed), *Unfinished constitutional business? Rethinking Indigenous self-determination*, Canberra: Aboriginal Studies Press, pp. 32–46

Brady, Wendy, 2007, 'That sovereign being: History matters', in A. Moreton-Robinson, *Sovereign subjects: Indigenous sovereignty matters*, Sydney: Allen & Unwin, pp. 140–151

Bray, Rob J., 2016, 'Seven years of evaluating income management—what have we learnt? Placing the findings of the New Income Management in the Northern Territory evaluation in context', *Australian Journal of Social Issues*, vol.51, no.4, pp. 449–468

Brennan, Bridget, 2016, '"Education is power": This childcare centre aims for an equal start', *ABC News*, 29 November, <http://www.abc.net.au/news/2016-11-29/indigenous-childcare-closing-the-gap/8042930>

——2017a, 'Garma festival: Turnbull, Shorten criticised for "empty platitudes" over Indigenous recognition', *ABC News*, 5 August, <http://mobile.abc.net.au/news/2017-08-05/indigenous-anger-of-turnbull-shorten-response-to-uluru-statement/8776812>

——2017b, 'Australia's progress on Closing the Gap "woefully inadequate", UN says', *ABC News*, 11 September, <http://www.abc.net.au/news/2017-09-11/closing-the-gap-progress-woeful-un-says/8892980>

——2018, 'Removing children from Indigenous communities "a national disaster"', *ABC News*, 31 January, <http://www.abc.net.au/news/2018-01-31/removing-children-indigenous-communities-national-disaster/9374866>

Brennan, Sean, Behrendt, Larissa, Strelein, Lisa & Williams, George, 2005, *Treaty*, Sydney: The Federation Press

Brigg, Morgan & Murphy, Lyndon, 2003, 'Whitegoods', *Arena Magazine*, no. 67, Oct–Nov, pp. 30–31

——2011, 'Beyond captives and captors: Settler-Indigenous governance for the 21st century', in S. Maddison & M. Brigg (eds), *Unsettling the settler state: Creativity and resistance in Indigenous settler-state governance*, Sydney: The Federation Press, pp. 16–32

Briscoe, Luke, 2017, 'Could the Redfern Statement reform the failing Indigenous affairs policies?', *NITV News*, 14 February, <http://www.sbs.com.au/nitv/article/2017/02/14/could-redfern-statement-reform-failing-indigenous-affairs-policies>

Briskman, Linda, 2003, *The black grapevine: Aboriginal activism and the stolen generations*, Sydney: The Federation Press

Brown, Bill, 2016, 'Historic meeting of Yuin nation agrees to massive native title claim in south-east New South Wales', *ABC News*, December 23, <http://www.abc.net.au/news/2016-12-23/yuin-nation-native-title-claim/8145798>

Brunton, Ron, 1993, *Black suffering, white guilt? Aboriginal disadvantage and the Royal Commission into Deaths in Custody*, Perth: Institute of Public Affairs

Buckmaster, Luke & Ey, Carol, 2012, *Is income management working?*, Background note, Canberra: Parliamentary Library, Parliament of Australia, <http://parlinfo.aph.gov.au/parlInfo/download/library/prspub/1603602/upload_binary/1603602.pdf>

Buckmaster, Luke, Ey, Carol & Klapdor, Michael, 2012, *Income management: An overview*, Canberra: Parliamentary Library, Parliament of Australia, <https://www.aph.gov.au/About_Parliament/Parliamentary_Departments/Parliamentary_Library/pubs/BN/2011-2012/IncomeManagementOverview#_Toc328056496>

Burgess, Katie, 2016, 'Intergenerational trauma leading to higher incarceration rates, forum told', *Canberra Times*, 5 August, <http://www.canberratimes.com.au/act-news/intergenerational-trauma-leading-to-higher-indigenous-incarceration-rates-forum-told-20160803-gqko56.html>

Burgmann, Verity, 2003, *Power, profit and protest*, Sydney: Allen & Unwin

Caccetta, Wendy, 2016a, 'Don Dale, NT v Abu Ghraib, Iraq—Spot the difference', *National Indigenous Times*, 26 July, <http://nit.com.au/don-dale-nt-v-abu-ghraib-iraq-spot-difference/>

——2016b, 'Social workers, leaders lament cycle of violence', *National Indigenous Times*, 9 November, <http://nit.com.au/social-worker-laments-cycle-violence/>

——2016c, 'Men must join the fight against violence, says leader Mason', *National Indigenous Times*, 14 October, <http://nit.com.au/men-must-join-fight-violence-says-leader-mason/>

——2017a, 'Land use deals kill native title: Pat Dodson', *National Indigenous Times*, 28 June, <http://nit.com.au/land-use-deals-kill-native-title-pat-dodson/>

——2017b, 'Bombshell ruling overturns "traditional owners"', *National Indigenous Times*, 23 November, <https://nit.com.au/bombshell-ruling-overturns-traditional-owners/>

Calma, Tom, 2007, 'Maximising economic and community development opportunities through native title and other forms of agreement-making', Paper presented to the National Native Title Conference 2007: Tides of Native Title, Cairns, 6–8 June

Calma, Tom & Dick, Darren, 2011, 'The National Congress of Australia's First Peoples: Changing the relationship between Aboriginal and Torres Strait Islander peoples and the state?', in S. Maddison & M. Brigg (eds), *Unsettling the settler state: Creativity and resistance in Indigenous settler-state governance*, The Federation Press: Sydney, pp. 168–188

Campbell, Claire, 2017, 'Youth detention royal commission: Aboriginal elder says another Stolen Generation is being created', *ABC News*, 30 May, <http://www.abc.net.au/news/2017-05-30/claims-another-stolen-generation-is-being-created-in-nt/8573528>

CAR see Council for Aboriginal Reconciliation

Carson, Bronwyn, Dunbar, Terry, Chenhall, Richard & Bailie, Ross, 2007, *Social determinants of Indigenous health*, Sydney: Allen & Unwin

Cavanagh, Edward, 2012, 'History, time and the indigenist critique', *Arena Journal*, no. 37/38, pp. 16–39

Cave, Damien, 2017, '4,000 kilometers, 10 Months: One Australian's march for Indigenous rights', *New York Times*, 7 August, <https://mobile.nytimes.com/2017/08/07/world/australia/clinton-pryor-aboriginal-walk.html>

Central and Northern Land Councils, 1991, *Our land, our life: Aboriginal land rights in Australia's Northern Territory*, Alice Springs: Northern Land Council

Central Land Council, 1994, *The land is always alive: The story of the Central Land Council*, Alice Springs: Central Land Council

Chadwick, Vince, 2013, 'Nation risks a new stolen generation, leaders warn', *Sydney Morning Herald*, 15 June, <http://www.smh.com.au/national/nation-risks-a-new-stolen-generation-leaders-warn-20130614-2o9ua.html>

Chan, Gabrielle, 2017, 'Labor sets up Indigenous caucus in push to improve representation across all parties', *The Guardian*, 20 February, <https://www.theguardian.com/australia-news/2017/feb/20/labor-sets-up-indigenous-caucus-in-push-to-improve-representation-across-all-parties>

Chan, Janet, 1997, *Changing police culture: Policing in a multicultural society*, Cambridge: Cambridge University Press

Chesterman, John, 2005, *Civil rights: how Indigenous Australians won formal equality*, Brisbane: University of Queensland Press

Children's Ground, 2017, 'William Tilmouth: You won't Close the Gap by trying to "fix" people', *Children's Ground News*, 14 February, <https://www.childrensground.org.au/news/86/you-wont-close-the-gap-by-trying-to-fix-people>

Clarke, Allan, 2017, 'Aboriginal people are victims of violence too, it's time to bring the perpetrators to account', *NITV News*, 18 December, <https://www.sbs.com.au/nitv/nitv-news/article/2017/12/18/aboriginal-people-are-victims-violence-too-its-time-bring-perpetrators-account>

Clarke, Connie, 2016, 'To hell and back: How June Oscar dried out Fitzroy Crossing', *Perth Now*, 15 August, <http://www.perthnow.com.au/news/western-australia/stm/to-hell-and-back--how-june-oscar-dried-out-fitzroy-crossing/news-story/d13f9f1fa535c6a9d5b57b582d118f67>

Clayton-Dixon, Callum, 2015, 'I can't call myself an Indigenous Australian and also say sovereignty never ceded', *IndigenousX*, 11 December, <http://indigenousx.com.au/i-cant-call-myself-an-indigenous-australian-and-also-say-sovereignty-never-ceded/>

Coleman, Claire, 2018, 'We will not accept Australia Day on 26 January without resistance', *The Guardian*, 25 September, <https://www.theguardian.com/commentisfree/2018/sep/25/you-can-have-australia-day-any-other-day-we-wont-accept-26-january-without-resistance>

Commonwealth of Australia, 2002, *Commonwealth Government response to the Council for Aboriginal Reconciliation final report—Reconciliation: Australia's challenge*, Canberra: Commonwealth of Australia

Conor, Liz, 2016, '"Piccaninnies" and other expendables: What we've always done to black kids in Australia', *New Matilda*, 26 July, <https://newmatilda.com/2016/07/26/piccaninnies-and-other-expendables-what-weve-always-done-to-black-kids-in-australia/>

Copp, Amanda, 2017, 'Can't put a price tag on Great Barrier Reef's value, say Traditional Owners', *NITV News*, 26 June, <http://www.sbs.com.au/nitv/nitv-news/article/2017/06/26/cant-put-price-tag-great-barrier-reefs-value-say-traditional-owners>

Cornell, Stephen, 2004, 'Indigenous jurisdiction and daily life: Evidence from North America', Paper presented to the National Forum on Indigenous health and the treaty debate: Rights governance and responsibility, Sydney: University of New South Wales, 11 September

——2006, *Indigenous peoples, poverty and self-determination in Australia, New Zealand, Canada and the United States*, Joint Occasional Papers on Native Affairs, No. 2006-02, Native Nations Institute, Tucson: University of Arizona

——2015, 'Processes of Native Nationhood: The Indigenous politics of self-government', *International Indigenous Policy Journal*, vol. 6, no. 4, pp. 1–27

Corntassel, Jeff, 2012, 'Re-envisioning resurgence: Indigenous pathways to decolonization and sustainable self-determination', *Decolonization: Indigeneity, Education & Society*, vol. 1, no. 1, pp. 86–101

Coulthard, Glen S., 2014, *Red skin, white masks: Rejecting the colonial politics of recognition*, Minneapolis: Minnesota University Press

Council for Aboriginal Reconciliation, 2000, *Reconciliation: Australia's challenge— Final report of the Council for Aboriginal Reconciliation to the Prime Minister and the Commonwealth Parliament*, Canberra: Commonwealth of Australia

Cromb, Natalie, 2017a, 'Comment: We need Aboriginal control of Aboriginal affairs', *NITV*, 23 March, <http://www.sbs.com.au/nitv/article/2017/03/23/comment-we-need-aboriginal-control-aboriginal-affairs>

——2017b, 'Nat Cromb: Justice for Elijah Doughty, now', *IndigenousX*, 25 July, <http://indigenousx.com.au/nat-cromb-justice-for-elijah-now/>

——2017c, 'Drowning in white privilege', *Independent Australia*, 29 July, <https://independentaustralia.net/life/life-display/drowning-in-white-privilege>

——2017d, 'We are the lucky country for a privileged white majority. A republic could turn this around', *The Guardian*, 1 August, <https://www.theguardian.com/commentisfree/2017/aug/01/we-are-the-lucky-country-for-a-privileged-white-majority-a-republic-could-turn-this-around>

——2018a, 'Political divisiveness happens every time Indigenous people are the topic of national debate', *NITV News*, 17 January, <https://www.sbs.com.au/nitv/article/2018/01/16/opinion-political-divisiveness-happens-every-time-indigenous-people-are-topic1>

——2018b, 'Still waiting 21 years after the Bringing Them Home Report', IndigenousX, 5 April, <https://indigenousx.com.au/natalie-cromb-still-waiting-21-years-after-the-bringing-them-home-report/>

Cubillo, Eddie, 2018, 'On the personal toll for Indigenous advocates and people when governments fail to act', *Croakey*, 18 June, <https://croakey.org/on-the-personal-toll-for-indigenous-advocates-and-people-when-governments-fail-to-act/>

Cunneen, Chris, 2001, *Conflict, politics and crime: Aboriginal communities and the police*, Sydney: Allen & Unwin

——2005, 'Consensus and sovereignty: rethinking policing in the light of Indigenous self-determination', in B.A. Hocking (ed), *Unfinished constitutional business? Rethinking Indigenous self-determination*, Canberra: Aboriginal Studies Press, pp. 47–60

Cunningham, Katie, 2017, '"It's not our opinion, it's fucking history": Dan Sultan on the Australia Day debate', *Junkee*, 3 August, <http://junkee.com/not-opinion-fucking-history-dan-sultan-australia-day-debate/116318>

Cunningham, Melissa & Carey, Adam, 2018, '"Invasion day" rally organiser says her comments Australia should "burn to the ground" should not be taken literally', *The Age*, 26 January, <http://www.theage.com.au/victoria/invasion-day-rally-organiser-says-her-comments-australia-should-burn-to-the-ground-should-not-be-taken-literally-20180126-p4yyxo.html>

Daly, Erin & Sarkin, Jeremy, 2007, *Reconciliation in divided societies: Finding common ground*, Philadelphia: University of Pennsylvania Press

Daley, Paul, 2017, 'Closing the gap isn't just a dramatic policy failure, it's a moral failure too', *The Guardian*, 14 February, <https://www.theguardian.com/commentisfree/2017/feb/14/closing-the-gap-isnt-just-a-dramatic-policy-failure-its-a-moral-failure-too>

Davidson, Helen, 2016a, 'Garma festival: Indigenous leaders say Land Rights Act is not protecting them', *The Guardian*, 30 July, <https://www.theguardian.com/australia-news/2016/jul/30/garma-festival-indigenous-leaders-say-land-rights-act-is-not-protecting-them>

——2016b, 'Jobs scheme doing "more harm than good" in Indigenous communities', *The Guardian*, 3 October, <https://www.theguardian.com/australia-news/2016/oct/03/jobs-scheme-doing-more-harm-than-good-in-indigenous-communities>

——2017a, '"We don't want to be dug out": The Indigenous art helping to protect the land from mining', *The Guardian*, 22 June, <https://www.theguardian.com/artanddesign/2017/jun/22/we-dont-want-to-be-dug-out-the-indigenous-art-helping-to-protect-the-land-from-mining>

——2017b, 'Child protection cases more than doubled after NT Intervention, inquiry told', *The Guardian*, 19 June, <https://www.theguardian.com/australia-news/2017/jun/19/child-protection-cases-more-than-doubled-after-nt-intervention-inquiry-told>

——2017c, 'Tackling alcohol in remote areas: Communities plead for local control', *The Guardian*, 4 July, <https://www.theguardian.com/australia-news/2017/jul/04/tackling-alcohol-remote-areas-communities-plead-local-control>

——2018a, 'Garma festival: Indigenous sovereignty would be a "gift for all Australians"', *The Guardian*, 4 August, <https://www.theguardian.com/australia-news/2018/aug/04/garma-festival-indigenous-sovereignty-would-be-a-gift-for-all-australians>

——2018b, 'Closing the Gap "refresh": Coalition accused of ignoring Indigenous Australians', *The Guardian*, 2 January, <https://www.theguardian.com/australia-news/2018/jan/02/coalition-accused-of-ignoring-indigenous-australians-in-closing-the-gap-refresh>

Davis, Lynne, Denis, Jeff & Sinclair, Raven, 2017, 'Pathways of settler decolonization', *Settler Colonial Studies*, vol. 7, no. 4, pp. 393–397

Davis, Megan, 2006, 'Treaty, Yeah? The utility of a treaty to advancing reconciliation in Australia', *Alternative Law Review*, vol. 31, no. 3, pp. 127–136

——2008, 'ATSIC and Indigenous women: Lessons for the future', *University of New South Wales Faculty of Law Research Series*, Paper 9, <http://law.bepress.com/unswwps/flrps08/art9>

——2012, 'A right that is fundamental to our aspirations', *Koori Mail*, 28 November, p. 24

——2015a, 'Gesture politics: Recognition alone won't fix Indigenous affairs', *The Monthly*, December, <https://www.themonthly.com.au/issue/2015/december/1448888400/megan davis/gesture-politics>

——2015b, 'Keating was right to intervene over recognition and Indigenous Australia's unfinished business', *The Guardian*, 21 October, <http://www.theguardian.com/commentisfree/2015/oct/21/soft-recognition-alone-will-not-resolve-indigenous-australias-unfinished-business>

——2016a, 'Listening but not hearing: Process has trumped substance in Indigenous affairs', *The Conversation*, 22 June, <https://theconversation.com/listening-but-not-hearing-process-has-trumped-substance-in-indigenous-affairs-55161>

——2016b, 'Scant recognition: Have Aboriginal and Torres Strait Islander peoples any reason to hope?' ABC Religion and Ethics, 11 August, <http://www.abc.net.au/religion/articles/2016/08/10/4515798.htm>

——2017a, 'To walk in two worlds: The Uluru Statement is a clear and urgent call for reform', *The Monthly*, July, <https://www.themonthly.com.au/issue/2017/july/1498831200/megan-davis/walk-two-worlds>

——2017b, 'Bad faith over Indigenous voice', *The Saturday Paper*, 4 November, <https://www.thesaturdaypaper.com.au/opinion/topic/2017/11/04/bad-faith-over-indigenous-voice/15097140005450>

Davis, Megan & Langton, Marcia, 2016, 'Introduction', in M. Davis & M. Langton (eds), *It's our country: Indigenous arguments for meaningful constitutional recognition and reform*, Melbourne: Melbourne University Press

Davis, Megan & Williams, George, 2015, *Everything you need to know about the referendum to recognise Indigenous Australians*, Sydney: NewSouth Publishing

Davis, Sharon, 2016, 'As an Aboriginal woman, I've learned education is essential to our freedom', *The Guardian*, 1 February, <https://www.theguardian.com/commentisfree/2016/feb/01/as-an-aboriginal-woman-ive-learned-education-is-essential-to-our-freedom>

Davis, Tony, 2010, 'Marching for a fresh beginning: The walks that took place across the country in 2000 gave new hope to Indigenous Australians', *Sydney Morning Herald*, 28 March, <http://www.smh.com.au/national/marching-for-a-fresh-beginning-20100527-whuu.html>

Decolonization, 2014, 'Leanne Simpson and Glen Coulthard on Dechinta Bush University, Indigenous land-based education and embodied resurgence', *Decolonization: Indigeneity, Education & Society*, 26 November, <https://decolonization.wordpress.com/2014/11/26/leanne-simpson-and-glen-coulthard-on-dechinta-bush-university-indigenous-land-based-education-and-embodied-resurgence/>

de Costa, Ravi, 2016, 'Two kinds of recognition: The politics of engagement in settler societies', in S. Maddison, T. Clark & R. de Costa (eds), *The limits of settler colonial reconciliation: Non-Indigenous people and the responsibility to engage*, Melbourne: Springer.

Department of Prime Minister and Cabinet (DPMC), 2017a, *Closing the Gap refresh: A public discussion paper*, Commonwealth of Australia, <https://closingthegaprefresh.pmc.gov.au/sites/.../ctg-next-phase-discussion-paper.pdf>

——2017b, *Closing the Gap Prime Minister's Report 2017*, Commonwealth of Australia, <https://closingthegap.pmc.gov.au/sites/default/files/ctg-report-2017.pdf>

Department of Social Services (DSS), 2016, *Third Action Plan 2016–2019 of the National Plan to Reduce Violence against Women and their Children 2010–2022*, Commonwealth of Australia, <https://www.dss.gov.au/sites/default/files/documents/10_2016/third_action_plan.pdf>

Dias, Avani, 2017, 'Arnhem Land community finds success blending Aboriginal culture with modern education', *ABC News*, 25 May, <http://www.abc.net.au/news/2017-05-25/indigenous-education-in-a-modern-world/8555368>

Dillon, Michael, 2018, 'The devil in the detail: The government's proposed Indigenous Land Fund legislation', on the blog *A walking shadow: Observations on Indigenous public policy and institutional transparency*, 2 April, <http://refragabledelusions.blogspot.com/2018/04/the-devil-in-detail-governments.html>

Dodson, Michael, 1997, 'Citizenship in Australia: An Indigenous perspective', *Alternative Law Journal*, vol. 22, no. 2, pp. 57–59

——2003, 'The end in the beginning: Re(de)finding Aboriginality', in M. Grossman (ed.), *Blacklines: Contemporary critical writing by Indigenous Australians*, Melbourne: Melbourne University Press, pp. 25–42

——2004, 'Indigenous Australians', in R. Manne (ed), *The Howard years*, Melbourne: Black Inc., pp. 119–143

——2007, 'Mabo Lecture: Asserting Our Sovereignty', in L. Strelein (ed), *Dialogue about Land justice: Papers from the National Native Title conferences*, Canberra: Aboriginal Studies Press, pp. 13–18

Dodson, Michael & Smith, Diane, 2003, *Governance for sustainable development: Strategic issues and principles for Indigenous Australian communities*, Discussion paper no. 250/2003, Canberra: Centre for Aboriginal Economic Policy Research, Australian National University

Dodson, Patrick, 1997, 'Reconciliation in crisis', in G. Yunupingu (ed), *Our land is our life: Land rights—Past, present and future*, St Lucia: University of Queensland Press, pp. 137–149

——2000, *Beyond the mourning gate: Dealing with unfinished business*, The Wentworth Lecture, 12 May, Canberra: Australian Institute of Aboriginal and Torres Strait Islander Studies

——2016, 'Locking in change', *Koori Mail*, 20 April, p. 22

——2017, 'Indigenous communities need to be part of the solution. Top-down measures don't work', *The Guardian*, 22 September, <https://www.theguardian.com/commentisfree/2017/sep/22/indigenous-communities-need-to-be-part-of-the-solution-top-down-measures-dont-work>

——2018, 'Challenge of negotiation: Learning the hard way', *Griffith Review*, 60, pp. 58–66

Donnelly, Beau, 2016, 'Could this be the place for a treaty to "end the war" on Indigenous Australia?', *The Age*, 4 November, <http://www.theage.com.au/victoria/could-this-be-the-place-for-a-treaty-to-end-the-war-on-indigenous-australia-20161104-gsi6z2.html>

Dovey, Ceridwen, 2017, 'The mapping of massacres', *The New Yorker*, 6 December, <https://www.newyorker.com/culture/culture-desk/mapping-massacres>

DPMC see Department of Prime Minister and Cabinet

DSS see Department of Social Security

Dudgeon, Pat, Milroy, Jill, Calma, Tom, Luxford, Yvonne, Ring, Ian, Walker, Roz, Cox, Adele, Georgatos, Gerry & Holland, Christopher, 2016, *Solutions that work: What the evidence and our people tell us*, Aboriginal and Torres Strait Islander Suicide Prevention Evaluation Project Report, Perth: University of Western Australia

Duffy, Sean & Parker, Kirstie, 2015, '24 years on, much more must change', *Koori Mail*, 22 April, p. 25

Elliott, Michael, 2016, 'Participatory parity and Indigenous decolonization struggles', *Constellations*, vol. 23, no. 3, pp. 413–424

Everingham, Sara, 2017, 'Remote Aboriginal community in the NT signs 99-year lease to control their own land', *ABC News*, 19 November, <http://www.abc.net.au/news/2017-11-19/gunyangara-community-sign-99-year-lease/9165490>

Expert Panel on Constitutional Recognition of Indigenous Australians, 2012, *Recognising Aboriginal and Torres Strait Islander peoples in the Constitution: Report of the Expert Panel*, Canberra: Commonwealth of Australia

Finlay, Summer May, Williams, Megan, McInerney, Marie, Sweet, Melissa & Ward, Mitchell (eds), 2016, *#JustJustice: Tackling the over-incarceration of Aboriginal and Torres Strait Islander peoples*, 2nd edn, croakey.org

Finnane, Mark, 1994, *Police and government: Histories of policing in Australia*, Melbourne: Oxford University Press

Fischer, Mez, 2014a, 'Division over treaty', *Koori Mail*, 12 February, p. 6

——2014b 'Women to tell UN of suicide shame', *Koori Mail*, 7 May, p. 12

——2014c, '7 years on, Intervention under attack', *Koori Mail*, 2 July, p. 11

——2014d, 'Sisters walk for freedom', *Koori Mail*, 19 November, p. 28

Fitzpatrick, Stephen, 2017a, 'Indigenous recognition: communities seek voice in consultation', *The Australian*, 1 April, <http://www.theaustralian.com.au/national-affairs/indigenous/indigenous-recognition-communities-seek-voice-in-consultation/news-story/1cbb1afe08dcd7357a1c7bebeadba972>

——2017b, 'Northern Territory Intervention just "another form of abuse"', *The Australian*, 3 April, <http://www.theaustralian.com.au/national-affairs/indigenousnorthern-territory-intervention-just-another-form-of-abuse/news-story/cbe127d8e6b11a699eba4452b90549c4>

——2017c, 'Senior leaders call for indigenous advisory body', *The Australian*, 24 July, <http://www.theaustralian.com.au/news/nation/senior-leaders-call-for-indigenous-advisory-body/news-story/ed5d490b767b630fc7e92abdc40512d5>

Flick, Isabel & Goodall, Heather, 2004, *Isabel Flick: The many lives of an extraordinary Aboriginal woman*, Sydney: Allen & Unwin

Flynn, Eugenia, 2018, 'Abolish Australia Day: Changing the date only seeks to further entrench Australian nationalism', *IndigenousX*, 23 January, <https://indigenousx.com.au/eugenia-flynn-abolish-australia-day-changing-the-date-only-seeks-to-further-entrench-australian-nationalism/#.W8S0jhNKiu4>

Foley, Gary, 2007, 'The Australian Labor Party and the *Native Title Act*' in A. Moreton-Robinson (ed), *Sovereign subjects: Indigenous sovereignty matters*, Sydney: Allen & Unwin, pp. 118–139

Fournier, Jean T., 2005, 'Preface' in B.A. Hocking (ed), *Unfinished constitutional business? Rethinking Indigenous self-determination*, Canberra: Aboriginal Studies Press, pp. vii–ix

Frankland, Richard, 2017, 'A treaty won't solve everything, but it could change this nation's cultural tapestry', *IndigenousX*, 7 March, <http://indigenousx.com.au/a-treaty-wont-solve-everything-but-it-could-change-this-nations-cultural-tapestry>

Gardiner, Greg & Bourke, Eleanor, 2000, 'Indigenous populations, "mixed" discourses and identities', *People and Place*, vol. 8, no. 2, pp. 43–52

Gardiner-Garden, John, 2000, *The Definition of Aboriginality*, Research Note No. 18, 2000–01, Canberra: Department of the Parliamentary Library

Gartry, Laura & Trigger, Rebecca, 2015, 'Police thought dying Aboriginal woman Ms Dhu was faking it, coronial inquest told', *ABC News*, 23 November, <http://www.abc.net.au/news/2015-11-23/inquest-into-death-of-dhu-in-police-custody/6963244>

Gibson, Paddy, 2017, '10 impacts of the NT Intervention', *NITV*, 21 June, <http://www.sbs.com.au/nitv/article/2017/06/21/10-impacts-nt-intervention>

Gilbert, Kevin, 1987, *Aboriginal Sovereignty, Justice, the Law and the Land*, Captains Flat: Burrambinga Books

Gilbert, Kevin, 2002 [1973], *Because a White Man'll Never Do It*, Sydney: Angus & Robertson Classics, HarperCollins Publishers

——1988, *Aboriginal sovereignty: Justice, the law and the land*, self-published, Canberra, <http://www.aiatsis.gov.au/lbry/dig_prgm/treaty/t88/m0066865_a/m0066865_p1_a.pdf>

Gondarra, Djiniyini, Kunoth-Monks, Rosalie, Ryan, Japata, Nelson, Harry, Murunggirritj, Djapirri, Shaw, Barbara & Mununggurr, Yananymul, 2011, 'Statement by Northern Territory Elders and community representatives: No more! Enough is enough!', *Concerned Australians*, 4 November, <http://www.concernedaustralians.com.au/media/Statement-4-11-11.pdf>

Goninan, Jason, 2018, 'There are no halves', in A. Heiss (ed), *Growing up Aboriginal in Australia*, Melbourne: Black Inc., pp. 93–99

Gooch, Declan, 2017, '"Entrenched racism" in NSW Police harming young people, Indigenous leader says', *ABC News*, 29 March, <http://www.abc.net.au/news/2017-03-29/entrenched-racism-in-nsw-police-harming-young-people-leader-says/8398122>

Goodall, Heather, 1996, *Invasion to embassy: Land in Aboriginal politics in New South Wales, 1770–1972*, Sydney: Allen & Unwin

Gordon, Michael, 2017, 'Shocking Close the Gap report shows need for new relationship between black and white Australians', *Sydney Morning Herald*, 14 February, <http://www.smh.com.au/federal-politics/political-opinion/shocking-close-the-gap-report-shows-need-for-new-relationship-between-black-and-white-australians-20170214-gucmo5.html>

Gordon, Sue, Hallahan, Kay & Henry, Darrell, 2002, *Putting the picture together: Inquiry into response by government agencies to complaints of family violence and child abuse in Aboriginal communities*, Perth: WA Department of Premier and Cabinet

Gorey, Michael, 2017, 'NT Aboriginal leader defends January 26 Australia Day', *Canberra Times*, 26 January, <http://www.canberratimes.com.au/act-news/nt-aboriginal-leader-defends-january-26-australia-day-20170126-gtzd74.html>

Gorrie, Nayuka 2016, 'On black rage, new funerals, and the exhausting resilience of our mob', *Junkee*, 1 September, <http://junkee.com/black-rage-new-funerals-exhausting-resilience-mob/84230>

——2017, 'Hope is like a key card I perpetually lose and find', *The Guardian*, 8 August, <https://www.theguardian.com/commentisfree/2017/aug/08/hope-is-like-a-key-card-i-perpetually-lose-and-find>

Graham, Chris, 2007, 'PM's reign a "living nightmare": leaders', *National Indigenous Times*, 6 September, p. 6

——2014, 'Congress staunch in face of uncertainty', *Koori Mail*, 12 February, pp. 7–8

——2017a, 'Bad Aunty: 10 years on, how ABC *Lateline* sparked the racist NT Intervention (with introduction by John Pilger)', *New Matilda*, 23 June, <https://newmatilda.com/2017/06/23/bad-aunty-seven-years-how-abc-lateline-sparked-racist-nt-intervention/>

——2017b, 'The killing fields: How we failed Elijah Doughty, and countless others', *New Matilda*, 23 July, <https://newmatilda.com/2017/07/23/groundhog-day-elijah-doughty-joins-a-long-list-of-deaths-with-no-justice/>

——2018, 'Apartheid state: Compensation for sexual abuse victims, betrayal for Stolen Generation', *New Matilda*, 11 February, <https://newmatilda.com/2018/02/11/apartheid-state-compensation-sexual-abuse-victims-betrayal-stolen-generations/>

Grant, Stan, 2016a, 'Four Corners: I can't see reason, I can only feel anger. And sometimes that's better', *The Guardian*, 26 July, <https://www.theguardian.com/australia-news/

commentisfree/2016/jul/26/four-corners-i-cant-see-reason-i-can-only-feel-anger-and-sometimes-thats-better>

——2016b, 'Without a treaty and constitutional recognition, no Australian is truly free', *The Guardian*, 14 June, <https://www.theguardian.com/commentisfree/2016/jun/15/without-a-treaty-and-constitutional-recognition-no-australian-is-truly-free>

——2016c, *Talking to my country*, Melbourne: Scribe Publications

——2017a, 'America tears down its racist history, we ignore ours', *ABC News*, 20 August, <http://www.abc.net.au/news/2017-08-18/america-tears-down-its-racist-history-we-ignore-ours-stan-grant/8821662>

——2017b, 'It is a damaging myth that Captain Cook discovered Australia', *ABC News*, 23 August, <http://www.abc.net.au/news/2017-08-23/stan-grant:-damaging-myth-captain-cook-discovered-australia/8833536>

——2017c, 'Between catastrophe and survival: The real journey Captain Cook set us on', *ABC News*, 25 August, <http://mobile.abc.net.au/news/2017-08-25/stan-grant-captain-cook-indigenous-culture-statues-history/8843172?pfmredir=sm>

Gray, Stephen, 2015, *The Northern Territory Intervention: An evaluation*, Melbourne: Castan Centre for Human Rights Law, Monash University <https://www.monash.edu/__data/assets/pdf_file/0008/406943/Caitlin-edit-of-NT-Intervention-page-1.pdf>

Gredley, Rebecca, 2017, 'Reform of Indigenous affairs sector in WA', *News.com*, 5 April, <http://www.news.com.au/national/breaking-news/reform-of-indigenous-affairs-sector-in-wa/news-story/2bee89d34e3c72923bd6ef2c7555c68d>

Guivarra, Nancia, 2016, 'Goat Island (or Me-mel) to be returned to Indigenous ownership', *NITV News*, 25 October, <http://www.sbs.com.au/nitv/nitv-news/article/2016/10/25/goat-island-or-me-mel-be-returned-indigenous-ownership>

——2017, 'Ross River referendum meetings focus on parliament and a treaty', *NITV News*, 4 April, <http://www.sbs.com.au/nitv/article/2017/04/04/ross-river-referendum-meetings-focus-parliament-and-treaty>

Gunstone, Andrew, 2009, *Unfinished business: The Australian formal reconciliation process*, 2nd edn, Melbourne: Australian Scholarly Publishing

Guyula, Yingiya Mark, 2010, 'NT Intervention review needed', Letter to the editor, *Koori Mail*, 13 January, p. 23

——2016, 'Yingiya Mark Guyula. Why I am running in the Northern Territory elections', *IndigenousX*, April 27, <http://indigenousx.com.au/why-i-am-running-in-the-northern-territory-elections-yingiya-mark-guyula/>

Hamilton, Fiona, 2017a, 'Securing our agency will require changing systems and structures', *IndigenousX*, 13 March, <http://indigenousx.com.au/securing-our-agency-will-require-changing-systems-and-structures/>

——2017b, 'We need safe housing for Aboriginal women and children. And we can't wait for an election', *IndigenousX*, 14 March, <http://indigenousx.com.au/we-need-safe-housing-for-aboriginal-women-and-children-and-we-cant-wait-for-an-election/>

Hamlyn, Charlotte, 2017, 'Elijah Doughty trial: Kalgoorlie searches for closure, elders fear issues being forgotten', *ABC News*, 22 July, <http://www.abc.net.au/news/2017-07-22/elija-doughty-kalgoorlie-closure-after-sentencing/8734538>

Havemann, Paul, 2000, 'Enmeshed in the web? Indigenous peoples' rights in the network society', in R. Cohen & S. Rai (eds), *Global social movements*, London: The Athlone Press, pp. 18–32

Hayman-Reber, Madeline, 2018, 'Community Development Program "racist, punitive, and expensive", report says,' *NITV News*, 2 May, <https://www.sbs.com.au/nitv/nitv-news/article/2018/05/02/community-development-program-racist-punitive-and-expensive-report-says>

Hinchliffe, Joe, 2017, 'Call to remove statue of John Batman, "founder of Melbourne", over role in Indigenous killings,' *Sydney Morning Herald*, 26 August, <http://amp.smh.com.au/victoria/call-to-remove-statue-of-john-batman-founder-of-melbourne-over-role-in-indigenous-killings-20170826-gy4snc.html>

Hinkson, Melinda, 2007, 'In the name of the child', in J. Altman & M. Hinkson (eds), *Coercive Reconciliation: Stabilise, normalise, exit Aboriginal Australia*, Melbourne: Arena Publications, pp. 1–12

——2010, 'Media images and the politics of hope', in J. Altman & M. Hinkson (eds), *Culture crisis: Anthropology and politics in Aboriginal Australia*, Sydney: UNSW Press, pp. 229–47

——2017a, 'Aftermath', *Arena Magazine*, no. 148, June–July, pp. 2–3

——2017b, '10 years after the Intervention, it's time to admit it has destroyed Aboriginal communities', *The Guardian*, 21 June, <https://www.theguardian.com/commentisfree/2017/jun/21/10-year-after-the-intervention-its-time-to-admit-it-has-destroyed-aboriginal-communities>

Hobbs, Harry, 2016, 'Will treaties with Indigenous Australians overtake constitutional recognition?', *The Conversation*, 20 December, <https://theconversation.com/will-treaties-with-indigenous-australians-overtake-constitutional-recognition-70524>

——2017a, 'Explainer: Why 300 Indigenous leaders are meeting at Uluru this week', *The Conversation*, 23 May, <https://theconversation.com/explainer-why-300-indigenous-leaders-are-meeting-at-uluru-this-week-77955>

——2017b, 'Response to Referendum Council report suggests a narrow path forward on Indigenous constitutional reform', *The Conversation*, 18 July, <https://theconversation.com/response-to-referendum-council-report-suggests-a-narrow-path-forward-on-indigenous-constitutional-reform-80315>

Hobbs, Harry and Williams, George, 2018, 'The Noongar Settlement: Australia's first treaty?', *Sydney Law Review*, vol. 40, no. 1, pp. 1–38

Hocking, Rachael, 2017a, 'Proposed changes to Native Title Act "undermines Aboriginal land rights": Activist', *NITV News*, 14 February, <http://www.sbs.com.au/nitv/nitv-news/article/2017/02/14/proposed-changes-native-title-act-undermines-aboriginal-land-rights-activist>

——2017b, '"Treated like animals" and isolated without toilets, Aboriginal Kids' Commissioner slams government', *NITV News*, 23 March, <http://www.sbs.com.au/nitv/nitv-news/article/2017/03/23/treated-animals-and-isolated-without-toilets-aboriginal-kids-commissioner-slams>

——2017c, 'NT Intervention: "It broke us," communities slam the government and offer solutions 10 years on', *NITV News*, 26 June, <http://www.sbs.com.au/nitv/nitv-news/article/2017/06/26/nt-intervention-it-broke-us-communities-slam-government-and-offer-solutions-10>

——2018, '2017 a "dismal year for Indigenous rights": Human Rights Watch', *NITV News*, 19 January, <https://www.sbs.com.au/nitv/nitv-news/article/2018/01/19/2017-dismal-year-indigenous-rights-human-rights-watch>

Hope, Alastair, 2009, *Record of investigation of the death of Mr Ward*, Western Australian Coronial Inquest 9/09, <http://www.safecom.org.au/pdfs/ward-inquest2009-alastair_hope-findings.pdf>

Hosch, Tanya, 2013, 'The call grows louder', *Koori Mail*, 27 February, p. 27

Howard, John, 1996, 'The liberal tradition: The beliefs and values which guide the federal government', Sir Robert Menzies Lecture, Sydney, 18 November

——2000, 'Interview with John Laws, 2UE Radio 29 May', *PM Transcripts: Transcripts from the prime ministers of Australia*, Canberra: Department of Prime Minister and Cabinet, Commonwealth of Australia, <http://pmtranscripts.pmc.gov.au/taxonomy/term/8?page=20>

Howard, John & Vanstone, Amanda, 2004, Transcript of the Prime Minister The Hon. John Howard MP Joint Press Conference with Senator Amanda Vanstone, Parliament House, Canberra, 15 April

Howard-Wagner, Deirdre, 2012, 'Reclaiming the Northern Territory as a settler colonial space', *Arena Journal*, no. 37/38, pp. 220–40

——2017, 'Governance of Indigenous policy in the neo-liberal age: Indigenous disadvantage and the intersecting of paternalism and neo-liberalism as a racial project', *Ethnic and Racial Studies*, <https://doi.org/10.1080/01419870.2017.1287415>, pp. 1–20

Howlett, Catherine, 2006, 'Mining and Indigenous peoples: Which theory "best fits"?', Paper presented to the Australasian Political Science Association Conference, University of Newcastle, 25–27 September

HREOC see Human Rights and Equal Opportunity Commission

Huggins, Jackie, 1998, *Sister girl: the writings of Aboriginal activist and historian Jackie Huggins*, St Lucia: University of Queensland Press

Human Rights and Equal Opportunities Commission, 1997, *Bringing them home: Report of the national inquiry into the separation of Aboriginal and Torres Strait Islander children from their families*, Human Rights and Equal Opportunities Commission, Sydney

Hunt, Janet, 2008, 'Between a rock and a hard place: Self-determination, mainstreaming and Indigenous community governance', in J. Hunt, D.E. Smith, S. Garling & W. Sanders (eds), *Contested governance: Culture, power and institutions in Indigenous Australia*, Canberra: ANU ePress, pp. 27–53.

Hunt, Janet & Smith, Diane, 2007, *Indigenous community governance project: Year 2 research findings*, Working paper no. 36/2007, Centre for Aboriginal Economic Policy Research, Australian National University, Canberra

Hunter, Fergus, 2017, 'Government rejection of referendum proposal sends "shockwaves" through Indigenous community', *Sydney Morning Herald*, 27 October, <http://www.smh.com.au/federal-politics/political-news/sad-day-turnbull-government-rejects-indigenous-referendum-proposal-20171026-gz8mpj.html>

Iorns Magallanes, Catherine, 2005, 'Indigenous political representation: identified parliamentary seats as a form of Indigenous self-determination', in B.A. Hocking (ed.), *Unfinished constitutional business?* Canberra: Aboriginal Studies Press, pp. 106–17

Jacobs, Genevieve & Walmsley, Hannah, 2015, 'Mental as: Winnunga Nimmityjah Aboriginal health service addresses Stolen Generations trauma', *ABC News*, 9 October, <http://www.abc.net.au/news/2015-10-08/canberras-aboriginal-health-service-addresses-stolen-generation/6834528>

James, Felicity, 2016, 'NT royal commission: Maningrida residents urge government to stop taking their children away', *ABC News*, 19 October, <http://www.abc.net.au/news/2016-10-18/nt-residents-urge-government-to-stop-taking-their-children/7944274>

——2017a, 'Arnhem Land school develops Indigenous wellbeing curriculum to improve mental health', *ABC News*, 9 March, <http://www.abc.net.au/news/2017-03-07/remote-school-teaching-indigenous-ideas-to-improve-mental-health/8332760>

——2017b, '"Fix this together": Arnhem Land island community leaders devise plan to deal with family violence', *ABC News*, 31 March, <http://www.abc.net.au/news/2017-03-31/arnhem-land-community-devises-plan-for-family-violence/8406136>

——2017c, 'Last fluent Ngandi speaker works to pass on endangered Indigenous language', *ABC News*, 17 April, <http://www.abc.net.au/news/2017-04-16/future-of-endangered-ngandi-language-rests-with-youth/8446414>

Jeffries, Sam, Maddison, Sarah & Menham, George, 2011, 'Murdi Paaki: Challenge, continuity and change', in S. Maddison & M. Brigg (eds), *Unsettling the settler state: Creativity and resistance in Indigenous settler-state governance*, Sydney: The Federation Press, pp. 116–130.

Jenkins, Keira, 2016a, 'Wiradjuri tours begin', *Koori Mail*, 10 February, p. 19

——2016b, 'How one man's positive change is helping others', *Koori Mail*, 19 October, p. 21

Jobs Australia, 2016, *What to do about CDP*, Melbourne: Jobs Australia

Johns, Gary (ed), 2001, *Waking up to Dreamtime: The illusion of Aboriginal self-determination*, Singapore: Media Masters

Johnson, Lissa, 2017, 'Best intentions: How we slaughter the Aboriginal race', *New Matilda*, 30 July, <https://newmatilda.com/2017/07/30/the-best-intentions-how-we-slaughter-the-aboriginal-race/>

Johnson, Murrawah, 2017, 'Black resistance is in resurgence in Australia', *Vice*, 26 January, <https://www.vice.com/en_au/article/black-resistance-is-in-resurgence-in-australia>

Jonas, William & Dick, Darren, 2004, 'The abolition of ATSIC: Silencing Indigenous voices?', *Dialogue*, 23, pp. 4–15

Jones, Delmos J. & Hill-Burnett, Jacquetta, 1982, 'The political context of ethnogenesis: an Australian example', in M.C. Howard (ed), *Aboriginal power in Australian society*, St Lucia: University of Queensland Press

Jones, Lucy H., 2017, 'NT Intervention achieved "nothing"', *The Australian*, 24 May, <http://www.theaustralian.com.au/news/latest-news/nt-intervention-achieved-nothing/news-story/57a6a8bef5d6a74fe2c5bf0405f3ee29>

Joyner, Tom, 2018, 'Warakurna welcomes first all-Indigenous police station, aiming to repair a community's mistrust', *ABC News*, 20 June, <http://www.abc.net.au/news/2018-06-20/this-is-the-first-indigenous-run-police-station-in-australia/9861778>

Jung, Courtney, 2011, 'Canada and the legacy of the Indian Residential Schools: Transitional justice for Indigenous people in a nontransitional society', in P. Arthur (ed), *Identities in transition: Challenges for transitional justice in divided societies*, New York: Cambridge University Press, pp. 217–250

KALACC see Kimberley Aboriginal Law and Culture Centre

Kimberley Aboriginal Law and Culture Centre (KALACC), 2006, *New legend: A story of law and culture and the fight for self-determination in the Kimberley*, Fitzroy Crossing: Kimberley Aboriginal Law and Culture Centre

Klein, Elise, 2016, 'Look up: How policy gaps and failure blind us to what's going on in Indigenous affairs', *The Conversation*, 2 December, <https://theconversation.com/look-up-how-policy-gaps-and-failure-blind-us-to-whats-going-on-in-indigenous-affairs-69465>

——2017, 'The Cashless Debit Card causes social and economic harm—so why trial it again?', *The Conversation*, 30 March, <https://theconversation.com/the-cashless-debit-card-causes-social-and-economic-harm-so-why-trial-it-again-74985>

Knaus, Christopher, 2018, 'Family violence rates rise in Kimberley towns with cashless welfare', *The Guardian*, 12 January, <https://www.theguardian.com/australia-news/2018/jan/12/family-violence-rates-rise-in-kimberley-towns-with-cashless-welfare>

*Koori Mail*, 2012a, 'Support "key" to union's success', 19 September, p. 17

——2012b, 'Reconciliation backed', 28 November, p. 17

——2012c, 'Gooda uses reports to call for new approach', 12 December, p. 27

——2013a, 'Recognition for Victorian tribal group', 10 April, p. 28

——2013b, 'Justice plan wins support', 14 August, p. 13

——2013c, 'Treaty tops agenda at Congress forum', 19 August, p. 18

——2013d, 'Gathering held in Canberra', 4 December, p. 34

——2014a, 'Tackling grog and violence', 7 May, p. 18

——2014b, 'Title victory for Kimberley mob', 4 June, p. 14

——2014c, 'Divisions run deep in battle for the Block', 27 August, pp. 6–7

——2014d, 'Good governance goal of program', 22 October, p. 34

——2014e, 'Summit a first in Torres Strait', 19 November, p. 26

——2014f, 'Working for our water rights', 17 December, p. 21

——2015a, 'Kimberley calls and the nation answers', 25 March, p. 5

——2015b, 'Murri School approach heads south', 25 March, p. 18

——2015c, 'More anger at closure plans', 22 April, p. 19

——2015d, 'Fight on to stop Qld mine', 15 July, p. 14

——2015e, 'Sights set on NT suicide', 9 September, p. 8

——2015f 'Anangu care for country', 7 October, p. 6

——2016a, 'Big plans for ACT', 13 January, p. 11

——2016b, 'Hope grows at Ali Curung', 13 January, p. 21

——2016c, 'Bourke gets justice', 19 October, p.15

——2017 'Redfern Statement handed to leaders', 22 February, p. 5

Koslowski, Max, 2018, 'It seems no one wants Tony Abbott to be special envoy for Indigenous affairs?' *Junkee*, 2 October, <https://junkee.com/tony-abbott-indigenous-affairs/176884>

Kowal, Emma, 2015, *Trapped in the gap: Doing good in Indigenous Australia*, New York: Bergahn Books

Lambert-Pennington, Katherine, 2012, "Real blackfellas": Constructions and meanings of urban Indigenous identity, *Transforming Anthropology*, vol. 20, no. 2, pp.131–145.

Land, Clare, 2015, *Decolonizing solidarity: Dilemmas and directions for supporters of Indigenous struggles*, London: Zed Books

Langton, Marcia, 2002, 'A new deal? Indigenous development and the politics of recovery', Dr Charles Perkins AO Memorial Oration, University of Sydney, 4 October

——2003 [1994], 'Aboriginal art and film: The politics of representation', in M. Grossman (ed.), *Blacklines: Contemporary critical writing by Indigenous Australians*, Melbourne: Melbourne University Press, pp. 109–124

——2008, 'Trapped in the Aboriginal reality show', *Griffith Review*, no. 19, pp. 145–162

——2013, *The quiet revolution: Indigenous people and the resources boom*, 2012 Boyer Lectures, Sydney: ABC Books

Langton, Marcia & Mazel, Odette, 2008, 'Poverty in the midst of plenty: Aboriginal people, the "resource curse" and Australia's mining boom', *Journal of Energy & Natural Resources Law*, vol. 26, no. 1, pp. 31–65

Latimore, Jack, 2018a, 'The stolen generations apology anniversary should stand as a day of shame', *The Guardian*, 13 February, <https://www.theguardian.com/commentisfree/2018/feb/13/the-stolen-generations-apology-anniversary-should-stand-as-a-day-of-shame>

——2018b, 'It's convenient to say Aboriginal people support Australia Day. But it's not true', *The Guardian*, 22 January, <https://www.theguardian.com/australia-news/2018/jan/22/its-convenient-to-say-aboriginal-people-support-australia-day-but-its-not-true>

Lattas, Andrew and Morris, Barry, 2010, 'The politics of suffering and the politics of anthropology' in *Culture crisis: Anthropology and politics in Aboriginal Australia*, Jon Altman & Melinda Hinkson (eds), Sydney: UNSW Press, pp. 61–87

Lawford, Elliana, 2017a, 'Treaty and sovereignty hot on the agenda at Uluru convention', *NITV News*, 25 May, <http://www.sbs.com.au/nitv/nitv-news/article/2017/05/24/treaty-and-sovereignty-hot-agenda-uluru-convention>

——2017b, 'Mutitjulu, the community that was ground zero for the NT Intervention, ten years on', *NITV*, 21 June, <http://www.sbs.com.au/nitv/nitv-news/article/2017/06/21/mutitjulu-community-was-ground-zero-nt-intervention-ten-years>

Liddle, Celeste, 2016, 'What we're missing while we argue over individual acts of blatant racism', *Sydney Morning Herald*, 22 August, <http://www.smh.com.au/lifestyle/news-and-views/opinion/what-were-missing-while-we-argue-over-individual-acts-of-blatant-racism-20160821-gqxsrr.html>

——2017a, 'Why I don't support changing the date of Amnesia Day', *Eureka Street*, 22 January, <https://www.eurekastreet.com.au/article.aspx?aeid=50528>

——2017b, 'Comment: Why the term "Australian" can be an imposition on Aboriginal people', *SBS Life*, 1 March, <http://www.sbs.com.au/topics/life/culture/article/2017/02/28/comment-why-term-australian-can-be-imposition-aboriginal-people>

——2017c, 'Elijah Doughty decision shows there is rarely justice for aboriginal victims', *Eureka Street*, 27 July, <https://www.eurekastreet.com.au/article.aspx?aeid=52789>

Lindsay, Kirstyn, 2017, 'Anangu Tribal Elders ask for the name of Uluru Statement from the Heart to be changed', SBS, 12 December, <https://www.sbs.com.au/yourlanguage/aboriginal/en/article/2017/12/08/anangu-tribal-elders-ask-name-uluru-statement-heart-be-changed>

Lino, Dylan, 2017, 'The Uluru Statement: Towards federalism with First Nations', *Australian Public Law*, 13 June, <https://auspublaw.org/2017/06/towards-federalism-with-first-nations/>

Lloyd, Brian, 2009, 'Dedicated Indigenous representation in the Australian Parliament', Research Paper no. 23 2008–09, Parliamentary Library, Parliament of Australia, Canberra. <http://www.aph.gov.au/Library/pubs/rp/2008-09/09rp23.htm>

Lyons, Kristen, 2017, 'Traditional owners expose Adani's relentless pursuit of W&J country', *New Matilda*, 23 November, <https://newmatilda.com/2017/11/23/traditional-owners-expose-adanis-relentless-pursuit-of-wj-country/>

Lyons, Kristen, Brigg, Morgan & Quiggin, John, 2017, *Unfinished business: Adani, the State, and the Indigenous rights struggle of the Wangan and Jagalingou Traditional Owners Council*, Technical Report, Brisbane: University of Queensland

Macklin, Jenny, 2009a, 'Australian Government response to "Our future in our hands"', Joint media release with Prime Minister Kevin Rudd and Bill Shorten MP, 22 November, <https://formerministers.dss.gov.au/14367/australian-government-response-to-our-future-in-our-hands/>

——2009b, 'Strengthening the Northern Territory emergency response', Joint media release with Warren Snowden MP, 25 November, <https://formerministers.dss.gov.au/14360/strengthening-the-northern-territory-emergency-response/>

Macoun, Alissa, 2011, 'Aboriginality and the Northern Territory Intervention', *Australian Journal of Political Science*, vol. 46, no. 3, pp. 519–534

——2016, 'Colonising white innocence: Complicity and colonial encounters', in S. Maddison, T. Clark & R. de Costa (eds), *The limits of settler colonial reconciliation: Non-Indigenous people and the responsibility to engage*, Melbourne: Springer

Macoun, Alissa & Strakosch, Elizabeth, 2013, 'The ethical demands of settler colonial theory', *Settler Colonial Studies*, vol. 3, no. 3–4, pp. 426–443

Maddison, Sarah, 2009, *Black politics: Inside the complexity of Aboriginal political culture*, Sydney: Allen & Unwin

——2013, 'Indigenous identity, "authenticity" and the structural violence of settler colonialism', *Identities: Global Studies in Culture and Power*, vol. 20, no. 3, pp. 288–303

——2015, *Conflict transformation and reconciliation: Multi-level challenges in deeply divided societies*, UK: Routledge

——2017 'Recognise what? The limitations of settler colonial constitutional reform', *Australian Journal of Political Science*, vol. 52, no. 1, pp. 3–18

Maddison, Sarah & Stastny, Angelique, 2016, 'Silence or deafness? Education and the non-Indigenous responsibility to engage', in S. Maddison, T. Clark & R. de Costa (eds), *The limits of settler colonial reconciliation: Non-Indigenous people and the responsibility to engage*, Melbourne: Springer

Mansell, Michael, 2003, 'Citizenship, assimilation and a treaty', in H. McGlade, *Treaty—let's get it right!*, Canberra: Aboriginal Studies Press, pp. 5–17

——2005, 'Why Norfolk Island but not Aborigines?' in B.A. Hocking, *Unfinished constitutional business? Rethinking Indigenous self-determination*, Canberra: Aboriginal Studies Press, pp. 82–92

——2016a, 'The longawaited consultation with Indigenous peoples on constitutional recognition has begun', *NITV*, 23 July, <http://www.sbs.com.au/nitv/article/2016/07/22/long-awaited-consultation-indigenous-peoples-constitutional-recognition-has-begun>

——2016b, 'Is the Constitution a better tool than simple legislation to advance the cause of Aboriginal peoples?' in M. Davis & M. Langton (eds), *It's our country: Indigenous arguments for meaningful constitutional recognition and reform*, Melbourne: Melbourne University Press

——2016c, *Treaty and statehood: Aboriginal self-determination*, Sydney: The Federation Press

——2017a, 'After Garma, we must learn from the failures of the referendum campaign', *The Guardian*, 7 August, <https://www.theguardian.com/commentisfree/2017/aug/07/after-garma-we-must-learn-from-the-failures-of-the-referendum-campaign>

——2017b, 'Uluru "Statement from the Heart" lacks real teeth and reality', *New Matilda*,

9 August, <https://newmatilda.com/2017/08/09/uluru-statement-heart-lacks-real-teeth-reality/>

Marika, R., 1999, 'The 1998 Wentworth lecture', *Australian Aboriginal Studies*, no. 1, pp. 3–9

Markham, Francis & Biddle, Nicholas, 2017, 'Radical rethink of Closing the Gap required, despite some progress', *The Conversation*, 4 December, <https://theconversation.com/radical-rethink-of-closing-the-gap-required-despite-some-progress-86203>

Mascarenhas, Carla, 2016, 'Aboriginal educator questions state government language revitalisation program', ABC Coffs Coast, 24 October, <http://www.abc.net.au/news/2016-10-24/aboriginal-language-concern/7959760>

Maxwell Rudi, 2013a, 'Language first for WA Parliament', *Koori Mail*, 24 April, p. 17

——2013b, 'Tas split on mining', *Koori Mail*, 14 August, p. 14

——2013c, 'Group will fight for justice in Qld', *Koori Mail*, 11 September, p. 8

——2013d, 'Co-chair is confident', *Koori Mail*, 9 October, p. 9

——2014, 'Elders want mine action', *Koori Mail*, 19 November, p. 19

——2015a, '"Stop trying to control our people"', *Koori Mail*, 28 January, p. 3

——2015b, 'Yawuru man battles CSG', *Koori Mail*, 4 November, p. 5

——2016a, 'Fight for justice', *Koori Mail*, 23 March, p. 5

——2016b, 'Our people deserve much, much better', *Koori Mail*, 15 June, p. 5

Maxwell, Rudi & Coyne, Darren, 2013, 'Elder in fight for "cultural survival"', *Koori Mail*, 4 December, p. 9

Maynard, John, 1997, 'Fred Maynard the Australian Aboriginal Progressive Association (AAPA): One God, one aim, one destiny', *Aboriginal History*, vol. 21, pp. 1–13

Mayor, Thomas, 2018, 'Getting the people behind the Uluru Statement', *The Saturday Paper*, 6 October, <https://www.thesaturdaypaper.com.au/opinion/topic/2018/10/06/getting-the-people-behind-the-uluru-statement/15387480006954>

McConchie, Peter, 2003, *Elders: Wisdom from Australia's Indigenous leaders*, Cambridge: Cambridge University Press

MacDonald, Lindsey Te Ata o Tu & Muldoon, Paul, 2006, 'Globalisation, neo-liberalism and the struggle for Indigenous citizenship', *Australian Journal of Political Science*, vol. 41, no. 2, pp. 209–223

McGlade, Hannah, 2017, 'Indigenous culture has a part to play in protecting the next generation of children', *ABC News*, 21 December, <http://www.abc.net.au/news/2017-12-21/forced-removal-aboriginal-children-at-all-time-high/9277170>

McGregor, Russell, 2011, *Indifferent inclusion: Aboriginal people and the Australian nation*, Canberra: Aboriginal Studies Press

McLoughlin, Liam, 2016a, 'We need to talk much less about Andrew Bolt and much more about treaty', *New Matilda*, 8 October, <https://newmatilda.com/2016/10/08/we-need-to-talk-much-less-about-andrew-bolt-and-much-more-about-treaty/>

——2016b, '"Nothing else works": Only self-determination can stop another Don Dale', *New Matilda*, 27 July, <https://newmatilda.com/2016/07/27/nothing-else-works-only-true-self-determination-can-stop-another-don-dale/>

McMillan, Mark & Rigney, Sophie, 2018, 'Race, reconciliation, and justice in Australia: from denial to acknowledgment', *Ethnic and Racial Studies*, vol. 41, no. 4, pp. 759–777

McQuire, Amy, 2015a, 'Recognise: The debate that is failing and dividing Black Australia', *New Matilda*, 5 March, <https://newmatilda.com/2015/03/05/recognise-debate-failing-and-dividing-black-australia>

——2015b, 'Recognise cracks deepen as Tasmanian leader says referendum won't bring justice', *New Matilda*, 15 April, <https://newmatilda.com//2015/04/15/recognise-cracks-deepen-tasmanian-leader-says-referendum-wont-bring-justice>

——2016, 'Amy McQuire on Don Dale: 200 years of trauma through a CCTV lens', *New Matilda*, 3 August, <https://newmatilda.com/2016/08/03/amy-mcquire-on-don-dale-200-years-of-trauma-through-a-cctv-lens/>

——2017a, 'To avoid another dead end, we need to know who's driving this Recognition bus', *The Guardian*, 12 June, <https://www.theguardian.com/commentisfree/2017/jun/12/to-avoid-another-dead-end-we-need-to-know-whos-driving-this-recognition-bus>

——2017b, 'Three years on, Ms Dhu's family continues its fight for justice', *BuzzFeed News*, 4 August, <https://www.buzzfeed.com/amymcquire/three-years-on-from-ms-dhus-death-her-family-hopes-there>

——2017c, '"It was a rude meeting," says an Aboriginal man who met the prime minister after walking 6,000km', *BuzzFeed News*, 6 September, <https://www.buzzfeed.com/amymcquire/it-was-a-rude-meeting-says-an-aboriginal-man-who-met-the?utm_term=.kbmJ10APg8#.ioBADr5LmV>

——2017d, '$1.1 million payment will not stop Ms Dhu's family from seeking justice over death in custody', *BuzzFeed News*, 20 September, <https://www.buzzfeed.com/amymcquire/11-million-payment-will-not-stop-ms-dhus-family-from?utm_term=.hqK6pjNlqD#.yk09ZRbQo7>

McQuire, Amy & O'Shea, Lizzie, 2017, 'White Australians celebrate, Aboriginal people mourn', *New York Times*, 25 January, <https://mobile.nytimes.com/2017/01/25/opinion/white-australians-celebrate-aboriginal-people-mourn.html>

Minow, Martha, 2000, 'The hope for healing: What can truth commissions do?', in R.I. Rotberg & D. Thompson (eds) *Truth v. justice: The morality of truth commissions*, Princeton: Princeton University Press.

Mitchell, Georgina, 2016, 'Stan Grant delivers fiery speech on Indigenous rights in wake of abuse scandal', *The Age*, 29 July, <http://www.theage.com.au/national/stan-grant-delivers-fiery-honorary-doctorate-of-letters-acceptance-speech-at-unsw-20160729-gqh0dh.html>

Mokak, Romlie, 2018, 'A question of value: Time to redress the price of silence', *Griffith Review*, 60, pp. 295–304

Moore, Gerry, 2016, 'From an Aboriginal mission to the UN: shifting perceptions on self-determination', *The Guardian*, 16 August, <https://www.theguardian.com/commentisfree/2016/aug/16/from-an-aboriginal-mission-to-the-un-shifting-percep-tions-on-self-determination?CMP=Share_iOSApp_Other>

Moore, Roxanne, 2017, 'Time to wake up Australia. Every child prison in this country is Don Dale', *IndigenousX*, 21 November, <http://indigenousx.com.au/roxanne-moore-time-to-wake-up-australia-every-child-prison-in-this-country-is-don-dale/#.WjsvtlT1V-U>

Moran, Mark, 2016, *Serious Whitefella stuff: When solutions became the problem in Indigenous affairs*, Melbourne: Melbourne University Press

——2018, 'The courage to reform', *Griffith Review*, 60, online only, <https://griffithreview.com/articles/courage-to-reform-commonwealth-indigenous-policies-moran/>

Morelli, Laura, 2017, 'Indigenous protected areas and rangers program prove positive in protecting Australia', *NITV News*, 30 March, <http://www.sbs.com.au/nitv/article/2017/03/30/indigenous-protected-areas-and-rangers-program-prove-positive-protecting>

Moreton-Robinson, Aileen, 2000, *Talkin' up to the white woman: Aboriginal women and feminism*, St Lucia: University of Queensland Press
——2003, 'Introduction: Resistance, recovery and revitalisation', in M. Grossman (ed.), *Blacklines: Contemporary critical writing by Indigenous Australians*, Melbourne: Melbourne University Press, pp. 127–131
——2005, 'Gendering and racialising self-determination: Indigenous women and patriarchal whiteness', in B. Hocking, *Unfinished Constitutional Business: Rethinking Indigenous self-determination*, Canberra: Aboriginal Studies Press, pp. 61–74
——2007a, 'Writing off Indigenous sovereignty: The discourse of security and patriarchal white sovereignty', in A. Moreton-Robinson, *Sovereign subjects: Indigenous sovereignty matters*, Sydney: Allen & Unwin, pp. 86–104
——2007b, 'Introduction', in A. Moreton-Robinson, *Sovereign subjects: Indigenous sovereignty matters*, Sydney: Allen & Unwin, pp. 1–12
——2015, *The white possessive: Property, power, and Indigenous sovereignty*, Minneapolis: University of Minnesota Press
Morgan, Myles, 2016, 'Marcia Langton: Why throw a "treaty bomb"?', *NITV*, 28 June, <http://www.sbs.com.au/nitv/article/2016/06/28/marcia-langton-why-throw-treaty-bomb>
Morrison, Joe, 2017, 'A smear on the nation', *Arena Magazine*, no. 148, June–July, pp. 18–20, 54
Morrissey, Philip, 2003, 'Aboriginality and corporatism', in M. Grossman (ed.), *Blacklines: Contemporary critical writing by Indigenous Australians*, Melbourne: Melbourne University Press, pp. 52–59
Moses, Dirk, 2017, 'Who is really airbrushing the past? Genocide, slavery and the return of the colonial repressed', *ABC Religion and Ethics*, 1 September, <http://www.abc.net.au/religion/articles/2017/09/01/4727499.htm>
Mudrooroo, 1995, *Us mob: History, culture, struggle. An introduction to Indigenous Australia*, Sydney: HarperCollins Publishers
Muldoon, Paul, 2005, 'Thinking responsibility differently: Reconciliation and the tragedy of colonisation', *Journal of Intercultural Studies*, vol. 26, no. 3, pp. 237–254
Muldoon, Paul & Schaap, Andrew, 2012, 'Confounded by recognition: The apology, the High Court and the Aboriginal Embassy in Australia', in A.K. Hirsch (ed), *Theorizing post-conflict reconciliation*, London: Routledge
Mundy, Jillian, 2013, 'Powerful words help heal', *Koori Mail*, 9 October, p. 12
——2014a, 'VAHS celebrates 40 vital years', *Koori Mail*, 9 April, p. 8
——2014b, 'New court launched', *Koori Mail*, 30 July, p. 11
——2014c, 'Redfern battle rages on', *Koori Mail*, 22 October, p. 5
——2017, 'Art helps prisoners', *Koori Mail*, 25 January, p. 8
Munkara, Marie, 2017, '"And still my family die." Marie Munkara on the commodification of life and death on the Tiwi islands', *Crikey*, 22 November, <https://blogs.crikey.com.au/northern/2017/11/22/still-family-die-marie-munkara-commodification-life-death-tiwi-islands/>
Murphy, Damien, 2017a, 'Cabinet papers 1992–93: Malcolm Turnbull must right the wrongs for Aboriginal Australians', *The Age*, 1 January, <http://www.theage.com.au/nsw/cabinet-papers-199293-released-malcolm-turnbull-must-right-the-wrongs-for-aboriginal-australians-20161216-gtczjs>

——2017b, 'Cabinet papers 1992–93: The Mabo debate made "Trump's campaign look like the free-flowing milk of human kindness"', *The Age*, 1 January, <http://www.theage.com. au/nsw/cabinet-papers-199293-the-mabo-debate-made-trumps-campaign-look-like-the-freeflowing-milk-of-human-kindness-20161216-gtd1oi>

Murphy, Katharine, 2017a, 'Indigenous people victims of "green" fight against Adani mine, says Marcia Langton', *The Guardian*, 7 June, <https://www.theguardian.com/ australia-news/2017/jun/07/indigenous-people-victims-of-green-fight-against-adani-mine-says-marcia-langton>

——2017b, 'Changing colonial statues is Stalinist, says Malcolm Turnbull', *The Guardian*, 25 August, <https://www.theguardian.com/australia-news/2017/aug/25/changing-colonial-statues-is-stalinist-says-malcolm-turnbull>

Murphy, Lyndon, Graham, Mary & Brigg, Morgan, 2017, 'The Uluru Statement: We never ceded sovereignty but can we join yours?', *NITV News*, 23 June, <http://www.sbs.com. au/nitv/nitv-news/article/2017/06/22/uluru-statement-we-never-ceded-sovereignty-can-we-join-yours>

Murphy-Oates, Laura, 2016, '"The national anthem does not represent our people": Indigenous sports star Joe Williams speaks out', *The Feed*, <http://www.sbs.com.au/ news/thefeed/article/2016/10/17/national-anthem-does-not-represent-our-people-indigenous-sports-star-joe-williams>

Nakata, Sana, 2017, 'The re-making of nation and Indigenous Australian children', *Australian Journal of Public Administration*, vol. 76, no. 4, pp. 397–399

——2018, 'The infantilisation of Indigenous Australians: A problem for democracy', *Griffith Review*, 60, pp. 104–116

*National Indigenous Times*, 2007, 'Heartbreak Hill', 23 August, pp. 16–18

——2008, 'A (dis)proportional voting system', 18 September p. 18.

——2016a, 'Traditional owners unite to protect Fitzroy River', 17 November, <http://nit.com. au/traditional-owners-unite-protect-fitzroy-river/>

——2016b, 'Leaders come out swinging against domestic violence', 17 November, <http://nit. com.au/leaders-come-swinging-domestic-violence/>

NSW Aboriginal Child Sexual Assault Taskforce, 2006, *Breaking the silence: Creating the future, addressing child sexual assault in Aboriginal communities in NSW*, Sydney: NSW Attorney General's Department

NSW Department of Education, n.d., 'Aboriginal education and communities: Language, culture, and communities', Sydney: NSW Department of Education, <https://education. nsw.gov.au/teaching-and-learning/aec/language-culture-and-communities>

Nicholson, Alastair, Behrendt, Larissa, Vivian, Alison, Watson, Nicole & Harris, Michele, 2009, *Will they be heard? A response to the NTER Consultations June to August 2009*, Sydney: Jumbunna Indigenous House of Learning, University of Technology Sydney

Nicol, Emily, 2017, 'What's the difference between Close the Gap and Closing the Gap?', *NITV*, 17 March, <http://www.sbs.com.au/nitv/article/2017/03/16/whats-difference-between-close-gap-and-closing-gap>

*NITV News*, 2017a, 'UN rapporteur slams the government's record on Indigenous issues, but hopeful for change', 3 April, <http://www.sbs.com.au/nitv/the-point-with-stan-grant/article/2017/04/03/un-rapporteur-slams-governments-record-indigenous-issues-hopeful-change>

——2017b, 'It's time to stop making decisions without us, co-chair tells constitution forum', 24 May, <http://www.sbs.com.au/nitv/nitv-news/article/2017/05/24/its-time-stop-making-decisions-without-us-co-chair-tells-constitution-forum>

——2017c, 'NT Elders tell royal commission they want children kept in community', 20 June, <http://www.sbs.com.au/nitv/nitv-news/article/2017/06/20/nt-elders-tell-royal-commission-they-want-children-kept-community>

——2017d, '"Racism" in child welfare and justice system', 23 June, <http://www.sbs.com.au/nitv/article/2017/06/23/racism-child-welfare-and-justice-system>

Noonan, Andie, 2017, 'Culture key to suicide prevention among Indigenous Australians, experts say, ahead of global discussion', ABC News, 4 April, <http://www.abc.net.au/news/2017-04-04/culture-key-to-suicide-prevention-among-indigenous-australians/8412338>

Norman, James, 2018, 'Native title and mining leases', The Saturday Paper, 24 April, <https://www.thesaturdaypaper.com.au/news/indigenous-affairs/2018/04/21/native-title-and-mining-leases/15242328006122>

O'Donoghue, Lowitja, 1995, 'Customary Law as a vehicle for community empowerment', Speech delivered to the Forum on Indigenous Customary Law, Canberra: Parliament House, 18 October

Oliver, Steven, 2018, 'Common ground: Steven Oliver on changing the date of Australia Day', New Matilda, 16 January, <https://newmatilda.com/2018/01/16/common-ground-steven-oliver-on-changing-the-date-of-australia-day/>

Onus, Lin, 2003 [1990], 'Language and lasers', in M. Grossman (ed.), Blacklines: Contemporary critical writing by Indigenous Australians, Melbourne: Melbourne University Press, pp. 92–6

Osborn, P., 2017, 'Wrongs can be righted, says indigenous MP', News.com, 14 February, <http://www.news.com.au/national/breaking-news/wrongs-can-be-righted-says-indigenous-mp/news-story/1c64073e2cf1a3e0f6304c3f1c554443>

Oscar, June, 2017, 'Address by the Aboriginal and Torres Strait Islander Social Justice Commissioner', National Suicide Prevention Conference 2017, Brisbane, 27 July, <https://www.humanrights.gov.au/news/speeches/national-suicide-prevention-conference>

——2017b, 'Address to the Rural and Remote Mental Health Conference', Notre Dame University, Broome, 27 October, <https://www.humanrights.gov.au/news/speeches/rural-and-remote-mental-health-conference-2017>

Oscar, June & Little, Rod (2018), 'Closing the gap on Indigenous health: this is our national shame, but it can be fixed', ABC News, 8 February, http://www.abc.net.au/news/2018-02-08/closing-the-gap/9407824?pfmredir=sm

Oscar, June & Pedersen, Howard, 2011, 'Alcohol restrictions in the Fitzroy Valley: Trauma and resilience', in S. Maddison & M. Brigg (eds), Unsettling the settler state: Creativity and resistance in Indigenous settler-state governance, Sydney: The Federation Press, pp. 83-97

O'Shane, Pat, 1998, 'Aboriginal political movements: Some observations', 13th Frank Archibald Memorial Lecture, 14 October, Armidale: University of New England

Parker, Kirstie, 2016, 'Building a new, better legacy', in M. Davis & M. Langton (eds), It's our country: Indigenous arguments for meaningful constitutional recognition and reform, Melbourne: Melbourne University Press

Parliamentary Debate, House of Representatives 2000, Questions without Notice: Aboriginals: Stolen Generations 3 April, 14 August

Partridge, Emma, Maddison, Sarah & Nicholson, Alastair, 2012, 'Human rights impera-
    tives and the failings of the Stronger Futures consultation process', *Australian Journal of
    Human Rights*, vol. 18, no. 2, pp. 21–44
Pascoe, Bruce, 2017, 'Aboriginal people do what we must to survive; 1967 didn't change
    that', *Awaye!*, ABC Radio National, 25 May, <http://mobile.abc.net.au/news/2017-05-25/
    bruce-pascoe-doesnt-think-much-about-the-1967-referendum/>
Patterson, Michelle, 2017, *Commonwealth machinery of government in Aboriginal and Torres
    Strait Islander affairs: 50 years of Commonwealth public administration in Aboriginal and
    Torres Strait Islander affairs*, IAG Working Paper Series, No. 1, Aboriginal and Torres
    Strait Islander Affairs Group, Canberra: Department of the Prime Minister and Cabinet
Pearson, Luke, 2015a, 'Another government review. Another disappointment',
    *IndigenousX*, 22 September, <http://indigenousx.com.au/another-government-review-
    another-disappointment/>
——2015b, 'The changes to the national curriculum have nothing to do with education',
    *IndigenousX*, 24 September, <http://indigenousx.com.au/the-changes-to-the-national-
    curriculum-have-nothing-to-do-with-education/>
——2016a, 'Can a treaty shift the racist ideology that plagues Indigenous affairs?
    I hope so', *IndigenousX*, 20 March, <http://indigenousx.com.au/can-a-treaty-shift-the-
    racist-ideology-that-plagues-indigenous-affairs-i-hope-so/>
——2016b, 'Don't tell me to "get over" a colonialism that is still being implemented today',
    *The Guardian*, 2 April, <http://www.theguardian.com/australia-news/commentisfree
    2016/apr/02/dont-tell-me-to-get-over-a-colonialism-that-is-still-being-implemented-
    today/>
——2017a, 'Indigenous affairs—no steps forward, two steps back', *NITV News*,
    3 April, <http://www.sbs.com.au/nitv/article/2017/04/03/comment-indigenous-affairs-
    no-steps-forward-two-steps-back>
——2017b, 'Growing up under the NT Intervention: 10 years later, what has changed?'
    *Speaking Out*, ABC Radio National, 26 June, <http://mobile.abc.net.au/news/2017-06-26/
    kylie-sambo-growing-up-under-the-nt-intervention>
——2017c, 'What is a Makarrata? The Yolŋu word is more than a synonym for treaty', *ABC
    News*, 10 August, <http://www.abc.net.au/news/2017-08-10/makarrata-explainer-Yolŋu-
    word-more-than-synonym-for-treaty/8790452>
——2017d, 'Statues, nationalism, and Trump's white pride bazaar', *IndigenousX*, 7 September,
    <https://indigenousx.com.au/luke-pearson-statues-nationalism-and-trumps-white-
    pride-bazaar/>
——2017e, 'Who identifies as a person of colour in Australia?', *It's not a race*, ABC
    *News*, 1 December, <http://www.abc.net.au/news/2017-12-01/who-identifies-as-poc-in-
    australia/9200288?pfmredir=sm>
——2017f, '2017 forced us to ask how far we have come in Indigenous affairs', *ABC News*,
    26 December, <http://www.abc.net.au/news/2017-12-23/2017-how-far-have-we-come-
    in-indigenous-affairs/9281920?>
——2018a, 'We do not need a special envoy, we need our leaders to listen', *IndigenousX*,
    29 August, <http://indigenousx.com.au/we-do-not-need-a-special-envoy-we-need-our-
    leaders-to-listen/#.W7VHyxMzb-Z>
——2018b, 'Unpacking "Is Australia a racist country?"', *IndigenousX*, 7 October, <https://
    indigenousx.com.au/unpacking-is-australia-a-racist-country/#.W7qrPhMzb-Y>

Pearson, Noel, 2000, *Our right to take responsibility*, Cairns: Noel Pearson and Associates

——2005, *The Cape York agenda: Fundamental transformation through radical reform*, Cairns: Cape York Institute for Policy and Leadership, <http://www.cyi.org.au/WEBSITE%20 uploads/Documents/Cape%20York%20Agenda%20final.pdf>

——2007, 'White guilt, victimhood and the quest for a radical centre', *Griffith Review*, no. 16, Winter, pp. 3–58

——2016, 'Conservative role essential in Indigenous recognition', *The Australian*, 11 March, <https://www.theaustralian.com.au/opinion/columnists/noel-pearson/conservative-role-essential-in-indigenous-recognition/news-story/c42b024e68b832dfad763da51855bf75>

——2017, 'A job half undone: Constitutional recognition for Indigenous Australians must be more than just tokenism', *The Monthly*, June, <https://www.themonthly.com.au/issue/2017/june/1496239200/noel-pearson/job-half-undone>

Perche, Diana, 2017, 'Ten years on, it's time we learned the lessons from the failed Northern Territory Intervention', *The Conversation*, 26 June, <https://theconversation.com/ten-years-on-its-time-we-learned-the-lessons-from-the-failed-northern-territory-intervention-79198>

Perkins, Charles, 1992, 'Aboriginal Australia and public administration', *Australian Journal of Public Administration*, vol. 51, no. 2, pp. 223-33

Perkins, Rachel, 2017, 'Indigenous declaration is an honest claim from the heart of our nation', *The Australian*, 29 May, <http://www.theaustralian.com.au/opinion/indigenous-declaration-is-an-honest-claim-from-the-heart-of-our-nation/news-story/e5adc80c44d2edc30c5b88540caa35bc>

Peterson, Nicholas & Sanders, Will (eds), 1998, *Citizenship and Indigenous Australians: Changing conceptions and possibilities*, Melbourne: Cambridge University Press

Phillips, Anne, 2001, 'Representation renewed', in M. Sawer & G. Zappalà, (eds), *Speaking for the people: Representation in Australian politics*, Melbourne: Melbourne University Press, pp. 19–35

Phillips, Gregory, 2018, 'No republic without a soul: Exorcising the ghosts of colonialism', *Griffith Review*, 60, pp. 97–103

Porter, Libby, 2016, 'How can we meaningfully recognise cities as Indigenous places?', *The Conversation*, 5 October, <https://theconversation.com/how-can-we-meaningfully-recognise-cities-as-indigenous-places-65561>

Povinelli, Elizabeth, 2002, *The cunning of recognition: Indigenous alterities and the making of Australian multiculturalism*, Durham: Duke University Press

Power, Julie, 2014, 'Fitzroy Crossing women tackle alcohol scourge', *Sydney Morning Herald*, 7 September, <http://www.smh.com.au/national/fitzroy-crossing-women-tackle-alcohol-scourge-20140904-10c9rv.html>

Pratt, Angela, 2005, *Practising reconciliation? The politics of reconciliation in the Australian Parliament, 1991–2000*, Canberra: Parliamentary Library, Parliament of Australia

Price, Jacinta, 2017, 'Men of violence', *The Spectator Australia*, 24 June, <https://spectator.com.au/2017/06/men-of-violence/>

Probyn, Fiona, 2004, 'Playing chicken at the intersection: the white critic of whiteness', *Borderlands*, vol. 3, no. 2, <http://www.borderlands.net.au/vol3no2_2004/probyn_playing.htm>

Prout Quicke, Sarah, Dockery, Alfred & Hoath, Aileen, 2017, 'Aboriginal assets? The impact of major agreements associated with native title in Western Australia', Report for the

Western Australian Department of Regional Development, Perth: Curtin University and the University of Western Australia

Pryor, Clinton, 2017, 'It's a long walk for Indigenous justice. That's why I'm crossing Australia one step at a time', IndigenousX, *The Guardian*, 29 June, <https://www.theguardian.com/commentisfree/2017/jun/29/clinton-pryor-walk-for-justice-indigenous-crossing-australia>

Ravens, Tara, 2007, 'NT child report authors "betrayed" by federal government', *National Indigenous Times*, 9 August, p. 3

RCIADIC see Royal Commission into Aboriginal Deaths in Custody

Read, Peter, 2010, 'Reconciliation without history: State crime and state punishment in Chile and Australia', in F. Peters-Little, A. Curthoys & J. Docker (eds), *Passionate histories: Myth, memory and Indigenous Australia*, Canberra: ANU E-Press, pp. 281–298

Referendum Council, 2017a, *Uluru Statement from the Heart*, 26 May, <https://www.referendumcouncil.org.au/sites/default/files/2017-05/Uluru_Statement_From_The_Heart_0.PDF>

——2017b, *Final report of the Referendum Council*, Canberra: Commonwealth of Australia

Reich, Hannah, 2017, 'Sovereign trax: One Wiradjuri woman's work to decolonise our music choices', *ABC News*, 11 July, <http://www.abc.net.au/news/2017-07-11/one-wiradjuri-womans-work-to-decolonise-our-music-choices/8694918>

Reilly, Alexander, 2001, 'Dedicated seats in the federal parliament for Indigenous Australians: The theoretical case and its practical possibility', *Balayi: Culture, Law and Colonialism*, vol. 2, no. 1, pp. 85–6

Reynolds, Henry, 1998, 'Sovereignty', in N. Peterson & W. Sanders (eds), *Citizenship and Indigenous Australians: Changing conceptions and possibilities*, Melbourne: Cambridge University Press, pp. 208–215

——2013, *Forgotten war*, Sydney: NewSouth Publishing

——2017, 'Triple J did the right thing, we need a new Australia Day', *The Conversation*, 29 November, <https://theconversation.com/henry-reynolds-triple-j-did-the-right-thing-we-need-a-new-australia-day-88249>

Ridgeway, Aden, 2000, 'An impasse or a relationship in the making?', in M. Grattan (ed.), *Reconciliation: Essays on Australian reconciliation*, Melbourne: Black Inc

——2003, 'We must all act to build on the legacy of Senator Neville Bonner', *Online Opinion*, 7 October, <http://www.onlineopinion.com.au/view.asp?article=769&page=0>

Rigney, Lester Irabinna, 2003, 'Indigenous education, languages and treaty: The redefinition of a new relationship with Australia', in H. McGlade (ed.) *Treaty—let's get it right!*, Canberra: Aboriginal Studies Press, pp. 72–87

Rind, Banok, 2017, 'I have seven weeks left of my nursing degree. I am scared', *IndigenousX*, 11 April, <http://indigenousx.com.au/i-have-seven-weeks-left-of-my-nursing-degree-i-am-scared/>

Robertson, Joshua, 2017a, 'Adani mine loses majority support of traditional owner representatives', *The Guardian*, 15 June, <https://www.theguardian.com/environment/2017/jun/15/adani-mine-loses-majority-support-of-traditional-owner-representatives>

——2017b, 'Leading Indigenous lawyer hits back at Marcia Langton over Adani', *The Guardian*, 9 June, <https://www.theguardian.com/environment/2017/jun/09/leading-indigenous-lawyer-hits-back-at-marcia-langton-over-adani>

Rogers, Jessa, 2017, 'Seats at the table: Our voices need to be heard', *NITV News*, 1 June, <http://www.sbs.com.au/nitv/article/2017/06/01/seats-table-our-voices-need-be-heard>

Rose, Deborah Bird, 1991, *Hidden histories: Black stories from Victoria River Downs, Humbert River, and Wave Hill Stations*, Canberra: Aboriginal Studies Press

Rouhana, Nadim N., 2008, 'Reconciling history and equal citizenship in Israel: Democracy and the politics of historical denial', in W. Kymlicka & B. Bashir (eds), *The politics of reconciliation in multicultural societies*, Oxford: Oxford University Press, pp. 70–93

Rowse, Tim, 1997, '"Out of hand": The battles of Neville Bonner', *Journal of Australian Studies*, Vol. 54–55, pp. 96–107

——2001, 'Democratic systems are an alien thing to the Aboriginal culture . . .', in M. Sawer & G. Zappala (eds), *Speaking for the people: Representation in Australian politics*, Melbourne: Melbourne University Press

——2002, *Indigenous futures: choice and development for Aboriginal and Islander Australia*, Sydney: UNSW Press

Royal Commission into Aboriginal Deaths in Custody (RCIADIC), 1991, *National report*, Canberra: Australian Government Publishing Service

Royal Commission into the Protection and Detention of Children and Young People in the Northern Territory, 2017, *Report overview*, <https://childdetentionnt.royalcommission. gov.au/Documents/Royal-Commission-NT-Report-Overview.pdf>

Rudd, Kevin, 2008, 'Apology to Australia's Indigenous peoples', House of Representatives, Parliament House, Canberra, 13 February, <http://www.pm.gov.au/media/Speech/2008/speech_0073.cfm>

Russell, Peter H., 2005, *Recognising Aboriginal title: The Mabo case and Indigenous resistance to English-settler colonialism*, Sydney: UNSW Press

Sanders, Will, 2004, 'Prospects for regionalism in Indigenous community governance', *Dialogue*, vol. 23, no. 2, pp. 56–61

——2005, 'Never even adequate: Reconciliation and Indigenous affairs', in C. Aulich & R. Wettenhall (eds), *Howard's second and third governments: Australian Commonwealth administration 1998–2004*, Sydney: UNSW Press, pp. 152–172

——2006, 'Indigenous affairs after the Howard decade: Administrative reforms and practical reconciliation or defying decolonisation?', *Journal of Australian Indigenous Issues*, vol. 9, no. 2–3, pp. 43–51

SBS News, 2018a, 'Turnbull distances himself from Abbott over First Fleet remarks', 23 January, <https://www.sbs.com.au/news/turnbull-distances-himself-from-abbott-over-first-fleet-remarks>

——2018b, 'Mark Latham launches dystopian Save Australia Day ads', 10 January, <https://www.sbs.com.au/news/mark-latham-launches-dystopian-save-australia-day-ads>

Schaap, Andrew, 2004, 'Political reconciliation through a struggle for recognition?', *Social and Legal Studies*, vol. 13, no. 4, pp. 523–540

——2007, 'The time of reconciliation and the space of politics', in S. Veitch (ed.), *Law and the politics of reconciliation*, Aldershot: Ashgate Publishing Ltd, pp. 9–31

Selvaratnam, Naomi, 2015, '"Whitefella" draws up own treaty for his land with traditional owners', *SBS News*, 23 December, <http://www.sbs.com.au/news/article/2015/12/23/whitefella-draws-own-treaty-his-land-traditional-owners>

Senate Standing Committee on Legal and Constitutional Affairs, 1983, *200 years later: The feasibility of a compact or 'Makarrata' between the Commonwealth and Aboriginal people*, Canberra: Australian Government Printing Service

Shine, Rhiannon, 2017, 'Tasmania on track to get Aboriginal reconciliation council, but not all are happy', *ABC News*, 24 February, <http://www.abc.net.au/news/2017-02-24/tasmania-aboriginal-reconciliation-council-local-disagreement/8301886>

Short, Damien, 2005, 'Reconciliation and the problem of internal colonialism', *Journal of Intercultural Studies*, vol. 26, no. 3, pp. 267–282

——2008, *Reconciliation and colonial power: Indigenous rights in Australia*, Aldershot: Ashgate Publishing Ltd

——2010, 'Australia: a continuing genocide?', *Journal of Genocide Research*, vol. 12, no. 1–2, pp. 45–68

Silva, Marlee, 2018, 'Cronulla to Papunya', in A. Heiss (ed), *Growing up Aboriginal in Australia*, Melbourne: Black Inc., pp. 211–218

Simpson, Audra, 2014, *Mohawk interruptus: Political life across the borders of settler states*, North Carolina: Duke University Press

——2016, 'Consent's Revenge', *Cultural Anthropology*, vol. 31, no. 3, pp. 326–333

Simpson, Leanne Betasamosake, 2017, *As we have always done: Indigenous freedom through radical resistance*, Minneapolis: University of Minnesota Press

Skelton, Russell, 2008, 'NT Intervention "creating unrest" in big towns', *The Age*, 26 April, <http://www.theage.com.au/news/national/nt-intervention-creating-unrest-in-big-towns/2008/04/26/1208743253119.html>

Sky News, 2017, 'Inquiry will become a joke: Mundine', *SkyNews*, 2 March, <http://www.skynews.com.au/news/national/2017/03/02/inquiry-will-become-a-joke--mundine.html>

Sleath, Emma, 2013, 'Traditional healers share their stories', ABC Alice Springs, 28 March, <http://www.abc.net.au/local/stories/2013/03/22/3721996.htm>

Smith, Diane, 1996, 'From cultural diversity to regionalism: The political culture of difference in ATSIC', in P. Sullivan (ed), *Shooting the banker: essays on ATSIC and self-determination*, Darwin: North Australia Research Unit, Australian National University

——2007, 'Networked governance: Issues of process, policy and power in a West Arnhem Land region initiative', *Ngiya: Talk the Law*, vol. 1, June, pp. 24–51

——2008, 'Cultures of governance and the governance of culture: Transforming and containing institutions in West Arnhem Land', in J. Hunt, D. Smith, S. Garling & W. Sanders (eds), *Contested governance: Culture, power and institutions in Indigenous Australia*, Research Monograph no. 29, Canberra: Centre for Aboriginal Economic Policy Research, ANU E-Press, pp. 75–111

Smith, Diane & Hunt, Janet, 2008, 'Understanding Indigenous Australian governance: Research, theory and representations', in J. Hunt, D. Smith, S. Garling & W. Sanders (eds), *Contested governance: Culture, power and institutions in Indigenous Australia*, Research Monograph no. 29, Canberra: Centre for Aboriginal Economic Policy Research, ANU E-Press, pp. 1–23

Snelgrove, Corey, Dhamoon Rita K. & Corntassel, Jeff, 2014, 'Unsettling settler colonialism: The discourse and politics of settlers and solidarity with Indigenous nations', *Decolonization: Indigeneity, Education and Society*, vol. 3, no. 2, pp. 1–32

Solonec, Tammy, 2014, 'The trauma of Oombulgurri's demolition will be repeated across Western Australia', *The Guardian*, 27 November, <https://www.theguardian.com/

commentisfree/2014/nov/27/the-trauma-of-oombulgurris-demolition-will-be-repeated-across-western-australia>

Sonti, Chalpat, 2010, 'Multimillion-dollar payout to Mr Ward's family after prison van death', *WA Today*, 29 July, <http://www.watoday.com.au/wa-news/multimilliondollar-payout-to-mr-wards-family-after-prison-van-death-20100729-10x1l.html>

Sorensen, Hayley, 2017, 'White people need to take a step back: CEO', *News.com*, 18 November, <http://www.news.com.au/national/northern-territory/white-people-need-to-take-a-step-back-ceo/news-story/a0b4208bc2e254e80759e6241b9b8fa3>

Stokes, Geoffrey, 2005, 'Why we went to Canberra', *Koori Mail*, 23 March, p. 24

Strakosch, Elizabeth, 2015, *Neoliberal Indigenous policy: Settler colonialism and the 'post-welfare' state*, Basingstoke: Palgrave Macmillan

——2016 'Beyond colonial completion: Arendt, settler colonialism and the end of politics', in S. Maddison, T. Clark & R. de Costa (eds), *The limits of settler colonial reconciliation: Non-Indigenous people and the responsibility to engage*, Melbourne: Springer

Strakosch, Elizabeth & Macoun, Alissa, 2012, 'The vanishing endpoint of settler colonialism', *Arena Journal*, no. 37/38, pp. 40–62

——2017, 'Patrick Wolfe and the settler-colonial Intervention', *Arena Magazine*, no. 148, June–July, pp. 35–37

Strohfeldt, Mhala, 2012, 'Bernie tells it straight', *Koori Mail*, 8 August, p. 21

Stunzner, Inga & Hendry, Megan, 2017, '"You can feel it in your heart": Indigenous groups celebrate landmark Gladstone-Bundaberg native title decision', *ABC News*, 28 November, <http://www.abc.net.au/news/2017-11-28/native-title-determination/9201258>

Sullivan, Patrick, 2011, *Belonging together: Dealing with the politics of disenchantment in Australian Indigenous policy*, Canberra: Aboriginal Studies Press

Sutton, Peter, 2001, 'The politics of suffering: Indigenous policy in Australia since the 1970s', *Anthropological Forum*, vol. 11, no. 2, pp. 125–173

——2009, *The politics of suffering: Indigenous Australia and the end of liberal consensus*, Melbourne: Melbourne University Press

Tallis, Wally, 2017, 'Wally Tallis: If you want progress on Indigenous issues, stop the paternal control and work with us', *IndigenousX*, 3 May, <http://indigenousx.com.au/if-you-want-progress-on-indigenous-issues-stop-the-paternal-control-and-work-with-us/>

Tatz, Colin, 1999, *Aboriginal suicide is different. Aboriginal youth suicide in New South Wales, the Australian Capital Territory and New Zealand: Towards a model of explanation and alleviation*, Report to the Criminology Research Council on CRC Project 25/96–7, <http://crg.aic.gov.au/reports/tatz/tatz.pdf>

Taylor, Andrew, 2017, 'Clover Moore refers concerns about Macquarie statue to Indigenous panel', *Sydney Morning Herald*, 23 August, <http://www.smh.com.au/nsw/clover-moore-refers-concerns-about-macquarie-statue--to-indigenous-panel-20170822-gy1jn4.html>

Taylor, Louise, 2003, '"Who's your mob?" The politics of Aboriginal identity and the implications for a treaty', in H. McGlade (ed), *Treaty—let's get it right!*, Canberra: Aboriginal Studies Press, pp. 88–99

——2016, 'Like that young fella shackled to a chair, it seems like we have little say in our fate', *The Guardian*, 2 August, <https://www.theguardian.com/commentisfree/2016/aug/02/like-that-young-fella-shackled-to-a-chair-it-seems-like-we-have-little-say-in-our-fate>

Taylor, Paige (2017), 'Elijah Doughty lost and Kalgoorlie simmers', *The Australian*, 22 July, <https://www.theaustralian.com.au/news/nation/elijah-doughty-lost-and-kalgoorlie-simmers/news-story/7265e77acaa0e01f696ff4ac0ffcdb72>

Terzon, Emilia, 2017, 'Indigenous elders join magistrates in special court for offenders willing to rehabilitate', *ABC News*, 7 June, <http://www.abc.net.au/news/2017-06-07/murri-court-look-inside-indigenous-queensland-court/8555416>

Thorpe, Lidia, 2017, 'Being Aboriginal is not all I am, but it's the centre of who I am', Maiden speech, 29 November, Melbourne: Parliament of Victoria

Thorpe, Nakari, 2017a, 'Labor to establish national caucus to increase Indigenous representation', *NITV News*, 20 February, <http://www.sbs.com.au/nitv/nitv-news/article/2017/02/20/labor-establish-national-caucus-increase-indigenous-representation>

——2017b, 'Native title being watered down for big mining, say traditional owners', *NITV News*, 3 March, <http://www.sbs.com.au/nitv/nitv-news/article/2017/03/02/native-title-being-watered-down-big-mining-say-traditional-owners>

——2017c, 'Indigenous youth join coalition in last ditch effort to stop Adani coal mine', *NITV News*, 22 March, <http://www.sbs.com.au/nitv/nitv-news/article/2017/03/22/indigenous-youth-join-coalition-last-ditch-effort-stop-adani-coal-mine>

——2017d, '"I don't see myself as a historic figure": Ken Wyatt on history, Indigenous politics, and what leadership means to him', *NITV News*, 4 April, <http://www.sbs.com.au/nitv/nitv-news/article/2017/04/04/i-dont-see-myself-historic-figure-ken-wyatt-history-indigenous-politics-and-what>

——2017e, '"Apartheid did exist in this country", Linda Burney reminds conservatives', *NITV News*, 19 May, <http://www.sbs.com.au/nitv/nitv-news/article/2017/05/18/apartheid-did-exist-country-linda-burney-reminds-conservatives>

——2017f, 'Rallies across the country call for justice for Elijah Doughty', *NITV*, 25 July, <http://www.sbs.com.au/nitv/article/2017/07/24/rallies-across-country-call-justice-elijah-doughty>

——2017g, 'Remote workforthe dole program, "stark reminder racism still endures": ACTU boss', *NITV News*, 6 August, <http://www.sbs.com.au/nitv/nitv-news/article/2017/08/06/remote-work-dole-program-stark-reminder-racism-still-endures-actu-boss/>

Tickner, Robert, 2001, *Taking a stand: Land rights to reconciliation*, Sydney: Allen & Unwin

Timms, Penny & Vidot, Anna, 2017, 'Murray–Darling: Indigenous leaders call for "meaningful" consultation over basin plan', *ABC News*, 27 June, <http://www.abc.net.au/news/2017-06-27/aboriginal-people-are-the-ones-who-speak-for-the-river/8653808>

Trigger, Rebecca & Hamlyn, Charlotte, 2017, 'Noongar native title agreement: $1.3b deal rejected by Federal Court', *ABC News*, 2 February, <http://www.abc.net.au/news/2017-02-02/billon-dollar-noongar-native-title-deal-rejected-by-court/8235138>

Troy, Jakelin, 2016, 'Songlines of my Country: belonging to land is a universal right that shouldn't be denied', *NITV*, 5 July, <http://www.sbs.com.au/nitv/article/2016/07/05/songlines-my-country-belonging-land-universal-right-shouldnt-be-denied>

Trudgen, Richard, 2000, *Why warriors lie down and die: Towards an understanding of why the Aboriginal people of Arnhem Land face the greatest crisis in health and education since European contact*, Darwin: Aboriginal Resource and Development Services

Tuck, Eve & Yang, K. Wayne, 2012, 'Decolonisation is not a metaphor', *Decolonization: Indigeneity, Education & Society*, vol. 1, no. 1, pp. 1–40

Tully, James, 2000, 'The struggles of Indigenous peoples for and of freedom', in D. Ivison, P. Patton & W. Sanders (eds), *Political theory and the rights of Indigenous peoples*, New York: Cambridge University Press, pp. 36–59

Turnbull, Malcolm, 2017, 'Response to the Referendum Council's report on constitutional recognition', Media release from the Prime Minister, Attorney General and the Minister for Indigenous Affairs, 26 October, <https://www.pm.gov.au/media/response-referendum-council's-report-constitutional-recognition>

Turpin, Eddie, 2017, 'Renewable Energy Empowering Communities', *NITV News*, 2 March, <http://www.sbs.com.au/nitv/article/2017/03/02/comment-renewable-energy-empowering-communities>

Vanovac, Neda, 2017, 'Barker College agrees to launch Aboriginal academy for girls in Utopia homelands', *ABC News*, 28 June, <http://www.abc.net.au/news/2017-06-27/barker-college-plans-for-aboriginal-girls-academy-in-utopia/8610654>

Veracini, Lorenzo, 2008, 'Settler collective, founding violence and disavowal: The settler colonial situation', *Journal of Intercultural Studies*, vol. 29, no. 4, pp. 363–379

——2010, *Settler colonialism: A theoretical overview*, Basingstoke: Palgrave Macmillan

——2015, *The settler colonial present*, Basingstoke: Palgrave Macmillan

——2017, 'Introduction: Settler colonialism as a distinct mode of domination', in E. Cavanagh & V. Lorenzo (eds), *The Routledge handbook of the history of settler colonialism*, Abingdon: Routledge, pp. 1–8

Verdeja, Ernesto, 2009, *Unchopping a tree: Reconciliation in the aftermath of political violence*, Philadelphia: Temple University Press

Wahlquist, Calla, 2016a, 'Treaty push should replace Indigenous Recognise campaign, says Yolŋu leader', *The Guardian*, 11 March, <https://www.theguardian.com/australia-news/2016/mar/11/treaty-push-should-replace-indigenous-recognise-campaign-says-Yolŋu-leader>

——2016b, 'Backing for Indigenous treaty grows as constitutional recognition loses support', *The Guardian*, 19 July, <https://www.theguardian.com/australia-news/2016/jul/19/backing-for-indigenous-treaty-grows-as-constitutional-recognition-loses-support>

——2016c, 'Indigenous advocate: "Jail is part of our life and part of being institutionalised"', *The Guardian*, 4 August, <https://www.theguardian.com/membership/2016/aug/04/indigenous-advocate-jail-is-part-of-our-life-and-part-of-being-institutionalised>

——2016d, '"Tell the world we want justice." Elijah Doughty's death exposes Kalgoorlie's racial faultline', *The Guardian*, 8 September, <https://www.theguardian.com/australia-news/2016/sep/08/tell-the-worldwe-want-justice-elijah-doughtys-death-exposes-kalgoorlies-racial-faultline>

——2017a, 'Indigenous incarceration: turning the tide on colonisation's cruel third act', *The Guardian*, 20 February, <https://www.theguardian.com/australia-news/2017/feb/20/indigenous-incarceration-turning-the-tide-on-colonisations-cruel-third-act>

——2017b, '"We want referendum": intensive Uluru talks call for an end to the fighting', *The Guardian*, 28 May, <https://www.theguardian.com/australia-news/2017/may/28/we-want-referendum-intensive-uluru-talks-call-for-an-end-to-the-fighting>

——2017c, 'Ms Dhu: family calls for criminal charges against ex-partner and three police', *The Guardian*, 4 June, <https://www.theguardian.com/australia-news/2017/jun/04/ms-dhu-family-calls-for-criminal-charges-against-ex-partner-and-three-police>

——2017d, '"The dream of our ancestors": Victorian bill gives Indigenous owners custodianship of Yarra', *The Guardian*, 22 June, <https://www.theguardian.com/australia-news/2017/jun/22/the-dream-of-our-ancestors-victorian-bill-gives-indigenous-owners-custodianship-of-yarra>

——2017e, 'Pat Dodson says cashless welfare card a "public whip" to control Indigenous people', *The Guardian*, 21 August, <https://www.theguardian.com/australia-news/2017/aug/22/pat-dodson-says-cashless-welfare-card-a-public-whip-to-control-indigenous-people>

——2017f, 'Adani coalmine: Traditional owners file injunction', *The Guardian*, 3 December, <https://www.theguardian.com/environment/2017/dec/03/adani-coalmine-traditional-owners-file-injunction>

——2017g, 'The killing of Elijah Doughty: Oil patch at crime scene fades but stain remains', *The Guardian*, 21 July, <https://www.theguardian.com/australia-news/2017/jul/21/the-killing-of-elijah-doughty-oil-patch-at-scene-fades-but-stain-remains>

——2018, 'Indigenous children in care doubled since Stolen Generations apology', *The Guardian*, 25 January, <https://www.theguardian.com/australia-news/2018/jan/25/indigenous-children-in-care-doubled-since-stolen-generations-apology>

Wahlquist, Calla & Karp, Paul, 2018, 'What our leaders say about Australia Day—and where did it start, anyway?', *The Guardian*, 19 January, <https://www.theguardian.com/australia-news/2018/jan/19/what-our-leaders-say-about-australia-day-and-where-did-it-start-anyway>

Wainwright, Sophie, 2017, 'Murray–Darling Aboriginal nations sign treaty, hoping for a stronger voice on Indigenous rights', *ABC News*, 11 May, <http://www.abc.net.au/news/2017-05-11/murray-darling-aboriginal-nations-sign-treaty/8518228>

Walter, Maggie, 2018, 'The voice of Indigenous data: Beyond the markers of disadvantage', *Griffith Review*, 60, pp. 256–263

Watson, Irene, 2002, 'Aboriginal laws and the sovereignty of *Terra Nullius*', *Borderlands*, vol. 1, no. 2, <http://www.borderlands.net.au/vol1no2_2002/watson_laws.html>

——2007a, 'Settled and unsettled spaces: Are we free to roam?', in A. Moreton-Robinson (ed.), *Sovereign subjects: Indigenous sovereignty matters*, Sydney: Allen & Unwin, pp. 15–32

——2007b, 'Aboriginal sovereignties: Past, present and future (im)possibilities', in S. Perera (ed.), *Our patch: Enacting Australian sovereignty post-2001*, Perth: Network Books

——2009, 'In the Northern Territory Intervention, what is saved or rescued and at what cost?', *Cultural Studies Review*, vol. 51, no. 2, pp. 45–60

——2018, 'Why celebrate on the day that marks crimes of colonialism and genocide?', *IndigenousX*, 25 January, <https://indigenousx.com.au/irene-watson-why-celebrate-on-the-day-that-marks-crimes-of-colonialism-and-genocide/>

Watson, Teila, 2017, 'Indigenous knowledge systems can help solve the problems of climate change', *The Guardian*, 2 June, <https://www.theguardian.com/commentisfree/2017/jun/02/indigenous-knowledge-systems-can-help-solve-the-problems-of-climate-change>

Watt, Steve Bunbadgee Hodder, 2017, 'Victories for Indigenous people are always short-lived. That's why we need a treaty—now', *IndigenousX*, 14 February, <http://indigenousx.com.au/victories-for-indigenous-people-are-always-short-lived-thats-why-we-need-a-treaty-now/>

Watts, Peter, Mitch & Muir, Kado, 2013, 'Taking issue with Langton', *Koori Mail*, 13 February, p. 24

West, Katie, 2016, 'My art is a personal antidote for the effects of colonisation', *IndigenousX*, 18 May, <https://www.theguardian.com/commentisfree/2016/may/18/my-art-is-a-personal-antidote-for-the-effects-of-colonisation>

Whyte, Kyle Powys, 2018, 'White allies, let's be honest about decolonization', *YES! Magazine*, 3 April, <http://www.yesmagazine.org/issues/decolonize/white-allies-lets-be-honest-about-decolonization-20180403>

Wild, Rex & Anderson, Pat, 2007, *Ampe akelyernemane meke mekarle: Little children are sacred*, Report of the Northern Territory Board of Inquiry into the protection of children from sexual abuse, Darwin: Northern Territory Government

Wilkins, David E., 2002, *American Indian politics and the American political system*, Lanham: Rowman and Littlefield

Williams, George, 2013, 'Race and the Australian Constitution', *Australasian Parliamentary Review*, vol. 28, no. 1, pp. 4–16

——2016, 'Australia needs a treaty and constitutional recognition for Indigenous people', *The Age*, 8 August, <http://www.theage.com.au/comment/australia-needs-a-treaty-and-constitutional-recognition-for-indigenous-people-20160805-gqm0xp.html>

Wilson, Alf, 2012, 'Outrage as Murri Court goes', *Koori Mail*, 19 September, p. 7

Wilson, Sammy, 2017, 'Statement by Sammy Wilson', *Central Land Council*, 2 November, <https://www.clc.org.au/index.php?%2Fpublications%2Fcontent%2Fstatement-by-sammy-wilson1%2F>

Wolfe, Patrick, 1999, *Settler colonialism and the transformation of anthropology: The politics and poetics of an ethnographic event*, London: Cassell

——2006, 'Settler colonialism and the elimination of the native', *Journal of Genocide Studies*, vol. 8, no. 4, pp. 387–409

——2016, *Traces of history: Elementary structures of race*, London: Verso

Wright, Alexis, 2006, 'Embracing the Indigenous vision', *Meanjin*, vol. 65, no. 1, pp. 104–108

——2016, 'The Northern Territory is a failed state', *Sydney Morning Herald*, 1 August, <http://www.smh.com.au/comment/the-northern-territory-is-a-failed-state-20160729-gqgf8w.html>

——2018, 'Hey Ancestor!' *Griffith Review*, 60, pp. 46–49

Wyld, Karen, 2016, 'Introduction/overview', in Summer May Finlay, Megan Williams, Marie McInerney, Melissa Sweet & Mitchell Ward (eds), 2016, *#JustJustice: Tackling the over-incarceration of Aboriginal and Torres Strait Islander peoples*, 2nd edn, croakey.org

——2018, 'What kind of morality do they want us to celebrate on that day?', *IndigenousX*, 22 January, <https://indigenousx.com.au/karen-wyld-what-kind-of-morality-do-they-want-us-to-celebrate-on-that-day/>

Wynne, Emma, 2011, 'Prison guard given record fine over Ward death', ABC Goldfields, 5 October, <http://www.abc.net.au/local/stories/2011/10/05/3333163.htm>

Young, Elspeth, 2005, 'Rhetoric to reality in sustainability: Meeting the challenges in Indigenous cattle station communities', in L. Taylor, G. Ward, G. Henderson, R. Davis & W. Lynley (eds), *The power of knowledge, the resonance of tradition*, Canberra: Aboriginal Studies Press, pp. 116–129

Yu, Peter, 1997, 'Multilateral agreements: A new accountability in Aboriginal Affairs', in G. Yunipingu (ed), *Our land is our life: Land rights—Past, present and future*, St Lucia: University of Queensland Press

Yu, Peter, Gray, Bill & Ella Duncan, Marcia, 2008, *Report of the NTER Review Board*, Department of Families, Housing, Community Services and Indigenous Affairs, Canberra, <http://www.nterreview.gov.au/docs/report_nter_review/docs/Report_NTER_Review_October08.pdf>

Yunupingu, Galarrwuy, 2007, 'The challenge begins', *The Australian*, 21 September, <http://www.theaustralian.news.com.au/story/0,25197,22453431-7583,00.html>

——2016, 'Rom Watangu: An Indigenous leader reflects on a lifetime following the law of the land', *The Monthly*, July, <https://www.themonthly.com.au/issue/2016/july/1467295200/galarrwuy-yunupingu/rom-watangu>

——2017, 'Makarrata the map to reconciliation: Over to you, leaders', *The Australian*, 31 July, <http://www.theaustralian.com.au/opinion/makarrata-the-map-to-reconciliation-over-to-you-leaders/news-story/a54bd329842f860a45a169c87ca020a0>

Zellerer, Evelyn & Cunneen, Chris, 2001, 'Restorative justice, Indigenous justice, and human rights', in G. Bazemore & M. Schiff (eds), *Restorative community justice: Repairing harm and transforming communities*, Cincinatti: Anderson Publishing

Zillman, Stephanie, 2016, 'Lost between two worlds', *ABC News*, 6 May, <http://www.abc.net.au/news/2016-05-06/the-indigenous-elders-left-behind-after-suicide/7386296>

——2017, 'The missing kids of the "second stolen generation"', *ABC News*, 28 February, <http://www.abc.net.au/news/2017-02-27/elders-speak-out-on-mission-kids-ahead-of-nt-royal-commission/8304628>

# INDEX

# INDEX